—Boundaries/Borders
—racial proportion

COLORMUTE

COLORMUTE

RACE TALK DILEMMAS IN
AN AMERICAN SCHOOL

Mica Pollock

PRINCETON UNIVERSITY PRESS   PRINCETON AND OXFORD

ISBN: 0-691-11695-4

British Library Cataloging-in-Publication Data is available

This book has been composed in Adobe Caslon

Printed on acid-free paper. ∞

pup.princeton.edu

Printed in the United States of America
10 9 8 7 6 5 4 3 2

To Columbus people, who lived this book; to my family, who never lost faith in its author; and especially to dear Joe, who weathered this book with infinitely more sweetness than I.

Contents _____

Preface

WHEN I ARRIVED in California City to teach at Columbus High School in 1994, I was 23 years old, one year out of college, and convinced that it was crucial to expose racial categories as social constructions. As I sit here completing this book on the other coast, I am 31 years old, a new professor, and convinced of the need to use racial categories to design solutions to racialized inequality. In between then and now, I became a teacher, an anthropologist, and an adult. I dedicate this book to the many people who helped me become all three.

In particular—though my family means the world to me—I dedicate this book to Columbus people, some of whom remain my dearest friends; for it is upon them that any critique present in this book may appear to rest. Yet though based at Columbus, this book is really about *American* race talk. I think that U.S. readers—whether they work in schools or not—will find Columbus people's dilemmas of talking racially distinctly familiar.

As both a former "native" of Columbus life and a person raised in the United States, throughout this research I have truly been my own fieldnote (Jean Jackson 1990), for I have myself lived all the dilemmas I describe here. After teaching at Columbus from 1994 to 1995, doing research with people I cared about very much—and in a culture I thought I knew well—was a project of exploring both self and other, one both enlightening and excruciating. Scribbling in a private journal in 1994–95 in the hopes of writing a memoir in the (tired) "first-year teacher" genre, and sitting at my kitchen table nearly every night in graduate school writing ethnographic fieldnotes in 1995–97, over the space of three years at Columbus I lived each day twice. Writing my fieldnotes—which were primarily, from the beginning, obsessive direct reconstructions of the countless conversations I had had throughout each day—both brought me closer to the people I cared about at Columbus and somehow distanced me painfully from them. Personalities, expressions, laughter, and struggles somehow got reduced to words on paper; yet reliving each turn of phrase, each muttered complaint, each joke and heated argument, also gave me a permanent appreciation for Columbus people, and for the complexity and importance of what they struggled with in their everyday lives.

Although retreading the words of my former students and colleagues often had me laughing at my computer, this analysis came to focus on the dilemmas of everyday American race talk and silence, a fact that made its writing particularly problematic. Investigating the use of race *labels* (rather than the nebulous "race," which I returned to Columbus originally to study) soon demanded that

I focus on communal descriptive problems—what I call American race talk dilemmas—rather than on all the lightheartednesses and small triumphs of daily life at Columbus. In focusing on the use and omission of race labels in everyday talk—actions, I argue, that embody all of our worries about how race matters in America—this story became a story of human confusion and uncertainty rather than joy. And in the endless rewriting of this book, I myself have lived such race-talk worries at multiple levels. Doing ethnography well is *about* worrying, about both research and writing—and worrying about worrying about race has been "reflexivity" at its most frenzied (Wolf 1992).

Had I been interested in a topic other than the dilemmas of talk and action, I could have written a far more celebratory book about life at Columbus, for plenty of people worked incredibly hard there to improve each other's lives. Instead, this became a book about good people struggling with difficult racialized orders, with the basic disparities of opportunity and power central to race in the United States. It became an analysis of the central traps of racial inequality, not the everyday joys of racial diversity that were also present at Columbus. While this project came to focus on the troubling traps of racial inequality rather than the positive aspects of racialized identity, friendship, and creative production, I have pursued the analysis precisely because I feel that a greater understanding of these shared traps and worries will assist us to overcome those aspects of race in America that are difficult. We can enjoy the friends and learning experiences that are the joyous aspect of everyday diversity in America without any book to help us; it is in navigating our everyday communal dilemmas of racial inequality and conflict that we could use more guidance. I have thus pursued a narrowed analysis of Columbus people's racialized dilemmas, at the unfortunate risk of making it appear that Columbus people were unusually troubled "about race" or that "race" at Columbus was always a "problem." Indeed, although the book might appear to some pessimistic— given that so many of our race talk dilemmas seem to lead us to paradoxical, damned-if-we-do-or-don't walls—it is in fact deeply optimistic. For in struggling with the everyday act of talking racially, people demonstrate that it is actually within the reach of everyday actions to make things better.

Ironically, it is Columbus people's own struggles to make their school better that prevents me from naming them. From 1994 on, as readers shall see, Columbus found itself at the eye of a very public school reform storm. "Columbus" and "California City," thus, are both pseudonyms promised to Columbus's second beleaguered principal, who allowed me to continue my research at Columbus after the entire staff I knew was summarily replaced by a critical school district administration in 1996.* She allowed a knowing eye to enter a

---

* Far too late in the process of writing and publishing this book, I learned that "California City" is in fact a real town in California. I beg forgiveness and understanding from its residents.

school to which she herself was a stranger, and for this act of kindness I am permanently grateful.

I particularly owe this book, then, to all the people at Columbus who worked so hard from 1994 to 1997 to teach and learn from one another, and to teach me. They taught me much of what I believe about the importance of the teaching profession, and that our public schools are places where we can struggle to take the good of "race" and eradicate the bad. For this was, despite their dilemmas, what Columbus people of all ages woke up every day to do.

Cambridge, Massachusetts
Winter 2003

Acknowledgments ⸺⸺⸺⸺⸺⸺⸺⸺⸺⸺⸺⸺

WRITING A BOOK seems like a very lonely process, even when the book is crowded with the voices of literally hundreds of people. Many people made the writing of this book pleasantly social. I would like to thank the individual readers who so valiantly encountered this book's many arguments at various stages of complexity, disrepair, and clarity: Peter Agree, John Baugh, Jodi Beder, Prudence Carter, Victor Cary, Gil Conchas, Catherine Cooper, Kristin Crosland, Larry Cuban, Robert Devens, Thea Abu El-Haj, Maya Fischhoff, Joby Gardner, Jonathan Gayles, Greta Gibson, Danny Gilbarg, Lani Guinier, Evelyn Jacob, Galen Joseph, David Kirp, Elizabeth Knoll, the generous Meira Levinson, Vivian Louie, Wendy Luttrell, Sunaina Maira, Tom Malarkey, Ray McDermott, Bud Mehan, Kathy Newman, Pedro Noguera, Gary Orfield, Margaret Perrow, Tom Rohlen, Roger Sanjek, Ingrid Seyer, Lissa Soep, George Spindler, Carol Stack, Barrie Thorne, David Tyack, Margery Wolf, Leisy Wyman, Princeton's anonymous reviewers, and the many readers young and old from Columbus High School (unnamed here for final anonymity). Students in my courses on race, ethnography, and youth at the Harvard Graduate School of Education were also particularly supportive of this work's final revisions; so were the members of HGSE's Junior Faculty Seminar. The Research Practitioner Council of the Minority Student Achievement Network was especially helpful in offering a final critique, as were the professional development specialists from the Columbus region. I thank the Spencer Foundation for supporting the initial writing of this manuscript, and I thank the American Anthropological Association's Council on Anthropology and Education for its blessing of the book's first incarnation. I also thank my colleagues at the Harvard Graduate School of Education for allowing me a kind introduction to professoring while this book was in its final stages. Finally, I thank Ian Malcolm, my editor at Princeton University Press, for his unflagging enthusiasm for this project.

My family's encouragement and support have been essential to my well-being throughout this journey. My father, Sheldon Pollock, was unflinchingly helpful, reading and critiquing sections for years; my sister, Nira Pollock, and my mother, Estera Milman, each also contributed mightily to individual chapters and to my overall mental health. My husband, Joe Castiglione, read all of these chapters dutifully in the bathtub, and he listened with astounding patience as I reconstructed this book's many arguments ad nauseam. Our relationship proved much stronger than any argument, and he deserves most of the credit for that success. Hallelujah, this book is done.

COLORMUTE

Introduction _____

"It is all rather complicated."—Edmund Leach,
Political Systems of Highland Burma (1954, 44)

THIS IS A BOOK about race talk—about people in one school and district struggling with the basic American choice of when and how to describe one another
racially. People in America have long struggled in various ways with racial
categories, arguably some of humanity's most conflicted creations. American
race categories have become a social truth without ever having had a legitimately biological basis: created to organize slavery, retooled with waves of immigration, and naturalized over centuries by law, policy, and science, race categories are now everywhere, alternately proud building blocks of our nation's
"diversity" and the shameful foundation of our most wrenching inequalities.[1]
Over the centuries, as people of various tribes, nations, and religions have
taken their places in the nation's taxonomy of "races," we have only sporadically
thought to ask each other whether these "races" actually exist: most of the time,
we have worried less about the reality of our race categories than about what
to do with the racialized orders we have made. Unwittingly or quite knowingly,
we have built systems of inequality around race categories; but we have also
built identities, friendships, and marriages around them. And Americans, now
never certain when race is a good thing and when it is a bad thing (and never
certain about the moral or political implications of using race labels to categorize human beings), keep struggling with a particularly daunting question:
When should we talk as if race matters?

Americans confront the question of whether and how race *should* matter, as
I argue in this book, every time we wonder whether to talk as if it does. As
this book will demonstrate, we encounter, every day, the pitfalls inherent in
this most basic act of racialization: using race labels to describe people. We
wrestle, for example, with the act of placing infinitely diverse human beings
into simple "racial" boxes; we then wrestle with the fact that these categories
of "racial" difference are central to the most troubling power struggles we have.
Ultimately, we wrestle with the paradoxical reality that in a world in which
racial inequality already exists, both talking and *not* talking about people in
racial terms seem alternately necessary to make things "fair."[2] Accordingly,
though people in the United States arguably use race labels more bluntly than
do many other citizens of the world, we also seem to worry about doing so
more than most other people. Many of us exhibit particular worries about
being "racist " with our very language: one anthropologist has described the

"fear of being labeled a racist" as "perhaps one of the most effective behavioral and verbal restraints in the United States today" (Van Den Berghe 1996).[3]

Given the amount of worrying that race-label use seems to require in America, it is perhaps unsurprising that many Americans have proposed we solve our "race problems" by talking as if race did not matter at all. We are, in fact, in the midst of major battles in the United States about the very future of race talk itself—and these controversies are a key context for this book. As Steven Gregory has noted, "diverse segments of U.S. society" claim that race "has become a tiresome topic, and one whose 'polite repression,' as Toni Morrison puts it, 'is understood to be a graceful, even generous, liberal gesture' " (Gregory 1996, 23). Lani Guinier and Gerald Torres (2002) claim that anti–race-talk arguments can be heard both on the American "right" and from "liberal progressives," both of whom tend to argue for "masking race in political discussion" (32). Spokespersons on the right, they argue, suggest that "when one notices race, one is implicitly manifesting racial enmity" (38), that "noticing race is in essence a throwback to racism" (39), and that "whoever mentions race first is the racist in the room" (308), while in turn, "liberal progressives" argue that "race is something that good people simply do not notice" (51), since "a frank engagement with race" would "only heighten social divisions" (32). Indeed, some public figures are now arguing loudly that even *using race labels* publicly is tantamount to reproducing racism itself. A public referendum currently being proposed in California, the Racial Privacy Initiative, argues for the elimination of *all* race labels from public records, declaring that "the state *shall not classify* any individual by race, ethnicity, color or national origin in the operation of public education, public contracting or public employment" (my emphasis). The referendum's key proponent, UC regent Ward Connerly, explains bluntly to the press that "The state should be blind to color, just as it is to religion or sexual orientation."

Many other quests to delete race talk from American life are implicit in our struggles over public policy. In 1996, when this ethnography was in the making in the under-resourced, "low-income minority" California school and district where I myself had taught, a majority of California voters marked the ballot for a state proposition vaguely entitled the "Equal Opportunity Initiative," which set out to make illegal not only "race-based" affirmative actions in the state's universities, but also every "race-based" educational program in the state. This Proposition 209, part of a nationwide wave of litigation intended to outlaw the consideration of race in college admissions, K–12 student enrollment plans, and programs for academic enrichment or student outreach, did not outlaw California's racial categories themselves, of course. It also did not erase racial categories from Californians' minds. Rather, it simply outlawed mentioning in official documents that these categories existed: in practice, the policy was less about being colorblind than being actively *colormute*.[4]

As Lawrence Blum (2002) notes of such "colorblind" policy, "A policy that makes explicit reference to race, or racial identity, is taken to stand condemned by that fact alone" (91). Indeed, "colorblindness" can often be more accurately described as a purposeful silencing of race words themselves. Proposition 209 effectively ordered district and university people to actively refuse to *talk* in racial terms. Yet actively deleting racial labels from applications and enrollment plans certainly didn't mean the disappearance of racial patterns in education. Policymakers could not stop Californians from viewing each other racially, or outlaw race as a system of categorization structuring people's social and economic lives. Nor could they outlaw daily racial references in school hallways and classrooms and at lunch tables. Instead, policymakers simply banned race words from the official policy analysis—they deleted the race labels that appeared in school applications, program descriptions, and brochures. As the mostly-white-and-Asian freshman enrollments at the UC schools after Proposition 209 quickly made clear, however, officially erasing race words had far from erased racial patterns at the state's universities. Indeed, the insistence on being colormute had actually allowed racial disparities in pre-college opportunity to proceed unhindered—helping increase racial disparities in UC enrollment and hinting that *deleting* race words can actually help *make race matter more*.[5]

Colormute policy and practice had specific consequences for this book's subjects. In the spring of 1996, around the time the campaign for Proposition 209 was in full swing, I was finishing my first year of formal research for this book at "Columbus High School" in "California City," where I had the previous year been a teacher. Over that summer, angry district officials replaced 90 percent of the Columbus staff in a reform called "reconstitution," wiping out not just the faculty themselves but also all the reform programs—career academies, small learning communities—the faculty had devised. As we will see, this tumultuous event also involved dilemmas of speaking racially—and race silence here too had consequences. For while the "reconstitution" reform stemmed from the city's desegregation order—a court action concerned on paper with achieving racially equal academic opportunities and outcomes for "African-Americans" and "Hispanics" in California City schools—for over a year of the "probation" period that preceded reconstitution, almost no one had even used the words "African-American" and "Hispanic" in any district- or school-level public conversations about school reform. And as 100 faculty and staff left Columbus as the result of a silently racialized policy, I watched a new staff of 100 well-meaning strangers reproduce all the prior staff's habits of deleting race words—and articulate identical dilemmas of race talk and colormuteness that would come to seem common American property.

This book, which uses everyday race talk controversies from Columbus High and California City as primary data, is an attempt to map the contours of six basic dilemmas of racial description that tie Americans up in communal knots, and that we must attempt to better understand. For these traps of discourse, I want to argue, are extremely consequential. Having witnessed three full years of struggles over talking and *not* talking in racial terms at Columbus—as a teacher in 1994–95 and as an anthropologist in 1995–97—I have come to argue explicitly what policy debates across the United States are currently implying: Race talk matters. All Americans, every day, *are* reinforcing racial distinctions and racialized thinking by using race labels; but we are also reinforcing racial inequality by refusing to use them. By using race words carelessly and particularly by *deleting* race words, I am convinced, both policymakers and laypeople in America help reproduce the very racial inequalities that plague us. It is thus crucial that we learn to navigate together the American dilemmas of race talk and colormuteness rather than be at their mercy; and that is the overarching purpose for this book.

Let me immediately explain my use here of an American "we."[7] Different racialized groups in the United States have very different experiences with racial description (Americans "of color" are described in racial terms far more often than are "whites," for example, while "white" people, the racialized category into which I myself fall, experience disproportionate anxiety over using race labels even as we experience their application least of all).[8] Yet Americans are a single giant speech community when it comes to some basic dilemmas of race talk: for we share not only our basic system of racial/ethnic categorization, but also the fundamental American question of when, how, and whether to take race "into account" in American life. We also share the racialized inequalities we most struggle to discuss.[9]

That this book focuses on schooling talk is no accident, for public struggles over race have long centered on this particular shared arena of national practice. From nineteenth-century laws denying basic literacy to slaves, through decades of twentieth-century battles over mixing "the races" in desegregated schools, to contemporary multiracial debates on "colorblind" college admissions or curricular "multiculturalism," our recurring debates over how race does and should matter in the United States have routinely circled back to address American schools.[10] Schools are key institutions where Americans "*make* each other racial" (Olsen 1997): not only are schools central places for forming racial "identities," but they are key places where we rank, sort, order, and differently equip our children along "racial" lines even as we hope for schooling to be the great societal equalizer.[11] School race talk, I argue, is thus one key version of American race talk: for the way we talk in school both reflects and helps shape our most basic racial orders.

Labeling (or not labeling) each other with race words is, of course, just one everyday way that Americans make each other racial—and make race matter. Sociolinguists and linguistic anthropologists have studied many other ways we reproduce "racial" difference through our everyday talk, such as through the patterned use of particular languages, dialects, styles, or vocabulary.[12] Going beyond talk, we make ourselves and each other racial through the hairstyles we sport, our gestures, and the friends we display; through the music we listen and dance to, the people we sit down next to, the organizations we belong to, the resources we distribute, and the neighborhoods we choose to live in or not to live in. Race is also reconstructed when people make meaning of the genetically insignificant physical characteristics, like skin color or nose shape or eye contour or hair texture, that we have used as markers of "racial" difference since pseudo-science codified this use centuries ago. Racial orders are built daily through movements of the body, through statistics and numbers, through glances across rooms to friends.[13] Racial orders in *school* are also built through the distribution of dollars, through the "tracking" of racialized bodies to designated schools and classrooms, through the false expectations that differential abilities reside in racialized minds, through an "institutional choreography" (Fine 1997) of everyday actions incessantly funneling opportunities to some students and not others.

In contrast to gestures, dollars, or knowing looks, the use of racial labels seems a bizarrely explicit way of making people racial. Race language is indeed itself a powerfully simple force: we *become* race-group members, or we must negotiate and resist so becoming, every time we are referred to in racial terms; and talking racially does prompt listeners to see the world anew in racialized ways.[14] This is no new claim: scholars have long viewed words as consequential actions that create the world rather than simply describe it.[15] Indeed, Americans, as this book will demonstrate, seem to know quite well that race words, in their bluntness, are extremely powerful agents. We seem somewhat less aware that our very resistance to using race words has major consequences as well.

We struggle over using race words, I argue, in part because the simplicity of racial descriptions so often seems to belie the complexity of human diversity. Imagine for yourself showing up for the first time at this book's infinitely complex field site: "Columbus High School" in "California City."

Trying to Describe Columbus

Entering Columbus at the end of a typical day and glancing around the building, you might notice that there are some adults "of color" at Columbus, including its principal; but you might label the majority of the adults you see "white" without much thought. As Columbus students pour out the doorway, however, they are likely to appear to you stunningly diverse, a population that seems to embody the country's breathtaking demographic complexity. Many Columbus students (or their parents) have immigrated to California City from various linguistically distinct islands in the Philippines, from numerous Central American and South American countries, from a list of Cantonese- and Mandarin- speaking regions of China, from both Samoas, and from a huge grab bag of other places, such as Vietnam and Tonga. Recently or some decades ago, the parents of many African-American students at Columbus migrated across the country from the American South. There are just a handful of students who are called "white" at Columbus, most with grandparents or great-grandparents hailing from Ireland, Italy, Germany, or other countries of Europe. Talking briefly to a few students, you might learn that they have lived across the street from Columbus their entire lives, or moved to the city as young children, or immigrated from another part of the globe just yesterday.

Watching the students emerge into the mid-afternoon sunlight, you might find yourself alternately framing them as a largely "of-color" unit, as divisible into a small list of presumed "ethnic" or "national" origins, or as a sea of faces of all shades of bronze and brown and beige. You might also begin to suspect that an accurate account of diversity at Columbus must take into consideration far more than what the classifying eye can comprehend. If someone were to hand you a sheet of the data that the California City Unified School District keeps on basic Columbus student demographics, for example, you would notice that students across Columbus are astonishingly diverse linguistically: one third of the student body is in the process of learning English for the first time. Listening to the other two-thirds of Columbus students chattering in the hallway, further, you might notice that some shift flawlessly between two or more languages or dialects. You might also notice from the district data that Columbus students seem diverse both economically and academically: the district gives a particularly low-income subset of Columbus students (40 percent) either free or reduced-price lunch (that is, 40 percent of Columbus students are willing to publicly claim such assistance), and the district also classifies 60 percent of Columbus students as "Educationally Disadvantaged Youth"—students that are both low-income and under the 40th percentile on a statewide standardized test.

Go to some classrooms during the day and try talking to and observing students, though, and you will learn that describing Columbus's academic and economic diversity is not so easy either. Some students write flawlessly, while others can barely read; a few can do calculus, while many others still struggle with basic fractions. Hearing more about students' outside lives, further, you might find that while some students sleep on spare beds in "the projects" or in foster homes, others live in aunts' extended family apartments, and still others wake up in stuccoed single-family, two-parent houses; some Columbus parents live on welfare, some clean hotels, others work as university librarians with master's degrees.

Talking at length to any student at Columbus, finally, you might find yourself challenged to describe the "diversity" of any individual. At Columbus, self-proclaimed "mixed" parentage is common enough that "what are you mixed with?" is a matter-of-fact student question. Indeed, ask any Columbus student "what" she "is," and you may find that she offers different answers at different times of the day, week, or year.

If the apparently infinite variety of ways available to describe Columbus's "diversity" now makes the task of description itself seem impossible, fear not. Columbus students and adults will often readily make describing the school's demographics exceedingly simple. One particular simplification of Columbus's diversity shows up daily in conversation, as people place one another into a few simple categories they call "racial."

There are, in fact, six words that people at Columbus use to describe what they call the school's main "races": "black," "Latino," "Filipino," "Chinese," "Samoan," and "white" (this last category includes mostly teachers). A student who told me in one conversation that he is both "black" and "mixed with Puerto Rican" thus still wrote this poem for a class, describing Columbus with easy numbers:

> 4 good teachers, with two bad ones a day
> every 5 bad kids copping one great student
> 2 fights, 0 body breaking them up
> 6 different groups, and nobody cares about anything
> over 1500 people different to the bone

In defining these "6 different groups," Columbus students call "racial" even the groups scholars typically term "ethnic" or "national," such as "Filipino," "Chinese," "Latino," and "Samoan." While some scholars would call this conflation of race, "ethnicity," and "nationality" theoretically problematic, merging the three is a process that is key to daily social analysis at Columbus, just as it is for young people in many areas of the world.[16] The word "race" at Columbus, as elsewhere, indeed denotes "groups" imagined to be easily physically distinguishable, yet rarely do Columbus students suggest that they frame these six "racial" groups as populations that are somehow genetically or "biologically" distinct. Rather, calling these six groups "racial" indicates primarily that they are all analogous parts in the school's simplest taxonomy of "diversity"—and importantly, often competitive parts in contests over social power.[17] While students occasionally change their nomenclature for categories, swapping "African-American" for "black" and "Mexican" for "Latino" (to the consternation of some "Latinos" of Guatemalan, Salvadoran, and Nicaraguan origin), students compress their diversity into six simple "racial" groups many times each day at Columbus. Adults at Columbus do the same.

This simple system of "racial" categorization, notably, is not limited to everyday life at Columbus. The California City Unified School District, for example, uses roughly these same six labels to keep records on what it calls Columbus's main "racial/ethnic groups": indeed, the district has been ordered by a federal court to distribute a set of nine such "groups" districtwide in proportional amounts. In the mid-1990s, district demographic records said Columbus enrolled "Filipinos" (28 percent), "Latinos" or "Hispanics" (29 percent), "African-Americans" or "blacks" (22 percent), "Chinese" (8 percent), "Other Non-Whites" (a bureaucratic category that included Columbus's "Samoans," roughly 8 percent), and "Other Whites" (5 percent). Columbus's teaching staff was listed as roughly 54 percent "Other White," 15 percent "African-American," 10 percent "Filipino," 13 percent "Latino," 5 percent "Other Non-White," and 3 percent "Chinese."

With Columbus's six main "racial" labels now in hand, you might with relief begin to describe the people pouring out of the building in their simplest racial terms. Yet you would have to take great care with what you were talking about, and to whom: for your "racial/ethnic" descriptions might well be met with uncomfortable silences or critical retorts. Descriptions of people at Columbus, you see, are only *sometimes* supposed to be racial. Stick around Columbus for a few days, and you will realize that to describe Columbus as it is described by people who spend every day there, you will have to decide based on circumstance the most accurate or appropriate way to frame Columbus's "diversity." No one around you will know when you *see* various groups at Columbus, but the moments when you *talk* about these groups as groups will be analyzable acts—and this fact may have you monitoring your speech rather carefully. The question this book asks is *when*—in relation to which topics and in which social or institutional situations—you might describe the people at Columbus *racially*, and when you might resist doing so. Three years of talk collected at and around Columbus High School suggests that there would be some moments in which you would consciously worry about using race labels, other moments when you would use race labels without thinking twice, and still other moments when you would erase race terms from your talk quite purposefully—and that all these actions would actually mimic the actions of others in an astonishingly precise choreography.

Using Race Labels: Three Main Acts of Racial Description

Three main patterns of race-label use ran throughout the fabric of Columbus's race talk, and they run throughout the fabric of this book as well: at different moments, speakers *contested* the use of racial labels, they *used* racial labels *matter-of-factly*, or they *suppressed* them altogether. First, speakers at Columbus and in California City often contested the use of racial labels quite heatedly. The inordinate complexity of Columbus's very Californian demographics—its *six* "race groups," and its multitude of self-consciously "mixed-race" students of color—actually accentuated the main pitfall of racial description anywhere in America. Racial descriptions of demographic patterns, as well as racial descriptions of individual people, can *always be wrong*. And people at and around Columbus, struggling tremendously with when it was either *accurate* or *appro-*

priate to talk in racial terms, often worried as much explicitly. Students worried daily, for example, about accurately classifying themselves and others as members of the school's six "races"; adults worried about accurately describing the racial demographics of patterns in schoolwide or classroom life. Students also occasionally apologized for comments about particular "races" at Columbus, or even for calling their teachers "white"; adults routinely questioned the appropriateness of speaking racially about school programs or school people, in conversations with the principal or the superintendent or their own peers.

In relation to some topics, though, such apparent anxiety over race-label use disappeared. Sometimes, everyone at Columbus talked quite matter-of-factly as if race mattered. Columbus people described classroom curricula and public assemblies, for example, in straightforward racial terms: classrooms provided units explicitly on "Latinos" or "Filipinos," and people chattered happily about "black" students who read poems at a Black History Month assembly or "Samoan" students who danced at a "multicultural" event. It seemed similarly easy for students, teachers, and administrators alike to describe conflicts between students with racial labels: the "Latinos" beat up the "Filipinos," people said matter-of-factly, or the "Samoans" beat up the "blacks." Especially when discussing pleasant aspects of "diversity" or topics of school life ostensibly confined to students, Columbus people often talked nonchalantly as if they assumed race to be matter-of-factly relevant.[18]

In contrast, there were moments at and around Columbus when talking in racial terms seemed to speakers either to indicate the existence of "racism," or risk *being* "racist"—and at these moments, people systematically suppressed race labels altogether from public talk. Adults, in particular, actively suppressed race labels when they were discussing inequitable patterns potentially implicating themselves. While adults spoke matter-of-factly in public about how race mattered to student-student peer relations, for example, they never spoke publicly at all about how race mattered to student-adult power relations: while "the Latinos fought the Samoans" was a possible public statement at Columbus, "the white teachers are having trouble with their Samoan students" was the sort of comment reserved only for private conversations. Similarly, while a teacher at a faculty meeting could nonchalantly announce a state writing contest targeted at "Chinese students" or a personal search for "Filipino literature," no public discussion of school reform goals at Columbus—goals for which adults would be held accountable—labeled students racially at all. Similarly, achievement patterns, which intertwined the roles of students and adults in a way that made adults particularly anxious, caused adult speakers particular consternation: while at department meetings adults matter-of-factly described the racial demographics of curriculum, for example ("we need more black literature"), they never assessed the racial demographics of student academic performance ("we need more black students in honors English").

As important as the topic of conversation, finally, was the question of whom one was speaking *to*: while Columbus adults spoke privately in the hallway about racial patterns in school suspensions, they never discussed these racial patterns with one another in faculty meetings. And while district administrators presented racial suspension statistics in matter-of-fact charts to the court monitors overseeing the city's desegregation plan, they deleted these very statistics from communiqués to be seen by school faculty. Race labels could be used easily in school talk, it seemed, only in certain places at certain times—and when they popped up had everything to do with who was speaking where about what.[19]

Some Central Considerations in This Study of Race Talk

In 1969, anthropologist Frederick Barth advised colleagues to stop studying the cultural practices presumed internal to individual "ethnic groups" and start looking instead at how boundaries between multiple such groups were socially maintained. This book takes an analogous approach to the study of "race groups": I am interested here not as much in what it *meant* in some internal fashion to Jake to be black, what it meant to Felicia to be Filipina, what it meant to Luis to be Latino, or what it meant to Steve to be white, as in *when*, in the institution of schooling, people drew lines around Jake or Felicia or Luis or Steve that categorized them as race-group members—and when Jake and Felicia and Luis and Steve drew such lines around themselves.[20] In privileging here this most basic simplifying social practice of racial *identification* over the dynamic complexities of racial *identity* (a distinction I explore further in chapter 1), I build here on anthropological work that has looked closely at the basic practice of description itself—work treating categorizing and delineating "classes of people," as Charles Frake (1980 [1975]) has put it, as a key piece of cultural practice.[21] I also build on historical explorations of how racial categories developed over time, explorations that have been particularly good at showing us people—including scholars of "anthropology," this relatively young "science of the races"—actively labeling people racially through law, policy, and science (indeed, these studies have reminded us that there was a time before racial categories existed).[22] Yet race is not something simply made in the past, but something we can watch being made in the present. We continue to *make race* and to *build racial orders*, I argue here, each and every day in the United States, with the help of the very racialized language we use and refuse.

This study's focus on race *talk* emerged gradually, over many months of struggling to understand racial practice at Columbus. I had originally embarked upon a more typical ethnographic investigation of how important "race" was to Columbus students' "identities"; research questions about race and schooling (which typically investigate one "race" at a time rather than framing "the races" as mutually constituted groups) regularly frame "race" as something students of color own, rather than as a shared set of racializing practices involving people of all ages and "races."[23] Making race words themselves the unit of analysis eventually displaced the study's more traditional research focus on students of color as "racial" actors—and in doing so, it revealed that all players inside and outside Columbus were actually producing racial orders together.

The reconstitution of Columbus itself created a bizarre natural experiment that demonstrated that everyday race talk habits, too, were shared, for some basic patterns of talking and *not* talking racially were reproduced by a new community of 100 almost complete strangers. Privileged to conduct research at Columbus both before and after reconstitution, I have here been an odd sort of anthropologist: with one year of teaching and one year of observing already completed in the spring of 1996, I was far more "native" than most of the new adult "natives" (educators) who arrived the following fall. Yet these new Columbus adults revealed quickly that they were already native to a much larger speech community, for they, like their predecessors, also resisted speaking publicly of racial achievement patterns; they, too, preferred to talk about reforms for "all" students rather than for racialized groups of them; they, too, used race words easily to describe student relations but not relations between students and themselves. Continuing to enjoy a researcher's privileged mobility to talk to players across the school building and school district, and with the time to read legal and district documents not readily accessible to school-level adults, I was now perfectly positioned to confirm that both district and school-level people talked in racial terms at predictable moments and conspicuously did not do so in others—and to learn to understand, over time, when people were deliberately *not* talking about race.

To study race talk like this—as a form of patterned cultural practice, with predictable scripts and silences—requires a special self-consciousness about ethnographic method. Scholars studying race far more often treat the talk they gather as simply quoted opinion to copy down: more rarely do researchers examine the everyday politics and patterns of talking racially.[24] I conducted a good number of interviews during this research, but in the end I decided not to use large portions of these, having become convinced that prompted race talk was always particularly packaged for a researcher and that the "informal logic of actual life" (Geertz 1973, 17) was best demonstrated by more naturalistic interaction with both students and adults. While I spent countless hours observing classrooms, too, much of the data presented in this book emerged in casual research conversations. Such casual conversations were already speech events central to Columbus daily life, and resembled those in which I had participated every day as a teacher: they were informal, impromptu discussions with students and adults in hallways, on outside benches, and in empty classrooms. During my years as a researcher at Columbus (1995–97), I spent almost every day embroiled in such discussions; as I was training to be an anthropologist, people understood that "hanging out" informally *was* my research. As I knew an omnipresent tape recorder would make these informal conversations stilted and awkward, I instead reconstructed these research conversations on paper immediately after they occurred. I did not need to recapture language at the level of grammatical detail required by most linguists, as I was interested primarily in the words and phrases that surrounded race labels in talk, the moments when race labels appeared and disappeared, and the apparent ease or anxiety with which people used them.

I thus participated in most of the school-level talk I present here (if I did not speak, I participated with my very presence), guided by the methodological mantra that I would allow others to bring race labels into any conversation first. Being "white" seemed to make me a more natural confidant of white adults, but being an ex-teacher sympathetic to and supportive of Columbus people's daily struggles positioned me as an acknowledged comrade to Columbus players of all ages and "races," both before and after reconstitution. I assisted administrators, teachers, and students throughout my years as a researcher at Columbus, and I remain friends with a subset of faculty and former students. Notes on my own teaching year in 1994–95 (which form the basis of much of chapter 1) were taken from a personal journal I kept in the hopes of writing a (never finished) first-year teacher memoir; over time, this diary became an important window onto a teacher's dilemmas.

The data eventually used for analysis, thus, was the talk of informal and public occasions when people at and around Columbus used racial labels—and the moments when they worried explicitly to me about doing so. Over time, as I realized that people were routinely talking to me *about* their concerns about race talk and silence, I learned to pay special attention to what linguists and linguistic anthropologists call the "metapragmatic" aspect of language—people talking *about* talking. While Columbus people had "limited awareness" (Silverstein 1981) of some of their racialized deletions and hesitations (no white adults pointed out how predictably they stuttered before saying the word "black," for example), they were brutally aware of many of their struggles with race words. Columbus adults talked to me most agitatedly about the pitfalls of racial description, and our in-depth discussions about the troubles of using race labels became a vital data source.

Finally, I also learned to go looking for race talk in multiple institutional locations. Seeking patterns in the use, contestation, and deletion of racial terms, I documented discourse from school board meetings, superintendent's addresses, conversations between teachers held in classrooms, hallways, and happy hours, conversations between teachers, students, parents, and administrators in and out of classrooms, and conversations between students both in and out of school. I also systematically gathered the written artifacts of legal opinions, district and school-level statistics, district pronouncements and press releases, union newsletters, faculty newsletters and memos, student assignments, newspaper articles, and educational research itself. Over time, comparing private to public talk became essential to this analysis, as Columbus people often conspicuously de-raced their public talk of the very topics (achievement, discipline, opportunity) to which they privately muttered that race mattered most problematically.[25] In the end, though, six core dilemmas of race talk and silence seemed to pervade all levels of schooling; as they started to become evident everywhere I looked, they soon came to seem fundamental to American race talk. Each chapter in the book fleshes out one of them.

Dilemmas Piled upon Paradoxes: The Organization of the Book

The book begins with Columbus students challenging the very idea of "racial groups" (chapter 1); it continues with adult and student debates over when race mattered to life at Columbus (chapter 2). After expanding the analysis to include district and legal struggles with race talk and racial inequality (chapters 3–5), it returns finally to Columbus to watch Columbus adults anxiously deleting one race label in particular, and in the process reproducing a racialized disparity despite themselves (chapter 6). The book concludes ("Moving Forward") by offering possible solutions to these dilemmas, arguing that we must become more proactively and critically conscious about race talk—that we must learn to discuss fruitfully not just our racial inequalities, but also the very question of when and how to use race talk strategically to address particular problems. A final section ("Practically Speaking") addresses educators in particular.

Chapter 1, then, begins by exploring the most fundamental dilemma of U.S. race talk, one demonstrated daily by Columbus students engaged explicitly in the very process of racial classification: *we don't belong to simple race groups, but we do.* Columbus students, many of whom proudly considered themselves multiracial or "mixed," always challenged the accuracy of simple race labels when discussing racial classification itself; when discussing other topics, however, they regularly placed themselves and one another into a handful of simplified groups they called "racial." These dynamics of racial identification were always intertwined with dynamics of power: while students' talk *about* racial classification routinely called the very borders and reality of "race groups" into question, such contestation over group membership ("*Is* he Samoan?" "What *is* 'white'?") vanished in everyday talk about racial *equality.* In classrooms and at public events, even "mixed" students demanded the equal curricular representation of Columbus's six "racial" groups, reifying these groups as things they should "learn about" in equal amounts; and adults and students speaking to one another typically proceeded as if people at Columbus belonged naturally to this simple, six-group "racial" taxonomy. Most school talk, in fact, takes no time to critique the boundaries or very notion of "race groups"—for school people typically worry about racial inequality rather than the very idea of racial

classification. Accordingly, the student challenge to racial categorization remains submerged until the conclusion of the book, where I discuss the possibility of modeling Columbus students' strategy of "race-bending": that is, strategically interrogating the very notion of "racial" difference even while keeping
race labels available for inequality analysis.

Chapter 2 begins to look at Columbus adults and students struggling not
with whether clear-cut "race groups" existed at Columbus, then, but with when
and how race mattered to everyday life there. In examining a particularly routine kind of everyday talk at Columbus—talk about social relations—the chapter explores a second fundamental dilemma plaguing U.S. race talk: in American logic, *race doesn't matter, but it does.* In the United States, it seems, we
expect and want race sometimes not to matter and sometimes to matter very
much; and daily talk at Columbus was accordingly routinely unclear about
when race "really mattered." Race labels waxed and waned in daily conversation, implying that race was only sometimes relevant; and when asked to sum
up whether race mattered, people often denied that it did. Yet at less self-
conscious moments, speakers used race labels matter-of-factly in public talk of
student-student relations as if such relations were *unequivocally* racial, speaking
so easily of student friendships and "riots" that the relevance of race to student
relations came to seem almost expected; and they *deleted* race labels from public
talk of student-*adult* relations that were perhaps racial too problematically. The
chapter concludes that the moments when we delete race labels from our talk
are perhaps the moments in which race matters most dangerously. Figuring
out *how* race matters thus involves attention not just to moments when we talk
overly easily "about race," but also to moments when we resist talking about
race at all—and the rest of the book follows this prescription.

Chapter 3 next tells a legal and school reform story about Columbus and its
district, in which race labels indeed vanished at the moments when they were
most relevant: namely, in talk of reforms designed to achieve racial equality.
Charting this tale historically and then over the turbulent spring of "reconstitution" at Columbus, the chapter demonstrates a third key dilemma of U.S. race
talk: *the de-raced words we use when discussing plans for achieving racial equality
can actually keep us from discussing ways to make opportunities racially equal.* Over
several decades of desegregation in California City, I demonstrate, a 1960s
concern for equalizing the educational opportunities of "black" students became submerged in a de-raced 1980s equality discourse of serving "*all* students." While this discourse of "all students" contained a decades-long quest
for racial equality, reform talk about serving "all" would itself replace discussion
of improving educational opportunities for specific racialized groups. Likewise,
during the reconstitution battles of Columbus's 1995–96 school year, district
representatives speaking of expected school reforms repeatedly submerged the
court's renewed concern for "African-American" and "Hispanic" students
within talk of reforms for "all students"; in turn, Columbus adults hoping to

avoid reconstitution spoke only of serving "all students" in the presence of district personnel. After the district finally fired all Columbus adults in 1996, the newly hired staff quickly reproduced this reform discourse of assisting "all"—completing a cycle in which no public analysis of assisting "African-Americans" and "Hispanics" in particular had occurred.

As chapter 4 shows next, the absence of race labels from public reform discourse was the result of confusion over inequality analysis as much as an explicit resistance to speaking racially. Analyzing inequality, I demonstrate, poses another fundamental challenge for U.S. speakers, especially in particularly diverse places: at and around "low-income," multi-"minority" Columbus, speakers seemed perennially unclear about whether race groups like "African-Americans" and "Hispanics" actually had fewer opportunities to succeed in school than anybody else. Speakers contested all available descriptions of educational "disadvantage," demonstrating deep uncertainty about who exactly was disadvantaged in comparison to whom; in trying to analyze opportunity citywide, speakers similarly shifted their analytic lenses both between "race" and "class" analyses and between an analysis framing all "minorities" as less advantaged than whites and one framing certain "minorities" as particularly "at risk." Through such analytic motion, ironically, speakers blurred *all* inequality analyses—and in the end, many abandoned altogether the task of determining how race mattered to educational opportunity. In our confusion over ascertaining the role race still plays in our complex multiracial and class-diverse inequalities, I warn, we often delete racial analyses of inequality prematurely. In doing so, we demonstrate another key dilemma of race talk: *the more complex inequality seems to get, the more simplistic inequality analysis seems to become.* The oversimplification of inequality analysis has real repercussions for students left to experience inequality without remedy: in the late 1990s in California City, policymakers dismantling the city's desegregation order and deleting race from the city's public inequality analysis (mirroring the statewide deletion of affirmative action remedies) would leave behind no sophisticated analytic framework for analyzing the distribution of educational opportunity at all.

Chapter 5 proceeds by examining a kind of race analysis that did keep rearing its head in district-and school-level discourse, even as analyses of educational opportunity were being erased: adults seemed mentally programmed to compare the *academic achievement* of the available "racial groups." District administrators routinely informed the newspapers and the courts of districtwide racial achievement patterns in the mid-1990s, while Columbus adults repeatedly compared race groups in private conversations about how students achieved at Columbus; yet such talk about existing racial achievement patterns appeared in public only sporadically, and only for specific audiences. The seemingly omnipresent question about how race groups achieved was the very question district and school adults most often refused to articulate when speaking publicly to one another—and when school and district speakers *did* mention racial achievement patterns, they routinely blamed these patterns on actors other than themselves. Examining the wider dynamics of race and blame in achievement talk at and around Columbus, chapter 5 argues that Americans actually *expect* school achievement to be racially ordered, yet we tend to *name* racial achievement patterns only when doing so does not seem to implicate ourselves personally. Paradoxically, the chapter thus reveals, *the questions we ask most about race are the very questions we most suppress.* I suggest that since both matter-of-fact talk blaming others for racial disparities and anxious *silence* about such disparities can serve to naturalize these very disparities, we might instead consider speaking proactively as if such disparities can be communally prevented and dismantled.

The final chapter addresses directly the most vexing paradox of racial description: *although talking in racial terms can make race matter, not talking in racial terms can make race matter too.* We return to the Columbus corridors to explore this final race talk dilemma. Listening to Columbus adults discuss an everyday school "problem"—students wandering through the hallways cutting class—we examine the use and deletion of one specific race label at Columbus: "black." In the hallways and in empty classrooms, adults privately muttered their perception that "black students" were overrepresented among the students wandering the halls. However, they admitted that even as they worried that this overrepresentation of "black students" among the "hall wanderers" "needed to be talked about"—since suppressing talk of "blacks" in Columbus's hallways effectively allowed black students to wander the halls in disproportionate numbers—they themselves self-consciously deleted the very word "black" from their public talk of the hall wandering "problem." Intending to avoid the potential "racism" of describing the hall wanderers as disproportionately "black," they explained, they omitted the word from public discourse quite purposefully. Yet few noticed an additional unintended consequence of these deletions: actively suppressing the word "black" from public talk of school "problems" served daily to *increase* the perceived relevance of blackness to these problems. In whispering anxiously in private about the isolated disproportionate role of "blacks" in school "problems," that is, adults deflected any analysis of their *own* role in producing the hallways' racial demographics—and they repeatedly framed "black" students themselves as an intrinsically "problematic" population. In knowingly saying nothing publicly about the overrepresentation of "blacks" in the hallway, further, Columbus adults effectively *ignored* black students *in racial terms.* In the end, such silence itself was a form of racializing action: for black students themselves remained both wandering disproportionately and quietly reviled. This book is, in the end, about how people anxiously remaining colormute risk institutionalizing the very racial patterns they abhor—and I conclude with recommendations about talking more skillfully.

Columbus Dilemmas as the Dilemmas of Us All

The description of "kinds of people" in the postmodern world, long acknowledged as a thorny analytic and social problem for anthropologists and other social scientists, is also a daily problem for "natives" themselves.[26] As both anthropologist and "native," I have found dealing with the dilemmas of race talk to be the central difficulty of writing this book. I want to make sure that readers see these dilemmas not as the fumblings and bumblings of strangers, but as dilemmas that belong to us all. Because this book focuses on one school's struggles, my analysis could backfire most on my teacher colleagues, since critiques of schooling seem to land most heavily on educators. I want to make clear that my position echoes that of George Spindler, the first champion of the anthropology of education, who stated in one of his earliest analyses that "It should also be clear that I have not been castigating teachers. They are the agents of their culture" (Spindler 1963, 156). All Americans, including this author, must fumble with race words often too clumsy to describe precise realities; we must fumble with the knowledge that both using and deleting race words can serve alternately to dismantle racial orders and to reinforce them. Most frustrating, we all must negotiate a world in which our very confusions over when to talk as if race matters help re-create a world in which it does.

A Note to Readers

Throughout the data segments presented in this book, I embed some of my analytic points within the data presented; within the quoted material from my own field notes, my own analysis appears in italics within square brackets. I have also often put racial and other labels in quotation marks to draw attention to them *as* labels. Such quotation marks are not meant to indicate any judgment of the speakers. More significantly, I use racial labels myself to describe speakers throughout this book, a practice that may strike some readers as a blatant attempt to make race seem relevant to speakers' words. Noting that speakers are "black," for example, may set up their words to be heard as critical; describing teachers as "white" may set up their words to be heard as "racist" (to many U.S. ears, "white teacher" primes us to expect racism in a way "teacher" does not.) Yet it would be a hypocritical silence, I think, to leave racial terms out of my own descriptions. For to me in this research, speakers almost always appeared racial.

One

We Don't Belong to Simple Race Groups, but We Do

> There is a yellow one that won't accept the black one
> that won't accept the red one that won't accept the
> white one
> Different strokes for different folks and so
> on and so on and scoobie doobie doo
>   —Sly and the Family Stone, "Everyday People"

ANALYSTS WRITING ON RACE in the United States often try to remind "everyday people" of a basic paradox about our categories of racial difference: "racial" categories are fake units of human diversity (the world's "racial" groups are more genetically diverse *within* themselves than *between* themselves), yet we have, over centuries of social racializing practice, created a country of "racially" "different folks."[1] We have long lumped together diverse people into simple "racial" units in a system of social relations and differentially distributed power: as Outlaw (1990) puts it, "That 'race' is without a scientific basis in biological terms does not mean, thereby, that it is without any social value" (77–78). Race categories are inherently paradoxical, many scholars have argued, since they are simultaneously invalid *and* now "a key component of our 'taken-for-granted valid reference schema' through which we get on in the world" (58).[2] Yet while analysts struggle to articulate this complex paradox of race to the public, every-day people themselves treat racial categories this paradoxically all the time. We can see this best in places where the very idea of "race groups" is both contested daily and repeatedly imposed.

Among Columbus students, as this chapter shows, the lines delineating "race groups" were daily both fundamentally blurred and constantly redrawn. Many students across Columbus, for example, listed strings of categories to describe themselves: at Columbus, being "mixed" was an exceedingly common way of life, and even students who did not consider themselves "mixed" acknowledged that it was often quite hard to tell "what" anybody at Columbus "was." At Columbus, where many students spoke of being uninformed about what "races" they were and joked about looking like races that they were not, racial categorization was routinely put up for debate. Yet these daily negotiations over race group membership coexisted with the described simplicity of "six different groups": while racialized *identities* at Columbus were admittedly in-finitely complex, racial *identification* was an accepted process of social simplification.[3] Often seemingly forgetting the widespread complications of individual "mixture," students routinely divided the student body into a basic taxonomy of six groups they called "racial"—"Latinos," "blacks," "Filipinos," "Samoans," "Chinese," and "whites."[4] I call this paradoxical treatment of race categories "race-bending," as Columbus students both defied and strategically imposed such simple "racial" labels every day—and in the process, they demonstrated that racial categories will for some time remain key social ordering devices. Indeed, as this chapter shows, Columbus students demonstrated quite gracefully a basic paradox of U.S. racial practice that professional analysts of race articulate only rather clumsily: *we don't belong to simple race groups, but we do.*

So many of the symbols displayed by Columbus students signified a pan-Columbus and, some might argue, increasingly global youth identity—the key chains dangling pounds of plastic ornaments, the baseball caps, the signatures or "tags" upon folders and backpacks, the omnipresent Nike symbol splattered upon shirts and shoes and caps and necklaces and earrings.[5] When I asked students to take my camera for a day and capture images that seemed particularly representative of their daily lives, students who often labeled themselves "black," "Latin," "Filipino," or "white" photographed themselves in front of identical bedroom posters of Tupac Shakur. Many of the homes I visited of students who called themselves "Filipino" or "Latino" or "black" or "Samoan," further, displayed crosses on walls or on shelves, just as students displayed crosses on their bodies; the graduation speeches of students of all "races" routinely included thanks to a Christian God.

Yet homes also displayed subtle symbols of so-called "race"-group particularity—an African drum in a corner of a room, a map of the Philippines on the refrigerator. Students would often comment that these objects were really important only to their parents, but at the same time they displayed various symbols of group affiliation on their own bodies—a flat square pendant from the Philippines, a similar dangling religious icon from Mexico or Nicaragua or Guatemala, a jade ornament from China, a tiny necklace or tricolored earring of the African continent. Along with words and actions and negotiations over physical appearances, such symbols contributed to race practice at Columbus, practice in which a central contradiction reigned: students were both boxed into "racial" categorizations, and exploding out of such boxes all the time.

Student *talk* at Columbus itself demonstrated this contradiction exquisitely. Within many single interactions and even within single sentences at Columbus, student talk both struggled against racial categories and gave in to them. That is, students talked alternately as if "race" labels were a perfectly adequate summation of human diversity and as if such single labels did not accurately fit people at all. Whether they talked one way or the other depended, tautologically, on whether they were debating the very process of racial categorization or simply describing the world as racially ordered. As the first part of this chapter shows, students always wound up contesting easy accounts of race-group membership in casual and classroom discussions *about racial classification itself*. Yet throughout these very conversations and almost always when talking with adults about other things, as Part 2 argues, students employed a shorthand language of simple race terms that assumed people fit easily into a simple, six-group race taxonomy. This simple language of what I call "lump-sum" racial terms dominated Columbus's daily race talk, and it was particularly fundamental to talk of school's preeminent racial anxiety: equality (see Part 3). When calling for students' equal "race"-group representation in the various public arenas of school life, that is, nobody contested the placement of people *into* "racial groups"—they simply asked whether each of these groups got its due attention. In keeping simple racial identifications strategically available for inequality analysis despite their startling diversity of identities, Columbus students demonstrated that racial categories are in fact always birthed in inequality contexts—and that in a nation with a legacy of simple-race logic, negotiating toward equality will accordingly require using "racial" categories strategically even as we alternately call them into question.[6]

We start, then, by listening to students talking about racial classification itself. As the following fieldnotes demonstrate, students debating the classification of specific people always made the boundaries of race categories seem negotiable rather than firm; talking *about* racial classification always exposed racialization itself as a negotiated human process of differentiating "peoples."[7] Yet throughout these very recurrent games of "guessing" one another's race group membership, students hinted that everyone in the end was somehow supposed to be racially identifiable—and in doing so, they indicated that they would accept the use of simple race categories at certain times and for certain purposes to describe complex people.

Part 1: Students Talking about Racial Classification Itself

I had already finished a year's tenure at Columbus as an Ethnic Literature teacher when I participated in the following conversation as a researcher hanging out in a school library study hall. The study hall teacher, a former colleague, had asked me to request that a student take his hat off. "School rule," I explained to the student, smiling; he was small, wiry, light-brown-skinned, with a pointed nose and freckles, enveloped in baggy clothes and a big black ski cap. He was "allergic to Columbus," he joked as he removed his cap, taking care to add that he was "just playin'." Pointing out another student, he suddenly started a guessing game:

> "Does that girl over there look Mexican to you?" he asked. "I don't know, do you think she does?" I asked. "Don't you think she looks Mexican?" he repeated. "I guess so, why?" I asked. " 'Cause she's not Mexican, she's Samoan!" he said, smiling. "Samoan and white, with some black," he added. "Hey, don't be pointing!" the girl yelled

over at us, smiling slightly. "I ain't no Mexican!" she added. "How do you know so much about her?" I asked him. "She's my cousin. And she's his cousin too, and he's mine!" he said, pointing to a guy sitting next to him who was somewhat bigger, with curlier hair, fewer freckles, and a wider nose. "So are you Samoan too?" I asked. "Yeah, Samoan . . . and part white, and part Chinese," he said. "So do you call yourself Samoan?" I asked [*I myself keep imposing this lump-sum categorization*]. "Yeah . . . and part white, and part Chinese!" he said, laughing.

The girl next to him said, "I'm Samoan, black, Puerto Rican, Filipino, and Indian." She was tall, freckled, with long braid extensions wrapped up into a loose knot on her head; I had met her earlier that day. "Indian from India, or Native American?" I asked, pointing at the table to mean "the U.S." "Native American," she said, mimicking my gesture. "How do you know all this about yourself?" I asked her. "My mom! My mom tells me," she replied. "What does she call herself?" I asked. "Others," she said matter-of-factly. "What?" I asked. "Others, like that's what she puts down," she said. "Oh, on forms and stuff. What do you put?" I asked. "Other," she said. "That's what I put, too," said the small guy, adding, "I don't know what to put. Or I put 'Polynesian.'"

"What'd you say you were?" called over a girl with straightened-looking hair and slightly darker skin. "Samoan, black, Puerto Rican, Filipino, and Indian," the freckled girl repeated. "Hey, you tryin' to be like ME," the other girl called back, smiling slightly. "Nobody's tryin' to be like nobody," said the small boy. [*Guessing game starts again:*] "I bet I can tell what everybody is," he said. "Like you, you're black and Filipino, right?" he said to a guy down the table. "What?" the guy replied. "You're black and Filipino, right?" he repeated. "Yeah," this guy said, nodding slowly. "And he's part Samoan and part white," the small boy said, gesturing toward a guy with a long braid sitting two seats away. "What's your dad?" a girl asked this braided kid. "He's French," he replied, very softly. "I can always tell a Samoan," said the small guy, shaking his head and smiling. "How?" I asked. "I just can," he said.

The simple identification "Samoan" triumphed at the close of this brief exchange, despite the students' proudly announced complexity. While racial identities were being treated here as infinitely expandable—a "Samoan" could actually be "Samoan and white, with some black," or "Samoan and part white and part Chinese"—the complexity of "being" "Samoan, black, Puerto Rican, Filipino, and Indian" could easily be reduced to a one-word identification prioritizing one label on the list. Both the single-word options of "forms" requiring respondents to "put down" single identifications (even the bottomless, hypersimplified "other") and the simplifying language of one's study-hall peers enforced this simple identification process. Still, as the small boy turned to another student to continue the guessing game (momentarily replacing "race" with the sporadic synonym "nationality"), the students demonstrated that being a "full" member of any single "group" at Columbus still often seemed an exception to the normality of "mixture":

"What's your nationality?" he asked another girl, who was sitting at our table. "Full black, right?" he added. She nodded slowly, her lips pursed. "Full black?" I repeated. She nodded. "Nothing of anything else?" I asked. She shook her head slowly. "I don't think so," she said. "So you call yourself black—you don't ever use 'African-American' or whatever . . . ?" I asked. "I'm BLACK," she said, shrugging her shoulders and shaking her head. "She's full Samoan," said the smaller guy, pointing to another girl at our table.

He and the bigger guy started asking the five-ethnicity girl about Samoan words. She translated the first five or ten words they said as "shit," or some variation thereof. "Where'd you learn all *these*, your mother?!" I asked her. We laughed. Then she started translating different words they tested her with—"nose," and "pregnant woman." When she got that one they seemed surprised, and somehow convinced that she really knew her stuff. "Wow! Are you fluent in Samoan?" I asked, also surprised. She nodded. "Do you speak 'Puerto Rican'?" I asked, smiling. "No, I don't really speak Spanish," she said. "What else did you say you were?" I asked. [*I'm in the race talk groove now: one "is" a group or a combination of groups.*] She repeated her list. "Do you speak Tagalog?" I asked. She shook her head. " 'Did you ever live in Samoa?" I asked. Yes, she said, she lived there with her grandmother for two years when she was younger. "Do you speak Samoan at home?" I asked. She nodded.

[*Trying to join the game more explicitly, I find that the category "white" is not expected to be much fun:*] "So what do I look like?" I asked the guys. "White," said the smaller one. "No more specific than that?" I asked. "What do you mean—you're white," he said. "So you get to be Samoan, white, and Chinese and I just get to be 'white'?" I asked. He smiled. "Like what kind of things?" he asked. "I dunno," I said, shrugging. "German?" one of the guys said. I kept shrugging, and eventually said that I had grandparents from Russia. "So you're Russian," said the smaller guy. [*Simple identification triumphs—the label is a new one for me, but I accept it.*] I shrugged and nodded. "I guess so," I said.

[*Now, someone starts dividing the category "Samoan" into even smaller parts:*] "Are you from Western Samoa or American?" the small guy asked the 5-ethnicity girl. "American," she said. "Is there a difference?" I asked. "Yeah," the boys said. "Then there's Tongans, and Fijians," the small guy said. "Are Tongans different?" I asked. "Yeah—we don't eat horses!" said the bigger guy. Several people laughed. "WE eat the pig, and chicken," he continued. "Everyone eats chicken!" said the smaller guy. "And ___, and ___," continued the guys, naming foods in Samoan and laughing. "Who's 'we'?!" I asked. "Samoans," they answered.

Simple identification triumphed again here. Struggling throughout the conversation to understand the students' constantly shifting lines of differentiation (hence my overwhelmed "who's 'we'?!"), I myself, of course, kept fueling the quest to draw simpler classificatory lines, with questions like "Is there a difference?" and "Are Tongans different?"[8] Yet as the students themselves contrasted the lump-sum category "Samoan" to absent groups like "Tongans" and "Fijians," they melted their own sub-distinctions of national origin (Western vs. American Samoa) back into the simplicity of "Samoanness." Mystified by the suddenly simplified self-identification of this now-assembled group of "Samoans," I next asked who in the group had actually been to Samoa. The "5-ethnicity girl," the bigger boy, and the braided boy said they had, while the small boy who could "always tell a Samoan" said he had actually never visited. Yet whether one had actually been to Samoa, he indicated, seemed less important to claiming "Samoanness" than whether one had people around to tell stories about it:

"So you've never been to Samoa?" I asked the smaller guy. "No," he said. "How do you know this stuff?" I asked. "My mom told me," he said. "And they eat __," added the 5-ethnicity girl, still harking back to the food list with a word in Samoan. "Who's 'they'?" I asked her. "Oh, well, 'us,' I guess . . . but I don't EAT spinach," she said. "And Tongans have big noses," added the small guy. "Like some Samoans, too, hella big!" added the bigger guy. A girl at the table raised her head from her magazine (*Ebony*) and said, "Don't be putting us down like that, I ain't no Tongan, we don't got noses nearly that big."

The "Samoan," "white," and "black" girl cousin who supposedly looked "Mexican" came nearby. "Hella heavy lipstick, man!" said one of the guys. "Hey, you better wash off that eye stuff, you look like a Mexican," said the small guy, smiling. "Is that an insult?" I asked him quizzically. "No," he replied. "Mehicano," he mused, seeming to like the way it sounded. "You guys act Mexican, cause you're from LA," the kid with a braid said to him, adding, "I never seen a Samoan that looks like you."

Group boundaries were simultaneously blurred and reinscribed here. The students had spent much of this conversation debating the very category "Samoan," but somehow through all this contestation the category "Samoan" survived. With the telling "oh, well, 'us,' I guess," the "5-ethnicity girl" indicated that a sense of one's "Samoan" *identity* could suddenly hinge precariously on whether or not one ate spinach, or whether or not one knew a Samoan word; yet people could be simply *identified* as "Samoan" even if they were only "part" Samoan, or even if they didn't really "look" Samoan, with or without knowledge of the Samoan language or a taste for Samoan foods.[9] They could wash off temporary "Mexican" appearances or cease "Mexican"/"LA" behaviors and return to Samoanness; they could *be* Samoan having grown up in Samoa, spent two years there, or never been. A "Samoan" girl reading a magazine targeted toward "blacks," a boy who was "Samoan and part white and part Chinese," a boy who was "part Samoan and part white," and a girl who was "Samoan, black, Puerto Rican, Filipino, and Indian" all finally identified themselves as matter-of-factly "Samoan" in comparison to other matter-of-factly bounded groups ("Mexicans," "Tongans," "Fijians") said to have bigger noses, wear more makeup, or eat stranger foods. Despite the complexities of "mixture," migration, and family history, it seemed, one was strategically *still* "*Samoan*"—particularly when ranking "Samoans" in comparison to other lump-sum groups.

Such games of classification and labeling thus bent race categories, but did not break them. While the boundaries encircling the groups mentioned could open to include different people at different moments, the basic structure of available categories remained sturdy. Indeed, to even answer questions like "what are you mixed with?" and "what are you?", students had to describe themselves or others with a host of simple race terms, as the sum of numerable matter-of-fact parts; although each individual's string of code could be different, these racial "parts" always seemed to add up to some articulable identification.[10] In boasting that he could "tell what everybody was," the boy spearheading the classification game had indicated both that it took considerable skill to identify people at hyper-"mixed" Columbus and that everybody in the end would be racially categorizable.

Occasionally, as I found one summer school day visiting a teacher friend at a nearby junior high, students even merged existing race terms into new race terms to identify "mixed" people racially. Indeed, my notes' own imposed physically descriptive language ("Filipino-looking," "black guys") demonstrated a cultural context in which racialized phrases seemed almost obvious shorthand for describing people:

> A Filipino-looking guy is speaking to two black guys and one Filipino-looking guy sitting in an informal circle. He says, "I know who's a niggapino—my auntie. And that one guy, he's a niggapino; my cousin's a pino; she's (points across room) a japapino."

In inventing such new race terms (and to me, disturbing ones, in the case of using "nigga" to denote a category I presumed to be "black") to describe the complex "mixture" of specific people, of course, students were indicating that the very practice of racial classification was a human act that could be actively contested. Yet they were also imposing the received idea of racial categories upon people who defied the very concept. During a discussion about "assumptions" in one of my own classes in 1994, similarly, Lani suddenly started trying to explain to me how she could "tell who was Filipino," and while everybody was soon indicating that in a place like Columbus using physical or linguistic signals to identify strangers was actually quite problematic, all but one of us left the conversation racially identified:

Lani: I can tell who's Filipino 'cause I'm Filipino.

Nando: Yeah, I can tell who's Latino 'cause I am. Like her (points to Anita), she looks white but I know she's Latino 'cause of how she talks.

Me: Did you grow up speaking Spanish?

Nando: Yeah.

Me: What about someone who grows up speaking English at home? (I see Mina [*a Filipina student*] nodding.)

Nando: I can still tell. Like you, I can tell you're, well, white 'cause of the color of your hair [*reddish brown*]. Michael, I can tell he's white, just 'cause.

Michael: But I'm not.

Me (to Michael): How would you describe yourself? (He shrugs.) Okay, you don't want to? (He shakes his head.) Okay, he doesn't have to.

Carrie: You can't always tell—people never know I'm Hawaiian.

Me: Do you think you look Hawaiian?

Carrie: (She shakes her head.) I look white.

Nando: Really? I would've thought you were white or Latino.

Me: Do people assume anything about you when they find out you're Hawaiian?

Carrie: No, 'cause they hardly ever find out or guess.

Although Lani and Nando had first framed racial classification as a simple task, our conversation about classification quickly demonstrated that people throughout the room claimed identities as members of unsuspected groups (later that year, similarly, Anita read an original poem about being "Chicana" that included the line, "I look white, but I'm not!"). Michael, whose very shrugging silence proved that racial identity was not always something you could "find out or guess," said to me later in an informal interview with his best friend Justin (who did classify himself as "white" in his own Ethnic Literature class) that although he himself "*appeared* white," "there are hecka races in me." Michael now called himself a "white black kid," adding that he got along with "black kids" because he grew up with them and with "Filipino kids" because he had "Filipino cousins." He had no interest in hanging out with "Samoans," though, he said—they always "caused trouble."

Michael wasn't easily categorized, we might note, but his friends and relatives suddenly seemed to be. While talk about racial classification itself had Michael describing his own blend of "hecka races," that is, matter-of-fact talk about social relations had him slotting others into simple racial groups. When *not* focused explicitly on contesting racial classification, students at Columbus often demonstrated what seemed to be mass amnesia about the blurred complexity of their racial demographics. The day before Thanksgiving vacation during my teaching year, for example, a conflict erupted that, within hours, was termed a "racial riot" between "blacks" and "Latinos": a "Latino" student and a "black" student had confronted each other, people said, and after some individual retaliations, black and Latino students rushed to join their respective sides. I myself spent one class period that day convincing several students, who were breathless with anxious excitement, not to run into the hall to join the shouts and running footsteps outside our classroom. School closed early to reduce tensions, and a number of students ended up arrested as the conflict moved to a nearby street.

It seemed necessary to me at the time to remind my students that these simple race categories did not matter-of-factly fit Columbus's complex people, and when I returned from vacation I decided to work more on deconstructing race in class. Planning a day of wrestling with a purposefully impossible question ("What makes one 'racial group' different from another?"), I asked the students for permission to tape-record our conversation, thinking we might critique our own comments at the end of the year. We giggled throughout the day about this "talk show" format, but our initial "embarrassment" soon was replaced by heated debate. As the following segment from one class demonstrates, students actually needed little prodding to contest the school's race categories—that is, when they were talking about racial categorization itself rather than simply operating in its terms. In the following transcript portion, "student" represents various student voices:

> **Me**: What I said before—all right, don't be embarrassed by this tape recorder! The reason why I have race in quotation marks on the board, is because it's sort of something that people have constructed, and what I mean by that is, they've *made* it. They've *made* race an important issue, OK? So the first question is, "What makes one race different from another?" One thing about race is that people thought of it to make people *different*—you're in one race, I'm in another race, he's in another race, she's in another race. OK? First of all, if one of you guys were to name the races that exist in this world, what would they be?
> **Student**: (muffled, softly) Black and white.
> **Me**: You would just say black and white?
> **Another Student**: (softly, but decisively/defiantly) No. [*Contestation begins*]
> **Me**: OK. What would you say?
> **Student**: African-American, um, white, Filipino, (mumbles): there's a lot of 'em. (some laughter)
> **Me**: OK, African-American, wait! (Writing on the board)
> **Student**: White. (some laughs)
> **Me**: African-American . . .
> **Student**: (mumbling)
> **Student**: African-American, Caucasian, Asian, um . . . Indian-American, um, Native, (softer) is it Native American? I dunno which one it is, is it a Native American race? And, there's a red . . . (mumbles) there IS, there's a red, um . . . on the application they also have a red.
> **Me**: OK, on the applications. [*Again, bureaucratic forms play a key role in teaching simple identifications.*]
> **Student**: Mm-hmm.
> **Me**: So you're talking about race coming from—
> **Student**: From (muffled)
> **Me**: Categories coming from applications.
> **Student**: (breaks in) NOOOO! It don't say red, (mumbles) it'd say yellow.
> **Me**: OK. So let's say you said African American. [*Here I try deliberately to complicate this racial category.*] Remember when we were talking about Barbados as being one

of the places where slaves went in that triangle trade, remember when we were talking about that?

Student: Uh-huh. (mumbles)

M: OK? What would someone—that's in the Caribbean Ocean, OK?—what would someone who grew up there be called, in those categories? What would someone be called?

Student (male): (unintelligible)

(pause)

Me: Would some—

Student (female): In the Caribbean?

Me: Yeah! Someone who was very dark-skinned but grew up, didn't grow up in the United States.

Student (female): Cuban.

Student (another girl): Cuban.

Me: You would call them Cuban?

Students: (many voices): (Amalia's emerges): Not really, if they're—if they're from the Caribbean and they speak Spanish they'd be Latino.

Me: You'd call them Latino.

Amalia: Latino—

Student (female): Not really. [*Contestation heightens.*]

Me: OK.

Student: (female): Cuban!

Student: (other female): They could be Cuban, or . . .

Student: Cubans are Latino.

Student: No . . .

Student: Yeah, but they call them Cuban. [*Boundaries of "Latino" becoming unclear.*]

Student: Everybody's (*muffled*)

Student: Cuban and Latino are two different things.

Me: OK, I see, what do you mean by that, what, wait—

Student: (wailing) What're you talking about, that Cuban isn't Latino!

Me: As she just said, everyone's different . . .

(male voice: unintelligible)

Student: Why don't they just say Latino then? Why do you put the Cuban and then . . .

Student: OKAY!

Student (Amalia): 'Cause that's what I AM, I'm Cuban and Salvadoran. [*Given the students' own admissions, I should add here that I had assumed for several months that Amalia labeled herself as "black."*]

Student: No . . .

Student: (loudly) You just said it was the same!

Various student voices: Latino . . . but Latino's the same THING! It's Latino! / Why didn't you say Cuban AND Latino . . . / the system here . . . / (laughter) / it's Latino . . .

In several minutes of discussing racial classification directly, we had made clear that the familiar label "Latino," ironically a key category in the recent "riot," was human-made: "Latino" was not a natural unit of human diversity, but rather a socially produced unit of "the system here."[11] Such simple identifications, the students noted further, were routinely superimposed upon complex identities: human classifiers, like themselves, often "called people" names that were simplifications (or misrepresentations) of what people truly "were." While the conversation here focused mostly on the labeling practices of others (the omnipotent "they"), students talking at length about how they learned to identify *themselves* in racial terms suggested that self-classification was no less fraught with potential error. One day in 1995, for example, I ran into Robert, a former student, outside in the main quad, and I asked how he was doing. Our simple conversation about "Latin American Studies" turned quickly into a discussion of his own fluctuating self-labeling process:

> Robert told me he was taking some courses at California City College in the afternoons; one of them was "Latin American Studies." I asked what he was reading and he showed me *Down These Mean Streets* by Piri Thomas, saying he liked it. "What's it about?" I asked. "A Puerto Rican kid growing up," he said. "Do you feel like you relate to it at all?" I asked. "Yeah—the gangs and stuff. Not that I really relate to gangs, but like that stuff, and the fights he gets into," he said. "Do you relate to the Puerto Rican part?" I asked [*an unusually leading question for me, but with an unexpected answer*]. "Yeah, 'cause I'm actually part Puerto Rican," he said.[12] "Really?" I asked (he hadn't mentioned this last year in class). "Yeah—my mom's Filipino and Puerto Rican, and my dad's Mexican and Puerto Rican, so I'm mostly Puerto Rican," he said. "Have you ever been there?" I asked. "No—I just did some research on it, on my culture," he said. A friend standing next to him snickered a little bit when Robert said "research." "How?" I asked. "I asked some friends, the friends I have from Puerto Rico and stuff, what it's like," he said. " 'Cause I don't even remember you mentioning this in class," I said. " 'Cause I didn't KNOW I was Puerto Rican!" he said, smiling. He continued: "I thought I was Hawaiian, but I was curious about my grandfather's last name. I asked my mom, 'cause I was like, that doesn't sound Hawaiian. And my mom said no, he was born in Puerto Rico." "You never mentioned the Hawaiian part in class either," I said, smiling. "No—I was all confused last year. What did I say I was?" he asked. "Uh, I think Mexican and part Filipino, you definitely didn't mention Hawaiian," I said. "I didn't? I thought I did," he said, continuing, "Well, I went to Mexico last year, you remember—met my family. I don't have much family around here, and I feel sort of, you know, alienated, and then I met all this family and I was like, wow! I didn't know I had so much family! I want to go to Puerto Rico and meet that part, and go to the Philippines and meet that part. And I think I have some family in Hawaii, so I want to meet them," he said. The bell was ringing so we had to leave.

In the assignments in my Ethnic Literature class the previous year that had prompted written self-identification, Robert had actually described himself simply as "Latin" (on one assignment about "racial discrimination," notably, he had recounted particularly matter-of-factly how he and his friends had been harassed in clothing stores "just because we were Latins"). He had also described himself in some class discussions about classification as "part Mexican and part Filipino." But he now presented all of these prior descriptions as somewhat inaccurate: at Columbus, how students identified themselves in one conversation was not necessarily how they would do so in another. Beginning with a few questions to his mother about his grandfather's name, Robert had jump-started a process of learning anew what he "was," and his smiling description of his "confusion" suggested that the racial identifications students asserted in class discussions or even casual interactions could never be taken for granted as fixed.

Self-classifications could shift particularly dramatically over the space of years. On the day of a schoolwide "multicultural" festival in 1997, I saw another former student, Rosie, who had described herself as "Filipina" in the 10th grade. She was sporting a lei made out of plastic-wrapped Snickers bars, an item sold often at school events by students in the simply labeled "Samoan club." I asked what significance it had for her, and we were quickly discussing the shifting process of classification itself:

> She says, "It's tradition . . . I dunno! Some necklaces with the big conch shell, it means the warrior. Like that," she says, pointing to another girl coming out of the Student Association office. "But in what culture?" I ask. "Pacific Islander," she says, adding, "there are no full-blooded Filipinos or Samoans, so . . ." "So it's like you're all related?" I ask. "Exactly," she replies. "You never talked about that when you were in my class. You'd say 'Filipino,' not 'Pacific Islander,'" I say. "Really?" Rosie says, as another "Filipino" former student, also listening, says "true." "We just weren't—as aware, informed, I guess," she finishes.

Over time, as students became more "informed" about the history and politics of various classifications, they began to treat some racialized identifications as false; sometimes new information had them imposing new categories upon themselves and one another.[13] Students talked about relatives, for example, who had gradually mapped out for them the simple structure of American racial orders (Leslie, who labeled herself "black," remarked in one class discussion about racial categorization that "My dad told me, there's only people who are black and people who aren't black."). Some students gradually took charge of reclassifying themselves: as one "Filipina" girl said with a smile in her English class, "I used to be Chinese." And some students were told abruptly by others that they "were" members of one group rather than another:

June 5th, 1996

I overhear a Samoan girl in the library talking to a black guy. [*I had heard this girl describe herself as "Samoan" in multiple public contexts; to my own racializing eyes, the boy looked "black."*] She tells him her mother said to her one day, "Do you know you're black?" "And I was like, '. . . OK!' " she says, raising her eyebrows. "She was saying my father was black," she adds.[14]

While many Columbus students received racialized classificatory information from adults (again, my own notes are evidence of the adult tendency to impose such classifications), they also took cues from one another on how to identify themselves in simple racial terms. In one meeting of a school club, the club president demonstrated just how forceful this identification process could be:

> Tuli said she had to make an announcement, and if the bell rang, she didn't want anyone to leave. After a long pause and looking up at the ceiling, she said that she was resigning as president. "I will no longer be a part of the organization," she said. "I will be Tuli Jenkins, going to class, and getting an education. I'm tired of people saying 'you're acting too white,' 'you're acting too black,' 'you're not being the president.' Well, I'm not going to be a doormat. I can't do it no more. Nobody comes up to my face—I just hear Tuli this, Tuli that. All this talkin' shit—I can't take it. I just want to try to be a Samoan person—not too white, not too black," she said. She was still looking up at the ceiling, her eyes tearing, speaking in alternately measured and rushed speeds, shaking her head side to side. As others spoke in support of her, she moved to stand over by the corner. The last thing I remember her saying was: "People say 'you talk like you white, you got a black last name.' I can't take it any more." She finally did walk out.

"Being a Samoan person" was something other students were pushing Tuli to do in school—and accusations that she was not doing it correctly had brought her to tears in front of students and adults. While they routinely played games with racial classification, Columbus students also forced one another to "choose" sides over racial lines drawn firmly in the social sand.[15]

Classroom talk, which rarely ended up debating racial classification itself, typically did not play games with racial classification at all. As Part 2 describes, particularly when Columbus students talked with school adults, they usually employed single race labels as if such labels matter-of-factly described people. Adults themselves rarely suggested that race-group boundaries at Columbus or elsewhere were blurred; school and classroom life typically just proceeded as if people were members of simple lump-sum groups.

Part 2: Using Simple Race Labels in School Conversations with Adults

On my second day of teaching at Columbus in 1994, I surmised that a teacher talking as if she did *not* take racial categorizations for granted seemed to sound ridiculous to some students. Talking in the hallway during class with three boys who had been gleefully baiting my every word, I tried to explain that I was hoping to elicit their perspectives in our classroom conversations on "ethnic literature." Anticipating that they might well be immigrants from the Caribbean like the young people I had known recently in Boston, I asked, "Do you all consider yourselves African-American?" "No," one boy replied sarcastically. "I'm a gorilla."

As a year of teaching "Ethnic Literature" was to prove, the classroom world typically prompted a simple discourse of lump-sum groups, alternately called "races," "ethnicities," and "cultures" in the presence of adults. "Ethnic Literature," a citywide English course designed to inject explicit considerations of "ethnic experience" into the 10th grade curriculum before students encountered the more homogeneously titled "American Literature" of 11th grade English, was a main conduit for the very word "ethnicity" to enter the Columbus student vocabulary; a discourse of "learning about other cultures" was typical to classrooms across Columbus as well. Wielded by both students and adults, the very discourse of "cultural" exchange itself typically took the existence of clear-cut groups for granted.[16] On one of my own class assignments (to comment on the pros and cons of "integrated" schooling), for example, students wrote almost uniformly about the importance of learning about "different cultures" and "races" in school:

> "I think that integration is good for us young students because we all (all races) need to know more about each other's background."
>
> "I think it's good because everybody needs to know about different races and cultures so that they won't be ignorant and start being prejudice."
>
> "It's better to learn about other cultures because the whole world isn't segregated. You will bump into someone who isn't your race. You need to know about these people and know why the things they do are done."

At Columbus, further, as at schools throughout the United States, adults and students typically "learned about" "different races and cultures" one at a time: curricular activities designed to sequentially flesh out single "cultures" were ubiquitous. When I arrived to teach at Columbus in 1994, my first teaching task involved joining other Ethnic Literature teachers in an attempt to make curriculum materials sequentially "representative" of the grade's major "ethnic groups." The coordinated social studies curriculum was to begin with a unit on imperialism in Africa, and then turn to units on Latin America and the Philippines. As the Ethnic Literature teacher, I was to lead concurrent examination of U.S.-based "African-American," "Latino," and "Filipino" literature (as the Samoan population in the 10th grade happened to be particularly small, we had no "Samoan unit"; as the "Chinese" students in our classes were all immigrants or the children of immigrants, "Chinese" literature was to be covered in a unit on immigration). Moving sequentially from group to group seemed a given for a teacher of "Ethnic Literature." As one white teacher would say several years later of her own Ethnic Literature class, "we're moving from Hispanic to Asian poetry, and then we'll be doing crazy white guys, the Beat poets."

Classroom curriculum itself, it seemed, played a key role in simplifying Columbus' infinite diversity into manageable units. Seth, a former student who said that peers routinely asked him what he was "mixed with," told me in one informal interview that while being "mixed" had actually started to become a "conformity thing" back in middle school (as people started "getting into family history," he said, people started saying things like " 'I'm black and this, Chicano and this'—They never just said '*I'm this*,' you never heard that"), Columbus's simple taxonomy of "races" had simultaneously started to solidify around texts in junior high classrooms.[17] As students began to investigate cultural "heritages" with the help of adults, he recalled, they started forging a new sense of pride in specific "race"-group histories (students, he said, began to say things like, "My momma used to pick cotton, or my grandmother used to pick rice, or my grandparents were like the women in *The Joy Luck Club*."). At Columbus, even as students reveled privately in the complexities of multiple "heritages" (one "Filipino and Portuguese" student suggested to me that a person of "only two" backgrounds at Columbus could sometimes feel an inadequate "half-breed," in comparison both to "full" Filipinos and to students who could list five or six "backgrounds"), the classroom was still a key place for stating publicly that one wanted to learn about one's own distinct "culture." Several girls who regularly called themselves "Filipina" (one had been born in the Philippines, the other two were raised in California City) demonstrated as much in reacting to a reading I had selected to begin a classroom unit on "Filipinos":

> March 16th, 1995
>
> We are working on a reading entitled "Pinoy," first person memoirs about the first Filipinos in California. Aza: "Why'd you give this to us?" Me: "To challenge you." Her: "But it's boring!" Lizzie: "No it's not, I'm interested in this!" (She pauses) "That's the only reason why I'm reading this," she says loudly, adding to Aza, "You should be interested in your peoples!" Sheryl and Aza smile.

In many Columbus classrooms, further, questions or assignments from teachers implicitly or explicitly requested students to classify themselves quickly as members of single "peoples," "cultures," and "races." Students asked to model a famous "Chicano pride" poem in my own classroom in 1994 typically wrote poems beginning with blunt analogous phrases like "I am black," "I am a Latin warrior," and "I am Filipino." In one white teacher's classroom in 1995, an interview assignment (common around Columbus) asked students to question one another briefly about their birthplace and "nationality," leading Pelton, who had actually participated in similar assignments in my own class the previous year, toward a notably matter-of-fact exchange of simple-race labels with Charla, a girl who also looked African-American:

Charla said Pelton's name was cute. She asked his mother's name, and then asked, "What nationality is she?" Pelton paused, then nodded his head with a sideways motion and lifted his hand in a gesture of apparent nonchalance. "Black," he said, as Charla simultaneously said, "black?"

Those students in my classes who considered themselves "mixed," I found out over time, often left the full complexities of their identities outside the classroom. Seth, who described himself in one private conversation as "a melting pot" (his father was "African-American," his mother was "Italian," his grandmother was "Irish and Italian," and his dad's parents were "black and Filipino," he said, so he considered himself "part Italian, part Irish, part African-American, and part Filipino") admitted that in our class discussions the previous year, he had never mentioned his African-American or Irish or Filipino "parts" and had simply "picked Italian," mostly because he had more ties with his mother. "Most people knew," he explained. I myself silently recalled Seth framing himself several times simply as "white" in the classroom. He now said emphatically that he was, if anything, "*not white.*"

While students often conformed to the student world by proclaiming racial mixture, then, the classroom world typically prompted students to select single, lump sum identifications within a finite system of options. In my own classroom curriculum, simple lines delineating the classroom into a small handful of "races" persisted to the end, despite my own intermittent attempts to have discussions challenging the very concept of "racial" classification. In response to the year's last assignment, which asked students to bring in music that they felt "represented themselves" or had something to say about "ethnicity," students squashed the complexity of their everyday media usage into neat racial categories, announcing that Tupac Shakur songs were about being "black"; "corridos" were "Mexican"; traditional folk songs expressed the experience of "Samoans"; national songs made one "very proud to be Filipina"; and music from the "Chinese New Year" demonstrated, as one student put it, "what my culture's mostly about." Robert, who as we have seen framed himself gradually as "part Mexican," potentially "Hawaiian," "part Filipino," and—over the course of several years—"mostly Puerto Rican," brought a song that, as he put it, "represents how Latins have come up a long way from Christopher Columbus." Although some students of all "groups" brought in the same hip-hop songs on this last day of Ethnic Literature, demonstrating the border-crossing appeal of the genre (Leslie, a "black" student, summed up paradoxically that "It's my ethnicity—everybody that's my ethnic group and that isn't listens to it"), most students throughout the day still talked as if music was designed for uncontested racial or "ethnic groups." My assignment, of course, had prompted such simple identifications even while suggesting that students be their complex "selves."

— curriculum can dictate racial conversation

With sequential discussion of distinct "races" or "cultures" or "peoples" in classroom life, finally, came another crucial question—namely, whether each lump-sum group was equally represented. As Part 3 describes, pleas or demands for equal racial representation in Columbus classroom curricula and school events were routine, and these demands rarely suggested that racial, ethnic, or "cultural" groups had blurry boundaries. Michael—the boy of "hecka races" who had refused to identify himself in our class conversation on "assumptions"—suggested in a private conversation with a "Latina" teacher and me after school one day that this logic and strategic practice of simple racial identification extended far beyond the Columbus walls. He himself actually had to "pick" a "culture," he said, in part to acquire resources within an existing structure of resource allocation:

> "I feel like I don't have a culture. My mom's Mexican and Irish, my dad's Filipino and, uh, Portuguese," he says. "You're American then, it doesn't get more American than that," Ms. Duran says. "My dad says, 'You're white,' and I'm like, 'No I'm not, just 'cause *you* wanna be white,' " he says. "What does being white mean to you?" asks Ms. Duran. "Plain . . . no culture. Eating hamburgers and hotdogs—that's it. *Blank*," he says. "It sounds like you feel like you're missing a culture, you want one," Ms. Duran says. "I do—my grandmother acts like I was never born," he replies, adding, "My mom doesn't tell me stories like about rituals and stuff, so I don't have a culture. But I have to pick one." "Why do you have to choose?" asks Ms. Duran. "Well, it says 'Other White' on my transcript. And I can't get *any*thing with that," he smirks, adding, "even though I live in the projects or whatever."

As inequitable racial orders were built with simple racial blocks, Michael noted, *equalizing* resources in turn required simple race groups: and every day at Columbus, students returned routinely to the discourse of simple racial equality.

Part 3: The School Discourse of Simple Racial Equality

One afternoon in 1996 at a traditional assembly where juniors parodied seniors, an equity-minded call from the audience caught my attention: "Where're the black people at?" I had noticed the same pattern myself: out of around twenty juniors performing on stage, only two regularly identified themselves as "black." One of the two was the event's emcee, and when he greeted the audience, several students, all of whom also looked black, stood up and shouted out, "reeeeee!"—it was Columbus students' colloquial form of the word "represent." Moments later, I heard a girl next to me ask another, "why don't they do any black people?"

In 1998, I called Tina, a former student who had graduated the previous spring, to ask her opinion about this question of equal "representation" in Co-

lumbus life. In my classroom, Tina had described herself as "black and Filipino" in several conversations that had addressed racial classification itself; in
later years, as she finished up at Columbus and went to college, she repeatedly
described herself to me as "black." Notably, she did so during our phone conversation, in suggesting that adults at Columbus had neither "represented"
"black people" sufficiently in school nor assisted her adequately to learn about
other "cultures":

> "It would have been nice if we would have had some African-American history," she
> said. There was "no black history until February, and then suddenly all the black
> people came out—and as soon as February was over they put them back in the closet
> again. And the only people you ever heard about were Martin Luther King and
> Malcolm X." In her history classes, she said, they "never learned anything about black
> people, Latin people, Filipino, Chinese—immigrants—nothing about culture really."
> Other graduates, she said, had similarly complained to her that they "didn't learn
> anything about cultures at Columbus." In the school talent shows, further, "they
> always had Samoans dancing, the Filipinos, the Latinos doing their little thing," she
> said. But there were a lot of "black kids with talent" at Columbus, and she never saw
> too many of them onstage. She said she didn't know whether this was because black
> students weren't recruited for the events, or because they didn't volunteer. I men-
> tioned to her that at the senior parody I had heard students say things like, "Where're
> the black people at?" "Mm-hmm," she replied. "But who organized that event? All
> Filipinos," she added, who only portrayed their friends.

While students like Tina sporadically admitted the nuances of their own
racial "mixture," analyses of resource distribution had them comparing a short
list of simple race groups. When articulating their needs for material and educational resources, students similarly prioritized simple "race" identifications
over the nuances of national origin. Carlo, a former student who at other moments sporadically called himself "Nicaraguan," argued fervently in one interview for more "Latino" history by contrasting "Latino" representation in school
with the representation of "blacks" and "whites":

> He mentioned the conquistadors, and I asked where he had learned about them.
> "Not in school—we don't learn about our race," he said decisively, adding, "Most
> teachers worry about keeping the blacks and the whites happy. They give blacks a
> whole month—for us, it's one day." "One day," his friend Miguel echoed, "Cinco de
> Mayo." "All we learn about is Christopher Columbus. Or slavery, and the under-
> ground railroad," Carlo continued, adding, "They don't teach us about how Latinos
> didn't have disease, that the Spanish brought diseases." "Smallpox," Miguel added
> seriously. "They just teach us black history and white history," Carlo finished.

Miguel had immigrated a few years earlier from El Salvador, and Carlo
came from a family that had spent several generations in Los Angeles. Both
framed themselves as "Latinos" in their analyses of the "race's" representation

in the school's curricular order. At Columbus, the label "Latino" grouped kids who had just immigrated from Central America together with third-generation California City students who acknowledged sheepishly that they could not roll their "r"s; student and adult participants in the school's "Latino" club, "La Raza," noted that such diversity of origins could actually cause deep social rifts between the club's members. Still, during discussions of racial representation, lump-sum communities like "Latinos" (and, in Tina's case, "black people") demanded equal time in public performances and on the school and classroom calendar. Noting the structural constraints of resource distribution inside and outside Columbus, students strategically prioritized racialized solidarities over the endless complexities of their diversity.[18]

While students strategically appropriated the school's short list of racial identifications for themselves, adults struggled circularly to equalize curricular resources distributed to the school's racialized "groups." Every year clubs sponsored by adults posted recruitment signs inviting "black sisters and my black brothers," "La Raza," or "Polynesian brothers and sisters" to show up and be counted at specific events, and each Columbus "group" had its club; and both student and adult organizers of "multicultural" activities were fairly meticulous about presenting sequential appearances of students representing the major groups of Columbus's simple race taxonomy. As one 1995 student newspaper calendar put it, "the multi-cultural assembly and fair" would "have people from different cultures perform, and during lunch there will be booths with different types of food from each culture, like Latino, Chinese, and Filipino."

An observer relying on a quick glance at these occasional "cultural" events would likely produce an artificially simple analysis of Columbus's complex demographics, for such "cultural" events themselves drew artificially clear racial boundaries. Looking more closely at the details of the school's performatively "multicultural" assemblies, for example, one could notice that racial categorizations were actually leaking all over the place. Although performances typically involved Samoan students in grass skirts performing traditional Samoan dances, Latino students dancing merengue in billowy shirts, and black students rapping, Latino students also sometimes rapped in these performances, Filipino students sometimes played hard rock, an occasional black student danced merengue, and Samoan students routinely sang R&B tunes. Still, talk *about* "multicultural" events and classroom curriculum continually referenced simple racial groups *as if* these groups had clear-cut borders. Indeed, talk of equal representation in events and texts itself seemed to organize students into measurable "racial" groups, even as everyday actions repeatedly demonstrated the blurred complexity of racial practice. When I showed "Menace to Society" as a class reward one day (a movie whose cast appeared almost entirely "black"), for example, Carlo approached my desk to say that he himself owned the video and had seen it countless times. But anyway, he complained, he "thought this was supposed to be Latino week!"

As Lipsitz (1998) argues, such simplifying practices of "encouraging allegiance to [single] group interests" (66)—often derisively called "identity politics" in the United States—can serve both to challenge racialized power hierarchies and to reinforce them. "Investment in individual group identities," he
notes, can inhibit cross-"racial" allegiances and even "run the risk of reifying
the very categories they seek to destroy" (252). Indeed, at Columbus, simple-
group conflict—what we might call competitive diversity—sometimes seemed
part and parcel of sequential curricular units and public events: as one self-
described "black" teacher remarked of "multicultural" assemblies, "Now in assemblies, it's the same old thing all the time—see who can outclap who." In
meetings the summer after my teaching year, my partner teachers and I discussed how setting up our own curriculum as a series of "ethnic" units had
seemed to foster what we called "ethnic cheerleading": if all "cultures" were
not given equal time, students had sometimes stated, they didn't want to learn
about "other cultures" at all. As a teacher, I had repeatedly found myself arguing defensively to students that in our attempts to "do" one lump-sum racial
group "before the next," we were learning about these groups in equal amounts:

> Miguel comes in before school, saying Jimmy [*a student who labeled himself as
> "black"*] made fun of him for his accent when Miguel answered the classroom phone.
> Jimmy "was laughing at me and I was like 'what, motherfucker, we don't want to
> read those mayate books!'" he said [*At Columbus, "mayate" was well known as a deroga-
> tory Spanish word for "black"*]. "What am I going to say to them, when we get to Latin
> American books and they say 'we don't want to read *their* books'?" I reply. I reiterate
> that we all need to learn about each other, then say that in all my classes I've been
> hearing that some people are frustrated that we're only doing "their" culture. "We
> have to focus on one thing at a time so we know what we're learning. The plan is to
> do Latin America second, and then the Philippines. We gotta do one before the
> next," I say. "I'd rather do #2," he says. "Number two's coming!" I say.

"Focusing" on one group at a time indeed simplified the learning process, but
in truth, equity-minded, sequential presentation of simple race groups seemed
paradoxically to prime people to measure such representation as unequal.[19]
When we began the next unit, which I described to my classes as "on Latin
America and Latinos in the U.S.," Nando, another self-described "Latino"
student, muttered to me quietly, "It's about time." In my partner teacher's class,
he said, "All we've been doing is Africa since the beginning." David, who had
been habitually absent for a number of weeks, asked a similar comparative
question a bit more audibly:

> David [*"black"*]: What happened to Africa? Me (wailing): You missed it! That's
> why you're getting an F! Lizzie (*"Filipina"*): How about the Philippines? Me: They're
> last. Lizzie: Why they gotta be last? Me: Someone has to be last. Michael [*"hecka
> races"*] (smiling): you're biased!

In challenging the proportions and sequence in which they "learned about other cultures," Columbus students critiqued both adults for allowing unequal representation and one another for monopolizing institutional or classroom time. And as all players struggled to avoid "bias" through additional sequential performances, conflict occasionally pit one "culture" against another. After an April 1995 "multicultural fair," I described in my diary how a can of soda thrown during a performance had sparked controversy over "respect" between "cultures." Again, my own descriptive language indicates the event's basic lump-sum logic:

April 28th, 1995

Twice during the multicultural fair, a can of pop started flying through the air—once at students, once at a multi-performer Chinese dragon, which had been throwing lettuce and oranges into the crowd as part of its performance (this troupe was hired from outside). Mel, a huge Samoan security guard, got up and said, "Move *back*!" and then, "If you guys don't stop throwing stuff we're gonna shut this thing *down*!" The sound system had broken down at the beginning of the performance, while Latino girls and guys were dancing. Apparently, a speaker blew out. There were about 25 minutes of no music. Then the Samoan/Polynesian club: rhythmic ughs, level chanting, mostly bald boys wearing chains of flowers and flowered wraps. During the Latino dance (girls in cropped tight tops and short skirts, boys in flowy white shirts and dress pants, doing salsa and merengue), a can of soda came flying through the air and (almost?) hit Kia and some African-American girls around her. According to Simon [*a teacher who labeled himself as "Latino"*], a big Latino guy went over to the group of African-American guys from which the can had come and said, "you're disrespecting my culture!" Nobody would admit to it; he started trying to fight, but he was taken away to the office. Then, according to Simon, a group of African-American guys followed him there, got him out of the office, took him out and beat him up! Simon said, "It really depressed me. I'd been feeling how great it was to share each other's cultures, but now, I kinda feel like maybe a mixed school isn't such a great idea!"

At Columbus, the project of "sharing each other's cultures" typically reverted to positioning these "cultures" as separate and sequential entities, and this very framework prompted assessments of allotted time and "respect." In my classroom after lunch, Takisha and Frankie, both of whom usually labeled themselves "black" (Frankie sometimes called himself "Jamaican"), had grumpily measured the assembly's inadequate representation of "blacks":

Takisha: This school's *racist*, I swear.
Frankie: The rapper didn't even get to finish!
Me: But the sound system broke, Frankie.
Takisha: It didn't break down during the *other* performances.
Me: You think they broke it on purpose?!
Frankie: He was gonna do free flow, they didn't let him do it.

Takisha: And the Samoan group got hella time!

Me: But the system was broken at the beginning, so *everything* got smushed—and they had to get in the last group before the bell rang.

Frankie: Yeah, well they should have made the thing longer—they stopped it early.

As Columbus students and adults struggled to equalize race-group representation within a limited curricular space and time, then, conflict routinely erupted over these very racial proportions. Yet these very shared attempts at racial equalization also served to clarify when resources *were* distributed equally: by making Columbus's seemingly infinite diversity manageable, sequential efforts attempted to ensure that every student at Columbus could feel in some way represented.[20] "Multicultural" rites were, in one sense, *about* simplification—about creating an equalizable set of "groups."[21] In the very act of reproducing together a reliably simple racial taxonomy, that is, Columbus people clarified the set of "groups" to which equal curricular resources *could* be distributed—and with relief, they proceeded to distribute resources accordingly.

Sometimes, it was students themselves who noted self-consciously that confronting a world in which resources constantly appeared inequitably distributed along simple racial lines seemed paradoxically to *require* the strategic use of lump-sum terms. Not surprisingly, they articulated this analysis of racial power relations best when talking directly about racial classification—and notably, they did so with special clarity in the rare moments when they analyzed directly the racial label "white." While the notion of whiteness (as later chapters will demonstrate) was daily made central to certain quiet analyses of race relations at Columbus, the *word* "white" was, at Columbus, a particularly unexamined race word—in part because "white" adults, who formed the vast majority of "whites" at Columbus, rarely joined in race-bending debates (recall that when I tried to join the race game that began this chapter, students had reacted with surprise, replying, "What do you mean—you're white!"). Yet talking about the very word "white" seemed inevitably to expose racial classification *as* a system of differentiating "peoples" in order to distribute power; and it demonstrated that racialized people negotiating *over* power had to remain racial precisely for the purpose of equalization.[22]

When we started to debate the category "white" in my own classroom near the end of 1994–95, my opening question "Are white people an ethnic group?" produced a surprised response; as one student put it excitedly, "White people? OK, let's *do* this!" Clarence, a student who described himself alternately as "Jamaican" and "black," next responded hesitatingly, "Well . . . if white people aren't an ethnic group, then black people aren't an ethnic group." And within moments, Michael, the student of "hecka races," offered the year's most piercing analysis of the racial identification process:

> Michael says: "They say all people from Europe are supposed to be white, right? And all the people from Africa are supposed to be black, right? And all the people—

Indians are supposed to be red, right? And all the Asian people are supposed to be yellow, right? These are the colors people are givin' 'em. So it seems just like sports— they put 'em all in teams, like categories," he says. "*Yes*!! And why do they put 'em into teams?" I ask. "To make 'em compete!" he finishes.

Although people didn't necessarily belong to simple race categories, "they" had already lumped together the people who were "supposed to be" racially similar—and now, the categories were bricks in a wall of power relations. Accepting the idea that race categories existed, of course, itself maintained this artificially simple and competitive racial structure—but as Columbus life demonstrated, people also strategically had to be racial in order to make things "fair."

Conclusion

Student life at Columbus was always inordinately complicated, and so it often seemed that placing "racial" boundaries on Columbus students was an inherently inaccurate exercise. At Columbus, a "Filipino" student speaking Tagalog to a friend at one moment might call him "homie" the next, just as a "Latino" student might switch from speaking rapid Spanish to chanting rhythmic English rap lyrics under his breath; students across Columbus dished out and responded to the adult-baffling, racialized friendship term "nigga." (As one self-described "Filipino" owner of a nearby convenience store put it, "These are the most racist people I've ever seen. They say they don't want to be called niggers, and then that's what the kids call each other. Even the Filipino kids call each other niggers. I don't understand it.") At assemblies, speakers of all languages would address the assembled student body with the obligatory "Columbus in the house!", just as speakers of all languages greeted each other in the hallway with terms of endearment like "hey, blood." When a student hardrock band of several Filipino-looking students and a black-looking drummer stunned the traditionally hip-hop crowd in one student assembly, one teacher called the performance a "culture shock."

Columbus, which often seemed to present a shared youth "culture," was not always carved into six simple racial groups. Yet the daily motions of complex racial identities did not erase racial categories as crucial and strategic social ordering devices. The reality of racial practice at Columbus was the coexistence of limitless complexity and pointed simplification: the routine defiance of racial categories alternated with a continually imposed simple categorical order. There are times, of course, when "natives" themselves impose simple categories upon their own complex societies, and for Columbus students, this imposition of simplification was itself a strategic cultural act.[23] Daily, Columbus students employed the logic of racial difference even as they deconstructed it, only "partially penetrating" the racial classificatory system.[24] Every day, they knowingly sacrificed the detailed complexities of individual "identity" to a national habit of simple racial identification, as a strategic response within an inequitable country that has for generations bluntly asked us what we "are."

Some analysts have argued that contemporary U.S. youths' self-conscious announcements of "mixed" ancestry, combined with their often seemingly easy association with one another (when desegregated demographics allow), are signals that U.S. racial categories themselves are finally near their demise.[25] Indeed, some public figures are actively attacking politically the very practice of racial classification in the name of the nation's growing population of "multiracial" youth. In California, Ward Connerly, the UC regent behind the state's anti–affirmative-action Proposition 209, has explained his current "Racial Privacy" public initiative (which hopes to ban race data altogether from public school records in the state) by pleading openly with voters to let "mixed" youth have "freedom from race" and "just be Americans."[26] Yet young Americans, as this chapter has shown, themselves employ simple "race" categories daily, in concert with the adults around them—especially in school, perhaps, and especially for the purposes of "fairness."[27] Both defying and utilizing the racial logic available for use in America, Columbus students bent racial categories rather than fully breaking them—and in doing so, they demonstrated that as racial classification itself is still a complicated part of struggles over power, creating equality will for a time longer require speaking categorically while alternately interrogating the very reality of categories themselves.

Youth at Columbus, then, gracefully lived race paradoxically; adult analysts seem to have a bit more trouble with this necessarily paradoxical treatment of race, this necessity of alternately employing and contesting simple notions of "racial" difference. Many scholars of race, for example, now routinely exhibit uncertainty about whether to contest the very notion of racial categories or simply employ such categories in analyses of social orders. In a recent ethnography about a New York high school, John Devine (1996) handles the dilemma by simply moving to a footnote a qualification of his own racial description of the school as "approximately 75 percent Hispanic and 25 percent African American":

> The term *Hispanic* covered students from Panama, Honduras, Nicaragua, El Salvador, Guatemala, Colombia, Venezuela, Costa Rica, Puerto Rico, and the Dominican Republic; the term *black* covered students from Liberia; Angola; Nigeria; Antigua; Jamaica; Barbados; Trinidad; Grenada; Surinam; Guyana; Nevis; British Virgin Islands; U.S Virgin Islands; St. George; St. Kitts; St. Lucia; St. Vincent; Haiti; St. Lucia; Canada; Britain; Germany; and the United States (i.e., native-born African Americans). In addition, there were students from Cambodia and from Yemen. Immigrant students may, of course, also enter the United States after having moved for a few years to a third country, e.g., Canada, England, France.[244]

While some adults relegate discussion of the diversity within U.S. "race groups" to footnotes, others are openly reluctant to describe simple race groups at all. Anxieties about publicly continuing to impose artificial racial lines upon a fundamentally porous human population have many anthropologists, for example, using the word "race" only in skeptical quotation marks (see, e.g., the American Anthropological Association's "Statement on 'Race,'" 1998). A subset of scholars, lamenting that the "race concept" has been used for centuries to disempower and destroy populations, have long asserted that any uncontested use of the word "race" to imply human difference is itself "racist" (see Patterson 1997; for a foundational example in anthropology, see Montagu 1997 [1942]). Other scholars, imploring their peers to avoid dismissing the possibility of analyzing social structures that still very much exist and operate in racial terms, write about racial orders in some books and question the very validity of race in others (see, e.g., Gilroy 1993b, 2000). The paradoxical twenty-first-century task of trying simultaneously to think and *not* think in terms of simple race groups is embedded in much adult educational prose as well. Authors in the most recent *Handbook of Research on Multicultural Education*, for example, strive to counter accusations that "multicultural" scholarship itself oversimplifies human diversity for the purposes of "recognition," warning anxiously that readers should avoid assuming that the group characteristics explored in their papers on various "cultures" are actually shared by all members of "groups" (Banks and Banks 1995).[28]

Overt anxiety over speaking as if people belong to clear-cut race groups seems widespread throughout social science, yet analyses calling for racial *equality* usually do not seem to be the place for interrogating the theoretical or social validity of racial categories themselves. For example, most researchers commenting on educational opportunity in the United States continue to compare how lump-sum racial groups fare in schools, as titles like *The Education of African-Americans* (Willie, Garibaldi, and Reed 1991) or *Latino High School Graduation* (Romo and Falbo 1996) make explicit.[29] When the distribution of resources *is* simply racially ordered, as we shall see, achieving equality requires some simple race talk: as Guinier and Torres (2002) warn, those who continually question the existence of race groups actually cede the definition of race to those who would like to "purge legal and political discourse of all racial references and who may be indifferent to whether this move preserves unjust hierarchies" (42).[30]

Equality itself is a simple-race idea, and at Columbus, the simple racial identifications of equality logic seemed to drown out complex descriptions of flexible or multiple identities. When Columbus adults spoke racially—which, as we shall see, was only some of the time—they referenced only the small number of simplified racial groups identified as competing for resources or power within the school taxonomy. While such talk of lump-sum racial groups indeed oversimplified the complexity of *people*, such simple-race talk, as we shall see, seemed to accurately describe many social *patterns*: and it was also the only kind of race talk pervasive in talk about educational policy, which was typically wrestling with racial inequality rather than with "race" itself. In one way only, for example, did the California City Unified School District—busy distributing the city's "races" across California City schools per a desegregation order—acknowledge that its nine "racial/ethnic" categories might not adequately describe the city's infinitely complex population. The district allowed parents to change their children's recorded "racial/ethnic" classifications once or twice to facilitate their enrollment in particular schools. Students were allowed simply to shift from one lump-sum race category to another—that is, as long as parents could produce some sort of official "proof."

I deliberately started this book with students talking about themselves because this is where studies of race in school all too often finish. Yet racialization, as this chapter has started to demonstrate, is a communal process of social simplification: often seemingly in battle, all Columbus players actually enforced together the logic of simple racial terms. Although "race groups" are a mind-boggling oversimplification of human diversity, we all practice this oversimplification daily, often drowning out rather than encouraging the "creative analysis *of* difference" destabilizing "race" every day in the margins of our institutions (Fine, Weis, and Powell 1997, 249). Paradoxically, however, we must often simplify diversity in order to purposefully challenge an existing simple race system, in which the distribution of social and tangible resources remains perennially unequal. The task, perhaps, is to bend race more self-consciously, to openly proceed as if people both belong to race groups and do not. Taking cues from youth, we can keep creating moments to talk about racial categorization as a human and contestable process, even while keeping race labels strategically available for analyzing social inequality.

As our analytic lens expands to include more adults at and outside Columbus, however, we will not see people struggling much more with the question of whether simple "race groups" even exist. Most race talk does not allow time for this complication: we are typically "prisoners of our own vocabularies" when it comes to race (Montagu 1997 [1942]), worried less about the existence of "racial" groups than about what to make of racial orders. Throughout public life and in our private conversations, we struggle far more often with the thorny question of race's relevance. At Columbus, daily talk begged the question, as people did not talk as if "race" was relevant consistently: the very presence of race labels waxed and waned in Columbus life, and chapter 2 starts to address the timing of this fluctuation. *When*, chapter 2 asks, did Columbus people *talk as if race mattered?* In beginning to explore this question, we encounter a second basic dilemma of racial description. In American logic, it seems, *race doesn't matter, but it does*—and as we shall see, people talking in de-raced terms as if race does *not* matter often expose the ways in which race matters to them most explosively.

Two

Race Doesn't Matter, but It Does

"The Samoans are gonna get you! No, we're all the same though."—Columbus student

ON MY FIRST DAY as a teacher at Columbus in 1994, I asked my students to introduce themselves and suggest some notable detail I could jot down to remember them. They suggested physical markers like hairstyles, glasses, and certain pieces of jewelry, or personality traits like "always goofing around." As an additional memory aid, I wrote brief physical descriptions next to their names. Most were simply racialized labels ("black," "Latino," "Chinese"), some followed by a question mark for students I had trouble identifying. I used this list many times until I learned names, but I kept it hidden under other papers and books. I did not want students to know that my first impressions of them had been racial.

As chapter 1 demonstrated, people at Columbus seemed socialized to frame one another daily as race-group members; as my own nervously hidden lists suggested, they also tended to resist this very socialization. Calls for "color-blindness," for proceeding as if we do not see people in racialized terms, have for over a century been a key trope in American equality discourse, and color-muteness—active *resistance to describing* people as racial—was as central to daily race practice at Columbus as was the act of framing people racially.[1] Indeed, across the United States, even as we categorize one another relentlessly as "racial" beings, we insist just as routinely that race should not affect our perceptions of one another. We often refuse racial *descriptions* as a way of refusing racial *categorization*. Yet as we keep framing each other racially even when we decline to say so, as this chapter demonstrates, it seems that when ideology meets practice, *race doesn't matter, but it does*—and everyday talk thus wrestles always between professing anti-racial beliefs and exposing actual racializing behavior.

In the daily clutter of Columbus life, indeed, people even suggested differently at different moments whether they *wanted* to be treated as racialized beings, a basic duality that presented speakers with a fundamental practical dilemma. Calls for "fairness" at Columbus, as chapter 1 started to demonstrate, sometimes asked people to highlight race, yet people across Columbus also argued alternately that fairness required ignoring race.[2] Columbus students, we have seen, expected adults to take student race purposefully into account in order to represent student "race" groups in assemblies and curricula in equal amounts. Yet when demanding the fair distribution of punishments, Columbus students argued explicitly that they should *not* be framed in racial terms, and that adults should treat students "all the same"—even as they insisted that adults monitor disciplinary demographics through a racialized lens. In arguing at some moments that making race relevant was a good thing and at other moments that making race relevant was a bad thing, Columbus students presented the adults in their midst with a troubled choice that is actually the reality of negotiating toward racial equality in the contemporary United States. To make things "fair," we need sometimes to treat one another as race-group members and sometimes actively to try to treat one another without "regard to race."[3]

Everyday *talk* at Columbus, as this chapter will begin to show, demonstrated well the anxious nature of this choice. For in talking about the everyday things of school life, speakers tended to speak confidently at some moments as if race mattered very much and nervously at other moments as if race should not matter at all. This chapter focuses on talk of social relations at Columbus—talk of how people "got along"—because it demonstrates this contrast particularly explicitly: such talk was sometimes matter-of-factly racial and sometimes anxiously de-raced. Columbus adults and students talked often about student-*student* relations, for example, in blunt and easy racial terms, with the same confidence employed for remarking on curriculum and public events: that race mattered to how students "got along" was widely and publicly taken for granted, and indeed, talking racially about these relations was viewed as a necessary and positive step toward solving conflicts and equalizing power between "the races."[4] Just as they spoke matter-of-factly of "Chinese literature" or "the Samoan dancers," then, both adults and students often remarked easily and publicly on how "Filipinos" or "blacks" hung out in certain areas at lunchtime, or how "Latinos" fought "Samoans" in a recent "racial riot." Yet while people easily highlighted the role of race when talking about student-student relations, they left the role of race in student-*adult* relations at Columbus only to anxious and muted debate. In particular, talk of student-adult conflicts was *never* casually made racial: Columbus students typically spoke only angrily about race's role in teacher-student conflicts, and when adults talked publicly of their conflicts with students, race labels vanished altogether with a remarkable predictability. Not one public adult discussion of "discipline" that I heard during my three years around Columbus even insinuated that racial groups existed at Columbus. Race simply was *not supposed to matter* to how students and adults "got along."

At Columbus, then, the predictably easy appearance of race labels in school-wide talk of student relations suggested at first glance that race at Columbus was "really" an issue between students; yet the predictable *absence* of race labels from adults' public talk of "discipline" belied a simmering schoolwide perception that race mattered to student-adult relations even more anxiously. Students occasionally complained angrily to one another or in classrooms that race mattered to their relations with adults, claiming that Columbus adults were themselves race-group members who apportioned favors or punishment in racially biased ways. Confronted sporadically by the student accusation of race's troubling relevance to classroom discipline, however, adults typically responded just as heatedly that race did not matter to disciplinary relations with students at all. Navigating daily between race's hoped-for relevance and irrelevance, Columbus adults avoided any sustained conversation with students or other adults on *how* race mattered to relationships at Columbus—and everyday relationships were thus described publicly primarily in polarized terms, as relations that were undeniably racial or not racial at all.

As this chapter will finally demonstrate, both too-easy race talk and race silence could cause Columbus people problems—for both kinds of public talk masked important forms of ongoing, if quiet, contestation over race's actual relevance to Columbus relationships. Relentless matter-of-fact talk of student race relations, for one, drowned out more complex quiet student analyses of the fluctuating role race actually played in student relationships—and also deflected analysis of the role race played in relations between students and adults. For while adults across Columbus muttered privately that disciplinary relations with students were in fact *deeply* racialized, matter-of-fact talk of student race relations reinforced daily the public script that only *these* relations were unequivocally racial. Indeed, matter-of-fact talk of "racial" student conflicts at Columbus actually helped solidify assumptions that race was *supposed* to matter to such relations, while the adult habit of deleting race labels from most discussions of "discipline" actually left the question of race's relevance just festering within all student-adult conflicts. And with race words alternately appearing and vanishing in Columbus talk of social relations, finally, proving when race "*really*" mattered to those relations was itself cause for daily school controversy.

This ambiguity of daily race talk also became a central issue in my own research. Returning to Columbus as a researcher interested (unsurprisingly) in Columbus's most publicly asked race question—how race was relevant to how students "got along"—I was initially drawn to ask students directly about this very question. Yet I found quickly that students who were asked directly to assess race's relevance to their relations often actually responded with a fundamental ambiguity: they routinely denied that race mattered to them only minutes before speaking matter-of-factly as if race did. In addition, students navigating knowingly a pervasive shared logic that race should *not* really matter to how people in general "got along" often flaunted scripted rhetoric about race's *irrelevance* with apparent glee: in a practice I call "race teasing," Columbus students talking directly about the relevance of race to their friendships and identities could suggest smirkingly both that race mattered a lot and that it did not matter at all (Part 1).

Realizing quickly that asking students to sum up quickly the relevance of race to their own lives could lead students either to dismiss the relevance of race or dutifully to highlight race's importance, I started listening more closely to unprompted everyday talk of how Columbus students "got along." Columbus people of all ages, I began to realize, actually turned to matter-of-fact talk of student race relations a bit *too* easily when talking generally about the relevance of "race" at Columbus. Students talking at greater length about student conflicts, for one, often suggested that these relations were *not* purely racial—and adults' quick and comfortable gravitation to the topic of student relations started to appear in stark contrast to muted analysis of relations between students and themselves (Part 2). Expanding my own analytic lens to include Columbus adults (who spoke effortlessly, as I once had, of students' racial friendships and "race riots"), I started to suspect that the daily power relations between students and adults were perhaps far *more* consistently racial than peer relations between students—and private conversations with adults clarified that de-raced public talk of "discipline" itself communicated this danger (Part 3). I concluded that understanding the full relevance of race at Columbus would entail looking for patterns in the scripted *absence* of racial terms, as well as questioning their scripted presence (the rest of my research would follow this prescription).[5] I also realized that *improving* "race relations" at Columbus would require that Columbus people replace both silence and easy summative statements of race's relevance or irrelevance with more critical and time-consuming debate on the very complex question of *how*, exactly, race mattered to various institutional relationships.

We begin, then, by listening to some students—Columbus students and, briefly, students appearing in others' research—attempting to express in various adult-controlled contexts the reality of race's fluctuating relevance to their own relationships and lives. We begin with student talk because it was students who were most often *asked* to "talk about race"; as we shall see later in the chapter and throughout the book, adults typically struggled mostly in private with the question of how race mattered. Adults often expected students to talk about race and student life in public settings, however, and while students (as Part 2 demonstrates) often fell into a shared race-talk script suggesting that race indeed mattered matter-of-factly to their own relations, a more careful listening to students' comments about race's relevance demonstrated that students were often almost gleefully ambiguous in assessing race's relevance to their own lives. When it came to speaking to adults about their *shared* relations, in fact, students' own occasional tendency to tease about race's relevance would complicate their own sporadic angry claims of adult "racism," while adults' nervous reluctance to publicly debate *any* relevance race had to their own actions could easily silence student claims that race mattered at all.

Part 1: Students' "Race Teasing," or Making Ambiguous How Much Race "Really Matters"

As chapter 1 demonstrated, "multicultural" assemblies were particular adult-sanctioned moments when students were expected to speak directly about the school's race groups. In doing so, I noticed upon closer reflection, students at times ironically made the very question of race's relevance to students highly ambiguous. In April 1996, for example, the Columbus student association president, a girl widely described as "Filipina," introduced a multicultural assembly with a speech in front of a banner that read "DIVERSITY IS OUR STRENGTH!" "When we go out into the world," she began, "we know how to get along with others, people of different ethnic groups. Students from areas not as diverse don't know how to do this":

> "We're going to have some performances by some of the ethnic groups represented on our campus," she said. "We're happy to be here to celebrate multiculturalism. We're different, but we are all similar, so we'd like you to appreciate what we have for you today."

In its simultaneous invocation of "difference" and "similarity," her preface to the day's "ethnic group" performances was a classic statement of two coexisting student treatments of "diversity" at Columbus: "difference" was alternately to be highlighted and actively downplayed. Even in informal conversations, Columbus students regularly proffered explicit anti-race rhetoric even as they simultaneously prompted listeners to think in terms of racial groups. When a girl rose angrily out of the stands during a spirit rally in September 1996 and headed toward a player on the girls' soccer team roaring "I'm gonna kick your butt!", for example, Beaux, a black student who was sitting next to me and watching the interaction, yelled down an overtly racialized warning to the soccer player: "The Samoans are gonna get you!" "No," he added, smiling down at his feet, "we're all the same though."

Students regularly parroted such popular clichés about how race should not matter ("can't we all get along?" was a prime example) at the same time that they were suggesting more explicitly that race *did* matter. Through such paradoxical citations, they similarly complicated popular arguments for the relevance of race. In October 1995, for example, I noticed several black students citing the overtly racialized statements of Louis Farrakhan's upcoming "Million Man March" in neatly double-edged tones:

> As people were sitting down during passing time between classes, an African-American boy came in and raised his fist, said "black power!", laughed, and walked out.

Often laughing even as they publicly presented solemn gestures of racialized solidarity, students somehow managed to mock and broadcast race's impor-

"Keeping the Yolk, changing the joke"

tance simultaneously. Students talking in classrooms about racial "pride"—a topic that classroom assignments and discussions raised routinely—often treated the subject of race's importance no less ambiguously. In my own classroom in 1994, for example, giggles complicated invited readings of student poems modeled on a famous "Chicano power" manifesto. As a teacher, I described this multilayered presentation as "pride with a smirk":

> I convince Emilio to read his poem, saying it was really good. He sits at his desk, reads his poem about "Mexican pride." Everyone claps and whistles at the end! Really *good* feeling! In fifth period, Takisha reads hers, which concludes with "I'm black! I—*am*—*black*!" She raises her fist with a small smirk on her face, separating the last three words with measured pauses. I am impressed. "Isn't she a powerful speaker?" I ask the class. Everyone agrees. Then James gets up and reads his own poem in a tone I can only describe as pride with a smirk. He finishes by looking straight ahead and saying "Filipino!" with his fist outstretched, laughing. Everyone laughs with him.

Such race teasing occurred throughout Columbus classrooms, in which adults were, of course, routinely asking students to frame themselves in race-group terms. In a class I observed in 1997, I watched a young Filipino teacher directing students in a public reading of a poem entitled "La Raza, Mejicano" encounter some similarly ambiguous talk of "pride." He had asked Al, a self-labeled "Samoan" student who was reading the poem aloud, to let another student, Jose, "pronounce the Spanish words." Al, however, turned on an exemplary Spanish accent and continued reading loudly:

> Jose: "He know how! He got the skills!" Al (smiling): "Go ahead, cuz!" Jose (smiling): "No, you do it, cuz!" Al lets Jose read the verse again (Jose does it with even more of a Spanish accent). Al then finishes the poem, ending with "in the name of Jesus Christ Amen" (not in the poem). Class continues with students reading several other poems, including a poem by a Chinese author. The teacher then asks a question about "cultural identity vs. dominant identity." "Are you African or American?" he asks a student. Al shouts out, "I'm Samoan! FULL BLOOD SAMOAN." When they arrive at the next "Chicano power" poem, "I Am Joaquin," Jose says Joaquin "is Mexican." "Are you?" asks the teacher. "I'm *Mexican* and I'm *proud* and if you don't *like* it we can have it out *right* now," Jose replies. Al shouts, "I'm *Samoan* and I'm *proud* and if you don't *like* it I'll take you *any* time, *any* place, *any* place, *any*where!" He is smiling as he shouts this fiercely.

Both Al and Jose were smirking while shouting theatrically militant statements of racial pride, teasing responses to a teacher's typically sober requests for speedy student self-identification. Remarking on Columbus students' displayed lack of seriousness about "cultural identity," some Columbus adults even sighed in exasperation that students—adolescent and seemingly politically uninformed—could stand to exhibit far more "*real*" pride." Charla, a black teacher who sponsored the "Black Student Union," complained one day that "black students" around Columbus had no "pride in their heritage," just "superficial priorities" like shoes, hair, and clothes (these days, she tsked, African-American students were even wearing hazel contact lenses). Lamenting that "the kids never come," she said she had to tempt students into the BSU with "Disney" and then "stick in stuff about heritage." She couldn't just advertise the club as a "learn your heritage" club, she said—"black kids wouldn't come to that." The Cinco de Mayo assembly scheduled for the following month was an example of *real* pride, she muttered. "Those kids are practicing *now*."

Sometimes students, like the rigorously rehearsing salsa and merengue dancers to which Charla referred, publicly highlighted racial solidarity with apparent seriousness. While pride talk teetered always on the boundary between fiction and "reality," seemingly solemn talk about "pride" popped up regularly at Columbus too: at a "black history assembly" in 1997, for example, one girl gave a stirring reading of a poem about a "black queen" (minutes later, another student danced to James Brown in a stuffed rear end and huge Afro wig as the audience guffawed). A graffiti "brown pride" emblazoned on the school's back entrance stayed up for years.

Still, for Columbus students, direct requests from adults to assess the importance of race to student life could produce giggles and disclaimers. Even as classroom curriculum regularly requested that students talk directly "about race," for example, such requests could easily prompt students to assert quickly in summation that race was not relevant at all. For example, in a 1997 summer school session I taught at Columbus, a video students produced to analyze "race at Columbus High" as a final assignment in Ethnic Literature filled quickly with blunt student commentary on how race was basically irrelevant to their "generation." The video (entitled "Generation X: The '90s and Beyond") included a taped conversation students planned to denounce racial "stereotypes," in which those not speaking held back laughs as they doodled. After a semi-ad-libbed conversation critiquing racial assumptions about "doing doughnuts" (spinning one's car around by putting the brakes on suddenly) that involved the scintillating interchange "They say black people be doin' doughnuts". . . "Some *Samoans* be doin' doughnuts though". . . "I'm Filipino and *I* do doughnuts!," one student smirked from behind mirrored glasses as she concluded solemnly to the camera, "That's wrong, man . . . [stereotypes] not even cool." In another skit, students choked with laughter as they portrayed an angry racist mob behind two giggling boys representing warring "races" in slow motion.

An adult request for students to directly sum up the relevance of race to student life, I realized quickly as a researcher, seemed just as likely to prompt tongue-in-cheek dismissals as blunt affirmative analysis. Yet the research literature provided few other strategies: researchers have typically assumed that direct questions asked in interviews, on surveys, or even during participant observation produce unmediated summative views on race's importance or irrelevance.[6] Interviewers often appear to forget the particularly strategic nature of race talk, which contends always, even when unprompted, with the pervasive American ideology that race should *not* really matter, or matter only at certain times. Note this classic dismissal of race's importance during an exchange between a researcher and a "black" student interviewee (Grant and Sleeter 1986):

R: Are you going to date just black boys, or what?
Frances: Nope. I'm not just gonna date black ones.
R: Are you going to date just who you want to?
Frances: Yeah, regardless of race. [32]

Direct questions asking respondents to sum up race's relevance often have respondents obligingly denying that race is relevant at all. In a study of "ethnicity" in a California high school, for example, when researcher Alan Peshkin asked students directly his main research question, "To what extent, if at all, is ethnicity a fact in the students' lives?" interviewees summed up repeatedly that race was unimportant, "not salient," or "not really a big thing" (Peshkin 1991, 171).[7] Yet interview questions demanding to know the salience of race in respondents' lives can also lead respondents to highlight race with expected zeal. In the Grant and Sleeter (1986) study quoted above, interview questions asking students to state the "importance" of "background" could actually lead them to emphasize the salience of race-group membership just as bluntly:

R: How important do you think a person's background is?
Rakia: It's important.
R: Do you intend to pass down your Egyptian background to your kids?
Rakia: Yes. [34]

Such direct questions about race's relevance can, of course, prompt similarly brusque acknowledgments or denials from adults.[8] At Columbus, for example, I found that adults answering blunt student questions about race's relevance often provided conveniently oversimplified answers. Stevie, an African-American security guard interviewed on the "Generation X" video (who talked to me often about "race groups" within Columbus and in Columbus neighborhoods), asserted immediately in response to student questions "about race" that he saw everyone at Columbus as "the same." Acknowledging the likelihood of such responses, some Columbus adults hinted that direct research questions about race's relevance would produce little data of interest: when Rob, a self-described "black" teacher, asked me over lunch one day if he could help me do any of my research, he started laughing, his mouth full of pink milk shake, as I reminded him that the official research question on file with the district was "How people talk about diversity." "What's so funny?" I asked. "People don't talk about that! That's '*We Are the World*' stuff!" he said, shaking his head.

Asking respondents to assess race's relevance in a few words, interviewers routinely seem to overlook the possibly scripted nature of both question and response.[9] Indeed, even in informal conversations about the relevance of race, Columbus students replied to blunt evaluative questions with scripted acknowledgments or dismissals, at times even seemingly defending themselves preemptively from possible accusations that race mattered to them too much. One day in a study hall in 1995, for example, I asked Leyla, a former student who had immigrated from Jordan as a child, whether she had "ever found very many Jordanian people to hang out with" at Columbus. "No," she said. "So do you care? That you don't have any Jordanian friends?" I asked. "No. I hang out with everybody, black, Filipino, Spanish," she said, looking me in the eye. "I'm not racist."

In research situations or in daily life, as such conversations indicated, when responding to blunt questions about whether race matters to our relationships, we are routinely expected to assert simply that race does not matter (Leyla: "No . . . I'm not racist") and occasionally expected to assert simply that race does (Rakia: "it's important"). Such simplifying race-talk scripts organize unprompted comments on race's relevance as well. At less self-conscious moments, Columbus students who often suggested when asked directly that race did not matter to their relations could be found speaking bluntly as if race matter-of-factly did. Carlo, for example, told me quite nonchalantly one day that he had "spent a week in lockup" for "stabbing a black dude"; Michael remarked on another occasion that his friend Justin got beat up on the bus because he "looks white." Nina (who described herself as "Filipina and Chinese") informed me that she was jumped in the tacqueria on Hacienda Street "by Samoans." And one day in 1997, a student-made poster appeared on the walls of Columbus announcing "The Top Five Races of the Week":

"**1.** Samoan
2. Filipino
3. African American
4. Latino
5. Asian

Rules: Do things positive with your race to get moved up on the chart like perform in a rally or play football in the quad or just about anything just *get along with one another.*

Congratulation Samoans"

Talking in racial terms about how students "got along" was, I came to realize, one of Columbus students' and adults' most scripted ways of claiming to one another that race mattered: as the following section shows, talk about student relations routinely became matter-of-factly and bluntly racial. Despite the way that their routinely ambiguous statements unsettled whether race *did* really matter to their friendships and conflicts, Columbus students—and adults along with them—repeatedly and casually made race relevant in talk of student-student relations. Almost, it would come to seem, too casually.

Part 2: Topics Scripted to Be Matter-of-Factly Racial

When I began my initial research on student race relations at Columbus, I found quickly that for Columbus students, the question "who do you hang out with?" often prompted preemptively universalistic responses (like Leyla's) about being friends with "everyone"; it also prompted matter-of-fact descriptions of racial groups. Three girls in one study hall demonstrated these dual responses well:

> I asked the girls who they hung out with. "Even at Columbus, some people hang with they own," one girl replied. Another girl said, "I hang with everyone." I asked the third girl, Chavanne, who she hung out with. "My cousin," she said, taking out a picture and showing it to me. "That's it? Just her?" I asked. "And a few other black people," she said.

When speaking to me about student relations, Columbus adults more typically just asserted bluntly that such relations were racially ordered. A white art teacher striking up a conversation about my research at lunch one day, for example, immediately started describing a friendship group of "Spanish girls" from his seventh-period class who he said had "really been included" after he encouraged them to use Spanish in a shared art project. "It was so great," he said. "Otherwise it would have stayed like them over here, the Samoans over here . . . *everybody in their little group.*"

When talking of student relations, both adults and students often focused like this—quickly, and usually critically—on perceived racial patterns in student "groups'" physical arrangement, with one group "over here" and another "over there." Such spatial organization of "groups" was the subject of many general complaints about classroom dynamics: in the fall of 1996, for example, a new white teacher, Mr. Fitsner, complained to me repeatedly after classes that "all the black students" in his classroom had clustered at a round table in the center of his room, while one black student ejected from a Latina teacher's classroom in 1997 sighed similarly that the classroom was "all divided between Spanish and black" because the teacher didn't "know how to mix it." In private discussion with me before class one day in 1996, similarly, Mr. J, a white teacher, lamented at length a pattern of "racial tensions" in his classroom seating, in which "black kids" congregated in one section and "Latino kids" congregated in another:

> I ask Mr. J why he seems to have moved his desks since the previous day. "To integrate the room," he says. "We've got real tensions—racial tensions, black kids at one table, Latino kids at another. So I moved the desks, and now the black kids all sit over there" (he points to the wall) "and the Latino kids sit over there. The black kids won't let the Latino kids sit with them." "Have you discussed the issue with them?" I ask. "That's what I'll do today," he says.

As the period starts, Mr. J immediately asks two Filipino guys to move from tables to desks. "Why?" one guy asks. "I don't need a reason!" Mr. J replies. As he begins talking, a black student and a Latino student come in late; each reluctantly sits where he is told. Mr. J tells another black student to move from a desk to a table. "Yeah, I'm smelling too many XX here," the student says, muttering something I cannot hear. "And that's another thing!" Mr. J says. "This class is composed of people of different backgrounds, including a white teacher. We all have heritages we're proud of. Nobody owns a table here, nobody orders anyone away from a table. We have black people in here, Latin people, Filipino people, Jewish people, Irish people, German people." "Who's German?" somebody asks. "Me," Mr. J says. "Who's Jewish?" someone else asks. "Ms. Pollock," Mr. J replies.

With a rapid list of his class's "heritages," Mr. J pointedly condemned the huddling together of people of shared "backgrounds"; while student "pride" in "heritage" was implicitly acceptable in the classroom, spatial student segregation along the lines of "race" was not. Columbus people complained fairly openly like this when students sat in racial groups in classrooms; they complained even more easily and openly that students arranged themselves racially at lunchtime. In the fall of 1996, for example, another white teacher talking to me about the Columbus social climate started complaining to me immediately about students' lunchtime seating patterns:

"It's gotten much more segregated," he says. "I went out to the quad at lunchtime and it was the Filipinos here, the Latinos over here, the Samoans over here, blacks over here."

Some scribbled notes of my own from a lunchtime scene a year earlier demonstrated that as a teacher, I had unself-consciously described the spatial organization of the school's different groups of "color" just as easily:

March 29th, 1995
Lunchtime. They stream out, and colors merge. Big coats have been tossed aside for tight tops, pants saggin' off butts. A food sale table has been set up and a number of students, those too tired or lazy to walk all the way up to Hacienda St. for Burger King or the tacqueria, crowd around. As I watch the student colors they align themselves—black skin groups together, braids flapping or straightened hair shining; Filipino students from my different classes meet each other and slap hands, curling lips around carefully cultivated mustaches . . . Chinese laughter is exchanged as students bound to meet one another. I see a clump of my Latino students swaggering up the stairs . . .

When analyzing student relations, students themselves focused just as readily on racialized spatial arrangements at lunchtime. Once we broached the general subject of student relations in one informal interview, my former student Michael (the student of "hecka races") even started spontaneously drawing a diagram of lunchtime racial patterns for me in his notebook:

Michael brought up how different ethnic groups have their own little places in the quad as evidence of people not getting along. According to him, Filipinos hang out along the main building wall; Latinos along the library building wall; Samoans in the arcade by the theater; blacks in the arcade by the deans office; Trisha [*a self-described "white" student*] is over under the tree in the corner by the theater; the ESL kids hang out in the hallway leading to the gym; and they (Justin, Michael, Kurt, Martin) [*mostly self-described "white" students*] sit at a four-person table in the cafeteria![10]

Noting over years the repeated appearance of such matter-of-fact descriptions in Columbus talk, I came to call easy accounts of students separating themselves racially at lunch the "lunchtime cliché." Indeed, such descriptions pervade academic and popular writing on school race relations.[11] And at Columbus, such matter-of-fact race talk itself had consequences for how people *viewed* "race relations": as Mehan (1996) summarizes much scholarship on language, "we know the world through the representations we make of it" (263). Routine, comfortable complaints of lunchtime spatial arrangements— which seemed to prove to Columbus people that student "race groups" did *not* "get along"—masked the fact that the quad's actual demographics were often far more blurred. Scanning the lunchtime crowd more critically with diagrams like Michael's in mind, for example, I found that I never saw the clean racial orders such diagrams suggested. While students did seem somewhat homogeneously grouped at first glance, a closer look revealed no "Latino" clump over near the ROTC door; a mixed crowd eating in the supposedly "Filipino" section; and "black" students chatting with other students in various areas throughout the school. Still, since people analyzing student relations relentlessly described lunchtime as if problematically clear-cut groupings existed, the perception that race *would* order such student friendships became a matter-of-fact assumption. Even after several years of noting exceptions to lunchtime spatial patterns, I found myself wandering through the quad at lunchtime looking for racial friendship groups—and any simple question about how kids were "getting along" at Columbus prompted immediate descriptions of lunchtime racial orders from other adults. On one day in 1996 when I told Mr. Vane, a black teacher, that my primary interest was in how Columbus kids were "getting along," for example, he replied bluntly that "At lunch time you see them all in separate groups—blacks here, Latinos there, Filipinos here."

Like talk of classroom seating or lunchtime space, discussion of student-student violence at Columbus seemed scripted to become matter-of-factly racial. And similarly, routine racial talk of student violence itself seemed to help compress complex social relations *into* simple "racial" orders: as such matter-of-fact summations almost never took the time to delve deeper into the underlying dynamics of assumedly "racial" conflicts, such talk itself played a role in organizing student conflict in simple racial terms. That is, every casual discussion of conflicts between presumably antagonistic lump-sum student groups helped to write the script for the next racialized clash: as routine talk of "the ___ vs. the ___" simply substituted one "group" for another, the notion that student "race groups" would fight one another came to seem to Columbus people almost natural.

In 1995–96, for example, Columbus students who were implementing a school district program called "Students Talking About Race" (STAR) led brief student discussions "about race" in classrooms around the school that inevitably came to focus on one particular "racial" topic: student violence. One discussion that took place in the class of a Filipino teacher, Mr. Cortado, demonstrated this scripted focus particularly well. After the STAR leaders began the 50-minute class with introductions by "name, age, and ethnicity, and something you like about your ethnicity" (most introductions went something like "I'm 15 and Chinese, and I like the food"), the leaders, who introduced themselves respectively as "Samoan," "Mexican," and "African-American," started off discussion after reading some definitions of "prejudice" and "discrimination" out of a book:

> "Has anybody been discriminated?" Nellie ("Samoan") said. Nobody answered. "You might not have known," said Mariana ("Mexican"). No answer. The team went on to "racism." Enrique [*a lone student in the audience "from Nicaragua"—the class, designed for students learning English, was composed almost entirely of students who identified themselves as "Filipino" or "Chinese"*] volunteered to define it. "You don't like a certain person because of their color or nationality," he said. "C'mon, people, this is confidential!" he added, trying to get other people in the class to talk. Mariana read the book definition. Nobody responded. Pedro (an "African-American" leader) said, "when you hate a race, like Filipino and Latin, or Filipino and black." "Or the KKK, that's SERIOUS racism," said one of the other African-American girl leaders. "The purpose of this," said Nellie, "is that all those things are everywhere we go, because we don't live in a world where everyone's the same." [*Now, the conversation narrows exclusively to the topic of student violence:*] "What does this all lead to?" she finished. "Violence," said someone in the class. "You can't stop it—sooner or later, there'll always be violence. People judging each other—it won't stop," Enrique said. "Even if everyone tries?" asked another student in the audience. "Everyone might try, but not everyone's gonna listen," Enrique replied. "What cultures have you seen that have been violent in Columbus? Don't be afraid to talk," asked one of the African-American girl leaders. Nobody answered. The group had run out of time. Nellie wrapped up the class, asking, "What can you do to prevent the violence that happens between different ethnic groups? Like I said, when people in my culture, Samoan, get into a conflict, everyone thinks *I'll* beat 'em up 'cause I'm Samoan." This was the last comment of the day.

Both in and out of the classroom, STAR discussions seemed inevitably to wrap up by referencing "the violence that happens between different ethnic groups," and a few students suggested that such brief exchanges themselves might exacerbate student "racial tensions": the next day in the STAR leaders' debriefing, the leaders were told by an adult adviser that some of Mr. Cortado's students were apparently worried the conversation might fuel problems between "black and Filipino" students at Columbus. One STAR leader responded that the students need not worry, as the main "drama" at Columbus was no longer a "black versus Filipino drama"—it now pitted "Samoans vs. Mexicans."

Such quick conversations "about race" led to matter-of-fact descriptions of student violence in every STAR discussion I attended—and when adults in the STAR classrooms occasionally joined in the conversation, they typically helped guide students rapidly toward the same conclusions. In a subsequent STAR session in the class of Mr. Ingot, a white teacher, the day's leader, a "Samoan" girl, recounted a painful story about a relative who was "shot by an African-American male." She said she and her cousins had first wanted to "beat up every black person we saw," but she had soon realized that such generic racialized violence was pointless:

> "So I tried to make a difference by being somebody in this school, to bring all races together so we can unite, make some of these racial tensions go down," she said. "Samoans are a big part of the violence here. You can stop stereotypes, but it starts with you," she finished. Mr. Ingot agreed. He ended the discussion by pointing to the audience and saying to the leaders, "They need to understand that they can make a difference—they can change their behavior."

As both concluding remarks about how students should "change their behavior" suggested, conversations led by STAR—whose very title suggested that it was a student task to "talk about race" in the classroom, despite the inevitable presence of adults during these conversations—always demonstrated an underlying taken-for-granted logic: "racial tensions" at Columbus were about students battling students. Oddly, both adults' and students' talk of student relations became perhaps *most* uninhibitedly racial in quick references to the school's largest-scale and most violent student disturbances—what people often called racial "riots."

On a Saturday morning in October 1994, an article in the California City paper entitled "School Dance Melee Puts Youth in Hospital" reported "bludgeoning" and "kicking" as "youth rivalries boiled over in a melee at a Columbus High School dance" the previous evening. It quoted a police officer who "said the incident had racial overtones. He said most of the initial assailants were black and the victims were Asian-American." A teacher that year, I had not chaperoned this particular dance, but I read about it in the paper, and I came to school Monday prepared to discuss the incident with my students. School administrators were clearly thinking along the same lines, for a conversation "about race" and student conflict was literally ordered: during first period, the principal came over the loudspeaker to suggest that classes take 20 minutes "to do group work discussions of the racial violence that occurred on Friday night."

In the more extended conversations that lasted throughout the day in my own classroom, students finally pointed out that such incidents of "racial violence" at Columbus were actually *not* purely racial: the fights actually often occurred over affiliations involving "turf" or "set" (neighborhood), gang or "colors," and these conflicts regularly occurred within "racial" groups rather than between them. The "Filipino vs. black" fight at this particular dance, they said, had actually stemmed from a personal romantic conflict and a shoe thrown across the room as a provocation. After security demanded that the core combatants "take it outside" in the street, some older kids not from Columbus who had somehow been allowed into the dance showed up with canes and a bat, someone pushed someone else, and the fight *became* both large-scale and "racial."

Despite these more in-depth deconstructions of "racial riots," however, the people I heard talking more briefly about the conflict throughout the day framed student tensions as matter-of-factly racial problems. In an emergency faculty meeting called after school that day, adults glumly assessed the fallout from the "black versus Filipino" student "riot"; as a white vice principal announced an apparently bluff threat to "finish the job" called in by "Filipino gang members" to a local TV station, everyone rolled their eyes in mock fear, and conversation turned to the need to find funding to hire more security guards. In one meeting earlier that afternoon between student representatives and several teachers, in which a Latina "Peer Resource" teacher led groups through a brainstorm of ways to deal with the "racial violence," a couple of self-labeled "Samoan" girls in my group had suggested briefly that conflicts were not *necessarily* racial ("people cause trouble because there's nowhere to go," they said), yet as the conversation rapidly moved on, they quickly had agreed that Columbus's student "racial" groups just did not "get along." One girl announced that she had been planning for some time to start a multicultural student group that would serve to "educate other races about each other," or educate students "on what other cultures are like." The girls' first suggestion of how to deal with the school's "racial violence," notably, was "start with ourselves."

Home sick in bed a month later, I wrote a letter to a friend describing a second "racial riot" that had shut Columbus down the day before Thanksgiving. Although I myself (as my quotation marks indicate) was skeptical about describing the incident matter-of-factly as "racial," my letter indicated that across Columbus the fight had been framed matter-of-factly as such:

> We've been having pretty bad "racial" problems at the school—we got let out early on the Wednesday before Thanksgiving because of a fight that started brewing at lunchtime between a "black guy" and a "Mexican guy" (according to school lingo) and expanded into a brawl that included a good deal of people in the school. There

were 32 substitutes in the building that day, and many of them couldn't keep their kids in the rooms, apparently, so it got bigger and bigger. The front window of the school got broken, people were running out of class, and the principal made an announcement to let everyone out. I thought this was a stupid idea, but I guess the idea was to not let a full-scale riot erupt inside the building.

When we returned to school after vacation in early December, all faculty members received a copy of a public letter of explanation about the incident that the principal had sent to Columbus parents and guardians. The letter's blunt racial terms made it sound strikingly like a police report. Indeed, the very repetition of the terms "African-American" and "Latino" in the document's treatment of "the facts" reinforced the running public summary of the violence as indisputably racial fact:

> Several incidents occurred on the afternoon of Wednesday, Nov. 23rd, which led to the early dismissal of our students. We want to report the facts of these incidents, the actions that were taken then and that we are taking now to ensure the safety and security of your child. . . .
>
> First incident: a Latino male student and an African-American male student fought one-on-one in front of London Middle School. The fight was arranged the day before because one student was "staring" at the other.
>
> Second incident: during lunchtime on the bus, an African-American, male, non-student, reportedly robbed a Latino Columbus student of his jacket. The two Latino Columbus students were then chased by the non-student assailant into Columbus. They ran to the third floor where a garbage can was thrown down to the second floor. It is not confirmed, but it is believed, that the student in the third incident, the African-American male, was hit by the garbage can.
>
> Third incident: at approximately 1:00 p.m., an African American male student was assaulted by a Latino student and received a bloody nose. This victim lost control, panicked and pushed the glass through the front door, badly cutting his hand.
>
> Fourth incident: after the students were dismissed for the day and at a location off campus, an African-American male student was "jumped" by 3 or 4 Latinos. It is not certain whether these are Columbus students.
>
> Fifth incident: after school a Latino female student reported that she was jumped by some African-American female students at a bus stop on Hacienda Street. She was not seriously injured . . .
>
> Please be assured that we were and will continue to place the safety and security of your child as our primary responsibility . . .

Such racial "riot talk" describing two lump-sum racial groups battling one another persisted for years after these incidents; indeed, such shorthand description served to solidify the institutional analysis of such conflicts as matter-of-factly racial events. Jake, who described himself as "black," summarized the "Filipino versus black" school dance "melee" two years after the fact in terms of battling "peoples": "Everybody got together—one Filipino, one black—everybody jumped in for his people," he said. Miguel (who sometimes described himself as "Latino," and sometimes as "Salvadoran") recalled the same incident as a "mayate vs. Filipino thing." In describing another "riot" in 1996, a Filipino teacher recalled "a huge fight between Filipinos and Latinos"; a white teacher referred to yet another incident as a "Samoan/Latino blowout." Reported talk of lump-sum race groups in battle framed the incidents as simply racial even for people who had not been present, as Edwin, a former student who usually called himself "black," indicated a year after the Thanksgiving incident:

> He recalled that "Some Mexicans whipped on a black dude; we were fittin' to get those Mexicans; they all got together; black folks were bangin' on Mexicans, and then the Mexicans got together." Different groups of "black" students had forgotten their neighborhood differences, he said, discarding "sets" to "get revenge on the Mexicans." He heard that a "Mexican jumped a black dude, and then the black dude went and got his friends, said they jumped 'em; after that, the black people stuck together," he said. This was what he had heard, anyway—he actually hadn't been at school that day.

Matter-of-fact talk of conflicts between assumedly clear-cut student racial "groups" not only passed the word retrospectively of who had been "bangin' on" whom; as Edwin's narrative demonstrates, such talk in the moment could also show newcomers to a battle in progress who was supposed to "stick together." After such fights, further, summarized "riot talk" became so nonchalantly racial that it somehow served to instruct listeners in the way race was *supposed* to matter at Columbus; easy descriptions of "riots" not only naturalized racial conflicts as predictable Columbus events, but also enforced the pervasive public logic about who really cared about race at Columbus—the kids. Columbus adults turned just as immediately and comfortably to talk of student-student conflict when asked generally about the role of "race" at Columbus. When I asked one white teacher in 1996 what she made of "race issues" at Columbus, for example, she replied that there usually "weren't many problems: if there's a fight, it's Mexicans vs. blacks." A new white teacher answering the same question in 1997 responded that she didn't "think it's a problem— the kids get along fine."

Talk of student relations at Columbus, then, proceeded as if race mattered unequivocally; talk of student-adult relations proceeded quite differently. Adults, who talked easily over loudspeakers and in public missives about how students fit into race groups that did not "get along," talked only privately and anxiously about how they themselves belonged to race groups that had to get along with students on a daily basis.[12] As with student relations, student-adult conflict was *not* by any means a constant at Columbus—adult and student laughter poured out routinely from Columbus classrooms into the halls—yet student-teacher conflict over power and authority happened often, and such conflicts seemed to most adults and students to be deeply racialized. Yet race labels, I came to realize, were conspicuously *absent* from largely adult-controlled public talk of "discipline"—and this notable absence indicated that the topic was perhaps *more* upsettingly racial than those topics in connection to which race labels were used quickly without apparent anxiety.

Part 3: Topics from Which Race Labels Are Conspicuously Absent

In classrooms and in interactions with individual adults, students—with few regular forums like faculty meetings for more public speech—often framed student-adult conflicts in basic racial terms. A young white teacher told me, for example, that some students in the hallway had suddenly called her "white bitch" at a moment of confrontation; a year after I had taught at Columbus, a former student explained to me that I, like many other teachers, had been constantly tested disciplinarily (generally "bugged") by my students specifically "because you're white." And, one day in 1994, when I told Lon, a black student with whom I was battling repeatedly in my classroom, to be quiet, he immediately yelled out a racial critique of both my actions and faculty demographics: "We need some more black teachers!"

Students talking to me about their conflicts with adults often framed themselves in racial terms as well. One day in 1996, for example, I was sitting in the dean's office talking to a girl about which students tended to get sent to the office by teachers. It was, she offered momentarily, "mostly black people" like herself. As a white-looking police officer led a boy who looked African-American out of an adjacent office in handcuffs, she grumbled, "OOH, he didn't do anything wrong . . . I *hate* white people." She then told me the story of the only "referral," or disciplinary write-up, she herself had ever received; it was for telling the previous year's librarian, the "tall skinny mean white man," around the time of the O.J. trial, that he looked like Mark Fuhrman.[13] She said he had written up a "whole page-long referral" about how she had called him a "racist," and how she had "said he hated black people." "I guess all that comes with 'Mark Fuhrman,' but I really didn't mean it that way . . . I don't remember any of that coming out of my mouth!" she said with pristine innocence. I looked at her. We laughed.

As a beginning researcher, I spent several months struggling with the key analytic dilemma that incidents like this presented: while the student-adult conflicts at Columbus routinely *felt* racialized, the race labels that could "prove" such racialization were absent from most actual interactions. My difficulties with ascertaining race's relevance to such disciplinary incidents—individually or in the aggregate—were compounded by a phenomenon of Columbus talk that I realized only gradually. While Columbus adults announced the actions of "Filipino gangs" at staff meetings, sent home letters about conflicts between "Latino" and "African-American" students, and referred nonchalantly to "Samoan/Latino blowouts," they never used race labels at all in public talk of conflicts between students and themselves. When planning together to improve "discipline" schoolwide and when publicly describing any example of individual clashes over authority, adults typically described conflicts with named individuals, "students," or various kinds of "problem student"—not with race group members. Except when quoting students who spit out race words in anger, adults discussing discipline almost never described *themselves* as racialized beings either. In fact, they only occasionally used race labels to describe either set of players when they were speaking in small private groupings of adults.

In the late fall of 1996, I went to a party at a local restaurant organized by former Columbus faculty who had gathered to trade stories of life since "reconstitution," which had replaced the faculty over the summer. One administrator, a Latino man, came over to talk to a small group of former colleagues who were still at Columbus. "Haven't they got rid of any Samoans yet?" he asked, munching some food. "No," one teacher replied, sipping a drink. Another added that "the Samoans are ruling the school." This explicitly racialized claim—that "Samoans" were particularly allowed to run amok over adult rules—circulated quietly in private conversations at Columbus for the entire year; yet as Columbus adults themselves occasionally pointed out, it was completely absent from any public conversation on discipline. In October of 1998, for example, when I was no longer around Columbus, I saw a white teacher (new the previous year) reading in a coffee shop in my neighborhood:

> He said that "troublemakers" were getting all the attention this year. "It's amazing how different groups of kids shape school policy. You could do a whole dissertation on how Samoans get treated there," he said. He told me about how a small group of "Samoans" had decided to get up and do an impromptu dance at the beginning of the most recent school rally. No one had stopped them for 15 or 20 minutes. The other kids noticed things like this, he said. I asked whether the disciplinary treatment of "Samoans" had been made a public conversation at Columbus. He said no, but it had been a common private discussion topic among the people that he knew.

During my years at Columbus as a researcher, Columbus adults regularly, but privately, described to me various other racial patterns in schoolwide discipline. Sitting with a white dean looking at a stack of disciplinary referrals one day, I asked, "Any sense of who's getting in trouble?" "Mostly girls," he replied. "Really?" I asked. "... Of the same culture," he added. "What do you mean?" I asked. "Blacks—and Latinos," he replied. Adults also privately used race labels to tell me which students supposedly were *not* "getting in trouble." Another white staff member whispered to me one day in the hallway, for example, that several Columbus teachers reassigned to another district high school had privately reported to her that they didn't "have to deal with the discipline problems that we have here ... I think it really has to do with the ethnic breakdown. They have more *Chinese* kids I think." And when Mr. Jones, a black administrator, motioned me over to talk to him one day in the hallway, he started explaining in comparative racial terms his theory that school adults "needed to take control of their students":

> "Look at the Afro-American, black American students here—and the Latino students. The district says they're not learning anything in class. How can they, when they've got people getting up, walking around, walking out of class? The black students—getting up, cursing the teacher, and the teachers don't do anything?" he says. "Is this so widespread?" I ask. "It's not everybody, but it's some. You've got to hold the kids to a high standard. The first thing I noticed when I came here was that they didn't hold kids to that standard. It's like I tell the kids, you can fight the system, but you will win one out of ten times—nine times out of ten you're gonna lose. I talk to the kids, the black students, and I say, 'Who runs this country? Who runs it? You know who runs it, the white man. And if he runs it, whose standard are you going to be held to? When you are out in the work world, are you going to go by his standards or yours?' And they say 'his,'" he finishes. "You have this conversation a lot with students?" I ask. "I have it to get their attention. It's a mean world out there—they'll end up in jail or on the street," he says, adding, "I say to them, look at the Chinese kids—they get the model. They're not disruptive, shouting as they walk down the halls. They get out of here and get good jobs."

Such quiet comparisons of student race-group behavior appeared often in private adult conversations; and as Mr. Jones's muttered analysis of "the white man's" "standards" indicated, many adults privately analyzing student-adult conflict framed the school's adults in racial terms as well. Many privately racialized analyses of disciplinary power dynamics, like those of Mr. Jones, focused on the school's "white" teachers, claiming that "white" adults in particular seemed to fear disciplining students or that students particularly challenged the validity of "white" adult authority. Ms. Tubbs, a black teacher, told me in her car one day about "the white woman who's afraid to say things to black students"; describing to me on another ride home how the mostly black cheerleading team refused to obey her, a white teacher sighed, "They basically said, 'you white girl, what can *you* teach *us?*'" "White" teachers were also said to discipline or fear certain "race groups" of students disproportionately. To my dismay, a white teachers' assistant who had worked with me in my classes in 1994–95 framed as racial the disciplinary incidents that had occurred not just in the classroom of a white male teacher, but in mine as well:

> "Kids would come in to his class, be pretty much right out the door. He kind of wanted to separate those who wanted to work from those who didn't. And he especially seemed to have a problem with the black kids. I told him that, and he denied it. But I said, 'no, you do—you just don't see it.'" She says he went and thought about it, and has since changed. She adds that she enjoyed working with me, since I

"had control of the class, so many of these teachers don't have control. But you were scared of some of those kids," she says. "Really? What makes you say that? Which kids?" I ask. "Well . . . particularly the black and Latino students, when they would get into groups against each other, I could see your anxiety level rising," she says. "Wow, that's interesting," I say.

As a teacher, I had thought daily about the role my own "whiteness" played in my relations with students; while *discussing* "whiteness" in my curriculum was enjoyable for me, *being* white at disciplinary moments was not. My "whiteness" seemed to come into relief at disciplinary moments as a state of being involuntarily wrapped up in dynamics of power struggle.[14] As for many new teachers of all "races," however, maintaining "control" was indeed a key part of human relations in my own classroom, and as a beginning teacher who had rarely *felt* so "white," I had come quickly to assume that sharing "race"-group membership with students would make asserting such authority easier.[15] When I revealed to a Latina colleague my own disciplinary troubles with a student we shared in 1994, she too explained that her relationship with the student, whom we labeled as "Latino," was indeed perhaps easier "because I'm Latin." Over my years at Columbus, however, I heard many other adults suggest that shared group membership had exactly the opposite effect. One comment overheard in the dean's office one day was particularly telling in this regard. After one black student got into consecutive heated arguments with a black social worker and the black assistant principal, his mother, also black, arrived at the office and asked him about the dean they were waiting to see. "Is she black?" she asked. Her son nodded. "They're the ones always trying to get you put out of here," she said with a frown. "Do your work and shut your mouth—don't do nothing to none of these teachers here. They got their education, they don't give a shit about you."

In many private analyses, faculty of color at Columbus argued that race indeed infused their conflicts with students. Speaking privately to me in the hallway on another afternoon, Mr. Vane suggested that being "black" did not lessen the likelihood of racialized conflicts with students, but instead set him up for *more* such conflicts:

> He says he feels many black students call him "an Uncle Tom, you see, or an Oreo, white on the inside, black on the outside," because he makes them "toe the line, and they expect me to give them a break because I'm black, and I don't. You know, 'come on, soul brother, gimme a break,' they'll say." We laugh. "In so many words they say this?" I ask. "Yes! 'C'mon, brother,' they'll say, and I say 'I'm not your brother, I'm Mr. Vane, now do your work!' I'm not going to give them a break, because I know what the world outside is like, and that's not going to give them a break," he explains. "They come in with all this anger inside them. It's not directed at me personally, but they see me as part of the institution, because I follow and enforce the institution's rules. And they believe I don't have legitimate power," he says. "Why?" I ask. "Be-

cause I'm a black—they're used to seeing white males in power—look around! So they see me as an Uncle Tom," he says. "They call you this to your face?" I ask. "No, but I can get it," he says.

Sitting in the back of her classroom as students worked on an assignment one day in 1997, I had an especially informative quiet conversation about this issue of power and "shared race" with Mrs. King, an experienced black teacher new to Columbus. While Mrs. King suggested that students who were frustrated with adults' attempts at "class management" were possibly *too* "sensitive" to the role race played in their relations with adults, she argued that adults made things far worse by *never* publicly broaching the subject of how race mattered to student-adult relations. The issue, she suggested in a whisper, was perhaps just too "sticky" for adults to handle:

> "I think there are a lot of very good, well-educated, motivated teachers here. Some of them have trouble with class management, dealing with the kids we have here. You can hear the frustration in the faculty meetings. When I say 'them' I mean the inexperienced, young teachers," she says, adding that she feels many really weren't prepared to deal with the situation at Columbus. "And many of them," she says, her voice dropping lower to an almost-whisper, "many of them don't share the same race as the majority of their students." "Did you say race?" I ask, actually not sure. She nods. "How would you say race factors in to what goes on here?" I ask. "It's something the *kids* are *extremely* sensitive to," she says, adding that she hadn't realized when she came that it would be that way, but now she sees that it's a "big deal" to the kids. "Samoan students are especially sensitive," she says, her low voice dropping again to add, "even more so than some of the black kids." (She totally whispers the phrase "the black kids," her eyes shifting to look at the students near her.) "Filipino kids are sensitive too," she adds. "Sensitive to what?" "To race," she says, "like 'he doesn't like me because I'm whatever.'"

She says that students often want to talk to her about other teachers, but she tells them she doesn't think it's professional, and that they should go talk to the teacher themselves. She says that at every school she has taught in, students go to her privately to discuss other teachers. "I think it's because I'm black," she says. Across the board, she says, students immediately see "the race of the teacher": "You walk in and all they see is this," she says, pointing at her bare arm. Students also expect that she will be less competent, she says, "because of this," she repeats, pointing to her arm again. This too has happened in every school she has been in. "You think black students expect this too?" I ask. "Oh yes," she replies. "I actually have the *most* trouble with black students, because of what they've learned." "In the world?" I ask. "Yes . . . in the community, at home or the lack thereof," she says. But all the students at Columbus have race-based expectations of teachers, she adds.

"These race issues, are they something the faculty talks about?" I ask. She looks at me. "Because I haven't heard any conversations like that, unless I've missed something," I ask. "No . . . they don't. I mean, I've looked at all those *lists*, like this morning—and I've never seen anything about it. I'm *so tired of lists*!" she says agitatedly. [*In a faculty meeting that morning, staff had made one of their many lists of suggestions for school improvement.*] "Do you think that's because the lists are public, or because they actually don't think about it?" I ask. "That's a good question," she says, thinking. "I don't know," she says finally, adding that she thinks they just don't want to get into it. "Like in the O.J. trial. I got really irritated with the media," she mused. "They kept saying with a black jury he would be innocent, with a white jury he would be guilty. They shaved it all down to that *one thing*," she says. "How is that analogous to here?" I ask. "It's the same as 'he doesn't like me because he's white'!" she says, adding, "In every O.J. interview, they missed the point. They don't want to get into the real issue, which is that everyone's really afraid to get *into* race. It's *hard* . . . it's *sticky*," she says. We are both smiling. "What are your thoughts?" she asks me. "Well, I'm amazed that it's something people aren't talking about," I say. "Oh . . . okay then!" she says, smiling, pulling her chair closer. She says that faculty never "get down to" this issue, but that they really should. "You can see it, hear it, in the faculty meetings," she says. "You mean you can hear race under the conversation?" I ask. "Yes," she says. "How do you hear it?" I ask. She says in people talking about discipline. But instead, they just take it all personally if they have problems, she says, tsking. "You think it would help to talk about it?" I ask. "Yes," she says. "How would it be worded if it came up in a meeting, on one of those lists?" I ask. "As relating to each other better," she says.

Throughout this conversation, Mrs. King implied that overcoming the racialized aspects of student-adult tensions at Columbus would require more direct discussions of how race *did* matter to the daily project of "relating to each other"; yet such whispered analyses stayed on the sidelines at Columbus, even as private talk demonstrated repeatedly that adult and student players across Columbus both framed "relating to each other" as heavily race-loaded. While Mrs. King expressed skepticism that student-adult relations could be "shaved down" to race alone—and while she indicated that both racial difference and "shared race" could foster racialized conflicts over power—she noted that the absence of *any* discussion of race's role in student-adult relations left both sets of players struggling in racialized "frustration."

I want to provide one final extended conversation about student-adult conflict—overheard one day in a school office in 1995—that made the racial framing of power relations at Columbus unusually explicit. The conversation took place between two African-American students (a boy and a girl who had apparently been thrown out of their classes) and an African-American man who worked part time at Columbus as a counselor; I was sitting over in the corner of the room grading papers when the three entered, and I stayed there with my back to them during the conversation. As race labels appeared seamlessly in all three's comments about discipline, it quickly became clear that their prior talk of "respect" and "authority" contained a deeply racialized analysis of struggle over power and control. The teacher as "authority figure" seemed always an exemplar of the fact that this was "the white man's country" (a phrase introduced into the conversation by the counselor):

May 11th, 1995

The counselor began telling the boy that he was setting himself up for failure if he lost his head and made a teacher more angry. Counselor: "If a policeman pulls you over and starts saying, 'you got a license, boy?' are you gonna keep buggin' him so he gets more mad at you?" Boy: "Yeah!" (The girl agreed.) Counselor: "But you're putting yourself in that situation, setting yourself up!" Boy: "I *like* to argue!" (The counselor said that for 50 minutes a day the boy had to play by the rules. He couldn't talk in class.) Counselor: "The teacher's an authority figure. You've got to learn how to respect authority figures. Someday you'll have a job and you'll have a boss. You have six now—they're called teachers." Boy: "Teachers ain't my boss. Teachers think they're your momma and daddy." Counselor: "That's how it's supposed to be—an extension of the family. Kids gotta learn how to *respect*." Boy: "They take it too far." Girl: "Don't try to stick up for these teachers—these teachers is *devils*, that's what they are, *devils*." [*Now race labels enter seamlessly into the conversation.*] Counselor: "This is the white man's country. You can't change that. You gotta learn how to deal with it. If you walk into class with headphones on, *I* don't want to help you, and I'm black!" Boy: "Teachers don't help me, except Miss Tubbs." Counselor: "But I've seen you disrespect *her*! And she's not white, she's black! So what's your excuse? You gotta learn to control your mouth. You're gonna walk into a white man's institution, eat when he lets you, shower when he lets you. And why is it like that?" Girl: "Because black people is crazy." Counselor: "No, because we're not educating *ourselves*."

[*Having framed Columbus as a "white"-controlled institution, they shift without pause to address a web of ways in which race matters to student-adult relations at Columbus.*] Girl: "What can you learn from a white teacher?" Boy: "They just teach you about white folks." Girl: "They don't even teach us English!" Counselor: "This country is run by Europeans. They make the laws and rules. If you want to change that, you educate yourself. Then you educate someone else. Work within the system to change it." Girl: "Can I ask you something? What do books teach us about black people?" Counselor: "You go on your *own* time and find it out!" Boy: "Nobody else got to do that! White people don't. Why should we take our own time?" Counselor: "Science doesn't have a color!" Girl: "What about US History?" Counselor: "You need to get a grade here—go learn on your own time." Boy: "They need to change the books!" Counselor: "You need to educate yourself—come with some ideas, come organized to say what you want!" Boy [*referring to a recent multicultural fair*]: "Just like how quick they was at the assembly to rush the black people off the stage." Counselor: "But you guys were throwing cans out there, man!" Boy: "But that's how I get into the most trouble, for what other kids do—they don't get blamed 'cause they're athletes! They won't tell on each other!" Counselor: "Use your mind instead of your mouth to get yourself out of trouble." Boy: "Sending people home just makes things worse—it don't do nothin.' " Counselor: "School is training you to come to a place every day, to listen to an authority figure, and to do what you're told." Girl: "What, to learn bullshit?" Counselor: "You gotta learn to listen to authority!" Boy: "They don't *want* you to learn, man!" Counselor: "People like Martin Luther King *died* to get you to learn! So you can go to the same school to get the education—" Girl: "That the white people get." Counselor: "Don't *let* yourself get kicked out—learn!" Girl: "Why learn?" Counselor: "Get educated, educate another person, so maybe down the line you can start to *initiate* change!"

Boy: "I'm gonna transfer anyway." Girl: "I won't, that's what they *want* you to do." Boy: "Some teachers bring it on themselves. Like Hull [*a white teacher*]—he'd say I was stupid and should be in kindergarten. And I told Harley [*a white dean*], and she *laughed*!" Counselor: "What did that make you want to do, talk back?" Boy (laughing): "Hit him." (He and the girl were getting up to leave.) Counselor: "You should stay here, not in front of the school. Why are you giving them the excuse to say 'why're you in the hallway?' " Girl: "Because the sons of bitches *made* me be there." Boy: "I'm telling teachers what I *feel*." Girl (to the counselor): "You ain't knowing how we feel because you're not in our *predicament*—you don't know what we've been through!" Boy: "Teachers can say whatever they want to you because they *know* they can get away with it!" (They left the room. When I finally turned around, the counselor looked frustrated.)

This pickup conversation in the office had moved transitively from mention of the police to teacher "devils" to "the white man"; over its course, the intergenerational analysis of faculty "authority" had broadened to critique the cumulative curricular and intellectual "predicament" weathered by young "black people" struggling to learn in a "white man's institution." For the students, interactions with adults over books, public events, and assumed intelligence all were saturated with actual or looming racialized injustice; the counselor's admonition to accept white "authority" during the school day evoked from the students both resentment and rage. In both the argument taking place and the incidents with teachers being debated, race was alternately explosively present and simmering just below the surface: that Columbus adults never admitted publicly that race mattered to student-adult conflicts and relations, then, was precisely because race often seemed to be simmering within these relations too dangerously. Ironically, the boy's complaint that "teachers can say whatever they want" did not indicate an awareness that teachers anxiously deleted from their public conversation any insinuation that relations with students at Columbus might be racialized at all.

As Mrs. King put it, the systematic absence of race analysis from most discussions of improving student-adult relations kept frustrated adults and students from exploring ways of "relating to each other better"; the literal absence

of race words from adults' public talk about discipline had a final specific consequence for Columbus students. While nonchalant public talk of student relations took the relevance of race *too* much for granted, no such public schoolwide script stood ready to support *any* student argument that race mattered to
student-adult relations—and any student claims that race *did* matter to student-adult conflicts in particular could thus always be trumped by the polarized
adult assertion that race did not. The subset of students who became embroiled
regularly in conflicts with adults often resorted to puncturing this silence with
sporadic and strategic accusations of adult "racism"; yet adults, suddenly confronted in their classrooms with the inflammatory student claim that race mattered problematically, typically protected themselves by claiming that race's
relevance was impossible to prove.

One day in 1994, Ms. Miller, a white teacher, entered the counseling office
to write referrals on a number of students who had left class despite her announcement that no one would be dismissed until she recovered a stolen phone
cord. Her voice sputtering with anger, she told the story to me and Mr. J:

> When the bell rang, she said, David and Lon [*black*] had stormed out, then Lizzie
> [*Filipina*], "the first of the good kids," and then finally and "reluctantly," Emilio
> [*Latino*]. David was calling her a racist because she was giving him a bad grade for
> the class. He and Lon actually came back after storming out, she said, her voice
> rising in frustration, thinking they could smooth it over with her and "because they
> wanted to make sure that I was writing up the non-black kids too." Mr. J, listening
> with a sympathetic smile, added that David had come in yesterday during a class
> period and "accused me of not caring about him because I was trying to eat lunch
> and he tried to take some fries. I said, 'I don't ask you for food, don't ask me,' and
> so I was a racist for not giving him a french fry."

As some students strategically wielded the word "racist" as a weapon to
garner power in battles with adults, most adults dismissed such accusations
of "racism," suggesting that these students argued far too cavalierly that race
mattered in student-teacher conflicts over french fries or referrals.[16] Many
months later, Mr. J himself complained in frustration that student accusations
of disciplinary "racism" had become a counterproductive "mockery":

> "Some people have taken the word 'racism' and made a mockery of it. Anything
> said negative is racist," he said. "If I tell a student to be quiet, and that student is
> there next to a student from another group, they'll say 'you just hate me because I'm
> whatever.' "

Noting that adult power would always be challenged in a high school setting,
many adults privately held student critiques of adult "racism" to be jibes designed to wound teachers personally rather than descriptions of inequitable
realities, and they would occasionally use the expression "pulling the race card"
to describe such moments. As Crenshaw (1997) notes, in the legal system, too,

the metaphor "playing the race card" has been "frequently deployed to stigmatize attempts to question the role that racial power might play" (99).[17] In muttered adult logic, students "pulled the race card" most often when they suggested publicly (usually in front of other students) that adults disciplined particular race groups of students disproportionately. The expression came into play at a brunch with several white and Asian-American teachers in 1997, when we started talking about a white teacher who had moved to a different city to teach:

> **Teacher 1**: He's teaching in an all-black school.
> **Teacher 2**: Oh, wow.
> **Teacher 1**: He says it's pretty good, motivated kids.
> **Teacher 2**: Well, if it's a *good* school.
> **Teacher 3**: It's probably one of those magnet schools.
> **Teacher 1**: He says it's good—for one thing, they can't pull the race card on you because they're all black! (All laugh)

At multiracial Columbus, as this conversation demonstrated, students' sporadic accusations of adults' disciplinary "prejudice" often claimed that particular "race groups" received unusually harsh punishment. In some cases, raw numbers demonstrated that students pulling this so-called "race card" were critiquing reality: statistics on Columbus suspensions available at the district office, for example, demonstrated a large overrepresentation of the school's "black" students among the harshly disciplined, and Columbus suspension lists floating around the school often demonstrated "black" (and, occasionally, "Samoan") names disproportionately. Such statistics were never debated openly at Columbus, however, and indeed, some adults who knew the district was collecting racialized disciplinary data often muttered quietly that they *resisted* suspending black students, and students in general, for the very reason that the district counted.[18] Given the school-level silence on the issue of racial patterns in discipline, however, students' accusations of disciplinary "prejudice" typically received ambivalent reactions from Columbus adults of all "races."[19] In November of 1996, Maverick, a black security guard, expressed a typical mix of sympathy and skepticism about some "stories" from students ("black, and some Latino kids") who were saying that several white teachers treated them unfairly based on race:

> He says he thinks the teachers are doing as well as they can under the circumstances. "There are a few that shouldn't be here . . . they're prejudiced," he says. I ask him what the kids reported. "Things about fairness. That things happen and consequences aren't consistent for certain kids. Grades—certain kids not being given chances to make up things." He mentions a teacher downstairs and a woman across the hall from her [*both white women*] who "have trouble with the kids. The kids talk about them. But you never know whether that's what it really is. The kids tell stories too, they don't get *their* work done, and say 'she's prejudiced.' "

As Maverick's comments suggested, the everyday ambiguity of Columbus students' "race teasing" about race's relevance itself also played a role in complicating student claims of adult "prejudice." That is, Columbus students' own tendency to complicate the question of whether race was "truly" relevant to them helped deflate their occasional angry claims that race was. Indeed, in quintessentially self-contradictory form, Columbus students sometimes dismissed as "jokes" their own classroom claims of adults' disciplinary racism. I noted one such incident in my own class one day in 1995:

> I tell Ralph's [*"black"*] group that I'm "up to here" with them wasting time. Sink or swim, both them and Luis' [*"Latino"*] group. I tell them they're all at risk of getting Fs. At one point, I gesture to Ralph's group, and he freaks about how I didn't include Michael [*the student of "hecka races"*] in the gesture. "Just because we're black!!" Ralph says. I get really mad and say I included the whole group in my gesture, repeating, "You all will get Fs if you don't do anything." "Nope, nope, I'm not gonna hear it," Ralph says. "I'm starting to feel really angry," I say to him, and finally he's quiet. I turn to the rest of the group and say, "If you don't get something done you're all looking at Fs, and it's not because of your skin color, it's because of the work you haven't been doing!" Darlene (*"black"*) says quietly, "That was just a joke." "I've had it up to here with that joke!" I say.

As the sole voices suggesting openly, if sporadically, that race mattered to student-adult relations at Columbus, students often cloaked these arguments in safely "joking" tones, blunting with ambiguous teasing the very accusation that adults could least stand to hear. Jake told me in one informal interview, for example, that students' public accusations of teacher "racism" were often "just play—getting on teachers' nerves." He admitted that he often did this "just to get a teacher mad," since openly suggesting that race mattered precisely at moments of student-teacher conflict could drive teachers over the edge:

> "Why does it make them so mad?" I ask. "Saying the things teachers don't wanna hear—especially white teachers. That's what they don't want to hear, so I tell them that, especially if they give you a bad grade. You go off because you feel bad, you want to make them feel bad too." He talks about how it's funny to see teachers get mad. "You ain't used to seeing it, teachers going off—people want to see it. It's funny, teachers making fools of themselves." He adds that if teachers were "*really*" racist, this school wouldn't be the way it is—it would be crazy, with race wars."

At Columbus, where people often asserted race's irrelevance and where students were also the only people publicly said to have "race wars," it was always possible to dismiss any student's angry claim that adults were "really racist." Students, grinning or in anger, regularly raised the basic question of how race mattered to student-adult conflicts; yet adults, trying anxiously to wield control, would not openly discuss the very topic to which race often mattered to them most problematically.

Conclusion

During my teaching year, as my notes reminded me years later, I myself had started advising students to avoid saying race mattered to student-adult relations if it "really" did not. Fearing that students were wearing out the accusation on minor disagreements with teachers, I called many such accusations "crying wolf," and I counseled students to save their energy for moments when there was "serious" racism to fight. When my partner teacher (a white man) decided not to give Arnold (a Latino student) extra credit for his outfit in a school event called "Dress for Success," for example, Arnold privately called it "racism." "He said it was because I wasn't wearing a tie. I've tried to get someone to tie it all day but they won't and I don't know how," he said, holding up a limp tie. "That's racist," he added. "What's racist?" I ask. "That he wouldn't give me my extra credit!" he said. "Alex—you gotta be real careful about saying people are racist," I sighed promptly, adding, "If you keep saying it all the time, nobody's gonna listen to you when somebody really is racist." He looked away and nodded once or twice. Surprisingly confident at the time that I could help students isolate the conflicts at Columbus that were "really racist," I took to asking students for "evidence" of adult "racism" to support their angry accusations. On the day my student Lon had yelled out that Columbus "needed more black teachers," for example, I had asked him if he had "evidence" to defend his next claim about "racist" teachers:

Me: What's wrong with us teachers?
Lon: They're racist, like Miss Miller.
Me: How? Give me some evidence.
Lon: Like when she always tells us to take our hats off in class, but she doesn't tell the other kids to 'til we point them out. And if we come in late, she's always pushing paper up into our faces and stuff.
Me: So why don't you go to her calmly and tell her this? (I summarize the story of "the boy who cried wolf.") I'm not saying this isn't legitimate, Lon. If you really think so, then go to her calmly and tell her what you feel. You have to go stand up for yourself calmly and defend yourself. You can't just accuse someone without explanation—they'll blow you off, say "oh, that's just Lon."

At Columbus, as my own advice to Lon demonstrated, students carried the burden of proving that race mattered to their interactions with adults; Lon himself was supposed to collect "evidence" and go to Ms. Miller "calmly" with his accusation. Yet with so few adults openly analyzing together how race might be relevant to their interactions with students, even proffered evidence produced little consequence: notably, I myself never discussed Lon's allegations with Miss Miller, even though I saw her daily. Rather than foster analysis of power relations between students and adults at Columbus, race talk at Columbus simply focused incessantly on other aspects of social relations: a public script suggesting that race relations took place between students drowned out sporadic accusations that race was relevant to how adults and students "got along." Daily, summative statements of race's alternate centrality and irrelevance to various Columbus relationships substituted for in-depth analysis of *how* race "really" mattered to those relations.[20] And in the scripted absence of *debate* on race's relevance to student-adult tensions in particular, the silenced anxiety that race mattered a lot was often left to thrive inside student-adult interactions.

Proving when race "really" matters is a dilemma of everyday life as well as research. Indeed, daily conversation begs the question, as race labels appear and vanish from our descriptions of the world. If you picked the right moment at Columbus, you could put "the races" up on stage in a festival for everyone to label and applaud; at other moments, it seemed you could only mutter about race groups privately with friends. In truth, Columbus demonstrated, both *too* matter-of-fact talk "about race" and *refusals* to talk at all about race's relevance can be acts with troubling consequences; and adults outside of Columbus, too, accordingly struggled regularly—sometimes unconsciously, often quite explicitly—over *when to talk as if race mattered*. The next chapter expands our analytic lens to include them.

Three _____

The De-Raced Words We Use When Discussing Plans for Racial Equality Can Actually Keep Us from Discussing Ways to Make Opportunities Racially Equal

THERE IS A WORD that pervades contemporary educational discourse, revolutionary to some and evasive to others. It functions as both a strikingly precise and a strikingly vague call for educational equality. The word is "all." Talk about educating "all students"—phrases like "high standards for all students," for example—has become almost standard in national conversations on schooling. Race is nowhere explicit in talk of education for "all," yet the phrase seems to generate a lot of controversy over how race does or should matter to educational policy. To some, talk of education for "all" specifically demands the active pursuit of racial equality; to others, the word demands that educational policy actively ignore race. Either way, this chapter argues, race is deeply buried in the word—and as a policy word that is colormute and race-loaded simultaneously, "all" can be both a useful and a dangerous word for equality efforts.

Looking at school reform talk in California City in general as well as at Columbus in particular, this chapter briefly tracks the way that race got buried over years in this apparently non-racial word (Part 1); it then watches people at and around Columbus struggle to conduct school reform business using it (Part 2).[1] To expose the racial history within talk of "all students," we first expand our analysis to include the language of educational policymakers and desegregation law. A historical look at two decades of education reform talk in California City reveals how talk of "all students" in the city's school district evolved over time out of an explicitly racial, 1960s discussion of desegregation reforms intended to make "black" students equal to "whites." By the 1980s, de-raced talk of "all" remained loaded with silent contestation over how race mattered to the district's educational policies; as a colormute call for racial equality, "all" talk would ironically also exclude conversations about race's relevance to educational reforms. By the 1990s in California City, as the chapter's second half shows, the absence of race labels from talk of school reform for "all" would foster a descriptive vagueness that would become a key policy problem—one that had particularly dire consequences for Columbus itself. At both the school and district levels, people describing education policy in the discourse of "all students" would fail to discuss the details of expected *or* existing reforms for racial equality. And as discussion of education for "all" obfuscated genuine dialogue about Columbus's own reform efforts, Columbus people would experience the consequences of a core dilemma of racial description: *the de-raced words we use when discussing plans for achieving racial equality can actually keep us from discussing ways to make opportunities racially equal.*

We begin in Part 1 with California City history, to demonstrate how talk of "all" emerged in the first place. Starting in the 1960s, California City's school reform talk first wrestled surprisingly explicitly with the question of whether race should matter at all to the city's educational reforms—and then with the question of which racial groups, if any, would be their target. Court desegregation opinions themselves would become key texts for this debate. In California City, a battle over undertaking the classic desegregation task of moving "black" students into schools with "whites" was to be quickly complicated by the presence of many "minorities"—and de-raced talk of plans for "all" students would quickly replace debate over serving specific "race/ethnic" groups.[2]

As the debate over racialized enrollment policies began in California City in the early 1960s, policy and legal discourse focused initially on the desegregation of "black" students, who were clustered far away from "white" students in a ghettoized neighborhood ("Port Place") in the city's corner and made up the largest and most segregated "minority" group in the city. The NAACP, which came to represent a group of plaintiffs from Port Place in the courts, would remain at the forefront of the desegregation case for its duration. Over the space of two decades in California City, however, the legal language of desegregation opinions would actively bury any mention of the needs of "blacks"—and crucially, the privilege of "whites"—within a policy language of increasingly generalized reform. As the city diversified throughout the 1970s, that is, its discourse of school reform would ironically once again become less explicitly racial.[3]

Part 1: From "Black" and "White" to "All"

The 1960s: The Opening Battle over Saying Race Mattered to District Policies

In 1960, the California City superintendent announced to the public that racial discrimination was simply not a problem in the city's public schools, hinting through his defensive stance that a public battle was brewing that suggested just the opposite. Indeed, debate ignited quickly over the racially ordered distribution of both educational opportunities and students themselves. When several leaders of the city's black community demanded public admission from the superintendent that California City's schools were in fact racially segregated, the superintendent countered by issuing a report in 1962 that argued preemptively that there was "no educationally sound program to suggest to the board to eliminate the schools in which the children are predominantly of one race." However, after an NAACP education committee study concluded not only that widespread segregation existed in California City but that educational resources were being denied black students in segregated schools, the NAACP filed a lawsuit to press the school district to desegregate. By 1963 the school board acquiesced somewhat, reassigning a few hundred black students to predominantly white schools and mandating that "wherever practicable and reasonable and consistent with the neighborhood school plan, the factor of race be included in the criteria used in establishing new attendance zones, and in redrawing existing boundaries." With this mild success, the NAACP dropped its suit, and local civil rights groups temporarily turned their attention to other issues.

As the battle smoldered over acknowledging and remedying the existence of racial disparities in the city's schools, not all black residents of California City at the time were calling for employing a desegregation strategy to racially equalize educational opportunity in the district. Many community leaders called instead for improving all-black community schools, by inaugurating black studies courses, hiring additional black teachers, and increasing district support for black parent involvement. In 1965, in fact, residents of Port Place approved a local bond measure to build two new schools in their neighborhood that would de facto be primarily "black," approving the very "racially identifiable" schools the NAACP was describing as "educationally indefensible." But after a 1965 census of California City schools revealed that the city's elementary schools were substantially racially imbalanced (four schools were over 90 percent white, and seven were over 90 percent black), the call for desegregation heated up again. The superintendent finally resigned, telling the newspapers agitatedly that "the number of whites in a school has no bearing on the quality of education." When city voters rejected a local referendum proposing desegregative busing in 1970, the NAACP finally decided to file a desegregation suit in federal court. The lawsuit demanded student and faculty desegregation in the city's elementary schools, arguing that these early years were crucial for equal opportunity and for teaching children the benefits of diversity before their "racial attitudes hardened."

That spring, after the famous *Swann* desegregation verdict in North Carolina approved busing for the first time as a valid desegregation method to eliminate "all vestiges of state-imposed segregation" in public schools, California City's federal judge ruled swiftly that California City Unified had in fact practiced purposeful segregation—and he ordered the desegregation of California City's elementary schools for the coming fall. Yet debate was about to erupt over which "races" actually needed to be moved. While the plaintiffs' complaint had denounced the separation of "blacks" from "whites," the proposed desegregation remedy involved moving the city's multiple "minorities." "While plaintiffs complain only of segregation of black students," the judge wrote, "the plan they had filed, as well as that filed by defendants, provides for a balancing of *all races*."[4]

The district, the judge wrote, had purposefully segregated "blacks" from "whites," concentrating 80 percent of the district's black students in majority-black schools despite the fact that only 20 percent of the total student body was now black. The district had also "assigned black teachers and teachers with limited experience to 'black' schools while assigning few, if any, such teachers to 'white' schools." Yet students in California City who were neither "black" nor "white" had been harmed by segregation as well, the judge asserted: "All who testified on the subject," he wrote, "were unanimous in pointing out that the evils of racism and ethnic intolerance are not limited to blacks and whites."

The opinion's brewing tension between binary and multiracial analysis was an indication of the city's changing demographics. From 1950 onwards, the proportion of California City's population recorded as "white" had steadily declined, from 90 percent in 1950, to 80 percent in 1960, to 50 percent by 1975. From the 1960s on, further, as in cities nationwide, a decreasing proportion of the city's whites had been attending its public schools, and this trend was to continue after desegregation (half white in 1965, California City's public school enrollment would be only 20 percent white by the late 1970s). Further, while the city's white population was dropping, the non-"white" population of the city was diversifying substantially. With the loosening of federal immigration restrictions in the mid-1960s, the population of Asian and Latino immigrants in California City had started growing rapidly. But this increasing "multiplicity of racial backgrounds" in California City made "effective desegregation more, not less, important," the judge wrote: the harms of segregation affected all "minorities," and opposition to desegregation would further mean depriving students across the city of "meaningful opportunities to know members of different races." The community's response to desegregation, the judge concluded, would determine "whether California City is to be divided into hostile racial camps, breeding greater violence in the streets, or is to become a more unified city demonstrating its historic capacity for diversity without disunity."

Despite this analysis of multi-"minority" harm and hope for multiracial unity, however, the traditional legal logic defining "segregation" as a separation of "blacks" from "whites" remained central to the legal argument for the remedial plan. Even while requesting that the district, the NAACP, and a citizens advisory committee each suggest a plan to desegregate the city's "different races," the judge required only that the plans achieve a proportionate "ratio of whites to blacks" at each school. In sum, a stated violation against "blacks" was being addressed with a multiracial solution—and this analytic tension was reflected in community reaction.

In the early 1970s, the city was weathering community battles over serving the language needs of immigrant children as well. According to the opinion itself, many "Chinese" parents in particular had requested in pre-judgment community hearings that they be exempted from the desegregation plan, arguing that removing their children from mostly-Chinese schools in the city's Chinatown would be both linguistically and culturally detrimental. "Mexican-American" parents, similarly, had argued that the desegregation plan ignored Spanish-speaking children's linguistic and community needs by assuming that spreading Mexican-American children across the city would be educationally advantageous. Representatives of both communities had suggested that the court was paying undue attention to the needs of "blacks," and the judge's final opinion accordingly argued outright that the desegregation plan was not biased toward "blacks" at all: the plan "favor[ed] no race or ethnic group," he said, but had been "fashioned so that benefits and burdens are shared equally by *all*." Equality planning in a multiracial city, he indicated further, required creating multiracial schools: the district could, if it wished, provide students in the newly desegregated multiracial schools with courses on the "cultural background and heritages of various racial and ethnic groups," but the goal was really to fit all "racial and ethnic group" pieces into the enrollment jigsaw puzzle rather than to serve any one of them in isolation. Telling "Chinese" parents pointedly that their children too would be redistributed by the desegregation plan, the judge explained that "*Brown* . . . was not written for blacks alone."

Over the next decade, the court would enforce an increasingly multiracial analysis throughout the desegregation plan's various iterations. Mandating first that each school in the district enroll its "race or ethnic groups" in proportions roughly reflecting the racial demographics of the district (plus or minus 15 percent of any "group"), the city's desegregation plan was tailored in subsequent years so that no one "racial/ethnic group" could comprise more than 45 percent of any school's student body, and so that each school also had to enroll at least four out of the nine "racial/ethnic" groups recognized by the district. Even so, different "racial/ethnic groups" continued to have specific experiences with the plan. During the 1970s, for example, many "Chinese" parents removed their children altogether from California City's public schools, only to be enticed back later by school transfers that effectively exempted many "Chinese" children from their assigned school placements. In turn, the white students who remained in the public schools disproportionately found seats in "gifted" programs, while black students were disproportionately funneled into classes for the "disabled." Even within "integrated" schools, thus, "different races" did not necessarily interact: as one black teacher who had been a young student in California City during these early desegregation efforts summed up to me over lunch one day, "We got bused over to [a white neighborhood] but we ended up in classes with people who lived next door to us . . . they said we were supposed to meet new kids but in our classes we didn't meet anybody who wasn't black." The strategy of simply moving students to different buildings was starting to sour, and by 1977–78, when students from Port Place were slated to be bused out to racially balance the schools on an island outside California City, the NAACP was labeling the city's desegregation plan "clearly and blatantly unconstitutional." The island desegregation venture was abandoned—and in the early 1980s the schools in Port Place remained almost entirely black.

As Port Place lived out its segregated existence in the early 1980s, many members of the local NAACP were said to be ready to give up on desegregation altogether. Yet the national NAACP was standing firm on desegregation as the nation's most effective first step for equalizing educational resources, and California City's case landed in court once again. In this round of court debates, however, particular plans for "black" students—and, in fact, for "white" students—were to be deleted altogether from the court's policy talk, as the call to make the educational opportunities given "black" students equal to those given "white" students would be submerged fully in a plan for "all." By this time, according to the census, California City's population included substantial "Chinese," "Filipino," and "Hispanic" communities (respectively 11 percent, 5 percent and 8 percent), while black students, at 15 percent, were still California City's largest reported "minority." Less than one in five students in the public schools were now white. And as the district continued to recognize *nine* "racial/ ethnic groups" in its demographic records ("Latino," "Other White," "African-American," "Chinese," "Japanese," "Korean," "American Indian," "Filipino," and "Other Non-White"), desegregation in the 1980s—as some analysts would later lament—would largely come to mean reshuffling "disadvantaged minorities." While the NAACP continued to worry particularly about the welfare of blacks in the city's most ghettoized neighborhood, talk of "black" needs and "white" privilege would, paradoxically, be obfuscated by generalized equity-minded language.

Fully Deleting Race Labels from Talk of "All"

In 1982, the same federal judge ruled that California City's school district demonstrated "remaining problems flowing from racial/ethnic concentration," and he asked that the NAACP, the school district, and the California Department of Education together devise a new desegregation plan, or "Consent Decree," that would be implemented by force of law. Presented eventually in a legal opinion by the judge, the Consent Decree would serve as the city's key desegregation text throughout the 1990s. According to the text of the Consent Decree,

> The key objective of the student desegregation plan is to eliminate racial/ethnic segregation or identifiability in any school, classroom, or program, and to achieve throughout the system, the broadest practicable distribution of students from all the racial/ethnic groups comprising the general student population.

Eliminating "racial/ethnic identifiability," the Consent Decree made clear, would require at minimum documenting and distributing both students and teachers *by* race. Pointedly, the Consent Decree required the district to enforce more rigorously the requirement that each school have representation of at least four "racial/ethnic" groups, by restricting students from transferring out of the schools to which they were assigned. Ordering as well that the district distribute district faculty, administrators, and staff more equitably by race, the Consent Decree also mandated that the district provide professional development for all "staff undergoing desegregation." Expanding its quest further beyond student and teacher placement, the Consent Decree ordered the district to step up efforts at school sites to increase parent and community representation, and to monitor "equity" in extracurricular activities as well as school discipline. Finally, stepping determinedly (though uncharacteristically, for a legal opinion) onto academic turf, the Consent Decree directed the district to "monitor test scores and academic results in order to evaluate the continued effort to achieve academic excellence throughout the system."

The desegregation plan's goals for racial equality were unusually ambitious, yet its language was becoming less precise even as its expectations increased. In the opinion, the very *word* "black," along with the word "white," had fully disappeared into a plan for "all races": the original goal of redressing the particular segregation of *black* children from *white* children—and equalizing the educational opportunities offered to segregated "blacks"—had finally vanished within a class action suit on behalf of "all" students in the district.[5] Since the first desegregation plan, the *Keyes* Supreme Court opinion on Denver had extended the nation's desegregation logic to include "Hispanics" (as necessary), and California City's increasingly complex demographics were indeed making "blacks" seem just one "minority" group among many. But the plan's new language of "all," a purposeful step away from rhetorically targeting "blacks," redirected the logic of equality away from blacks with surprising force. While the Consent Decree opinion began by recognizing that the NAACP had brought the case in collaboration with "individual black parents proceeding on behalf of their own children," it stated explicitly that the case had turned into a class action suit that was "broader in scope" than the original desegregation case because it sought "relief for *a class of all California City public students, rather than a class solely of black students.*"

This new plaintiff class, as the opinion recognized, was actually not necessarily glued together by common needs. The class consisted of "at least four, and as many as nine distinct racial/ethnic groups" (ironically, the judge could not say conclusively how many such "distinct" "racial/ethnic" groups actually existed), and had the Consent Decree agreement not been reached, the judge suggested, further litigation could possibly have resulted in the "fragmentation of the plaintiff class during trial." In fact, if the city's various "racial/ethnic groups" had "begun to compete for solutions" tailored to "their specific concerns," he held, they would have risked losing altogether the benefits of the "comprehensive relief conferred on all the class members by the decree"—for the plaintiffs had actually "produced little or no evidence of discrimination against any racial/ethnic group other than Blacks."

As the new plaintiff class itself lost its former "racial/ethnic" specificity, so did the court's proposed remedies. The Consent Decree's primary "specific" provisions were for Port Place, but the judge stated that the plans were not designed "solely for the purpose of meeting black students' needs," but rather to desegregate "the most racially isolated area in the district." Indeed, not focusing on black schools *as* "black," he suggested, was a necessary part of attracting non-black students to them: "It is in fact this very notion that [Port Place] schools are 'black' schools," he wrote, "that the special desegregation plans are designed to alter." Focusing on school reform rather than on "blacks" per se, he intimated, was the key to school improvement *in* black neighborhoods: as an immediate action to begin "improving both the educational quality of the schools and the public perception of the area," he wrote, all staff in Port Place schools were to be replaced in a reform called "reconstitution," and existing Port Place schools would be converted into an "academic" middle school and high school to which "all California City public students" would be eligible to apply.

Class members who claimed they still heard an unfair focus on "black" students within this plan for "all" had been informed outright that "blacks" were no longer a specific focus of the court. Representatives from the Mexican-American Legal Defense and Educational Fund (MALDEF), for example, had complained that "the decree addressed only the specific needs of black students in California City, and that it [failed] to address the need for equal educational opportunities for Hispanic students as well"; the judge responded that the basic premise of the Consent Decree was "system-wide desegregation." The desegregation plan would disband not only five historically "black" schools, he explained, but also nine historically "Hispanic" schools and five historically "Chinese" schools, a fact that demonstrated the "comprehensive nature of the proposed remedy." Besides, "*all*" children would be eligible for enrollment at the newly converted "academic" schools in Port Place—and to this extent, the judge argued, the decree *did* address the needs of "Hispanic students." Meanwhile, black parents from Port Place had begun to argue that the planned conversion would "displace" *their* children from the neighborhood's new "academic" schools. The judge replied that the sacrifices of the black children displaced from all-black schools would ultimately be repaid by a districtwide remedy that would "redound to their benefit, as well as to the collective benefit of *every child in California City.*" The court's responsibility, the judge wrote, was now "to the class of *all children* in California City schools, and in fulfilling that responsibility it must examine the fairness and adequacy of the proposed plan as a whole."

With requests for specific aid to "black" children and "black" schools in Port Place now being answered in the language of "all children" and "every child," generalized talk of "all"—designed to promote racial equality—was now precluding racially specified actions. Addressing the "specific educational needs" of particular "racial/ethnic groups" in the plaintiff class, the judge argued with an almost audible sigh, "would necessitate the creation of as many as nine separate plans." Indeed, the decree, the judge wrote, now *precluded* entitlements to "certain programs to meet specific needs" and would not approach the city's various "racial" groups as "separate."

Containing and Excluding Race: The Paradoxical Function of "All" Talk in Schooling Discourse

Two decades of struggle over achieving racial equality were infused into the district's new reform plans for "all students"; yet in practice, talk of "all" could also be used to counteract any racially particular demands for equalizing opportunity. Somehow, paradoxically, talk of reform for "all" could be used simultaneously to call for racial equality and to drown out any dialogue on defining racially equitable opportunity; and once such multiuse "all" talk reigned in California City, it would become all too easy to exclude race words altogether from the public policy debate.[6]

In California City in 1992, at the request of the court, a committee of outside researchers convened to review the implementation record of the Consent Decree over the past decade. Their subsequent report to the judge, referred to later by district administrators simply as "the expert report," reminded readers in its first sentence that the city's original desegregation case had meant to address discrimination against "African-American school children." In the past decade, they argued, the district had largely achieved the Consent Decree's general goals for physically desegregating the district's student population, even as the enrollment of both "Chinese" and "Hispanic" students had come to surpass that of "African Americans" (California City was, they noted, "a multiethnic community in which Chinese students are now the largest single group"). Yet the district had not achieved the Consent Decree's loftier desegregation goal: racially equalizing academic achievement. In particular, they concluded, "The overwhelming majority of African American and Hispanic students" were not yet achieving at the levels of other "groups."

The experts argued that these achievement disparities had ironically resulted in part from the Consent Decree's own multiracial school assignment policies, which had treated all of the district's "racial/ethnic" groups as interchangeable jigsaw pieces instead of treating particular "groups" with particular care. Designed not only to integrate "African Americans" with "whites" but also to permit "the desegregation of African Americans with Chinese and Hispanics

with Vietnamese among many other possibilities," they argued, the desegregation plan had actually "achieved little contact between the most successful and
least successful groups of students in the School District." "Because the plan
defines a school overwhelmingly occupied by African Americans and Hispanics, for example, to be desegregated so long as there is any presence of two
other ethnic groups," the report stated, "it is quite possible for a school occupied
by low-scoring African American students to be desegregated by low-scoring
Hispanic students or by large groups of new immigrants who do not speak
English." While the improvements in Port Place's schools had been designed
to "encourage white and Asian students to enroll there," the experts argued
further (in an unusually explicit racial description of this reform), most parents
of "white and Asian students" had squeezed their children through loopholes in
the district's placement process rather than transfer them to Port Place schools.
While the Port Place schools successfully "reconstituted" since the Consent
Decree had managed to import a new student body of non-poor and non-
black children from elsewhere in the district (what the report called "attracting
strong students from other parts of the city"), these reconstituted schools had
enrolled only a minimal number of poor *black* students, while many black students had actually transferred out of Port Place into "high-poverty minority"
schools that seemed worse for them than the ones they left behind. In sum,
"the number of African American children directly benefiting from the more
effective components of the Consent Decree was small"—and "Hispanics,"
too, had been both ineffectively desegregated and left to flounder in largely
inferior schools. It was time, they concluded, to focus more explicitly on the
needs of these *two* still underachieving "minorities": the experts recommended
that the district "build upon those programs developed under the Decree that
have succeeded for African American and Hispanic students."

It was the very first "reconstitutions" of the Consent Decree, the experts
suggested, that seemed to be the district's most successful reform efforts for
these two "groups": most schools reformed later in the 1980s had overlooked
both "African-Americans" and "Hispanics" with overgeneralized reforms that
lacked a real focus on racial equality. Such schools that had simply treated
Consent Decree funds as a general funding source to improve their existing
programs without reconstitution had developed no "new approaches to teaching minority students," they argued, and had thus seen "no overall academic
gains for African American and Hispanic students according to the District's
own data." In the district's first reconstituted schools, in contrast, "all of the
existing leaders were replaced with committed new principals and very substantial resources were made available to carry out the philosophical tenets of
the new plan which strongly emphasized high expectations and positive race
relations," and student achievement had improved accordingly. The experts
suggested, in sum, that the district reinstitute "reconstitution," the Consent
Decree's original racial-equity school reform, and that it start making its basic

reform goals more explicitly racial—that it start monitoring specifically whether or not schools attempting other reforms were improving the particular achievement of "African Americans" and "Hispanics." They then added a predictable caveat to this racially specific recommendation: "The district remains responsible for ensuring that *all children irrespective of race and ethnicity* shall receive high quality and effective educational programs and services"; "An improved plan for the Consent Decree will not subtract from some groups to pull others up."

By the report's logic, providing a quality education to "all children irrespective of race and ethnicity" required retargeting reforms toward particularly underserved "African-Americans and Hispanics"; yet targeting students racially while operating with the hegemonic discourse of "all children" was not to be so easy. By now, talk of serving "all students," made central to the Consent Decree's equity language, pervaded the district's "Philosophical Tenets"; "all" talk appeared in school mission statements, on posters taped to classroom walls, and in brochures distributed to parents. The discourse of "all" contained decades of struggle over equality for the district's racialized "groups," yet talk of "all" now erased "racial identifiability" itself: in most public school reform talk by the mid-1990s, talk of the needs of specific race "groups" was nowhere to be found.

As the second part of this chapter shows, after the "expert report" of 1992 rekindled the district's interest in reconstitution as a strategy for achieving racial equality for "African-Americans" and "Hispanics" in particular, district officials started seeking out schools to charge with not successfully serving "all students." In the spring of 1995, the year I taught at Columbus, they focused their evaluative lenses on Columbus, itself already straining to succeed at its own schoolwide reforms. Yet over the coming year of the Columbus faculty's attempts to avoid reconstitution, the very words "African-American" and "Hispanic" would be conspicuously absent from most district-*and* school-level reform policy talk of serving "all" at Columbus. On the day at the end of the 1995–96 "probation" year when bewildered Columbus staff were told they would indeed be reconstituted for the following fall, a district representative sent to deliver the news distributed an explanatory document entitled "Basic Information about School Reconstitution" that simply explained:

> The Consent Decree became law in December of 1982. The purpose of the Consent Decree was twofold:
> 1. To integrate all aspects of the CCUSD; and,
> 2. To achieve academic excellence for all students.

Such reform policy talk of needing to serve "all" was race-loaded and colormute simultaneously—it was both a call for racial equality and a seeming mandate to proceed in de-raced terms. In daily talk of reform at the school level, "all" policy talk produced a response that was similarly ambiguous. What happens when race is buried rather than explicit in reform discourse? When vague policy and everyday reform talk interact, as Part 2 demonstrates, de-raced equality words can actually sabotage discussions of efforts to make opportunities racially equal.

Part 2: The Reconstitution Story

"In spite of our program, we have not saved all of
our kids."—Columbus principal

In late May of 1995, the faculty of Columbus High School gathered in the school library to hear whether they were all in danger of being fired. Rumors had been circulating among the staff, of which I was a one-year rookie member, that the school had been placed on the district's secret list of low-performing schools. If Columbus was on this list and did not rise to district expectations within one probation year, all adults at the school, from principal to secretary, would be "reconstituted"—"vacated," as one district document put it. The staff would be evicted and replaced with adults the district thought could handle the job.

Having just weathered a year of intensive schoolwide reform as a Columbus teacher, I was honestly surprised by the district's implication of Columbus's abject failure. The staff had spent several jam-packed years creating a "house" program grouping freshmen and sophomores in small teacher-student cohorts for interdisciplinary courses, social and academic counseling, and elaborate student research projects. In the past year, the staff had also created career academies offering juniors and seniors coursework and internships in media arts, the health sciences, and international business. Both reforms, consistent with reforms of coalitions reinvisioning large high schools across the country, were beginning to receive national recognition for their impact on teaching and learning at Columbus. Like most other teachers in the room, I was exhausted. The staff waited pessimistically, slumped on the library's rectangular wooden tables, for word of the list.

The principal, an Asian-American woman in a suit, stood to prepare us for a district representative's announcement. "Yes, we've made mistakes," she began. "But when we designed the program we're implementing now, we really had the idea to help the at-risk kids," she said. "Still, a lot of kids are continuing behavior that's not helping; we can focus on those kids. There is a small group of students who are still not responding—the highly at-risk kids. In spite of our program, we have not saved all of our kids," she finished dejectedly, pursing her lips.

Mystified, I scribbled down her comments on the back of a letter from the superintendent that had been distributed at the beginning of the meeting.

Glancing at the letter quickly, I noted that it simply stated that the district had "identified" six city schools, including Columbus, as "low-performing." Despite the principal's pointed mention of a "highly at-risk" subset of Columbus students, further, pages of state standardized test scores attached to the letter revealed only an aggregated Columbus score. As other staff squinted at the pages thick with black numbers, tension in the room began to build.

The district administrator, a white man with a sweater slung over his shoulders, now stepped forward from behind the principal. "I see he dressed up for the occasion," hissed a teacher next to me. I smiled nervously. Slowly, quietly, with a knit brow and an exasperated frown, the administrator began to recount a brief history of this reform called "reconstitution." In the early 1980s, he said, a case called "the Consent Decree" had resolved an NAACP lawsuit against the California City Unified School District by mandating two missions for the CCUSD: "the elimination of racial identifiability," and "academic excellence for all students." At that time, he said, a number of "racially isolated" and "low-achieving" schools had been targeted immediately for reconstitution. By the 1990s, the district had started targeting other schools that were "low-achieving," and this year, Columbus was one of nine elementary and secondary schools that would be given one year on probation to improve. If it did not, he said, reconstitution would fire and replace a faculty that perhaps, like a family, had become "dysfunctional." As a number of teachers gasped resentfully, he added that with reconstitution, all adults' association with the school would end and a new faculty with "homogeneity of belief" would be selected.

Shocked into silence and then galvanized by a surge of angry energy, the faculty peppered him with questions. Why weren't schools in the district with test scores lower than Columbus's also being put on probation for reconstitution? Had reports describing Columbus's growing successes with its house and academy programs been taken into account when making this decision? And what about the psychological toll on students, who would be labeled publicly as representatives of a failing school? The administrator sighed. "I happen to believe," he said cryptically in response, "that *all students can learn.*"

The response seemed to me an evasion of the questions, but the silent fury of the grimacing teachers around me suggested something deeper still. More questions about the evaluation process followed. Still bewildered after a brief discussion of quantitative and qualitative variables, I finally asked the administrator to simply explain the qualitative criteria upon which Columbus was going to be evaluated. "I can't tell you that," he responded. Dumbfounded, I looked around and saw the older teachers shaking their heads with wry smiles.

I went home that night wondering why the district had such a negative impression of Columbus—and why the district administrator had been so inarticulate about Columbus's impending evaluation. In particular, I mulled over his reply to questions about Columbus's predicament: "all students can learn." It was only when I became a graduate student the following fall and started reading the CCUSD's legal and policy documents myself that I came to recognize the administrator's remark as one of the district's "Philosophical Tenets," a list of principles written to embody the Consent Decree's desegregation ideology. After one year of living and working as a teacher in California City, I had never heard of this "Consent Decree"—in fact, I had never even imagined that desegregation orders existed in California. It was also only after reading policy and legal documents myself that I came to recognize a particularly racialized point about "reconstitution" that the administrator himself, positioning Columbus simply as a "low-achieving school," had not articulated: the district wanted to reform schools that did not adequately serve two particular racial groups.

Coming upon the 1992 "expert report" in my research one day, for example, I was startled to find its explicitly racial conclusions—to find that in recommending the reinstatement of a "reconstitution" policy, its authors had advised evaluating other school reforms and expenditures "by the extent to which they actually improve educational opportunity for African-American and Hispanic students." I was also surprised to learn from subsequent judicial opinions that the court monitoring the district's desegregation efforts had taken the "experts' " advice quite literally and ordered additional school reconstitutions until a very specific "task" was complete: improving "African-American" and "Hispanic" academic performance.

The administrator who came to announce Columbus's probation had said nothing so explicitly racial about the school's alleged shortcomings. Over the following probationary year at Columbus, in fact, *no* district representative would suggest publicly that to avoid reconstitution Columbus would have to demonstrate specific efforts to serve "African-American and Hispanic students"—and no one at Columbus would, either. Indeed, Columbus would be reconstituted in the spring of 1996 without *any* sustained district-led or school-level conversation on how "African-Americans and Hispanics" were being served by the current reforms at the school—or even how or whether the reconstitution reform was an attempt to serve them better.

California City's school reform policy talk, as I found that year, was actually characterized not by the total absence of race talk, but by the inconsistency of it. That is, while the language of "all" was hegemonic in California City's reform talk, race labels did surface occasionally within school reform policy documents and speech. Yet any speakers who started talking or writing of school or district reforms in racial terms themselves abruptly reaggregated these descriptions into talk of "students" or "all students"—making perennially unclear how race mattered or was expected to matter to reforms. During the probation year, the "all" talk of school reform discourse itself would repeatedly erase talk of "African-Americans" and "Hispanics"—and of the court's racially specific goals for serving them.

Disaggregated Descriptions

In any talk about schooling, one might argue, speakers shift back and forth along a continuum of descriptive specificity, moving from talk of "students" in general to talk of particular individuals. Policy discourse, rarely interested in individuals, speaks most often of "students"; policy talk calls such talk "aggregated" (such that we might call talk of "all students" "hyper-aggregated"). Policy discourse thus calls descriptions of more specific student subgroups *disaggregated*. "Disaggregated" descriptions of policy-relevant populations can be overtly racial ("the Latino students"), or not ("our highly at-risk students," "the Special Ed kids," or "the kids under the 40th percentile"). In practice, people speaking and writing about policy routinely disaggregate and reaggregate their descriptions of students, displaying an interest in different sizes and shapes of populations at different times.[7] In California City, policy talk was alternately specific and general, as speakers abruptly disaggregated and reaggregated descriptions of students depending on the situation.

During the year Columbus was on probation for reconstitution (1995–96), district representatives typically spoke in public in hyper-aggregated terms about school reform for "all," blurting out race words only at moments when confusion over the aims of school reform had reached its limit. Meanwhile, Columbus teachers and administrators interacting with district personnel matched the district's hyper-aggregated discourse by speaking hopefully of their work to improve education for "all students." After reconstitution, the new Columbus staff talked in aggregated terms of "all students" even more vigorously than did the old, reproducing an identical equity-minded reform discourse that similarly made no specific mention of "blacks" or "Latinos" at all. Although race labels had begun to emerge a bit more regularly from "all students" talk during the heat of the reconstitution battle in spring 1996, after reconstitution the waters of "all" talk closed over racial terms once again—ending a cycle in which no public analysis of assisting "blacks" and "Latinos" in particular had occurred.

Probation Year, 1995–96: Reform Talk

In the spring of 1996, near the end of the probation year, I attended a summative formal presentation on Columbus programs given by Columbus students in the school library, for a district evaluative panel that included the superintendent (a Latino man) and several representatives from the NAACP. As I noted at the time, almost all of the student presenters at this "qualitative presentation" appeared to me to be Filipino or Chinese; one or two of the students looked Latino to me, and only one, a well-known honors student in the student government, typically described herself as "black." The hopeful presentation, which proudly outlined Columbus's "houses" and career academies, included no specific focus on programs or activities for "black" or "Latino" students; indeed, it did not reference students in racial terms at all.

According to some Columbus adults, such omission of explicitly racial reform discourse from Columbus's school improvement planning had been somewhat purposeful. In an interview several years later, Columbus's former principal implied that the omission of race words from reform discourse had been on her part something of an intentional equity strategy. Her personal philosophy about the school's house and academy reforms, she said, had been to "nurture all students" rather than "segregate" different groups in the school's programs: while certain disaffected staff members at Columbus possibly saw the need to frame student needs in racial terms (one staff member, she heard, had reported to a "Latino" board member that Columbus was "not doing things to make Latinos successful"), she herself had decided that a strategy for serving "all students" would most equitably catch "African-Americans and Latinos" in the programmatic net. But anyway, district officials had not discussed the Consent Decree's racialized mandate much with principals, she said, either the reasons for it or how the district wanted it actualized. At one district meeting for principals in the spring of 1995, she recalled, she and the principals of the other schools just placed on probation had simply been handed documents outlining the Consent Decree's mandate for school reforms improving the lot of "African-Americans" and "Hispanics." There was no discussion at all at the meeting of serving "African-American" and "Hispanic" students, she said, perhaps because the principals were being told in writing that these groups were the district's priority. But since principals were also subordinate to district administrators, they just accepted the mandate, she added, with "no clue as to how they wanted you to do it." It had seemed a waste of time at such meetings to try to question things or get clarification. "You needed to figure it out yourself. You just wondered, 'What *are* we not doing?'—and you tried to be innovative. It was a hit and miss approach."

Throughout the probation year, it came to seem later, school reform documents written both by the district and for the district had been similarly rather "hit and miss" about articulating the question of racially targeted reforms. In 1998, going through my stack of papers from my teaching year, for example, I found the district document I had used for scratch paper on the day in the Columbus library when the district administrator had announced Columbus's probation status. I now noticed that the document included, in its back pages, some assessment criteria that were racially disaggregated. Several "qualitative" criteria—the criteria the administrator had protested that day that he "couldn't tell" the faculty—were printed here, and they called for a demonstrated targeting of reforms toward "African-Americans and Hispanics." One criterion required that the school's site plan include "activities that are being implemented and effective and which focus on improving academic performance of

African-American and Hispanic students"; a second required that the school portfolio "effectively document the school's program, direction, efforts and plans to improve achievement of all students, especially African-American and Hispanic students"; and a last criterion required that a "presentation to the superintendent and review panel effectively communicates the efforts, plans and commitment to improve the achievement of African-American and Hispanic students." Yet eight "quantitative" criteria, printed first in the document, called only for the improved achievement, attendance, grades, dropout rates, and suspension rates of "students."

While the district buried talk of "African-Americans" and "Hispanics" in the back pages of assessment documents, Columbus documents meant to communicate the school's reform efforts to district administrators spoke confidently of a quest for academic excellence for "all" and said almost nothing that labeled Columbus students racially in any way. The Columbus school site plan from the probation year, written for a district audience by the principal and a faculty committee, outlined Columbus's house and academy programs as activities designed to improve teaching, learning, and academic performance across Columbus. It announced that Columbus would "continue to develop and implement a rigorous, project-based curriculum that will strengthen the language and mathematical skills of all students," and that it would focus on "improv[-ing] teaching and learning so that all students will feel that the school community supports their success." Over its course, the site plan outlined current plans to assist several disaggregated subgroups of needy students, such as "students who received two or more Fs" (required to attend homework clinic), "Special Ed students" (to be more fully included in mainstream programs), "students in the bottom quartile on CTBS tests" (to receive help from resource teachers), and "kids who are not succeeding academically and behaviorally" (to receive a "personalized plan-of-action"). Professional development, it said, was helping teachers serve students who were "underprepared." A single paragraph, on "equitable student access and outcomes," referenced the school's "cultural" "diversity," stating simply that "our students come from richly diverse linguistic, cultural, and learning style backgrounds." Predictably, the paragraph reaggregated to conclude that "the challenge for teachers is to use and adapt instructional materials and methods to promote the educational success of all students."

In turn, several district documents attached to the back of this school site plan ordered schools to prepare programs for "targeted students" without identifying directly who these targeted students were. While one paragraph did state explicitly that "all CCUSD schools are expected to successfully educate students from all racial/ethnic groups" (each school, it said, was expected to "demonstrate at least a year's gain as measured by NCE scores for each racial/ethnic group represented at the school"), the paragraph quickly reaggregated its reform language and concluded, "To accomplish this, all schools are expected to achieve specified outcomes in terms of improving overall student achievement." The Columbus site plan itself concluded that the school's understood mission was "to improve teaching and learning to enhance the academic achievement of all students, and thereby to improve teaching and learning for all."

In Columbus-produced documents about school reforms in progress, talk about "all" students often seemed central to optimistic attempts to demonstrate these reforms' alignment with district equality rhetoric. However, to those at Columbus, the district often seemed to be almost deliberately obfuscating its own expectations. According to some teachers, direct requests for additional clarity from district administrators about the district's expectations during the probation year were seldom answered satisfactorily. Kay, a veteran white staff member, recalled one day the following fall—months after she and her colleagues had actually been reconstituted and removed from Columbus—that one day during the probation year she and several other teachers made an appointment with the district administrator who had informed the staff of its probation status that day in the library. They asked him, she recalled, what his suggestion was for improving the schoolwide attendance rate. With a shaking head, the administrator replied, "You folks at Columbus just don't have a *clue*." "We asked him what he meant by that and he said he couldn't say," she said. "If he had magic answers, why couldn't he tell us?"

Nodding, I told Kay about my recent surprise at finding a district document, passed out by this administrator, that had requested in its back pages an explicit "qualitative" focus on "African-American and Hispanic students." Kay looked at me in silence. "Well, that's always been the focus," she said. "Do you think the rest of the faculty knew about that?" I asked her in surprise. "Well, what can you *do*?" she asked, looking exhausted. Mystified, I raised the subject of this document and its three racialized "qualitative criteria" later that day with John, a young Asian-American teacher who had been among the few teachers rehired at Columbus after reconstitution. Driving me home, he said he was surprised to hear about a district desire to see plans focused on serving "black and Latino" students. He didn't recall this document, he said, but he had thought the school's goal during the probation year had been to help "all students who were failing." "Black and Latino students do make up the majority of those students," he mused, "but the house program was designed to help all failing students."

Throughout the probation year, it came to seem, no consistent conversation on whether schoolwide reforms sufficiently served "African-American" and "Latino" students had been promoted either by the district demanding reforms for "all" or by the subset of experienced Columbus educators who knew that the district's reform demands were deeply racialized. Those present at several school board meetings at the end of the probation year, though, had a rare opportunity to hear the district reveal its interest in racialized reform. The school board was moving to vote on a district recommendation to reconstitute Columbus and two other schools for the following year—and on several Tuesday nights at the end of May, the racial vagaries of the district's reform discourse hit the fan.

School vs. School District: A Hidden Racialization Revealed

At a school board meeting held in a middle school auditorium, representatives from the three schools (an elementary school, a middle school, and Columbus) chosen for reconstitution from the nine on probation were scheduled to speak on their own behalf. As usual, the six-member school board (consisting of two black men, one white woman, one white man, one Chinese-American man and one Latina) and superintendent faced the audience from a long table in the front of the auditorium. A standing microphone awaited speakers directly in front of the table.

The evening started off, tense yet subdued, with discussion of the elementary school slated for reconstitution. A woman who looked African-American walked in silence to the microphone. Announcing that she was a special education teacher, she told the crowd that 94 percent of her school's students were participants in free lunch and breakfast programs—a fact, she added, that was important only to indicate that her school had the largest population in the district of "educationally disadvantaged" and "high-risk students." She and her colleagues were thus quite puzzled, she said, that during the probation year they had not received more support from the district in consideration of their "special needs." She dramatically recounted how, at the district's request, her school had submitted a list, fourteen items long, of the supplies, equipment, and support they needed for that year. To date, she said, they hadn't received a single item on the list. As she sat down, one of her colleagues (a blond teacher with a Hispanic name) came forward to say that no representative from the district had ever set foot in the elementary school until the final day of evaluation. "We were told to measure up, to bolster our test scores—not that anything in particular had been done wrong," she said. It seemed as though the district had approached their school with the premise that it was a failure, she said. In fact, she reported, one school board member (a black man whom she named) had even attended an outside meeting on the school advertised only to parents with fliers stating "[this school] is failing your students."

After some representatives from the middle school implored the district to give them more time to improve (the superintendent and several school board members exchanged raised eyebrows as one white teacher recounted how "out of control" the school's students had been in the past), speakers rose to represent Columbus. A senior spoke first, describing how he had emerged out of Special Education classes and announcing that he had just been accepted to one of the top four black colleges in the country. The audience applauded; the board members sat in silence. As a Chinese-American junior described his personal fear of losing Columbus's science career academy, the superintendent quietly read a stack of papers on the table. A veteran white English teacher then described the five-year process of creating Columbus's house program, concluding, "I've never worked with a group of teachers that have worked harder to make effective change . . . I'm sort of at a loss." The superintendent, still reading, looked up only when a Latina student came to the microphone to say she represented the bilingual department. "You must take into account *our* opinions," she said. "Columbus has good teachers who want to teach us." After a Filipina junior, a high-ranking officer in the student association, demanded finally that teachers and staff not be blamed for any school failures as "some students, no matter how much teachers work, do not take learning *seriously*," the district's union president, a white woman famous for forceful pontification, finally rose to argue that reconstitution illogically infused Consent Decree money into schools only after they had been judged failures and also simply redistributed reconstituted teachers to other schools with similar demographics. It was time for the district, not the court, to run its schools, she concluded: "Desegregation is appropriate for a judge to rule on, but how to improve schools is not."

The union president's reference to "desegregation" was so far the only comment even to imply that race had some relevance to these reconstitution decisions; the evening's discussion had revealed nothing about the district's court-mandated interest in the welfare of "African-Americans and Hispanics." Fresh from studying the Consent Decree as a graduate student, I decided to approach the microphone myself. I had been thinking a lot about something I had learned from reading the "expert report": the Consent Decree had allotted a substantial amount of state money for the CCUSD to conduct staff development activities for "schools undergoing the desegregation process districtwide," specifically addressing "such key goals as equity in discipline, upgrading minority academic achievement, and teaching in a racially and ethnically diverse school." The district, according to the report, had used this staff development money to cover other district expenses. During a school board meeting several weeks earlier, I myself had quietly approached the district head of High School Operations, a white man seated in the audience, to ask what had happened to these monies earmarked for staff development on race relations. "Not 'race relations,' but 'multicultural education,' " he corrected me in a whisper, naming a woman who conducted these trainings in the district. Surprised, I asked him why she had never been to Columbus. "Probably because nobody ever asked her," he replied, whispering that the district really hadn't been conducting many of these workshops anyway. "It can get difficult, painful," he said. "Things get opened up that can't get closed."

Standing at the microphone now, I told the audience about the district's possibly unused staff development funds, and I concluded by suggesting to the board and superintendent that in not pursuing the Consent Decree's mandated staff development on the pointed issue of working with "black" and "Latino" students, the district could perhaps be seen as having broken the law. The superintendent looked up, his face somewhere between a dismissive growl and a grimace. I sat down, flushed, to audience applause.

Following my rather inflammatory accusation, one more Columbus student, a white sophomore, approached the mike and skewered the superintendent with a simple request—to explain why Columbus had received a score of 4 out of 25 possible points on the "qualitative presentation" of Columbus programs given some weeks earlier to district and NAACP evaluators. All night, teachers around me had been pointing to a list of scores handed out with the night's agenda, which showed clearly that all three schools slated for reconstitution had lost points primarily on these "qualitative presentations"—their quantitative scores, covering things like test scores and attendance rates, looked identical to the schools deemed "improved." Glancing at the other board members, the school board president replied that the superintendent would answer such questions later. With this deferral, the Columbus speakers' list resumed, and listeners witnessed the most bizarre disaggregation yet.

An older white man, a former Columbus teacher, approached the mike to tell a story. Imagine, he said, that some bakers are given peaches and told to make peach cobbler. One day, they are given some slightly different peaches with a slightly different taste and told to make the same cobbler with this fruit. The bakers make the cobbler and taste it; dissatisfied, they go to ask their supervisor for vanilla and sugar to make it taste right. The supervisor refuses, saying, "I pay you to make cobbler without those things." The bakers, cowed, try to make the cobbler without vanilla and sugar. They give it to the supervisor. He tastes it, doesn't like it, and fires them all.

As this teacher sat down, leaving listeners to muse over his strange extended analogy, the next speaker, a first-year Asian-American teacher at Columbus, spontaneously added the "peaches" metaphor to his own extended comments on reconstitution: "We don't have anything but peaches at our school—all our students are peaches," he said. As a child himself in California City, he added, he had attended a school that was reconstituted; and after losing all his teachers, he was a "bruised peach." "We'll have some bruised peaches at Columbus— please take care of them," he finished, sitting down in silence.

The superintendent finally rose to speak. In a flat tone, he began his remarks by citing, without reference, the same "expert report" I had cited: a number of "experts," he began, "from places like Harvard," had decided in 1992 that schools that were *not* reconstituted simply "did not do it for minority youngsters." That year, he said, the district had started selecting schools for reconstitution based on "variables both quantitative and qualitative": when a school needed to be reconstituted, he said, it had "something to do with the culture."

"The 'bruised peaches' analogy doesn't work," he added angrily. "We don't have any bruised peaches! We have *all great kids!*" His brow in a deep crease, he admitted that reconstitution was a very dramatic and difficult thing. But the discussion of reconstitution was becoming a process of "finger pointing and whining." Students could be "Vietnamese, Samoan, African-American, Latino, whatever—but if the kids are poor and haven't had as much opportunity, it gets harder to catch up," he finished.

Scribbling down his comments, I listed several of my own questions about this rather bizarre sequence of references to students. The "peaches" metaphor had seemed first a critique of inadequate resources at Columbus, as well as a potentially coded deficit analysis of the "sugar" Columbus students themselves supposedly lacked; in the statements of the Asian-American teacher, "peaches" had then suggested student innocence. The superintendent, finally, had seemingly taken the metaphor as evidence of the three schools' "culture" of reduced expectations for "minority youngsters." In the absence of any clear discussion of the students who were supposed to be assisted by the reconstitution reforms, this strangely potent disaggregation now referenced an entire silent conversation about students (at the next board meeting, a white Columbus teacher would introduce himself by saying, "so that you know where I'm coming from: I think of all our students as delicious, juicy, freestone peaches").

As I sat musing in my notes about the indirectness of the evening's discussion, the superintendent suddenly addressed the question of Columbus's score on its qualitative presentation, speaking directly to the student who had asked it. "If you put it up against any other school," he said in a serious tone, "I might not be able to justify it." He paused. "Because the 4 may have been *too high!*" he roared.

Gasps erupted around me. "The presentation was weak. It was *poor*," the superintendent added. Columbus teachers and students around me jumped to their feet, faces contorted with embarrassment and disbelief. Tripping into the auditorium aisles, they began a rush to leave the meeting. "Why were you clapping when you left?!" a white Columbus teacher shouted at the superintendent, waving his hand in the air. "Certain courtesies are necessary," the superintendent replied.

The rush of people became a stampede. Somewhere near the exit of the auditorium, the white student who had asked about the presentation score shook his finger at the superintendent and yelled with fury, "You see where our school is going? Out the door!! And it's all because of you!!" "Bad news is not appreciated," the superintendent replied calmly. He asked if there were any more questions, then ended the meeting without waiting for a reply. As remaining audience members shouted across the auditorium that there should be more time for questions, almost everybody from Columbus left the building. I struggled internally for a moment and then decided to stay. It was a fortuitous decision: the adults up front were about to proffer racial descriptions long deferred.

As the noise subsided, a Chinese-American school board member addressed the superintendent and the small number of remaining audience members with a question that demanded clarity about how race mattered. "I went back to the court records," he said. "African-American and Latino students are not doing well. But many other students are not doing well in the school district. It's a problem that the Consent Decree was tied so much to African-American and Latino youngsters," he finished. He was getting the impression from the superintendent that the board was compelled to reconstitute, that it had no choice, he added. But perhaps they first needed more evidence that reconstitution actually worked.

The superintendent countered with a de-raced response: the original desegregation case, he said, had been "about many parties." The district, he added, was currently expecting even more evidence to prove reconstitution's success. Frowning, the board member rephrased his racially disaggregated question even more directly. "*Does* the Consent Decree agreement refer to Latinos and African-Americans particularly?" he asked. There were several seconds of silence. A white district administrator in the front row, the same one who had addressed Columbus staff in the library the previous spring, sifted through a document and cleared his throat. "*Especially* African-American and Latino youth," he read, looking up at the board. The board member nodded and repeated his request for data on reconstitution.

A white board member further down the table next addressed his colleague's original race question, stating that "African-Americans have been historically discriminated against in educational areas across the country. I think targeting them is OK." He too was concerned, though, about troubling discrepancies between the schools' qualitative and quantitative evaluations. In response, the white administrator in the front row stood up, listed the schools' various scores off a sheet of data, and explained that the qualitative score was "like skating—you do it and somebody holds up a card." Looking surprised, another white school board member asked if she could see the records of the schools' presentations. The superintendent replied that they did not keep such records. "We talk, and ruminate later," he explained. "There are no notes even of meetings *on* the collective meetings?" the board member asked. "No. Just points," replied the superintendent. He would be happy to attempt to gather the videotapes of the presentations, he said, "but what you'll be looking at is a value judgment made by the four of us," he finished. The board members conferred, and after a quick vote, the board decided to postpone their reconstitution decision until these tapes had been retrieved and reviewed.

The night's events resulted in a weeklong reprieve for Columbus. Yet there had been, oddly, no talk about exactly what Columbus and the other two schools had done wrong. One district press release being circulated around Columbus stated that the district's reconstitution decisions had been "based on an extensive review of a school's culture and organization as well as student performance"; the comments appearing in the wee hours of the board meeting made the process seem a bit more vague. Startlingly, a school board member about to vote to fire three faculties had had to ask publicly whom these reforms were for, and a district representative had had to search the text of the law before answering.

School vs. School District, Take Two

One week later, the school board meeting began at 7:00 p.m. and stretched until past midnight. Though it was first on the printed agenda, the reconstitution decision was repeatedly postponed until many people had gone home and radio coverage had turned to static. Waiting at the back of the room while an out-of-order discussion of funding for early childhood programs raged on, Columbus people muttered nervously about the impending decision. By 11:00, Columbus students were slumped in their chairs yawning, struggling to hold up floppy signs saying "Save Our Teachers"; somebody had tried and failed to retape a Columbus banner that was half stuck to the wall. A Latina girl next to me shouted, "I have to go to bed. I have homework to do!" Several teachers around me passed a note up to the board saying Columbus students were exhausted. The superintendent, smirking, passed the note to a board member. Watching, a white teacher next to me muttered that this meeting was "totally demoralizing."

Speakers were just about to raise the ante. A young Asian-American woman who had spent the evening passing out fliers about pro–affirmative action activities at a nearby university took the microphone, first shouting at the board about the lateness of the hour and then loudly denouncing reconstitution as a school reform. In response, a black woman, probably a decade older, came up to the microphone and said loudly into her face, "you can't speak for black kids. Our kids are failing all over this district." And the reconstitution discussion—for a sudden moment bluntly racialized—now began in earnest.

After a brief series of laments from worried teachers at the three schools (during which the superintendent and board members intermittently shuffled papers), a young teacher—white or perhaps Latino, from one of the handful of high schools in the district officially labeled "academic"—stood up and approached the microphone. His voice shaking slightly, he said he came to speak in support of the faculty slated for reconstitution. Faculty at his own school were also struggling to "come up with solutions. We have problems, based on the nature of our students—on the nature of ourselves," he said. "The social conditions haven't changed. You can't just reshuffle bodies, because at my school the problems haven't gone away. Our students are still struggling—particularly our African-American and Latino students," he finished.

The meeting had now seen several direct racial descriptions, but it took some additional time, and another long list of speakers, for race labels to resurface. After a number of teachers addressed the bleary-eyed school board and superintendent, the black woman who had spoken earlier of "black kids" rose finally to speak again. She introduced herself as the leader of a community youth organization (which, I knew, had its headquarters two blocks from Columbus) and announced that she had been a parent at Eaton, a high school she said had been reconstituted several years earlier (actually, as teachers at Columbus liked to point out, Eaton had evicted its students as well as its faculty and reopened as an "academic" school requiring student applications). "I was happy when we got a man with enough courage to support us and reconstitute Eaton," she said, naming the superintendent. "Only twelve black males were graduating," she finished.

The racial descriptions became more frequent as the clock approached midnight. A white school board member read aloud a letter she had received from a Columbus teacher (a white man named Christopher), which argued that "African-American and Latino" failure was a districtwide rather than a school-specific problem. Putting down the letter, the board member recommended against reconstituting the three schools. The Latina board member to her left, however, countered in her own closing comments that "I've watched six superintendents try to deal with one problem: what to do with Latino and black students who are not achieving. Folks, we either educate them or we'll have to support them in jail." The superintendent finally leaned toward his desk mike, curving it toward him with a characteristically raised eyebrow. Stating that the data "flat-out indicated" the need for reconstituting the three schools, he began to slowly reaggregate the discussion of "kids":

> "Reconstitution," he said, "is not a simple or a happy issue. You've had lots of years of restructuring, reforming, re-this, re-that—go back to your data and see how many kids have been lost in that process. The academic achievement of Latino and black kids blasts out—but it blasts out on *all* kids of poverty. *Many* kids didn't get the opportunity for equality of achievement. The primary issue is not the comfort level and the morale of adults . . . this addresses the morale of *students*, and their academic achievement."

As a low growl of voices began to grow across the auditorium, the superintendent's words suddenly became racially disaggregated once again. Reconstitution, he said, had originally been one prong of a plan to create "desegregated schools"; a decade later, he said, "there were African-American and Latino kids" participating in all types of reform in the district, but those students were only achieving in the reconstituted schools. The reconstituted schools were superior, he added, because of their desire to achieve reform and their strong system of belief in their students. "Unless you have kids who have succeeded historically, a successful school has to be *made*," he said. It was necessary to build a "culture and a climate of success." "The issue is do nothing and feel good about it, or . . ." he said, trailing off into a silence heavy with implication.

"Thank you for your support!" yelled out an elementary teacher into the silence, her voice breaking. "No attempt has been made by the adult community to make reconstitution a positive process," the superintendent finished. "Columbus cooperated fully!" yelled a white Columbus teacher next to me. She leaned over and put her head in her hands.

An African-American board member now cleared his throat. "I feel a sense of moral urgency around these issues," he began. "When I walk the streets I'm hit up by panhandlers—many if not most are black men. It pains me. I feel we have to do something about that." He traced this situation to educational failure, he said, and he hadn't seen any reports on school improvement more "data-rich" than the data on the tactic of reconstitution. "The most effective schools for Latino and African-American students are the reconstituted ones," he said. "I appreciate the disruption of it, but when I balance it with the obligation to do something for these young people . . . I *want* us to have good relationships with our personnel. A critical challenge is to see if in this progressive city we can truly build a coalition between labor and people of color." "*Yes*—but this isn't the way to do it," muttered the white teacher next to me from behind her hands. "No one can stand before me," the board member concluded, his voice growing louder, "and say that African-American kids are being well served." Across the auditorium, the blond elementary teacher with a Hispanic name sprang to her feet and shouted, "How *dare* you tell us what we're like when you've never even been to our school!" The board member shouted back that he had been to the school and had talked to parents. Teachers screamed back that he had not, that he was lying, but the board member called for a vote. With solemn pledges of "aye," the majority of the six-member board voted to reconstitute all three schools, overruling the lone "nay" votes of the white female and Chinese-American board members.

Aftermath: "The Corpse of Columbus"

During the tense days following the meeting, I spoke on the phone one afternoon with a former Columbus teacher, a white woman who had left school midyear to take a district administrative job. She had asked me at that time, as I now recalled, to help her print, surreptitiously on a school computer, a proposal she had written with a small group of Columbus teachers, suggesting various tactics for improving education for "minorities" across the district. She had presented the proposal directly to the superintendent rather than to the Columbus faculty. She now told me with excitement that she was involved in formulating plans for the new Columbus staff that would be assembled over the summer. "Yes," she said. "We've *gotta* find a way to make black kids more successful!"

Lost in talk of "all students" throughout most of the probation year, public discussion of serving "black kids" in particular had taken place just minutes before the final reconstitution decision. Speaking last before the vote, one black board member had done what no other speaker in this debate had: he had articulated the district's claim that the educators in front of him represented schools in which "Latino and African-American students" were not "being well served." No district document preceding his words had articulated this claim so clearly. In a press release from the district's "Director of Communications and Public Relations" announcing the initial decision to reconstitute the three schools, the superintendent simply described reconstitution as a "dramatic and radical tactic for bringing positive development to a low performing school or organization" that "commits everyone associated with the school to the principles of excellence and equity for all children." Around this same time, a local newspaper article on reconstitution quoted the district press spokesperson as saying, "just because the test scores aren't really bad or showed some improvement doesn't necessarily mean that things in the school are working as they should."

On the morning immediately following one of the final board meetings, one of the superintendent's written announcements about reconstitution had been copied and placed in all faculty mailboxes at Columbus. The Columbus principal had attached a note addressed to all teachers and students that read,

> The decision has been made to reconstitute Columbus although you have all worked very hard. . . . Although it is extremely difficult to accept this decision, it is our obligation to our school community to model appropriate behavior so no one can point fingers. . . . This is the time to support each other and help students understand that life may not always seem fair, but that perseverance always prevails and the most important thing is their continued education.

The letter concluded by evoking one of the school's symbols, an exploring ship: "As proud sailors we will disembark from this ship with our heads held high."

Leaving the building on one of the last days that school year, I met one older white teacher in the hallway. "Come to see the corpse of Columbus?" she sighed. In June of 1996, Columbus adults took down their posters, gathered their papers, photographs, and potted plants, and left the building—quickly, before the locks were changed. Some took books and equipment with them.

Changing the Guard

As that school year ended, I wrote the members of the school board a final letter arguing what I had stated at the microphone: that the district had failed to conduct the staff development on serving "black" and "Latino" students funded by the Consent Decree. My only response came from the Chinese-American board member, who called me at home. "Columbus could have gotten help on their problems had they asked for it," he replied. Other schools were also covering up their "problems," though, as a race conversation would be "painful"—people would call each other "racist." My curiosity piqued, I walked into the district's Office of Integration in late June in search of a detailed Consent Decree budget. In the office, I recognized a man I had met at a school board meeting in the aftermath of the reconstitution hearings. Himself African-American, he had been introduced as the leader of a district program for improving "African-American student achievement." As the title had sounded unusually blunt, I had approached him after the meeting, and he had given me a treatise produced by the National Council on Educating Black Children. Greeting him in the integration office, I told him that I had enjoyed reading it:

"It's the bomb," he agrees. I tell him I am there in search of the Consent Decree budget for staff development. The discussion on race issues is totally shoved under the rug, I say. "No one wants to discuss race issues in America," he says, "except people out to uphold white supremacy. People don't even want to disaggregate the data. 'We don't have black students, or white students, or Asian students—we just have *students*,' " he imitates with sarcastic earnestness. He adds, "People just ignore the lower test scores. They say, 'Oh well, what can we expect from them—if their parents were more together they'd do better.' " I mention that no district staff development on race issues ever took place at Columbus. He says it was the principal's job to get it arranged. And, he asks me, did the teachers complain? Did they ask the principal for training? I reply that one teacher, a Latino man, had told me he had been in three Consent Decree schools and had not received one race-related training. "Well, then, he's an accomplice—he's part of the problem, not the solution," he responds. I agree, but add that the district was getting three million dollars a year for the purpose of promoting discussions on racial equality. He replies that he has faith in the superintendent. He just saw him out marching with the African-American achievement award winners. "He really supports black students," he says. "Other people just talk."

In July of that summer, I ran into Christopher, the white Columbus teacher who had written the letter about districtwide problems with "African-American and Latino achievement" read aloud at the final school board meeting. He said he had just interviewed with the incoming principal for a position on the new Columbus staff. In his interview, he said, he had urged the new principal to retain the health and science academy (she had replied, according to him, that she "wasn't interested in academies"); he had also told her that he thought there were "too few African-American juniors currently in the academy," and had mentioned one science teacher who perhaps turned students off to science by "sending out all the black students who acted up." The principal had raised her eyebrows at his report of these "racism issues," saying, "that'll change." "I told her, 'I hope you have a *plan* for it!' " he sighed. "She talked a lot about how great the new Columbus was going to be. She said, 'We'll do something that nobody ever did in this country, design a comprehensive high school that works for *all* students.' I felt like saying 'fuck you, we've been working on that for three years and you're dismantling it.' It wasn't perfect, but it was starting to work."

A year later, Christopher—who in the end declined an invitation from the principal to return to Columbus and went instead to teach in a neighboring city—told me he had realized something belatedly about reconstitution. The Columbus faculty had failed to address the district's racialized expectations explicitly during its probation year—and this omission, he said, had made the school's substantial reforms inevitably look inadequate. "It would have been so easy to address it in our qualitative presentation—with equal representation among student presenters, by showing statistics on black and Latino students choosing academy programs and receiving improved test scores. We really dropped the ball on that," he said.[8]

In a year of public debate, while district representatives had blurted out race labels only at the last minute before reconstitution, no one at Columbus had referenced "black and Latino students" in any public talk of school reform. No one would do so after reconstitution, either.

August 1996: The District Talks to Its Creation

In the late summer of 1996, I met with the new principal of the reconstituted Columbus, who graciously agreed to let me return to Columbus to finish my dissertation research. Weak with relief, I arrived at the start of several weeks of orientation and introduced myself as a researcher to the new staff on the morning they all met one another. The majority of the new teachers were white, though in total they were more diverse and much younger than the previous staff; they were friendly and energetic, and many were relatively new to teaching. About ten teachers and administrators from the old staff had been rehired, most of whom were white.

After some initial get-to-know-you activities, I was seated on the floor of the stage chatting to new teachers when the superintendent arrived for an initial address to the new faculty. As the stage became quiet, the teachers arranged themselves in concentric circles facing the superintendent, the principal staring up at him from his feet. I slouched behind a teacher seated in front of me, fearing that if the superintendent saw me he might recognize me as the graduate student who had accused him three months earlier of breaking the law.

Before reconstitution, the superintendent began, "things were working for many of the kids" at Columbus, "But they weren't working for *all* the kids— and *that* was the problem." The new faculty would have to make sure that "all kids" were well educated in four years, he said, no matter where they came from or the skill levels they came in with. "They might be in algebra and not know the fundamentals of math very well, but they're still going to learn algebra, or they'll be limited to incomes of $17,000 a year for the rest of their lives," he said. He was tired of hearing things like "they come from dysfunctional families," he said, tsking along with a number of seated teachers at the phrase. The majority of the kids they would be working with were "poor." They had to be well educated, and they had to get jobs. The school had to "know the needs of these kids and to meet these needs," he said. "In the first grade," he continued, "sixty percent of African-American students are in the lowest quartile. That's not how it should be. Latino kids are about the same. But when you look at other non-white kids, they are also at about forty percent in the bottom quartile. And even Michael Johnson can't start ten minutes behind and catch up," he finished. He didn't have a plan to bring to the staff, saying "this works," he said, but "radical change" was necessary. "The only people who are to be held accountable are on this stage," he finished.

Repositioning myself behind the safety of a teacher's head, I mulled over the superintendent's introductory words. While he was telling the teachers that "radical change" was necessary in order to make things "work" for "*all* the kids," he was rather vague about what approaches had not worked previously, and for whom. While he had presented some racially disaggregated statistics about young "African-American students" and "Latino kids" in the "lowest quartile," in adding that "other non-white kids" fared similarly and that Columbus students were mostly "poor," he had blurred any distinct analysis of the subset of kids the previous Columbus had apparently not been "working for." While he urged the new faculty to be "creative" in building a "school culture" that would work for "*all*"—and while he assured them that they would be held accountable for their creation—his discussion of the previous Columbus's "problem" was both strikingly racialized and strikingly vague.

Throughout the rest of the three-week orientation—indeed, throughout the rest of the year, my last around Columbus—public talk of the school's reforms would also reference Columbus students primarily as an aggregated needy unit. Over the coming weeks of orientation, many teachers made clear that they had heard little about "the kids" before arriving; some asked me in private for an "ethnic" breakdown of the student population. Throughout the orientation, as it turned out, teachers received no such data in public on Columbus's racial/ ethnic demographics: race labels appeared only to describe the race-group "clubs" (Black Student Union, Samoan Club) that needed new advisers. In- deed, in the name of student "unity," many administrators and teachers pro- posed dismantling any holdover institutional "divisions," as I noted on the second day of orientation:

> The principal says that she wants to fill in the cracks kids are falling through— before, she heard, 400 ninth graders would become 200 graduates. They start talking about "advisory," a proposed daily homeroom period. A female white teacher asks if someone will help her if she calls the home of an advisee and nobody there speaks English. The principal says that she is purposefully not grouping advisories by lan-

guage. "This has been a school where there has been a lot of division, and we don't want that to exist any more. We want to send a real clear message that in the real world, everyone works together," she says. Jerry [*a Latino administrator*] steps forward and says that they will be following Hillary Clinton's quote, "There's no such thing as other people's kids." "Any kid will become our kid, regardless of race, ethnicity, whatever," he says.

Later that day, I went to talk to the new music teacher, a man who appeared to be African-American. He was telling me about his plans for the music program, and thinking of the Samoan and Filipino students I had heard singing hymns, I commented that many Columbus students already sang in church:

> "I want to stay away from church stuff—gospel," he responds, pausing. "That's black. That's okay, but the students aren't all black. I don't want to have the male choir over here," he says (he mimics a student whispering "that's black!"), "and a Filipino percussion group over here" ("that's Filipino!" he whispers theatrically). "It's gonna be one group, the *Columbus band*, the *Columbus chorus*," he says.

Throughout public discussions about the "new Columbus" in the orientation weeks, the staff would repeatedly suggest purposefully aggregating the school's reform goals. In one small-group brainstorming session devoted to "thinking outside the box" and "reinventing high school," for example, one group reported back to the full faculty group a suggestion to utilize "strategies for helping all students to succeed instead of just targeting groups." One new white English teacher explained, "not just for the lower quartile students"; a returning Asian-American teacher added, "not just certain groups." As the principal stated on another day of orientation, she wanted Columbus to be "a school where *everybody* can succeed. This is really the most important message. This is *everybody's* school. And *everybody* will succeed here."

Department Talk: Aggregation in Action

As if scripted, "all" talk became the "new Columbus's" dominant reform discourse almost immediately. At a math department meeting held during the first days of the reconstituted Columbus, I even watched the hyper-aggregated language of "all students" quickly overpower a momentary suggestion to focus the conversation on "African-American" and "Latino" students. As some teachers proposed "narrowing down" math department goals, others countered quickly with the need to serve "all students"; by the time the conversation concluded with a reaggregated discussion of "students," suggestions of targeted efforts to increase the number of "African-American" and "Latino" students in advanced math courses had literally been erased from the department's plans. All teachers talking in the conversation (which I scribbled down in real time) were new, except for "White teacher #1" and "Latina teacher," who had been rehired from the previous staff. "Black teacher #1" himself left the faculty several days later:

Black teacher #1: We need to sell math.

Black teacher #2: Especially in this community—it's so diverse, there are so many students of color. We need to say the reasons for learning math. Like the political reasons: so few women and people of color are in the sciences.

Black teacher #1: Are you trying to narrow this down to say how *African-American* students are at the bottom? Because in *every* school it seems that African-American students are. Are we going to address what will get them into higher math courses? Will we build up their math strengths, or just place them in the higher level courses?

White teacher #1: [*reaggregates*] I don't—I understand that administrators look at statistics, but I think we should be helping all students.

Black teacher #1: That's the political thing to say—but the reality is, there are still printouts by ethnicity. In [a nearby city], students signed up for certain courses because they knew they wouldn't fail. It became a fad.

White teacher #2: We need peer support—selling math, that it's not a good thing to fail, it's *not* cool.

Black teacher #2: [*reaggregates*] We're trying to help *all* the students.

Black teacher #1: Exactly.

Black teacher #2: [*tries himself to disaggregate the conversation once again*] But it ties into the real world—African-American and Latino students and other students of color are not represented in science.

White teacher #1: How are we supposed to do this?

Black teacher #1: I want methods to employ. We *know* the goal.

Black teacher #2: We can use presentations and journals.

White teacher #2: We can also bring math to *them*.

White teacher #1: But all these things make a *math* class better. It doesn't suck *African-American* students, *Latino* students in. It's just a better product.

White teacher #3: [*overt reaggregation*] Yeah, not one group in particular. If the class is geared to *all* kids, to a community of workers. . .

Black teacher #1: I like the word 'if,' but what comes after that if?

White teacher #3: We will have to say what's not appropriate behavior if there are behavior problems. We'll say it's not appropriate, that you need to work with everybody, get along.

Black teacher #1: (with a wry laugh): I'm not *talking* about *behavior*—I'm talking about certain teaching strategies. I've heard seminars on special ways to teach certain students—some people are working on it.

White teacher #1: Like what strategies?

Black teacher #1: [*disaggregates slowly and carefully*] Please, when I speak, don't think we're dealing with 100 percent—it's not all African-American students. We're talking about a large percentage of African-American and Latino students at the bottom.

White teacher #1: Anita [*a returning Latina teacher*] has hundreds of students in her classroom at lunchtime—do you have any suggestions?

Latina teacher (Anita): You need to understand what's happening with students—a lot of Latino students have some problems in their house. They explain them to me, I have contact with parents. I have students in my class because it's my culture. I understand their problems, then I explain math. You need to understand the problems in the home life first.

White teacher #1: It's a long-term thing—not just 'I respect you, you respect me.'

Black teacher #1: [*begins a final reaggregation*:] Is there a standardized test measuring students in California City? In Texas, if you pass, you don't have to take more math.

Me: The CTBS [*California Test of Basic Skills*] can't be passed, it's just a score.

Black teacher #1 (laughing wryly and shaking his head): It's *not* just a score. What they're asking for is for us to bring up those CTBS scores. Is the bottom line to raise the CTBS scores? You can't ignore reality. If the school is going to be evaluated on if scores have risen, that's what we'll have to focus on.

White teacher #1: I think general progress will be reflected on the test—of course, this is a weird test with this population because of general language issues. Test scores were not clear as a reason for having reconstituted Columbus.

Black teacher #1: What was the failure rate at the school before?

White teacher #1: These are huge issues; maybe this is not the time . . . can you define failure rate?

Black teacher #1: The number of Fs given by teachers.

White teacher #1: Fifty percent of the kids who start don't finish. A giant percentage fails because they don't attend.

Black teacher #1: In Texas, when you give grades, teachers are listed by the percentage who passed.

White teacher #1: I firmly believe that judgment of teachers here is not based on this.

Black teacher #2 (laughing): Or your salary!

White teacher #1: Great teachers at Whitman [*the top "academic" school in the city*] would come in here and fail 93 percent of the kids because of their idea of math.

Black teacher #1: Exactly—we need to determine what the minimum standards for passing are.

White teacher #2: So we have to adapt to the students.

White teacher #1: I think people in charge wouldn't judge teachers as failing because of the failure rate of students. Students fail here because they just stop attending. We work hard. Some students, because of—problems in their house, like Anita said—they stop coming. First period is a big problem—you could have 75 percent absence.

Black teacher #1: Is 8:00 too early for some of the kids here?

At the end of that school year, after a year of watching Columbus's new faculty struggle to implement academic programs (many of which were eerily reminiscent of the reforms existing previously), I went to talk to Marivi, one of the handful of Columbus teachers who had applied and returned to teach at the post-reconstitution Columbus rather than accepting transfers to other district schools. Over lunch, she recalled that many members of the old staff had actually aggregated their reform plans quite self-consciously. Ironically, she suggested, they had done so in an attempt to meet the district's racialized expectations:

> She says it was clear to the faculty she knew that they were being judged on the performance of their African-American and Latino students. But they had decided that the house program they were already building was making "*all* students successful," so they would just keep working on that. She says she remembers one district consultant showing up at a faculty meeting "with numbers by ethnicity of test scores. But the district was never clear about what to *do* about it—what you *do* to raise the achievement of black and Latino students," she says. She says that she remembers having had a number of private conversations about this topic during the probation year; indeed, conversations among the teachers in her academic "house" often focused on assisting individual students from these groups anyway. "But the decision was to continue doing a program for *all* students," she reiterates, so a press packet she and another teacher had assembled to publicize Columbus successes during the probation year had focused on successful schoolwide programs. They took the probation year as "a mandate to improve the *whole school's* culture," she finishes.

So a new faculty had arrived at reconstituted Columbus, the product of over three decades of district and legal clashes over school reform and racial equality. Faculty were told by the energetic new principal, also a woman of color (who, as some teachers and students later pointed out, refused to publicly identify herself racially), that a culture of "failure" had to be transformed into a culture where "all students could learn." Although 100 adults had been evicted from Columbus supposedly because of the district's conviction that full academic racial equality had not been achieved there and 100 new adults had arrived supposedly to address this problem, the newcomers were not given a racialized framework with which to assess the past or plan for the future. Instead, they embarked upon a mission to help "all students" succeed—as had the previous staff. It was not until the spring of 1997 that a new teacher would reveal in the faculty newsletter her discovery—made via a belated presentation by a district consultant—that there was a desegregation order in California City focused on "black" and "Latino" student achievement. In questioning whether the school was in fact serving these students' needs, she marveled at "the immense silence surrounding this issue."

Conclusion

When race labels popped up in talk about school reform in California City, somebody usually reaggregated the conversation. It was far easier to speak in hopeful aggregated terms about reforms for "all" than to suggest that things were *not* working for particular racial groups. Paradoxically, district people typically communicated the court's racial equality reform expectations in de-raced language, while Columbus people continued on their quest for improved education for "all" in a discourse that obfuscated their own equality efforts. Trying to achieve racial equality—or demonstrate improvements toward it—with a largely colormute discourse often seemed like trying to have a group fix a machine without discussing where it was broken.

In 1998, I went to visit a reassigned Columbus teacher, a black woman who, ironically, had been reassigned to the middle school reconstituted at the same time as Columbus.[9] During an after-school staff meeting on the school's developing reform goals, I watched the school's new principal, who was standing at an overhead projector in front of a crew of exhausted teachers, gradually submerge the district's legal mandate for targeting "African-American and Latino students" within aggregated talk of school reforms. Reading aloud the school's new site plan, which was soon to be submitted to the district, he went from tacking on "especially for African-American and Latino students" to each officially phrased reform goal to saying "especially for targeted students" and then finally "etc. etc. etc." and "blah blah blah."

Throughout the exhausting reform waves in the mid-1990s, as we have seen, people had vigorously and often passionately enforced a language of serving "all students" in California City. Indeed, it often seemed that educators, policymakers, and lawyers believed they were somehow *achieving* equality by the very speech act of referring to opportunities for "all." Yet speaking of "all students" does not in itself produce equality. Neither, of course, does speaking of "all students" in itself analyze *inequality*. Most importantly, perhaps, aggregated school reform talk of serving "all" in California City had never allowed for serious and thorough discussion of the opportunities "African-American and Latino students" in the city's schools supposedly lacked.

As chapter 4 will demonstrate, the widespread resistance to racially targeted reform language in California City indicated not only a political or pragmatic preference for aggregated reform talk, but also a deep uncertainty about how race actually mattered to educational inequality. Every morning at Columbus, low-income "black" and "Latino" students walked in the door with low-income "Filipinos," "Samoans," and "Chinese"; one third of the students entering the building were impoverished recent immigrants learning English. In such a "low-income minority" context, many Columbus people muttered quietly, how *could* one accurately or appropriately call particular "race/ethnic groups" particularly needy? As the final chapters will show, even *acknowledged* racial inequalities would often be purposefully submerged within colormute talk; yet as chapter 4 shows first, confusion and anxiety over *how to analyze* the distribution of opportunity in this "low-income minority" school and its majority-"minority" district, too, manifested itself in the daily language of inequality analysis. We turn now to observe people wrestling with another central race talk dilemma: analyzing who, exactly, is being kept unequal to whom.

Four

The More Complex Inequality Seems to Get, the More Simplistic Inequality Analysis Seems to Become

We have a lot of different cultures at Columbus—we
also have a Columbus culture.
  —Columbus principal at a school assembly, fall 1996

Talking to a Latino student, Luis, one day, I mentioned that the superintendent seemed particularly interested in "black and Latino" students, but that at the school level people rarely talked about these groups of students as having specific needs. He nodded and said that things at the school were more general, for everyone. But that's better, though, he said—there shouldn't be things just for particular races, it should be equal for everyone.

We then talked about one of his friends, Emilio. Luis said Emilio "wasn't doing anything" after graduation except working at Costco. He said it was that way with a lot of Latin people—not going further academically. I asked how this process happened. He said basically people think that Latin kids aren't going to do anything after high school, that they're poor, that they'll just go get a job. I said that this was the problem I was working on—if these patterns existed, how to talk about them without offending someone. He said maybe you could have a program for Latin kids. But then, I said, people would say, "what about the Filipino students, or the Samoan students." He nodded, adding, "the other groups."

On another occasion, I was talking to Luis along with Emilio himself, who suggested that teachers could stand to learn to "relate" better, "to know that some Latinos have a lot of problems in their life, and there are a lot of things going on with their family, with making money, the household. Things like that, to see all the problems." "Treat 'em different," Luis now agreed, adding, "You treat different ethnicities different 'cause they been through different things."

In our schools and districts and around our dinner tables, daily analysis of educational inequality is plagued by a structural question of human comparison: *who is disadvantaged, and compared to whom?* In American educational discourse, the category "disadvantaged" embodies a national confusion over inequality analysis. Vaguely denoting a group of people with an unequal opportunity for school success (another phrase for the same concept is "at risk"), the very term "disadvantaged" gets applied to different populations at different

times, demonstrating that Americans measure such unequal educational opportunities in myriad ways. "Poor" children, "children of color," "inner-city
children," "Latin kids," housing "project children," rural children, girls, "black
kids," immigrants all are considered "disadvantaged" or "at risk" at different
moments. Yet as some definition of need must precede remedies, our everyday
plans to address unequal opportunity must define more specifically the grounds
upon which people are kept unequal—and as this chapter demonstrates, this
is where we run into problems.[1]

When debating who should be considered disadvantaged in comparison to
whom, Americans often particularly contest whether we should be analyzing
inequality in racial terms—and whether inequality remedies should accordingly be racial.[2] People wonder if, as Luis put it at one point, "there shouldn't
be things just for particular races, it should be equal for everyone." In their
battles over affirmative action in the 1990s, for example, Californians struggled
quite publicly with whether race should still be made explicitly relevant to
public policies designed to equalize educational opportunity. After a debate
over the validity of a race analysis of educational opportunity in contemporary
California, many voters marked the ballot for the blithely titled "Equal Opportunity Initiative" in 1996 and (often unwittingly, as surveys later revealed)
opted to delete race labels altogether from public education policy analysis.[3]
After the passage of Proposition 209, ironically, the language of state scholarships, K–12 enrichment programs, and university admission formulas was to
proceed using the very category up for debate: equal opportunity policies were
to assist not race groups, but "disadvantaged" kids.

Actions like Proposition 209's erasing of race words from policy efforts to
counter educational disadvantage suggest in part a new rejection, among voters,
of any race analysis of educational inequality. But a close look at daily inequality
analysis among California City residents at that time also suggests deep analytic confusion over the structure of inequality in a multiracial state.[4] At
multiracial, low-income Columbus and in multiracial, class-diverse California
City in the mid-1990s, as this chapter shows, people were also debating inequality in both everyday and official ways, and many analysts who resisted the
sharp focus of race-group labels in talk of educational inequality struggled
regularly with inequality analysis' thorniest question: whether particular "race
groups" in this complex place were actually any worse off than anyone else.

As we have seen, court and district analyses of inequality in California City
by the mid-1990s had sporadically marked first "black," and then "African-
American" and "Latino" students, as particularly disadvantaged: as Luis
phrased it, people suggested "programs for Latin kids." Among everyday analysts, however, such racialized lines of inequality seemed not nearly so clearly
drawn. At Columbus, a low-tracked school of low-income "Latino," "African-
American," "Filipino," "Chinese," and "Samoan" students (with a tiny handful

of "white" students), the question of who exactly was educationally disadvantaged in comparison to whom was a stymieing one. It often seemed that Columbus programs should indeed be for "everyone": to compare the disadvantaged to the advantaged, Columbus people most often looked not within Columbus itself, but out to other district schools that were more moneyed—and more white. Columbus adults' omissions in targeting "black" and "Latino" students within school reform discourse and practice were in part a product of analytic uncertainty about the very validity of comparing race groups *within* this complex multiracial place. Weren't all "low-income minorities," many reasoned, equally needy?

Within the district at large, too—which was by the 1990s, according to its own records, majority low-income and approximately 20 percent "Latino," 17 percent "African-American," 27 percent "Chinese," 13 percent "Other White," 7 percent "Filipino," and the rest a handful of "Other Non-White" "minorities"—people struggled with the basic issue of defining disadvantage in racial terms. By the late 1990s, in fact, renewed public contestation over how race still mattered to educational disadvantage within California City Unified's complex multiracial demographics would finally prompt the court to ban the use of race in the city's main equality remedy—its desegregation plan. Mirroring a national process of dismantling desegregation orders in U.S. cities (see Orfield and Eaton 1996), California City policymakers would gradually start abandoning the Consent Decree and would immediately discontinue altogether the Decree's racial student assignment policies. In the process of purposefully deleting a decades-old race analysis of "disadvantage," however, they would leave the city with *no* coherent understanding of "disadvantage"—or remedy for it. Indeed, in deleting a race analysis of inequality rather than struggling to thoroughly analyze local inequality dynamics that were to some degree still both racial and economic, they demonstrated a central dilemma of current American race talk: *the more complex inequality seems to get, the more simplistic inequality analysis seems to become.* Many Americans, I want to argue, now appear dangerously unwilling to navigate the substantial analytic difficulties of determining the role of race in our complex contemporary inequalities—indeed, analysts nationwide are abandoning the task.

This chapter examines everyday analysts struggling to describe the structure of educational inequality at Columbus and in California City at large in the mid-1990s, during the several years before the city's race-based desegregation strategies were formally abandoned. Speakers demonstrated the central importance of talk itself: for they continually contested one another's descriptions of educational disadvantage, by subtly rewording and qualifying all available descriptions of who was kept unequal to whom. Determining the role of race in local inequalities—and in particular, determining the intersection of race and class—was central to these quiet analytic debates. Rather than negotiating through the analytic complexity of multiple coexisting inequality patterns, however, speakers foundering upon the complexity of local inequality structures repeatedly replaced complex and detailed analyses of race-class inequality with simpler, blurrier analyses that deleted mention of racial inequality altogether.

Before beginning with Columbus's everyday analysts, I want to spend a few minutes describing California City, a city where any description of inequality could indeed easily seem inaccurate. Imagine that you stand in California City in the mid-to-late 1990s. It is quintessentially diverse, a city where people of multiple colors sometimes meet randomly in parks and beat on drums, and where people of multiple colors wave streaming sticks of incense at hip-hop concerts. It is also a city where a pedestrian realizes suddenly, starkly, that she is on a street where "black" people, or "Asian" people, or "Latino" people, or "white" people, make up the bulk of the visible. It is a city where people of multiple colors share bus seats, but also a city where bus lines suddenly become single-colored, or noticeably not-some-color. Passing cars blare music in multiple languages and styles—just as passing voices heard in the city park or downtown shopping center reveal snippets of innumerable dialects—but while race is fluid here, it also isn't. Right next to this bustling multiculturalism are stark segregated patterns. Just around the corner from the gleamingly diverse downtown shopping center, for example, several square blocks contain wandering and destitute people. Most of them look "black."

Yet—in descriptions of inequality in California City, there is always a "yet" or a "but"—*is* there a clear racial pattern here? Upon a closer look, one sees integration here too: on the street corners of this neighborhood, weathered pink men hold signs requesting money from passing cars. In another neighborhood regularly talked about as a "black" ghetto, similarly, Asian-looking teenagers and white-looking mothers of toddlers wait for the bus. In a neighborhood commonly described as "Latino" territory, white-looking neo-hippie kids emerge from apartments, Chinese restaurants dot the streets, and black-looking people descend from the trolleys. As two boys who described themselves as "Latin" put it to me once, their neighborhood—which wrapped around one side of Columbus—"seemed mostly Latin" simply because folks like "the white family" across the street never left their house and "Filipino families" in the area "stayed hidden."

California City is thus a city of simultaneous segregation and integration, where every race pattern has an exception upon a closer look. If one accepts the more basic patterns one can see at a quick glance, however, racial orders *are* immediately apparent—and one likely notices that these racial orders articulate with economic orders. That is, California City's more obvious racial patterns are patterns of inequality rather than an infinitely dynamic "diversity"— and they divide in part along a white/non-white axis.

In the 1990s, small single-family houses and condominiums in California City routinely went on the market for over half a million dollars. Many young-ish people in California City, sipping lattes in suede jackets, had higher in-comes than most people in the world, and they bought these homes. While the ranks of these wealthy young people were indeed diverse, the vast majority of them were white. And as the spoils of the booming technology industry afforded many young American immigrants to California City access to the gleam of freshly painted cottages, many students in the city's public schools graduated knowing little more about computers than how to use them to type. Despite the city's celebrated technological prosperity, the superintendent re-ferred often to students in California City as "kids of poverty." Sometimes he also called them "minorities," sometimes "low-income minorities": for most of the kids in the California City public school system were (and remain) "non-white." A relatively undiscussed exception are those "white" students who usu-ally attend the city's most prestigious public schools, which also tend to have far lower proportions of students from families on public assistance. White kids attend the "good" schools across California City's expanse, and they live in areas that are predominantly "white" and predominantly non-poor. Al-though the categories of racial inequality leak in California City, then, they still hold water: white students in California City typically have more money than do kids of color, and they more consistently get a decent education. Race in California City is not just about where you live or go to school: it is about the kind of lucky hand life has dealt you. Students at Columbus associate "growing up white" with "growing up spoiled" or "privileged"; they live at the other end of the spectrum, figures in a multicolored painting entitled "low-income minority."

Look closer at this painting again, though, and analytic trouble returns: for you might notice some race-class inequality patterns *within* California City's "low-income minority" population. "Black" people, for example, are still the most residentially segregated population in the city—segregated specifically from highly segregated whites. While very few "white" people live in California City's so-called "ghetto" areas—some of which are around the corner from white wealth, some miles away from it—only a fraction of "black" people in California City live *outside* its "ghetto" areas. Yet ask any resident of "the ghetto," and he or she will admit that California City's ghettos are both "black" and "not *all* black." On one day at Columbus as the last school bell rang, one former student who identified himself as "mixed" suddenly pointed to a bus heading toward a housing project where he himself lived and said, "Look, all the black kids will get on the 8." He himself was an exception, he added, as he was not "black"—but the project was *primarily* "black," he explained. Indeed, look more closely at who gets out of buses or cars in "the ghetto" and disappears into homes, and you will start to see some "Filipinos"; look at the housing projects more carefully and you will notice a sizable handful of "Samoans." Many California City residents do not know that some recently immigrated "Asians," particularly Southeast Asians, also live in California City's supposedly all-black "ghetto" housing projects. Far more prominent in the demographics and public imagination of California City are the city's "Chinese" "Asians"—a population that complicates all analyses of inequality in California City by living simultaneously in some of the city's richest areas and some of its poorest.

There are several neighborhoods in California City, for example—of varying degrees of wealth—that are predominantly "Chinese" (California City actually has two neighborhoods, one poor and one more middle class, that refer to themselves as "Chinatown"). Yet in housing and schooling, Chinese-American residents are also substantially more integrated into California City life than are other "minorities." Many "Chinese" people, particularly those who are long-time California City residents, live in expensive areas with "whites"; and unlike "Latino" students, further (who are also somewhat scattered around several neighborhoods in the city and are thus less ghettoized than "blacks"), "Chinese" students regularly join "whites" at the city's "academic" public schools. The most prestigious high school in the city, Whitman High, is actually *predominantly* "Chinese." Not all "people of color" in California City, one begins to sense, seem identically "disadvantaged"; not all well-off people are "white"; and indeed, not all people within any given "racial group" share identical disadvantages either.

If you keep your eyes from blurring on the infinite details of California City's demographic complexity, however, two basic and simultaneous systems of race-class inequality actually start to become apparent. One system has an axis dividing advantaged "white" people from all "people of color," and the other system contains multiple axes dividing the city into a multiracial complex of differently advantaged groups. In trying to describe such simultaneous and intricate systems of "disadvantage" in California City's schools in the mid-to-late 1990s, people sometimes started a sentence on inequality with one unit of analysis, qualified it, and shifted to another unit of analysis by the end. Comparisons of inequality in California City did not remain static long—and as some people struggled in particular to produce accurate descriptions of how *race* mattered to inequality, to others all descriptions of racial inequality came to seem inherently inaccurate.

Everyday Analyses of Inequality

In analyzing inequality at Columbus and in California City, people talked routinely as if they were viewing the social world through a very sophisticated camera, one that offered multiple analytic lenses and could zoom in and out to use these lenses at different levels of magnification. In their talk, they changed analytic lenses constantly to describe people as members of various kinds of groups (switching, for example, from the race lens of "Columbus students are *minorities*" to the class lens of "Columbus students are *low-income kids*"); they also often *combined* analytic lenses, describing people in race-class terms like "low-income minority." Speakers also set their analytic lenses at various levels of magnification, either zooming in to make their unit of analysis more focused (replacing the general "*minorities*" with the more specific "*Samoan* people"), or zooming out to make their unit of analysis more general (replacing the specific "*Special Ed students* at Columbus" with the more general "*Columbus students*").

Since it was Columbus students who were currently struggling most obviously to succeed—to pass tests, to graduate, to attend college, to pursue careers—they were the focus of most Columbus-level analyses of local opportunity and disadvantage. As we see in Part 1 of this chapter, Columbus people changed analytic lenses frequently when trying to describe what made "Columbus kids" disadvantaged as a group in comparison to kids at other California City schools (and, as we shall see, in comparison to people like Columbus teachers); they typically resolved such confusion with the basic binary framing of Columbus students as "low-income minorities" disadvantaged in comparison to "middle-class whites." When analyzing inequality *within* Columbus, however, as we see in Part 2, Columbus people young and old seemed suddenly plagued by analytic confusion over whether particular subgroups of students— especially race groups—could be deemed particularly disadvantaged. Loathe to navigate the complexities of analyzing inequality *within* Columbus, they typically zoomed out from focused subgroup analyses to generalized analyses of Columbus students as uniformly disadvantaged. As Part 3 concludes, even further analytic simplification characterized the citywide inequality analysis: stymied by the simultaneously binary and multiracial complexities of race-class inequality in California City, policymakers would eventually not only erase race from district analyses of student disadvantage but also start abandoning the very practice of formally analyzing educational inequality.

The assertion that Columbus students as a group got a raw deal within the district caused little controversy on Columbus grounds: by the time students congregated at Columbus as 9th graders, they seemed unarguably grossly undereducated in comparison to many of their district peers. Choosing an analytic lens to define this accrued disadvantage, however, caused some disagreement. Sometimes, people actually implied that Columbus students were low-tracked because they were somehow inherently "bad," or even "dumb"; at other moments they argued that Columbus students were disadvantaged by the district "system" because they were poor; and at still other moments they suggested that they faced citywide disadvantages because they were not "white." In comparison to other district kids and often in comparison to their own teachers, Columbus students were alternately framed as "low-tracked," "low-income," and "minority"—or most often, as a simplified combination of all three.

Part 1: Analyzing "Columbus Kids" as an Aggregated Disadvantaged Unit

Columbus as Low-Tracked Unit

Over three years at Columbus, I came to know "Columbus kids" as bright young people who seemed to despise school and, at certain moments, to really love it, resilient kids who somehow seemed to lack the corrosive cynicism presumed of their generation even as they dealt daily with the realities of splintered families and struggling communities. The majority had been allowed to arrive in high school tremendously underskilled, and they could, at times, offer much seemingly angry resistance to classroom tasks; at other times, they displayed a great love for figuring out complicated ideas. They were kids who seemed simultaneously old and young for their age. There were boys who shouldered the child care responsibilities of adults but cowered when a bee flew into the classroom; there were girls who would break windows with their fists in anger and later sit quietly, shoulders shuddering with silent sobs, during a bad date at the prom. As a student summed up once, Columbus kids somehow seemed "ALWAYS stressed."

Columbus adults, too, often seemed "always stressed." Working at Columbus was both human joy and superhuman trial, as the inherently exhausting labor of teaching had to be performed with inadequate resources (teachers routinely spent large sums of their own money to buy school supplies) and under the constant threat of district-judged failure, both before and after reconstitution. To my eyes, Columbus adults indeed seemed at times too weak to deal with Columbus life, yet they often seemed far stronger than their students. There were adults who came early to make coffee from aged pots for school functions, and who stayed until dark designing academic projects for the houses, writing curricula or grants for the career academies, and coaching and counseling students. There were also adults who ran in the door as the bell rang to start school and ran out the door as the bell rang to end it. There were adults who hugged kids regularly and adults who screamed at them regularly. Yet in the aggregate, before and after reconstitution I saw a changing cast of Columbus adults devote the majority of their days and nights to serving students who simultaneously resisted them with all their might and absorbed thirstily any drop of kindness.

As all Columbus people complained consistently, no one on the outside ever seemed to see this "real" Columbus. To many in California City, the name "Columbus" conjured up instead an unsavory world of graffiti, low achievement, gangs, pounding music, and violence; those who uttered it often smirked in silent critique or pity. Students told of parties where other teenagers ridiculed them for attending Columbus; Columbus teachers said that when they told others their place of employment, they were often greeted with murmurs of sympathy. Such public connotations reached incoming teachers and students before they themselves reached Columbus; newcomers had to work hard to form their own opinions. A public analysis of the school as a "bad school" for the low-achieving seeped in daily through the Columbus walls. Consider one conversation about "stereotypes" we had in my own classroom in 1994:

Me: What do people assume about you when they find out that you go to Columbus?
Students: We're all in gangs. We all have fights. We cut classes. We don't learn anything; they don't teach us anything here.
Me: Is it true?
Students: No . . . a little bit.
Me: If they spent a day walking around with you, would they still assume this?
Students: *NO!*

Columbus's cycles of reform, it seemed, never had quite enough time to rectify Columbus's districtwide image as a place of substandard teaching and learning. The first staff I knew was reconstituted before their house and academy reforms came to fruition; most of the second staff (who descended on the school in 1996 with just three weeks' preparation time to create a "new Columbus" from scratch)—was to disperse within two years of reconstitution. With many public evaluations of Columbus based on its low standardized test scores, further, Columbus students weathering the testing process throughout these years of change often confirmed the public's perceptions in a cycle of seeming self-sabotage. On one standardized testing day in 1996, for example, Katrina, a former student who self-identified as "black," noted that a lot of students hadn't shown up; she explained that the test was "important to Columbus, but not important to *us*—Columbus is always going to be looked at as a rowdy school." In 1997, students interrupted standardized testing with a series of mock fire alarms. Some student frustration about Columbus's negative public image came out in silly ways, some in tragic. When Takisha, another former student who self-identified as "black," found out in the spring of 1997 that she had missed too many classes in her senior year to graduate with her class, she sobbed to me on the front lawn that as a freshman she hadn't wanted to come to Columbus anyway. "Why?" I asked. " 'Cause that's where all the *dumb* kids go," she sniffled, looking glumly at the ground.

Both before and after reconstitution in 1996, the specter of public perceptions that Columbus kids were indeed the district's "dumb kids" hovered over Columbus at all times. During finals week, students incessantly asked teachers, "What if I fail?" At guest presentations about local colleges, students sometimes asked if they could get their money back if they failed their classes or were unable to finish. One day during the school's "probation" year, I went to talk to 10th graders waiting in the auditorium to take a new district math test. "I don't see why we have to take this. We're the guinea pigs," grumbled a

Latino boy to me. "Why should we even do this? We don't get anything out of it," a Filipina girl agreed, frowning. "Just to see how well you do, I guess," I replied. "Just to see how stupid we look," muttered a Samoan boy.

"We," Columbus kids in the aggregate, sometimes seemed to "look stupid" in comparison to the "smart" kids presumably attending other district schools. The districtwide notion that students' motivation and intellectual capacity were indicated by the school they attended seeped easily into everyday comparisons. One day in 1995, for example, two white Columbus teachers comparing Columbus's sparse academic decathlon team to the team from the district's most prestigious "academic" school remarked, "Whitman always wins because they have all the *smart* kids. They have an awards ceremony, and our kids just sit there . . . The Whitman kids are hustlers." Of course, that some schools in California City were officially labeled "academic" implied much about the ones *not* so labeled, as a Samoan security guard angry about the decision to reconstitute Columbus indicated in the spring of 1996: "I like to use that garbage can as a good analogy," he muttered, pointing to a can inside the gate. "The academic schools, they've taken the top trash. But no one, no one takes the trash at the bottom. That gets sent to us—and we have to deal with all the *losers!*"

California City's enrollment system, which quietly allowed savvy parents to transfer their children to schools already popularly viewed as successful, actually stoked the citywide perception that the families in the city without much interest in academic pursuits ended up where they deserved. An independent resource guide called *Getting the Public School You Want*, advertised at the district's student placement office, asked readers, "How did these children get into a good school in California City? Their parents did their homework." While many "good" schools required such parent application (a handful also required tests or certain grade-point averages), "comprehensive" schools like Columbus enrolled students based on attendance zone, and accepted midyear students who were having behavioral or academic problems at other schools. In the mid-to-late 1990s, only around 20 percent of the students at Columbus had chosen to go there, while the rest were assigned and did not protest. When the first Columbus staff attempted to create an application process for Columbus's house program, the district quickly dismantled the process, and teachers and students familiar with district enrollment procedures continued to grumble accordingly that comprehensive Columbus got "kids who didn't want to be here." Before and after reconstitution, both teachers and students complained that the "best" students who arrived at Columbus were soon skimmed away by the city's "academic" schools, leaving the remaining students with the additional disadvantage of thinking that they were the district's remnants.

California City's 1971 desegregation case had cited the testimony of one Board of Education member who argued that "black children and their parents view the segregation in California City as purposefully designed to separate the races," and that "this feeling reinforces the black child's feeling of inferiority." In the 1990s, many Columbus people sensed a purposeful segregation of the entire student body. In the back of one classroom, as I wrote in my notes, a black student weaving between desks offered a quintessential description of such academic segregation:

> "This school's for *rejects*. He's a reject," he says, tapping a Latino guy in duck duck goose style, walking to the next desk. "He's a reject," he says again, tapping a Filipino guy. "We're *all* rejects. That's why they got us locked up in here."

In such everyday analyses of educational opportunity, district tracking patterns gradually separating "good" students from the "rejects" were routinely framed in terms of student "smartness," "dumbness," and "hustle." They were also regularly framed in terms of economics. Analyses of Columbus's low-tracked status, that is, often triggered analyses through a class lens in everyday descriptions: Columbus became a "low-income" school. In a May 1996 school board meeting protesting reconstitution, for example, a former Columbus teacher framed his argument about educational opportunity in common economic/academic terms for the board:

> "You can't establish academic high schools and leave the comprehensive high schools alone. You have students going to the academic schools, and when they don't succeed they get dumped on our schools. You're not serving the *lower socioeconomic* kids. You're creating a two-tier system."

In such analyses of "disadvantage," Columbus kids became non-"academic" *because* they were "lower socioeconomic": Columbus kids ended up academic "rejects" primarily because they had less money.

Columbus as Low-Income Unit

Both before and after reconstitution, Columbus staff pooled into schoolwide programs federal funding targeting especially low-income students, arguing that all Columbus kids fit this description. While family financial problems were private matters (only in a handful of classrooms did I see the specifics of family poverty discussed), students indeed often commiserated about a general dearth of family funds. Some Columbus students flaunted sports team coats or shoes that cost a hundred dollars or more (some students even kept the price tags hanging on their jackets), but many confessed privately that they often cycled only two or three such outfits and hoped others would not notice. In one black teacher's class discussion about how Tupac Shakur's songs raised themes "about the communities we live in, or the world we see around us," the theme of "money" was suggested immediately. "Everything's money, really," said a Filipino student. "Lack of money," added a black student.

Some district descriptions of Columbus students combined analyses of economic and academic disadvantage: two-thirds of Columbus students were designated "EDY," or "Educationally Disadvantaged Youth," because they were "lower-income" based on free and reduced lunch records and had also scored low on state standardized tests. "Lack of money" indeed had negative consequences for many Columbus students' academic trajectories: some students dropped out of Columbus altogether to make money in fast food restaurants or in other low-tier service positions, sometimes to take care of children (ironically, of course, many graduates ended up in such service positions as well). In explaining academic troubles, students told their teachers privately of caring for siblings at night or in the morning while parents worked, of working to earn extra income for the family, and of lacking money to attend college. Career counselors at Columbus recommended to many graduating students that they attend a local community college before transferring to a four-year program, advising students that this strategy for pursuing higher education addressed disadvantages both financial and academic.

Other everyday analyses of Columbus's low-tracked status in the district suggested that the school as a whole "lacked money"—that Columbus was disadvantaged financially because of district negligence. At one Columbus alumni reunion in 1996, for example, I asked a white alumnus who had graduated in the 1940s what had changed since he attended Columbus; in response, he simply pointed to a sign that read "your bond dollars at work" and remarked that it hung right beneath a broken window. Later that day, similarly, I was looking at some old photographs with a Filipino teacher who had graduated from Columbus in the mid-1960s, when, as he put it, the schools in California City had still been "all equal" in status. "They were all the same—except Whitman. In the mid-eighties, when they made Eaton, then WSA," he said, mentioning two of the district's "academic" schools, "that's when it all started":

> "They started taking all the good students from Columbus. And all the resources started going to those schools. It's really a three-tiered system. You've got Whitman; then the schools like Eaton and WSA, and then—we're at the bottom, not even in the bottom *half*! It's a class thing, too. Those schools, they don't get a lot of kids from the projects," he said, leaning towards me.

As this teacher indicated, the concept of "the projects" also dominated many "class" analyses of Columbus's disadvantaged status in the district. Despite the fact that the majority of Columbus students actually lived in private apartments or houses, the very fact that a sizable subset of Columbus students lived in public housing explained for many people Columbus's placement on the bottom of the district's academic "tiers." Some argued that the district could systematically deny resources to a school full of clout-less kids and parents "from the projects"; others argued that the very funneling of "project kids" to a handful of district schools concentrated the district's pockets of poverty in a manner unfair to both students and teachers. Such analyses permeated talk about school differences throughout the district: one former Columbus teacher reconstituted to another district high school, for example, reported that her new colleagues reassured her privately that their school would be a far easier assignment than Columbus precisely because it was "two bus transfers away from the projects."

"The projects" stood as analytic shorthand for economic disadvantage in much public analysis. When a 1994 city newspaper article on the Columbus basketball team marveled at the success of a team composed of "project kids," I, a teacher at the time, wrote an exasperated letter to the editors:

> My students and I were appalled at the stock description of Columbus as "[a] monolithic edifice . . . covered with graffiti tags . . . huge, imposing, intimidating." My students also were especially incensed by the unsubtle description of the basketball team as "wildflowers sprouting from a weed-strewn lot," as it was perfectly clear to my students that they were being cast as "the weeds." My students easily recognized that this was yet another example of the 'bad press' given to our high school. As one student remarked, "That's all they *ever* say—why don't they come here and find out how we *really* are?"

Columbus students complained regularly about the assumptions thus made about their own economic circumstances and the effects these circumstances would have on their lives; but they often agreed that the school as a whole weathered aggregated economic disadvantages. They did, however, occasionally entangle this analysis of schoolwide economic disadvantage with analyses of their own presumed innate inferiority. When I complained about holes in my classroom walls one day in 1995, Antoine, a student who typically called himself "black," yelled with a smile, "This isn't the Ritz, this is *Columbus!*":

> "You don't see the district putting lots of money into this school like they do the other schools," Antoine says. Me: "Well, lemme give you an example. Earlier this year there was a math class that had new calculators and one day they went flying out the windows. Now some people said, 'why should we give these kids any more calculators?'" Michael ["*mixed*"] stands up, rips off his jacket, and says, "It's the kids! It's all on the kids! You don't see stuff like this happening at Whitman—and it's not all white, neither, there's lots of different races there. The kids here is brain-damaged! That's what they is!!" Everyone laughs. Antoine: "But y'know, at a place like Whitman you've got to have a certain grade point to get in. You have to have a 3.0!" Darlene ["*black*"]: "Not if you're black." Antoine: "Well, but you don't *have* to have a certain grade point to go here. So *everyone* comes here." Me: "That's called tracking." Clarence ["*black*"]: "You really think if we had carpets and stuff it would make us smarter?"

That Columbus, with its open enrollment of "everyone," was relentlessly made to appear inferior through numerous analytic lenses in the district sometimes made remedies for Columbus's low academic status seem unbearably unclear. For a painful moment here to Clarence and the others, it seemed that no material advantages would make Columbus's "brain-damaged" kids "smarter." Further, in comparing low-tracked, "money"-deprived Columbus to the district's "other schools," the students had offered yet another lens for analyzing Columbus's place in a district system of unequal opportunity. Michael had had to remind his classmates that Whitman was "*not all white*, neither": for analyses of school differences in California City often pointed out that Columbus, unlike some of "the other schools" in the district, was not "white" at all. In many everyday comparisons, that is, Columbus was framed not just as a low-tracked or a low-income unit, but also as an oxymoronically all-"*minority*" unit—a unit of "low-income minorities" academically disadvantaged in comparison to all the kids clustered at private or "academic" schools in the city and surrounding towns who were either well-off, white, or both.

Columbus as Low-Tracked, "Low-Income Minority" Unit

When I was teaching at Columbus in 1994–95, my aunt Marlene came to visit me from Massachusetts. The final bell had rung, and she reached my classroom as some of the last straggling students were slamming their lockers shut for the day. She said she had been standing outside for a while watching students emerge from the building. "So much for *Brown v Board*," she said with a raised brow. I asked her what she meant. "It's a million shades of black and brown," she said. "But aren't there any white kids in California City?"

Columbus's non-"white" student demographics had been half a century in the making. Since Columbus opened its doors in 1928, each graduating class of seniors has taken a panoramic picture, with one row of chairs in a semicircle and several rows of standing students behind. In the 1932 picture of the first graduating class, there are approximately 200 students; one dark-skinned girl stands, not smiling, on the far left side of the back row. A number of olive-skinned kids dot the photo, but they and all the rest of the students seem to be of European origin, and alumni stories of Depression-era "Greeks" and "Italians" support this assumption. Panoramic pictures from the 1990s show a complete demographic reversal. Almost all of the students are now people of color; a lone "white" student stands here and there in the crowd.

As we peered at an old graduation picture in the Columbus foyer at a 1996 reunion, an alumnus from the class of 1961 explained to me that Columbus's neighborhood had always been "blue collar, middle class." Yet the school's racial demographics had changed over the years, he said, as I wrote later in my notes:

> "It's changed . . . the diversity is different," he said, some thought between the two phrases. "What do you mean?" I asked. "There used to be a lot of Italians—they had their gardens out here. And there were some Greeks here, too, and some Spanish surname, and some Filipinos, and some Samoans, and some black families. It was a

real melting pot here," he said. He said he thought it was more diverse when he was here than it is now. "Some people moved out—a lot of the Italian families," he said.

To him, Columbus seemed somehow less diverse in the 1990s—implicitly, because there were no more children of Europeans. White students had indeed gone elsewhere, and to many, the white kids now absent from Columbus embodied educational advantage. Justin, one of the few former students of mine who self-identified as "white," explained that as a freshman he had considered moving to a neighboring city to live with a relative because "it's all white up there, and you learn more." Similarly, one black student waiting in the Columbus hallway to receive his graduation gown in the spring of 1997 grumbled that at his previous school in a neighboring city, "kids got an *education*, teachers were *prepared*. There were more white kids there."

Within California City, too, white students were clustered at "good" schools where parents perhaps figured they would "learn more"; under the Consent Decree, we might remember, white students could legally be clustered at a small set of schools, as they were just one of the nine "race/ethnic groups" making any school "integrated." Moments when students met one another in athletic competition often starkly demonstrated this racial pattern of school enrollment in California City. At one football game against "academic" Whitman in 1994, for example, I noticed that the players' legs, the only part of their bodies where their skin was visible, demonstrated a striking pattern: one was a team of dark legs, the other a team of light ones. As helmets came off, Columbus's team appeared almost completely African-American (with a few Samoan- and Latino-looking boys), while the majority of Whitman's players looked white. I said as much to an African-American teacher I was with, who agreed, "Yes, it's almost like night and day!" In 1995, I described a Columbus-Whitman baseball game in similar racial terms in my notes:

> Whitman has *such* a white team. Our "Juan" pitches to their "Zachary." Columbus team yells "COME ON BABY!" to Juan, while the Whitman coach tells Zachary to "hit the ball in the middle third of the bat." I can't believe these kids have grown up in the same city!

When I walked around the public baseball diamonds near my house during spring, I couldn't help but analyze high school demographics through a race lens—the private schools in the city had teams that were almost exclusively white, and white parents in polo shirts and school sweatshirts surrounded the field for mid-afternoon weekday games. But when one recalled that many of the private schools in California City charged tuition comparable to universities, one realized that such binary racial enrollment patterns were always also economic. Indeed, the racial demographics of the lowest-income public schools in California City demonstrated the same binary race-class pattern: while students of color abounded, upper- and middle-income white students were notably absent. People analyzing the Columbus neighborhood's compounded disadvantages, too, often invoked the same simultaneity of class and race: one Columbus teacher citing statistics from the health department demonstrating that Columbus had the largest proportion of kids in the city with mental health issues, asthma, lead poisoning, and other environment-related health problems, for example, explained simply that "this area of the city has the most immigrants and poor minorities." It indeed often seemed that Columbus students' various disadvantages could only be analyzed accurately through combined lenses of race *and* class, and in most everyday comparisons to kids at other schools, Columbus became not just low-tracked *or* "poor" *or* "non-white," but all three—a low-tracked, "low-income minority" unit.

Adults with a history at Columbus, for example, often implied that the economic resources Columbus received from its district had dwindled with the school's racial transformation. In 1996, Mr. D, a white Columbus teacher who had graduated from Columbus in the 1960s, recalled in one interview that that decade—the decade when Columbus first started becoming a predominantly "minority" school—had been the last time the district had had Columbus's windows washed twice a year. The greenery was kept up then, and there were no cracks in the walls; broken things got fixed immediately. These days, he said, nothing got repaired.

When describing Columbus students' current disadvantages, speakers sometimes merged economic and race analyses seamlessly as did Mr. D; with some regularity, they also shifted back and forth abruptly between explicit race and class analyses within several short sentences. Ms. Duran, a Latina teacher, offered such an intertwined analysis of race-class "challenges" in a discussion that emerged from talk of Steinbeck's *Mice and Men* one day:

> Ms. Duran said, [*race lens:*] "Most of you who are students of color—'cause I'm a person of color—you have to keep going. [*Now a class lens:*] Society sees us and thinks that just because we come from poor backgrounds, we won't make much of our lives. You might have less than kids in suburbs, other neighborhoods where people have all nice stuff in their schools; for you, it's more of a challenge. You gotta meet that challenge."

Everyday analyses of the inequalities plaguing Columbus often were a compilation of such alternating race and class comparisons ("of color" versus the implied "white"; "poor backgrounds" versus the implied well-off). As Ms. Duran's comparison between "poor-of-color" neighborhoods and "the suburbs" suggested, people also sometimes packed class and race analyses into single loaded descriptors. Talking to me privately on another occasion, Ms. Duran offered a classic collection of such race-class loaded academic words, first noting with exasperation that the district had labeled 60 percent of the population at Whitman High (which had the district's highest proportion of white students as well as its lowest proportion of poor students) as "Gifted and

Talented." The district needed to spread out Columbus's "so-called at-risk kids," she then sighed, adding that "this kind of school becomes a warehouse" for "low-income students with special needs":

> She got the sense from many new teachers, she said, that they were "getting brownie points for doing a stint in the inner city, to put it on the resume." Indeed, some teachers were so casual about their lack of teaching experience that they seemed almost to hold a "condescending" and "colorial" attitude toward students. "As a woman of color—a minority person—I feel a deep resentment," she said. "Minority kids are being used here as an experiment. Every year there are new programs and ideas introduced because they're trendy, without asking if it translates to our students. The seniors this year have seen things change every year they were here. This wouldn't happen at a middle-class Caucasian school—parents would be up in arms. Minority students' parents are in survival mode. Many don't speak English—they're intimidated. They have kids, no transportation. Our kids can't afford to be used as experiments."

Descriptors like "inner city," "at risk," and "Gifted and Talented"—which, as Ms. Duran talked, clearly seemed packed with race-class analytic categories like "minority," "of color," and "middle-class Caucasian"—were shorthand for the multiple inequality systems facing Columbus students and their parents. "Inner city," for example, seemed a word designed to connote a morass of race-class disadvantage: "inner-city" schools were inherently *not* "middle-class Caucasian," and thus were concerned more with "survival" than with fighting a deluge of inexperienced teachers or educational "experiments." Only a few miles away, in its own neighborhood of slightly larger pastel homes, stable, "academic" Whitman was never labeled "inner-city"; Columbus, a stately pink building surrounded by palm trees and located on the city's edge in a neighborhood of modest single-family houses, was routinely called an "inner-city school," making clear that the term "inner-city" often defies geography.

"Ghetto" was a similarly race-class loaded term used as shorthand to describe Columbus students: unpacked in various contexts, the term implied alternately that Columbus kids were low-income and that they were not white. At a happy hour convened by the former Columbus faculty in 1996, for example, a white teacher who had been transferred to majority "Asian" Roosevelt High framed her new assignment as non-"ghetto" in terms more explicitly classed than racialized:

> "If I had my chance I'd be back. I've always taught ghetto kids. I miss them . . . they needed me. The kids at Roosevelt are very middle-class. They're not worrying about survival. They're just worrying about adolescence."

In other comparisons, "ghetto" more directly connoted non-"white." One day at Columbus that same year, for example, Maverick, a new black security guard, was logging in students in a detention room as a new white teacher,

Ms. Orlan, got into a more explicitly racial conversation about "the ghetto" with a black student named Stephen. With a subtle smile, Stephen quickly framed Columbus for Ms. Orlan as an exaggeratedly dangerous foreign turf:

> Stephen says to Ms. Orlan, "You new?" "New this year," she says. "But new?" "New to here this year," she repeats. "After a while, teacher, you're gonna hate this school!" he says. "Why?" she asks. "Soon as there are drivebys, shootings," he says ominously. "I hope not, 'cause I'm here," Maverick says, going toward the door. "Right, not with Maverick here—Maverick'll take care of it," Stephen says, smiling. "He's got some help, too," says Ms. Orlan. "That's right," Maverick replies as he walks out. "He's got people who're working with him," Ms. Orlan continues. "We can all work together. Talking about it—don't you think talking about it can stop people from doing things, fighting?" she asks, walking towards Stephen. "I think they shouldn't even have brought all the new teachers up in here," Stephen replies matter-of-factly. "Why?" Ms. Orlan asks pleasantly. "They should've had people from the ghetto up in here—that's who goes to this school. If there were teachers from the ghetto, kids would listen," Stephen says. "I see what you're saying," Ms. Orlan replies, adding, "That was part of what they wanted. They tried to find people who came more from backgrounds like the students . . . I mean, I'm white, I'm a woman, I come from like a different background," she finishes. "You *do*?!" Stephen says, with impeccable seriousness.

Whether Columbus people imagined one another's "backgrounds" or described their own, they routinely placed "white," "middle-class," or "suburban" people on the opposite side of a binary race-class divide from Columbus students as "ghetto," "inner-city" "poor minorities." Indeed, "the ghetto" was presumed foreign to most Columbus adults: as Stephen and Ms. Orlan demonstrated, Columbus kids were framed as "ghetto" "low-income minorities" perhaps most often in comparisons to their own teachers. Such relentless shorthand comparisons could have dangerous consequences: Columbus students could come to seem a population defined *by* disadvantage, while the gulf between teachers and students could come to appear so vast as to be almost uncrossable.

Columbus as Low-Tracked, "Low-Income Minority" Unit, Continued: Comparing Columbus Students to Columbus Teachers

Sarah, a white teacher, once described to me an awkward conversation she had had with a "black student" who had been listening to her "ESL students" converse in the Columbus library:

> "I said, 'Isn't it amazing to think about what it would be like to come here and go to a school in a different language? It would be like me dropping off my child to school in Hong Kong and saying 'see ya!' " And he said, 'It'd be like you coming to live in the ghetto.' "

In such everyday comments, people at Columbus regularly distinguished students from teachers as populations primarily defined by their presumed relative experience and inexperience with race-class disadvantage. As Tina (a former student who usually identified herself as "black") put it, Columbus students needed to see teachers "of *their* culture, with *their* background, not with sheltered lives"; students even appropriated media representations of disadvantaged "inner-city youth" to frame themselves ironically through their presumed "sheltered" teachers' eyes (after reconstitution, for example, students complained that the crop of new teachers had descended upon Columbus to "fix it up like it was from *Dangerous Minds* or something."). As I wrote in my notes, a new Filipino teacher, Mr. T, also imagined diametrically opposed teacher-student "backgrounds" as he tried to explain to me Columbus adults' various "problems" with "the kids":

> He says he really doesn't have any problems with his classes, and that if I am doing research I should go to look at some of the classes where the teachers are really having problems. He says Ms. Ridgeway [*a white woman*], for example, is having real problems with classroom control—some students had a fight in her room and she just stood in the corner crying. "She doesn't have the respect of the kids. Though she's a very energetic and innocent person, she's afraid of the kids," he says. "How do you know?" I ask. "Oh, I know she's afraid of the kids," he says, smiling. "Did she tell you?" I ask. "She doesn't have to tell me!" he says, smiling. He mentions another teacher, Mr. Carter [*a black man recently graduated from a nearby elite university*], who also is always throwing students out. "Why, do you think?" I ask. "For him, it's a cultural thing. I think the place, the background he's coming from is *so* far removed from where the students are coming from—it couldn't get any farther," he says.
>
> He says that Ms. Ridgeway "has really good motives, coming to a place like this." [*Now his analytic lens becomes more specifically economic:*] "She wants to help poor kids—but these aren't the same kind of poor people there used to be. These people aren't all welcoming and thankful. This is a new kind of poor person," he says. We both smile. "You mean like she thought she would come here to help these poor kids who would welcome her with open arms and say *thank* you and it would all be a happy place?" I say, thinking of my own beginnings as a teacher. "*Exactly,*" he says, laughing. "These are kids of the '90s and they're *different*," he adds. "I just don't think Ms. Ridgeway knew what she was getting into," he says. [*Now he shifts to a lens that is more specifically racial.*] He adds, "She probably grew up in an all-white community." He thinks she went to "some Ivy League school. I dunno if it's like in Boston, where there's a big black-white polarization going on. She could have grown up somewhere like Minnesota, where it's like 98% white, there are no minorities. But it's not about being prejudiced and stuff, it's about your background, your experience. [*Struggling to define differences in "background," he now starts explicitly merging his race and class lenses:*] If there was a white guy who had grown up in Brooklyn, or let's say the Bronx,

who went to Harvard or something and then came out here—do you think he would do well here?" he asks. "I dunno," I say. "Sure! Over someone from the suburbs," he says, adding, "I mean, do you think Ms. Ridgeway ever was in a position where she had to defend herself, when she was about to get jacked?!"

In such comparisons, Columbus students became a unit summarized by the race-class experience of dealing with challenges their non-"poor," non-"minority," and "suburban" teachers presumably could not begin to understand. Like Mr. T, teachers of color, too, often themselves wondered aloud about the relative importance of race and class to such differences in teacher-student "background"; they typically prioritized differences of class over those of race. After one particularly raucous class I witnessed one day in 1997, for example, the class' Filipino teacher, apparently mortified, started to wonder aloud to me in private whether the difficulties he was having with his students were based on differences in "background, race, or color." After musing that he was "also pretty middle- or upper-middle-class, the way I talk," he quickly concluded that "The ones who really seem to value education are more middle-class. Yeah, I think more than race it's class."[5]

To help bridge the privately assumed divide in race-class "background" between Columbus students and their teachers, in the fall of 1996 Mr. T sent out a memo to faculty advertising that Maverick, the security guard, was an experienced motivational speaker. Word spread speedily that Maverick could come to classes to offer students words of experience and wisdom, and many new teachers came quickly to rely on Maverick's assistance. Maverick became known as a rare Columbus adult who could "relate" to "Columbus kids" because he shared their "background" along both race and class lines, and could therefore inspire them to do their work. Many teachers quietly described enlisting the assistance of Maverick as a response to the perceived gulf in race-class "background" between themselves and Columbus students. One new teacher suggested that as a "white chick" she had nowhere near the clout with Columbus kids that Maverick had; Maverick said in so many words in his presentations that being "black" afforded him necessary knowledge. Similarly, one black teacher who had attended a middle-class "suburban" high school where "chewing gum in class was the worst offense students ever committed" sighed, "it's the *way* he says it."

As O'Connor (1997) and Ward (2000) both argue, systematic analysis of hurdles upcoming for students of color can empower rather than discourage, and in his motivational talks, as students sat transfixed, Maverick indeed tended to outline the aggregated challenges they would face, focusing sometimes on the disadvantages of racialized status, sometimes on those of class status. Perhaps the biggest disadvantage of being poor and of color simultaneously, Maverick often slyly suggested in his classroom addresses, was that people tended to *assume* one's aggregated disadvantages—most dangerously, people assumed that one lacked basic abilities, intelligence, and drive. Maverick outlined the attitude that was accordingly necessary for survival in a racist world (he punctuated one talk by looking straight into students' eyes and saying, "I am no dumb black man"). Stressing his own poor background, he also argued that students needed to hold themselves to extremely high standards to make it in a world that would repeatedly assume their class inferiority. My notes indicated a classic Maverick quote:

> "Young folks, you live in a very mean, nasty world-society, and it's not getting any better. You have to be competitive. You're gonna get knocked down, spit on—maybe not physically, but emotionally," he said. He held up a sign saying "NEVER FEEL INFERIOR TO *ANYONE*."

Calling his own youth in "the ghetto" a key factor in his success with Columbus students, Maverick privately described inexperienced "suburban" Columbus teachers and administrators to me as "marshmallows," "cheerleaders," and "cotton candy." Such adults, he further suggested to me in exasperated commentaries on his work days, actually helped to exacerbate the disadvantages of race-class inequality when they held students to an artificially lowered set of behavioral and academic standards. A year earlier, Mr. Jones, an African-American administrator, had both employed and critiqued this same logic of binary student-teacher difference when explaining to me one day why he believed "inner-city kids are not getting the education they deserve":

> "Even if they have particularly difficult situations, we still have to require the maximum of them," he said. "A lot of teachers, they want to let it slide. Like when I came here, they said, 'These kids, where they come from, they can't do any better.' I do not like that. That's how we train these kids to fail. If you set the standard high and you hold it high, they will rise to it. These kids can achieve anything anybody else can achieve. When I got here, the kids didn't even know what the rules were. These teachers, some of them, would they send their kids here? No, because they let the kids get away with things that some all-white school out in the suburbs wouldn't let the kids get away with. How's a kid going to learn anything sitting in class wearing a walkman? When I got here, there were kids cussing teachers out and the teachers wouldn't do anything about it. The teachers are afraid of the kids! Now this is my personal opinion," he adds. He pauses, then says slowly, "Inner-city kids are not getting the education they deserve. I was there once—people told me I wouldn't make anything of myself. But I did."

Even as they themselves outlined the various academic disadvantages plaguing students struggling in the "inner city," thus, many adults at Columbus suggested privately that repetitive simplified analyses of compounded "low-income minority" or "inner-city" disadvantage were themselves an insidious form of additional disadvantage plaguing "Columbus kids." In one interview, similarly, Ms. Duran (who herself, as we have seen, often framed Columbus kids as a group of "low-income minorities" with "special needs") suddenly denounced the academic side effects of a school habit of framing Columbus students as an aggregated "needy" unit. Students, she suggested, used this aggregated framing to lower standards for themselves:

> "Why does education have to be always sugar-coated?" she asked. "I tell kids, 'You can't read very well. We need to fix that this year.' Stop pussyfooting around—that's abandoning them. Some kids know, they say, 'just tell that teacher you have a little headache, that you went to bed late, and he won't make you.' It's the welfare game— 'I'm needy, I'm poor, I need to be helped—don't ask me to do these things, because I'm a poor kid.' They get self-esteem from learning skills, not by being told they're wonderful. They need tough love—they play 'oh, you poor thing' to the hilt!" She says she's had African-American and Latino kids say to her, "Oh, Ms. Duran, he's a white teacher." (She says this in a mumble. I have to ask her to repeat it.) "Oh, that 'he's a white teacher and he's trying to be all nice to us, he'll go easy on us,' " she explains. "And I say, 'and you play that to the hilt, don't you,' " she adds, with a disapproving smile.

Compounding the various complex hurdles faced by Columbus's "poor" and non-"white" "kids," then, Columbus speakers repeatedly returned to frame Columbus students as uniformly disadvantaged by a binary race-class inequality system that kept all Columbus students as an aggregated group of "low-income minorities" unequal to "middle-class whites." The aggregated analysis was demographically accurate, but many argued that its relentless use as shorthand could dangerously reduce Columbus students *to* the sum of race and class disadvantage; and as we see next, further, this routine analysis of a uniformly disadvantaged Columbus student population also did not always seem sufficiently precise. While an understanding of Columbus students as a disadvantaged "low-income minority" unit preempted much analytic confusion (to my knowledge, no one ever contested the accuracy of the phrase), speakers who attempted to look *within* the Columbus student body for patterns of disadvantage never seemed sure whether certain groups of Columbus students could ever be considered particularly disadvantaged *in comparison to one another.* Foundering on the complexities of analyzing inequality *within* Columbus, speakers routinely simply deleted their most complex analyses of subgroup need, zooming out to simpler familiar descriptions of schoolwide Columbus disadvantage. As we shall see, *racial* analyses of subgroup needs within Columbus seemed to many to be particularly problematic. Yet giving particular attention even to a population *defined* by having "special needs"—Columbus's English-learner population—often gave way to generic analyses of "Columbus kids' " uniform "low-income minority" problems.

Part 2: Debating Disadvantage within Columbus

As mentioned earlier, the California City Unified School District classified two-thirds of Columbus students as "Educationally Disadvantaged Youth" (EDY) based on their low incomes and low test scores. It also classified another one-third of Columbus students, mostly recent immigrants, as "Limited English Proficient" (LEP). A large proportion of Columbus students actually spoke English as their second language, as they had been born to immigrant parents or had themselves immigrated as younger children, but only the subgroup of the Columbus population formally labeled "LEP" was deemed to need direct instruction in English as a second language ("ESL"). Throughout the three years I was at Columbus, a subset of teachers quietly monitored "LEP" students' academic progress, grouping "LEP" students as often as possible with content teachers who spoke their primary languages so they could learn grade-level subject matter in those languages (and more often, placing "LEP" students from numerous language groups together to learn subject matter and English through "sheltered" English techniques). The students designated for English language assistance were typically called "ESL students" around Columbus rather than "LEP," unless people were citing district policies—as, for example, when a black administrator announced to Columbus staff in 1997 that there was district money available to increase the performance of "EDY and LEP kids" at Columbus. He then zoomed out immediately from this subgroup analysis to a description of schoolwide disadvantage: "That's like everyone in the school!"

As his comments indicated, the category "ESL" or "LEP," which literally denoted the educational needs of a third of the school's student body, was an important demographic category at Columbus on paper; it rarely drove the school's public discussions of academic practice.[6] Structures explicitly set up to serve LEP students appeared and disappeared at Columbus over the years, often leaving academic monitoring dependent on individual committed teachers. While in the first two years that I was around Columbus an interdisciplinary "ESL department" and academic "house" formally linked "ESL" students and their "ESL teachers," after reconstitution administrators removed the "ESL department" and other structures specific to ESL students with the stated goal of ending ESL student "isolation." In the process, academic record-keeping on English language learners went into flux, and many English language learners were placed into "mainstream" subject classes with English-fluent students.

In February of that year, I asked an ESL teacher how she thought "the ESL kids" at Columbus were doing. She replied that they were "definitely getting shafted." She mentioned one new counselor who hadn't "fathomed the size of the program—500 ESL kids. He didn't have a comprehensive list of ESL kids until we got him one from the district in *December*. He didn't even know he could have such a list. So about 150 ESL kids are scattered all over mainstream classes in the school." Sighing, she described one "mainstream" English teacher who had insisted on keeping such an ESL student who had been placed mistakenly in her all-English-speaking class:

> "She said, 'I don't care what level they come in with. I won't turn anyone away because I don't want them to be *labeled*.' Then she came back to me in the middle of the semester and said, 'I made a big mistake. He needs to be out of my class!' So I said, 'We'll talk to the kid.' And the kid was like, 'why are you *punishing me?*' " she finished, looking pained. "I told the teacher, 'You should have *thought* this *through*.' "

The debate over "labeling" the LEP/ESL students at Columbus was both ideological and practical, as addressing English learners' particular language needs required documenting and analyzing their English proficiency.[7] Around this time, curious to see how the school at large dealt with "labeling" its English learners, I asked several administrators and the "bilingual counselor" for a numeric breakdown of ESL students' primary languages. The administrators sent me elsewhere for the information; the counselor said he didn't have it and didn't know how to get it. He suggested I go to another assistant principal or to the attendance office, and added, "And will you please let me know what they said? That would be good information for me to have." It was, finally, a secretary who printed the information for me off a mainframe computer.

Although roughly one-third of Columbus students required specialized English instruction, public talk of Columbus student needs very rarely framed "ESL" students as a particularly disadvantaged subgroup. Private conversations sometimes articulated the public absence of this analysis. On one staff development day in 1997, for example, I was sitting at a table with three other teachers (all of them white), two of whom taught classes of recent immigrants. They suddenly started talking about how the "ESL teachers" had no department:

> Sarah says, "It's ridiculous—the ESL kids have so many needs. What scares me is that the school operates as though ESL doesn't even exist. I'm not worried about the individual classroom teacher so much, but it's the administration I'm scared of. These kids have special money, they need special *programs* . . . there are compliance issues. The English department really operates as if ESL doesn't exist," she repeats. "Do the ESL teachers meet as a group?" I ask. Sarah says, "Not really, hardly ever. But there are so many kids—I don't think the regular teachers know." She says there "should be a lot more attention paid to ESL students." Kids come to her and say they are lost in their regular math classes. There aren't enough ESL teachers; they need bilingual paraprofessionals. "We should *discuss* this," she says.

In such private discussions, typically, "ESL" teachers at Columbus planned to assist ESL students; in meetings with the full English department, many admitted they rarely discussed Columbus's various language groups at all. In more public discussions of addressing Columbus students' needs, further, very few people would even remark that a subgroup of students faced additional linguistic disadvantages within the school. At the end of a 1997 staff meeting on "advisory," a homeroom period designed to foster more personal connections between teachers and students at Columbus, for example, a white teacher raised his hand and said, "I know a number of the students who only speak Spanish go to their advisory and are like, 'huh?!' " As a Spanish-speaking teacher next to him nodded emphatically, he continued: "I'm not saying we should have an all-Latino advisory, but maybe if we bunched five Spanish speakers with each Spanish-speaking teacher?" As the meeting proceeded, no one responded to his comment: public plans to address Columbus students' general neediness typically skirted more complex analysis of the needs of the third of Columbus students still struggling to learn English.

While comments on language-group needs could meet such silence, finally, talk of race-group needs tended to be more explicitly rejected. Race analyses of disadvantage *within* Columbus's low-income-minority student population did not stand uncontested for long. Indeed, even in private, people apologetically erased their *own* suggestions that particular race groups needed particular attention as soon as they articulated them. In typically zooming back out again to a simpler and safer analysis of the aggregated needs of "Columbus kids," speakers typically dismissed in so many words the validity of analyzing inequality within Columbus in racial terms.

Zooming Out: Resisting Descriptions of Race Groups in Need

Jimmy, a former student who typically identified himself as "black," zoomed in briefly to an analysis of "black students' " classroom needs while sitting talking to me in the counseling office one day. In response to my follow-up question about what "black students" particularly needed in comparison to "other students," however, Jimmy zoomed back out to what "students" and "kids" needed without missing a beat:

> Before reconstitution, he said, "A lot of teachers didn't relate to the students. They didn't really know where the students were coming from. And not all students can be taught the same way. [*Here he zooms in to his racial analysis:*] Especially black kids, they need a different style. I was talking to Mr. Drake [*a black teacher*] about how you can't just talk and lecture all day. You have to do hands-on projects, keep people interested." "Why do you think black students need more 'show' than other students?" I asked. [*Challenged, he zooms back out to analyze Columbus students as an aggregated unit:*] "They probably don't, not at a school like this," he said. "Teachers also need to get to know their students, to ask really what they're up to. Kids really need that, they *really* do," he added emphatically.

A race-group analysis, it often seemed, could always be trumped by a generalized one. In backtracking from his more precise analysis of what "black kids" needed, Jimmy shrugged that a race analysis of subgroup need was perhaps inaccurate at "a school like this"—and we dropped the subject. Policy talk, as we have seen, could dismiss its own sporadic race-group inequality analyses just as defensively: even the 1992 "expert report," while emphasizing the "serious needs of African-American and Hispanic students" in California City, predictably zoomed out to describe an "overall pattern of academic inequality in the district" and to add that the authors were aware that "other children were not doing well either." One 1996 interview with Jake, a student who also called himself "black," demonstrated neatly how this process of zooming out from specific race-group analyses to aggregated ones characterized everyday analyses of student needs at Columbus:

> I ask him if he knows why the school is being reconstituted. "Because of test scores," he replies. [*Uncharacteristically, I drop the words "black and Latino" purposefully into our analysis to test his reaction to race-group analysis:*] "They also say it's because black and Latino students aren't being given a good education," I say. "We ain't," he replies, adding, "They're letting us do whatever we want to. We can talk in the classroom for hours, and nobody is going to stop us." [*Now he starts zooming out, expanding the analysis to "minorities":*] "But it's mostly minorities who don't go to class—the people who school isn't interesting for," he says. "They don't wanna be here," he continues, "at a place for nothing. It's hella boring—you're gonna want to leave. It's eight hours of your life." He says again that it's "mostly minorities" who feel this way. "Meaning what?" I ask. [*He zooms out even more explicitly:*] "Blacks and Latinos—all of them—it's all of us," he says.

The process of zooming out from race-group analysis to generalized analysis characterized both student and adult talk at Columbus, and it became so familiar to me that I could predict that people would do it. Talking one day in the school quad to Martha, a Filipina teacher, for example, I tried asking her a race-group question I assumed she would resist:

> I say I have been talking to a security guard, who described the students wandering in the halls as really "diverse." Did she agree? She nods. I ask if she thinks the Filipino kids cut too, and she says yes. [*As predicted, she then zooms out from this racial description to a general one:*] "It's all of them. It's an exception *not* to cut. That's the point—it's a whole school culture," she says. A white teacher, Thomas, comes over to join us. The two of them are looking at their roll books. Martha notes that a number of her kids have 30 or more absences that grading period. She looks at the names. [*Ironically, she now speaks racially despite her disclaimer:*] Then she says to Thomas, "It's all the African-American kids who have that many absences."

When asked directly about the validity of race-group analysis, even speakers who tangentially articulated patterns of race-group need typically denounced the accuracy of such analysis, zooming out instead to simpler talk of schoolwide academic disadvantage that somehow always got accepted as if it were matter-of-factly accurate. Listening to Ms. Duran talk on another day about some test scores she had glimpsed, for example, I decided to ask her bluntly if the scores had been "racially disaggregated." As predicted, she too rejected racial analysis immediately: "Yes—and it's very interesting, because all of them are doing poorly—all the kids," she replied. Persistent, I added that I had seen scores showing "black students the lowest, then Latino students," and I asked her if it would make sense to her to "go after these groups' test scores." "No," she said emphatically. " 'Cause really, they're all low. In general the student body is performing below grade level. We should say this school was performing below—how to get the whole school to come up."

In explicitly rejecting such analysis of race-group educational "performance," Ms. Duran typically denounced most ways of dealing with Columbus students as members of race groups with particular needs. She was at odds with "multiculturalism," she continued here, even with having a course called "Ethnic Literature," since this was "treating ethnic groups in little boxes," and was thus "divisive." She argued that race-based academic assistance programs were "racist." Indeed, teachers sometimes came to ask her questions about "Hispanics," like "why are the Hispanic kids so apathetic about school?", she said, and she resented the very idea of such race-group thinking. "Maybe we should be asking this about all our students—not just Hispanics. Some of these things apply across the board," she finished.

Claiming at times that such analysis was "racist" and at other times that it was simply inaccurate in a place where students had needs "across the board," Columbus people privately offered various such reasons for their rejection of race-group analysis within Columbus. One Asian-American teacher telling me over the phone one day in 1997 that racial patterns in academic opportunity existed within his department then added that it really made no sense to "talk specifically" in race-group terms when analyzing Columbus students' academic needs:

> He says his department will be keeping a general computer database on students. "You'll be keeping records on what grades they're getting?" I ask. "No—their name, their teacher, their current class, the class they're recommended to, their grade level . . . (long pause) their ethnicity, I want to put that in there too," he says. "Why?" I ask. "One of my visions for the department is to have more Latinos, African-Americans, and Samoans take advanced courses," he says slowly. "Now if you look in those classes, it's almost all Chinese and Filipinos. Very few Latinos, African-Americans, or Samoans. I'd like to see it looking very different in three years or so," he says, adding, "The goal is to maintain the Asian kids there, but to make it more accessible to other ethnicities." "So will you talk about this stuff as a department?" I ask. "I don't really see the need to talk specifically . . . there's no need," he replies. [*Here he*

zooms out to include other groups:] "There are Filipino kids failing too, and Chinese. If our mission is to have all students succeed, you get African-Americans and Latinos in there too. If the goal is to get all to succeed regardless of ethnicity, you get them. I'd rather approach it that way, too. If they're failing, who cares what their ethnicity is?" he says.

As Columbus people typically zoomed out from race-group inequality analysis, often stating preferences for describing Columbus kids as an aggregated group of needy students "regardless of ethnicity," zooming in—making the analysis that specific race groups at Columbus had specific needs—was socially quite controversial.

Zooming In: Social Problems with Targeting Students in Racial Terms

As long as all race groups were being targeted equally, as chapter 1 demonstrated, racial targeting at Columbus caused little controversy: targeted activities for the "Filipino club," "Chinese club," "Black Student Union," and "Polynesian club," for example, were advertised sequentially and casually in public calendars. In contrast, speakers isolating single race groups for attention in their public talk had to work hard to justify such targeted analysis. In one "black history" assembly in 1997, for example, a guest speaker, a young black man who was a local graduate student, first zoomed in with unusual gusto to a focus on "black folks." Meeting a cautious response, he immediately started hedging this focus:

> The speaker walks out to the mike. "Hello Columbus! You out there?" he yells. [*Zooms in:*] "Any black folks at this school?" he asks. There is some scattered applause. "He askin' some *stupid* questions!" says a black girl behind me. The speaker says, "The legacy of black history is a lot about *pain*. [*He starts to zoom out again:*] Joining us in that legacy of pain are Samoans (four Samoan girls and one boy in front of me start clapping loudly), Chicanos. . . ." His voice is covered by loud applause as he lists, "Filipinos . . . [*finishing with a final expansion:*] "all people of color." [*He then re-targets his language:*] "But today we're gonna focus on black folks," he says. There is a *huge* roar of applause. The Samoan girl in front of me claps her hands over her eyes in exaggerated distress.

Even a stranger to Columbus knowingly hedged his focus on the pain of "black folks" with an acknowledgment that "all people of color" were in the same boat; in a "low-income minority" place like Columbus, such acknowledgment seemed social common sense. Indeed, even speakers momentarily describing their own plans for assisting specific race groups within Columbus tended to downplay the suggestion in favor of universalistic comments on schoolwide need. One Latino teacher briefly described to me his own idea for "ethnically" targeted parent nights at Columbus (such a strategy, he posited, might make parents more comfortable); but he quickly qualified his informal proposal with an admission that Columbus parents were generally disenfranchised. "I tend to think of things much more in class terms, socioeconomic terms, than in ethnic terms," he added earnestly.

In a school full of "people of color" of low "socioeconomics," district efforts at targeting specific "races" for particular attention also seemed to many to be premised on a faulty analysis of disadvantage. One day after reconstitution, for example, I went to talk to a new Asian-American teacher who had started SAT preparation classes for students, and within minutes she had wearily raised the subject of targeting "African-Americans" and "Latinos" within a school full of kids with "problems":

> "I just wanted to know about the SAT classes," I say, as she welcomes me in. "Yeah! We have about 80 students now," she says. The district is paying for a lot of it, and an outside agency, "Test Prep," is offering a discount so more kids can participate. "How did you recruit for it?" I ask. "Mostly private recruitment, asking teachers. It was race-based, so . . ." she says. "What do you mean?" I ask. "It was funded through Chapter something money, so it had to be for African-American and Latino students—which sucked, because most of the kids who volunteered were Filipino," she says. "There were volunteers?" I ask. "Yes—well, I'd been telling students about it and it was announced to everyone in the bulletin, but you know not too many people read that. Somehow my room has ended up being mostly Filipino, so they were the ones who volunteered," she says. "Your classes are mostly Filipino?" I ask, surprised. "My room, like at lunch—and yeah, my classes," she says, explaining that she teaches Communication classes. [*This was the last remaining "career academy" program from before reconstitution, itself based on voluntary student enrollment.*] "How did the Communication program become mostly Filipino?" I ask. "They signed up for it," she says.
>
> "So most of the volunteers for the SAT classes were Filipino," I repeat. "Yes. We had to recruit for diversity. Our classes are still mostly Chinese and Filipino. Rafael [*a Latino teacher*] did a great job of recruiting Latinos. We still," she says (rolling her eyes up in an "oops" expression), "need to work on the African-American population. But I don't know what else to do . . . if you know anyone who'd be a candidate," she says. "What makes them a candidate?" I ask. "Just being a junior," she replies.

Since all juniors were automatically eligible for the SAT classes, it was at first unclear to me why it had been hard to "recruit" the "African-American population." Yet her next comments suggested that recruiting students by race had seemed difficult socially as well as analytically:

> "Why did you have to recruit privately for the TestPrep program? Why couldn't you announce openly that you were looking for African-American and Latino students?" I ask. "Well, I felt strange doing that. I was shy about it. I felt the program was shitty already for being race-based. The idea of announcing to my classes, 'hey, we're looking for black and Latino students'—I didn't want the kids to get upset," she says. "Who would get upset? The Filipino kids, or the African-American and

Latino kids?" I ask. "Oh, I didn't think about *that* . . . that the African-American and Latino kids might get upset. I mean the Filipino kids," she says. "I mean, they have just as many problems in their communities, and they have the ESL thing, which is *really* screwing up their SAT scores."

The district had requested that its "Chapter something" funds be targeted toward "African-American and Latino students," yet in a place where everyone seemed to have "just as many problems in their communities, " many analysts displayed deep uncertainty about whether these two particular race groups were actually worse off than the others. Expressing a general discomfort with navigating the social and analytic complexities of framing disadvantage in racial terms within Columbus, some deleted such a race analysis altogether. This teacher did not target "races," as it turned out—and in the end, the SAT classes remained "mostly Chinese and Filipino."

People in the district's other "low-income minority" schools recounted similar controversies over analyzing student disadvantage in race-group terms. During a day at the district spent reviewing the district's English proficiency tests in spring 1997, for example, I spoke to two white teachers from Hacienda High, which was going through the same pre-reconstitution evaluation Columbus had just weathered and was viewed in the district as a school predominantly of low-income "Latinos":

> One says that the school's administration told the government club it couldn't go to Washington D.C., "even though they had spent all this time raising money, because they didn't have an African-American on the team—and they didn't have a female of color as a chaperone. This is racism at its worst! I mean, the clubs are open to everyone, all year. So an African-American student finally said 'I'll go.' He didn't want his friends not to go. [Sarcastically, he expands the analysis of those in need:] I mean, I don't see any Filipinos on the football team, so that should be closed down," he says. Bluntly, I ask whether the district's requested reform focus on "black" and "Latino" students was clear to Hacienda's faculty. "Well, there's not supposed to be more than 40% of any one group *at* the school, so I don't know *how* you're supposed to focus on them," replies the female teacher.

With analyses of disadvantage within schools like Hacienda or Columbus complicated both by the required presence of multiple racial "groups" and the preponderance of "low-income minorities," some called it "racist" to "focus on" some "minorities" rather than others. Racial targeting was complicated further by the fact that not all "race group" members were actually identically disadvantaged economically. In each of Columbus's "racial groups," for example, some parents held white-collar jobs as corporate or university administrators; some held community college associate degrees, while a few held master's degrees. While some families struggled to survive on workers compensation or public assistance, others had members holding single decent-paying or multiple low-wage jobs. Some students in each group worked 40-hour weeks to supplement household incomes, while some worked simply for extra pocket money for clothes and movies, and others did not work at all. Some students in each group lived in family-owned homes, some in crowded rented apartments, some in public housing, some in foster homes. Some, further, came from families able to pay for them to attend private Catholic elementary or middle school, where, according to Tina, a former student of mine who had attended Catholic elementary school, "the nuns *didn't play*—you were there to study, to learn, to do your work and *that was it*." Tina, who described herself as "black" and went immediately to college after graduation, often differentiated herself from a Columbus friend she also described as "black" (who remained living at home in a housing project with her family after graduation) by saying that they came from "different backgrounds." Tina herself had "grown up in a house with a father figure around," while her friend grew up in a housing project without a "father figure." "I'm a spoiled brat. I get more than what I need. She has only just what she needs," she explained.

In everyday analyses, such class diversity confounded specific efforts to target racial groups at Columbus for particular assistance. That not all "black" and "Latino" students seemed to be equally "at risk," for example, clouded enrollment in the "African-American and Latino retention programs," two programs based at the nearby community college that attempted to guide a subset of the district's black and Latino students to graduation by taking them off campus for college courses and motivational seminars. Jose, the Columbus-based adviser of the "Latino retention program" (who called himself "Latino"), confessed an analytic dilemma to me one day when I asked him to describe the demographics of his hand-picked class of 30 students: "Originally the program was designed for at-risk kids, but really, there are only about three at-risk kids in the program this semester," he said. It was similarly unclear to Silas, the Columbus-based adviser of the "African-American retention program" (who identified himself as "black"), whether his program was supposed to serve college-bound black students or black students at current "risk" of dropping out of Columbus. While I overheard an administrator in the fall of 1996 telling both men that they would get a sense of who "belonged" in their programs as they noticed the students repeatedly sent to the dean's office, each of them also sometimes described their programs to me as designed for stellar students who had completed their Columbus credits and were already planning the transition to college. By October of 1996, however, Silas was calling some of the parents who were involved in the African-American retention program (and the community college officials who ran it) "damn house niggers," saying, "They're only interested in their bourgeois students. A lot of those kids have parents with master's degrees. This program isn't for them—it's for the kids from the projects."

While Columbus people articulated many complexities of analyzing disadvantage within Columbus, analyses of race-group disadvantage were the ones most explicitly deemed inaccurate.[8] As the last section of this chapter shows, those analyzing inequality in California City at large also focused on openly challenging the accuracy of racial analyses, even as they navigated the analytic complexities of both race and class. Shifting, intricate analyses of how race mattered to the distribution of opportunities in a multiracial, class-diverse school district were necessary attempts at analytic precision; but to some they provoked the very question of whether race mattered to such inequalities at all.

Part 3: From Difficult Analyses of Racial Inequality to No Analyses of Racial Inequality

Speakers trying to analyze inequality outside Columbus often shifted in single sentences between referencing the city's two major inequality systems: a binary one that held all people of color to be unequal to whites, and a multiracial one that considered specific groups of color to be particularly disadvantaged. Carlo (a student who labeled himself sometimes "Nicaraguan," sometimes "Latino"), for example, mentioned to me in one informal interview that schools in California City seemed to give curriculum on "Latinos" short shrift when trying to keep "the blacks and the whites happy." Having framed "Latinos" as a particularly disadvantaged subgroup, however, Carlo suddenly shifted to a binary analysis pitting both "blacks" *and* "Latinos" against "whites":

> "Here in the US, all you see is white people having power, like 187," he said. [*In 1994, California's Proposition 187 had tried to eliminate public services for immigrants deemed "illegal."*] "If you're born here—a white person has the power," he said, adding, "Blacks and Latinos, we don't have rights."

Expanding their analyses of inequality to include the world outside of schools, too, Columbus speakers kept shifting the racial axes of power they argued divided the population. Similarly, in a classroom discussion on "prejudice" led by student leaders from the "Students Talking About Race" (STAR) program, Pedro, who labeled himself "African-American" in the opening round of student introductions, suddenly tried to describe a system of social inequality that seemed both binary and multiracial:

> Pedro said, "If an African-American goes into a white restaurant, they'll take their time to wait on you. *Any* people [will get this treatment], Mexican or whatever, if they don't like your color."

Pedro's description invited a similarly shifting analysis of employment inequality from Enrique, a student who moments earlier had labeled himself "Nicaraguan":

> "You go to the white folks over in the mall, like if you go to the Gap, people follow you," Enrique said. "My homie applied for a job, he's black. I hate white people, to tell you the truth! Why can't I get a job at the Gap, because I'm not white?!" Enrique said.

Having framed himself and his "black" friend as equally disadvantaged non-"whites," Enrique now suggested to Tuli, another STAR leader, that being "Latin" was what disadvantaged him specifically:

Tuli asked, "Why do you think they didn't hire you?" "Because I'm Latin," Enrique said. "How do you know that? It could be because you're underage, or because you're from Columbus," Tuli replied.

All of these comments described multiple systems of inequality that were indeed simultaneous in California City. Yet the very practice of sometimes saying the victims of racial discrimination were non-"whites," sometimes saying they were "Latinos" or "blacks," and sometimes saying that "any" or "all people" were the victims of discrimination seemed to blur the analysis of how such inequality worked. While shifting and multiple axes of power relations were indeed the reality of local inequality, such descriptive movement itself could support the dismissal of race analysis: following Enrique's unstable analysis of inequality at the Gap, Tuli suggested that perhaps getting hired at the Gap didn't involve race at all.

Such analytic instability over defining how race mattered to inequality in California City similarly permeated citywide discourse on who was disadvantaged in comparison to whom. In March of 1999, for example, I attended a presentation suggestively entitled "Beyond Black and White: Youth Perspectives on Affirmative Action" held at the California City Public Library. The event featured a panel of student representatives from three "comprehensive" high schools in the city answering questions about affirmative action posed by two teenage emcees. Most of the students on the panel promptly identified themselves as "Latino," "black," "Chinese," or "Filipino" (one student who looked Latina did not identify herself racially). The students' opinions on affirmative action quickly diverged, but they all agreed that although race should not "matter," people in California City were still judged by the "color of their skin"—and that race *did* still particularly affect the opportunities one was afforded in school.

The event's implied multiracial framework quickly metamorphosed into a binary analysis that included other non-"whites" *with* "blacks" in a dichotomous inequality system. Throughout the panel's discussion of opportunity in the city, the panel members typically described themselves as an aggregated group of "minorities," "blacks and browns," or "people of color" that had fewer opportunities than "whites" in the city (or "Anglos," as two Latino members of the panel put it; one student also referred to whites as "non-colored people"). There were, I noted, no white students present on this panel—in part, perhaps, because they did not regularly enroll at the three comprehensive schools in attendance. Students of color, the panelists also suggested, had fewer opportunities than "whites" because they were typically "low-income": the students referred to themselves several times as "low-income people" or "low minorities," repeatedly deeming California City's "low-income," "run-down," "minority" schools disadvantaged in comparison to "white" schools, particularly in the suburbs (as one black student stated, "Our schools are falling apart!"). However, the students' binary analysis of well-off white suburb/low-income minority city inequality was suddenly complicated by an allusion to an "advantaged" public school *within* multiracial California City: "academic" Whitman High, which not only enrolled "whites" but was actually predominantly "Chinese."

Leaving the complexities of Whitman's place in the city's inequality system largely unanalyzed, the panel described Whitman simply as a school with "more money"—and in skipping over the fact of Whitman's white enrollment and Chinese-American majority, they indicated that Whitman was both the city's icon of educational advantage and its analytic Achilles' heel. The antithesis to "disadvantaged" Columbus, Whitman High was in fact currently plaguing public analysis of how race mattered to the distribution of educational opportunities in the district. And in embodying the difficulties of analyzing a race-class inequality system that was simultaneously binary and multiracial, the particular case of Whitman's "Chinese" students would prompt analysts citywide to argue that perhaps race did not matter to the distribution of educational opportunity in California City at all.

By the 1990s in California City, public policy talk usually referenced only "black" and "Latino" students as the district's "disadvantaged minorities": the label "Chinese" had come almost exclusively to connote educational advantage in the district's desegregation and school enrollment discourse.[9] The "expert report" commissioned by the District Court in 1992, for example, framed "Chinese students" as "a group with a strong record of academic achievement," and it suggested, as legal analysts had once suggested about "whites," that the opportunity to learn in close proximity to "Chinese" students was the city's key educational asset. The report recommended that the district now encourage the voluntary transfer of "disadvantaged minority students" to "high achieving schools" within the district—that it now encourage mixing "black" and "Latino" students not only with "whites," but with "Chinese."

As Dana Takagi (1992) has noted in her discussion of talk of "Asians" throughout California, most public talk of "Chinese" students in California City (who, with a notable implication of persistent foreignness, were rarely called "Chinese-American" in public discourse[10]) placed them on the "white" side of a dichotomous axis dividing the advantaged "races" of the city from the city's "low-income minorities." Only occasionally did observers point out the complicating fact that a good percentage of the "Chinese" students in California City were actually low-income recent immigrants from China languishing, along with other recent immigrants and "low-income minorities," in "reject" schools like Columbus. As Wang and Wu (1996) argue, "the model minority myth ensures that poor Asian-Americans will be ignored," and indeed, in most public discourse on educational opportunity in California City by the 1990s, talk of an almost mythical "Chinese" advantage ignored the complicating reality of poor and underachieving Chinese immigrants. Such talk of successful "Chinese" also typically *replaced* talk of local *white* advantage: a citywide narrative of "Chinese" success, embodied in the unarguable fact that Whitman's high-achieving student body was disproportionately Chinese-American, overshadowed the fact that white students within the city's schools routinely enjoyed educational opportunities that most of their peers of color did not. In erasing talk of white advantage, further, talk of "Chinese" advantage prompted the public policy suggestion that educational inequality should not be analyzed in racial terms at all.[11] Complicated race analysis would soon be replaced by no race analysis, as analysts threw out the baby with the bath water: analysts foundering upon the complications of defining the role of race in the city's complex inequality system would topple the race-based provisions of the city's desegregation plan.

In the late 1990s, the parents of several Chinese-American students who had been denied admission to Whitman challenged the racial balancing provisions of California City's desegregation plan in court, and the vagaries of the city's discourse of inequality blew up. The plaintiffs themselves argued that a race analysis of inequality did *not* any longer accurately fit the city's complex demographics: alleging that their children had been unfairly denied admission to Whitman because of the Consent Decree's limits on any school's enrollment of a single "race/ethnic group," the plaintiffs wanted the entire race-based system of school enrollment in California City thrown out. Ensuing arguments over whether the school district should "take race into account" in enrolling students at Whitman, however, rarely made clear whether all "racial" groups in the city really had equal academic opportunities to become viable candidates for admission. As public debates raged over limiting "Chinese" enrollment at Whitman, the fact that the city's small proportion of "whites" would be well represented at Whitman was often assumed and rarely discussed; the districtwide disparities in pre–high school academic opportunity that had "Latinos" and "blacks" scoring too low on Whitman's admissions tests repeatedly went unexamined. Moreover, public policy discussions hardly registered the stark underrepresentation at Whitman of the city's "Filipino" and "Samoan" students, who tended to join "blacks," "Latinos," and recent immigrants from China at comprehensive, "low-income minority" schools like Columbus. Rather than attempting to deconstruct how race still actually mattered to the complex circumstances of inequality in California City, most debate hinged on the abstract issue of whether it was appropriate to analyze educational opportunity in California City through a "race" lens at all—and in rejecting the complexities and details of race analysis, the district was about to discard sophisticated inequality analysis altogether.

In 1999, the court banned the use of race in school enrollment planning in California City Unified and set an end date for the Consent Decree itself. As one commentator remarked in a California City newspaper in the summer of 2000, the judge had ordered that the district "remove race or use no priorities at all. The district chose the latter." Without a coherent system for distributing any pockets of persistent student "disadvantage" across the city's schools, the schools in California City, as newspapers soon reported, rapidly started resegregating by both race and class. Now prohibited specifically from using race-based desegregation strategies, the district would eventually be released altogether from its long-standing responsibility of remedying patterns of racially ordered educational disadvantage in California City schools.

Conclusion

In our schools and districts, everyday analysts are faced with the daunting task of analyzing how race matters to the opportunity to succeed, one of the most complex analytic and political questions facing academic and legal analysts as well. In California City schools, daily life indeed raised some paralyzing questions. Were all students in a mostly low-income, non-white district or school equally "needy"? Which populations, if any, were to be targeted for extra assistance? And finally, if assistance targeting *racial* subgroups was deemed necessary, how were people supposed to accomplish and justify such assistance within multiracial and class-diverse communities?

No one at "low-income minority" Columbus, where hardly any student was both "well-off" and "white," could argue that "race" was totally irrelevant to the school's disadvantaged status within the district. Indeed, no one ever did. Throughout California City, however—as in the state of California at large— debate over defining and addressing complex racial patterns in educational inequality routinely concluded simplistically that racial analyses of inequality were inherently inaccurate. In our confusion over how race matters to "disadvantage," and over how race should then matter to *remedying* "disadvantage," Americans often end up discarding the possibility of any sophisticated analysis of inequalities that are both racial and economic. Indeed, as we fail routinely to describe accurately the complex dynamics of our existing inequalities, we are choosing more and more not to analyze our inequalities at all.

As U.S. school districts become more and more diverse, our confusions are multiplying: we have little guidance in theorizing remedies for inequalities that are simultaneously binary and multiracial. Columbus offered innumerable snarly examples of such complex disadvantage. "Filipinos" at Columbus, for example—framed sometimes in research as California's most "disadvantaged" Asians (Kitano and Daniels 1988)—stood on a bizarre borderline between perceived advantage and disadvantage: many Columbus people described the school's "Filipinos," who were low income but lived in housing projects far more rarely than the school's "blacks" and "Samoans," as relatively well-off. As a self-described "Latin" student put it once, "Filipino kids" in the Columbus neighborhood often seemed to go to a more prestigious public school or even to private school because of "money." Sitting with me and one of her friends one day in 1998, Tina, a graduated student who described herself as "black," predicted that no "black people" would likely be going to any future Columbus reunions: it would be "all Filipinos," she said, people who had graduated and done things they were proud to come back and report on. Truly, at the 1997 Columbus graduation ceremony, the huge majority of students walking down the aisle in their caps and gowns were "Filipinos"; and far more of them were heading immediately to college than any other Columbus "group." Some inequality—some *racial* and possibly *race-class* inequality—*was* taking its toll within this low-income, kids-of-color community. But how is one to analyze and remedy an inequality this complex, especially without suggesting that Filipino students graduating from a low-tracked, underresourced school for discarded "rejects" had somehow gotten a good deal?

As our city schools and districts become predominantly "low-income minority," and as we acknowledge the complex "multi-polarity of racial identities (not just black and white, but also red, brown, and yellow)" within such communities (Omi and Winant 1994, 158), we are becoming less good at responding to the complicated question of who exactly is to be called disadvantaged, and in comparison to whom. Rarely do we successfully analyze race and class simultaneously, looking within "race groups" for class patterns and within class groups for race ones; rarely do we successfully add to our analyses the complexities of linguistic or neighborhood need. Policymakers wrestling with how *race* still matters to the distribution of educational opportunity founder upon the same social and logical problems as everyday analysts, and the result is sometimes de-raced policy based on the inherently imprecise category of "disadvantage" itself. Strangely, when we contest the accuracy of every description of inequality, our vaguest analyses of inequality are the ones that seem to triumph.

It is difficult to build remedies on such imprecise analyses of need. In November of 1996, immediately following the passage of California's anti–affirmative action referendum, Proposition 209, I noted that in a memo from a nearby UC campus all recruitment references had literally replaced race terms with the term "disadvantaged" (e.g., "new programs to help prepare more disadvantaged and low-income students for study at the University"). After the statistics of the first post-209 UC enrollment became public, however, it became clear that the erasure of race words had not erased racially patterned disadvantage itself: some race groups—"blacks," "Latinos," "Filipinos," "Native Americans"—were even *more* drastically underrepresented at the state's campuses. In California City in the fall of 1999, similarly, Whitman—now restricted from using race to balance its student body—enrolled only 56 new African-Americans and Latinos out of a mostly-white-and-Chinese-American freshman class of around 700. Yet policy analyses that now purposefully ignored the relevance of race could not even begin to address such continued patterns of complex inequality in educational opportunity. Both citywide and statewide, those California analysts who had publicly abandoned the complications of racial analysis offered no useful substitute for grasping the complexities of the state's actual inequalities, which remain to some degree racial even in its most diverse places.

So racial analyses of disadvantage were actively dismissed daily in California City and at Columbus; but certain ways of making race relevant kept reasserting themselves nonetheless. Despite the student population's often seemingly low-income-minority uniformity, there were actually many moments when different "race groups" *were* compared to one another. At Columbus, sometimes people made being "Samoan" different from being "Filipino"; sometimes they made being "Latino" different from being "black." If you were a Columbus student, you were always generally a "low-income minority" or "inner-city" kid in the eyes of your teachers, your school district, and the nation, but at many moments you were also framed as a member of a specific "racial" group. As the next two chapters show, Americans daily re-create ways in which *what* "race" you "are" matters substantially.

Five

The Questions We Ask Most about Race Are the Very Questions We Most Suppress

On a district high school staff development day in March 1997, the principal of a district high school, a man who appeared to be African-American, ran a "diversity" workshop for the small number of teachers who chose his session. He led the conversation directly to racial patterns in achievement, even while suggesting that such conversations were extremely rare:

He said he wanted to offer "a case study of one of our populations—African-Americans—in the district. African-Americans," he said, had been consistently at "a 2.0 grade point or less—Latinos the same. We've spent millions of dollars, the same all over the country." He then put up an overhead projection of the California City Unified School District's districtwide test scores by ethnicity. He told the eight of us who had shown up that he was preaching to the choir, "because you came to this session. Others avoided it like the plague. We generally try to avoid talking about race."

People interested in figuring out the role of race in U.S. schooling often approach the subject with one basic question: having assumed a basic taxonomy of racialized groups, they ask how these groups are achieving relative to one another. This comparative question, which often seems to shift to fit the "race groups" locally available, demonstrates both a fundamental correlation in the United States between race and school performance and a fundamental assumption of this very correlation. A national habit of matter-of-factly thinking racially about school achievement surfaces in both official and casual conversation about education. It emerges constantly in journalistic and public policy discourse. Indeed, it is central to educational research. A series on the "achievement gap" in *Education Week* begins by unself-consciously linking achievement to race, asserting the expectation that the future school performance of the 3.4 million students entering kindergarten in 2000 would be determined largely by "whether they are white, black, Hispanic, Native American, or Asian-American" (Johnston and Viadero 2000). The entry on "Race and Ethnicity in Education" in the *International Encyclopedia of Education* makes the same blunt connection in discussing existing achievement patterns. "The major question," it asks, "is: do differences in race and ethnicity account for differences in the educational achievement and attainment of students?" (Clifton 1994).

Americans routinely think about school achievement in such racial terms. Whether we so openly *describe* school achievement in racial terms, however, depends upon our institutional position—and on who is listening. While researchers of all political stripes regularly ask readers to consider how and why various "race" groups achieve differently in school, for example, this question linking achievement to race is not asked so publicly in all schooling locations. Indeed, many people within schools struggle instead to *erase* race labels from their public talk of school achievement. To many colleagues at school sites, framing achievement publicly in racial terms risks *being* "racist"—and when it comes to achievement, as the principal leading the "diversity" workshop put it, educators "generally try to avoid talking about race."

At Columbus, as we have seen, people sometimes spoke publicly in de-raced language, as if race did not matter, in regard to the very topics to which they privately suspected race mattered most problematically. Achievement was one such topic. In speaking of academic success or failure, it became clear, adults were just as likely to suppress racial labels as to use them. When discussing achievement in the relatively public settings of staff or department meetings, as chapter 4 began to indicate, Columbus adults typically framed the school's students as uniformly academically underperforming. Indeed, Columbus students themselves also typically described the student body as an underachieving unit: while students occasionally noted the representation of the school's various "race groups" in publicly presented honors and classroom rewards, they rarely compared the achievement of these groups in any setting. As Tina, a self-described "black" student, put it, race-group achievement comparisons within Columbus often seemed silly because Columbus was "all Latins, Filipinos, and blacks—it was an all-minority school." In *private* conversations about achievement, however—in hallways, empty classrooms, or off campus locations—Columbus adults were actually routinely comparing the school's "minorities" to one another. Adults privately noted that "Filipinos," elsewhere called an "at-risk" sector of the "Asian-American" community (see Flores 1998), were the school's top achievers along with its "Chinese" students; they framed "black," "Latino," and "Samoan" students as the school's underachievers, and they debated various explanations for these intra-Columbus patterns (the handful of students calling themselves "white" at Columbus was so minute that "whites" rarely made it into such comparisons). Indeed, any adult new to Columbus quickly learned its particular repertoire of privately racialized comparisons and explanations—demonstrating how racialized achievement comparisons often simply shift to fit local demographics.

At Columbus, then, teachers and administrators worried privately about the existence of racial achievement patterns within Columbus, even as they typically spoke publicly only of the achievement of an aggregated body of "students"—and often, as they allowed actual racial achievement disparities within Columbus to be reproduced unchallenged. In the meantime, district representatives and policymakers funneled racial achievement statistics to the court and referenced them in the city newspapers, yet they buried any mention of existing racial achievement patterns when in the presence of educators themselves. As adults at and around Columbus whispered comments about racial achievement patterns in some locations while delivering racial achievement data in matter-of-fact charts in others, they demonstrated a major paradox of U.S. race talk: *the questions we ask most about race are the very questions we most suppress.*

As this chapter will argue, the question of whether and how and why school achievement is racially patterned is also our most often deleted school question, precisely because it provokes our most tormented explanations. While people inside and outside schools seek to find and explain racial achievement patterns as a routine part of schooling analysis, I argue, we name existing patterns primarily when it seems possible to hold other players responsible for them. Indeed, it often seems a habit of both everyday and professional schooling analysis to frame the very racial patterns we expect as someone else's problem: an analytic habit of displacing blame for racial patterns, I argue, allows many of us to avoid the task of dismantling communally the racial patterns that actually exist. Both our silence and our routine *answers* about race-group achievement, I conclude, thus play a covert role in naturalizing such patterns as American "common sense."

In this chapter, then, we look at people at and around Columbus linking race and achievement almost naturally in their talk about schooling (Part 1); we then look at people at and around Columbus suppressing this very connection (Part 2). Finally, we explore the way that the dynamics of blame lead people to both promote and suppress talk of how various "race groups" achieve (Part 3)—and we note, in closing, how speakers routinely displace the responsibility of dismantling any racial patterns found. To demonstrate immediately that the dynamics of race and achievement talk far exceed the boundaries of Columbus or California City, we begin with a brief discussion of the race questions asked in educational research itself.

Part 1: Naturalizing the Link between Race and Achievement

Watching Researchers Frame Achievement Racially

For over a century, American researchers have ranked the school achievement of racial/ethnic groups, with different groups cycling in and out of the ranking system depending on current taxonomies of distinct ethnic or racial populations ("Italians," for example, appeared in achievement rankings in turn-of-the-century New York [Tyack 1993]). When researchers study achievement, any doubts about the boundaries of "race" groups vanish; students simply belong to groups that can be labeled and ranked, and this ranking in turn must be explained. A continuing quest to explain racial achievement patterns permeates many academic disciplines—all of which locate the cause of achievement patterns in different parts of the social world. U.S. researchers have long butted heads in repeated waves of battle over whether natural "ability" is distributed along racial lines (for debunking of such false propositions, see Gould 1981 on nineteenth-century "craniometric" research, and Fraser 1995 on the recent vicious *Bell Curve*),[1] but these days, researchers following the lead of anthropologists (who have spent a century challenging pseudo-scientific connections between "race" and "intelligence") more routinely delineate and compare the "cultural" achievement attitudes or school behaviors of racial/ethnic groups instead.[2] Examining the cumulative effects of many generations in which people in the United States have actively distributed educational opportunities unequally along racial lines,[3] sociologists of education also similarly compare and explain race-group achievement as a disciplinary habit. Policy studies veer effortlessly into statistical comparisons of race-group test scores when seeking evidence of the functioning of district, governmental, or school structures. Psychologists' experiments routinely compare the cognitive performance of children, grouped by "race," on schooling tasks, while psychometricians design academic tests using race as a matter-of-fact variable.

Whatever the discipline, race-group comparisons regularly and openly define educational research questions and methods; researchers routinely frame students matter-of-factly as members of racial groups expected to achieve more or less than one another. While researchers struggle often with documenting and understanding specific social mechanisms causing achievement patterns to be racial, the language of much research discourse unwittingly implies that racial achievement patterns themselves will exist regardless of circumstance (consider, in this regard, the well-meaning assumption of a timeless and universal racial achievement pattern buried in a title like "Asian-American Educational Achievement: A Phenomenon in Search of an Explanation" [Sue and Okazaki 1995]). Researchers rarely admit that their own matter-of-fact research questions about racial patterns, launched from a distance, are themselves evidence of culturally scripted expectations that achievement will *be* racially ordered—and more importantly, that such research questions routinely produce culturally scripted explanations for why racial patterns exist. In a U.S. context, for example, race-and-achievement questions routinely presume certain racial achievement patterns (such as the success of "Asian-Americans"); they also provoke familiar explanations about students' "cultural" or race-group achievement attitudes and behaviors—not analyses of how people across the educational system together produce and allow achievement that is racially ordered.

Consider, for example, an interview situation reported by anthropologist John Ogbu, one of the more influential "sociocultural" analysts of American schooling in recent decades. Despite his critique of the U.S. racialized opportunity structure, Ogbu is known primarily for locating the cause of racial achievement patterns in the behavior and attitudes of student "minorities" themselves. In his first ethnography of a diverse California school (1974), Ogbu proposed what would become his career's central thesis: that certain "minority" groups reacted oppositionally to schooling because of their status and experience in an American system of caste-like inequality. Ogbu set out to argue that racial achievement patterns were not the result of "cultural deprivation" in students' families and communities, as scholars at the time commonly believed; his argument highlighted student choices about how to navigate a system of structural inequality. Students of racialized "minority" groups that had experienced "involuntary" rather than "voluntary" immigration, he argued, recognized their persistent low-caste positions and joined with peer groups in rejecting schooling's potential for social mobility. The well-known conclusions of Ogbu and his colleagues now offer some of the country's most familiar explanations for why students of some "minority" groups pursue school achievement while others "give up."[4]

Ogbu's ethnography included some of his interview questions, which reveal a tendency to prompt informants to talk about achievement in terms both student-centered and racial. Consider the following:

"Some people have told me that black and Mexican-American students are not doing well in school because of the influence of their friends. Do you agree?" (127)

Ogbu not only chose racialized achievement patterns for students to discuss in these interviews; he also repeatedly urged explanations for them implicating students and "their friends." An example of a conversation with one student makes this explicit:

Anthropologist: why do you allow your friends to take you away from school?
Student: I don't.
Anthropologist: all right, why do you goof off then?
Student: that was last year?
Anthropologist: yes. But why? Why did you goof off last year?
Student: because I really don't want to go to school. I didn't care about school.
  [201–2]

Ogbu's rigorous use of student-centered "why" questions ("yes. But why? Why . . .") causes the student to provide a standard American "explanation" for the underachievement of black and Latino students: he himself just "didn't care about school." Throughout his interviews for *The Next Generation*, Ogbu prompted respondents to compare "failing" "racial" or "ethnic" groups ("blacks" and "Mexican-Americans") to "successful" ones ("Anglos" and "Orientals"), and to explain these patterns in familiar terms implicating students themselves. He asked students to rank their own classroom performance in comparison with "the performance of other students of their own race" (87), and then

[handwritten annotation: How do we ask race? Is that r not matter-of-fact? Push beyond expected racialized answers?]

wanted to know "how students from each ethnic group rank their group's performance in relation to other groups" (90). He also asked black and Mexican-American students to "compare the school work of students of their groups with that of Orientals," a race-and-achievement question which, he added in an unintentionally poignant footnote under one table of data, "some students refused to answer" (92).[5]

Such leading questions, routine to research on race and achievement, tend both to matter-of-factly organize discussion around researcher-selected racial achievement patterns and to prompt familiar explanations that locate responsibility for such patterns not in communally built social orders, but in the behaviors of groups of actors presumed to act almost in isolation. As Payne (1984) suggests, research on race and achievement focuses relentlessly on students themselves, rather than on the role played by powerful adult players in racialized systems; many researchers, Payne argues, have "too frequently assumed that understanding inequality is essentially a matter of describing those who suffered from it" (7). As Fine (1997) argues further, research often proceeds as if the achievement of any "race/ethnic" group is a "distinct, separable, and independent" phenomenon, rather than one "produced, coupled, and ranked" within a racializing system (64). Linda Powell (1997) notes, for example, that research focused exclusively on discovering the role of *black* students in "black underachievement" systematically ignores the role that whiteness and white people play in the "knot of minority student failure" (3). Another typical example of an isolated-race-group research question is, "*What is it about Asian students* that helps account for their above-average record?" (see Steinberg, et al. 1996, emphasis added).

[handwritten annotation left margin: ? role of whiteness]

All such research questions are themselves cultural acts, and so are typical answers. At private moments at Columbus, people tapped into this same comparative, matter-of-fact explanatory discourse, talking as if it was common sense that the school's different "race groups" would achieve differently—and often, that they would do so for reasons specific to "race groups" themselves.

Watching Columbus People Frame Achievement Racially

If asked directly in private to compare the school's racialized groups, Columbus adults could easily produce comparisons of these groups' "cultural" achievement behaviors. On one of the few occasions during my research when I asked a directly racialized question about which "groups" at Columbus were more "problematic," for example, Mr. Vane, a teacher who labeled himself as "black," started describing to me racial patterns in achievement behavior that he quickly defined as "cultural":

> "Well, when Latino kids aren't into school, they just don't come. Filipino kids tend to be more passive. They'll come, but they'll sit in class and just not do the work.

Black kids tend to be more verbal, and demonstrative, showy," he said. Later he added, "Like I said, Latinos don't come, Filipinos are more passive—I think it's in their culture to be more passive."

I typically resisted asking Columbus teachers such blunt questions about racial patterns in school achievement, both because such questions could produce predictably racialized answers and because I so rarely heard them ask these questions bluntly of one another. In an important paper entitled "Notes on Queries in Ethnography" (1980 [1964]; the title is a play on a then-classic fieldwork interview manual entitled "Notes *and* Queries in Ethnography"), anthropologist Charles Frake argued that researchers accustomed to arriving in the field with lists of pre-generated questions should instead take time to understand what questions would be behaviorally and logically appropriate to local people.[6] Conscious of such advice about asking culturally appropriate queries, for one year of fieldwork I privately asked teachers a more school-familiar question as a test of adults' propensity to frame achievement racially: "Do you see any patterns in achievement here?" Such "achievement" questions, as it turned out, still always privately produced race-group comparisons. Many teachers would respond first with a general commentary about "the kids"; eventually, however, persistent discussion of achievement "patterns" had teachers offering descriptions of patterns that were racial. In quiet and private analyses, it seemed, framing achievement racially seemed almost common sense.

A few teachers, especially some teachers of color, replied without hesitation to my achievement-related questions with descriptions of racial patterns:

Me: "Do you think all the students here are equally at risk?"
Charla [black teacher]: "I think the African-American students here are more at risk."

In contrast, white teachers talking about student achievement typically hedged for quite a while before finally offering racial comparisons. One day in 1996, for example, I stood talking to a new, young white teacher outside her classroom while her students finished a writing assignment; we were discussing a recent school controversy over giving students "incomplete" ("I") rather than failing grades at the end of the semester. She said she had given "incompletes" to "the students who never came to class." When I asked her if there was "any particular characteristic that ties together all the kids who don't come," she responded, "They seem to be the ones who are really totally disconnected from the community here." Within moments, she added, "It's mostly the RSP kids" (meaning a subset of Special Education students), and after a long pause, she continued:

"I think if you look at the numbers it would probably turn out schoolwide to be the African-American males . . . because they're the ones getting suspended, if you look at the list," she says, referring to a list of suspended students circulated recently to the staff. "I saw that list—did you know the kids? Were they all African-American?"

I ask. "For the most part," she says. "So you'd connect the ones failing to the ones on the list with discipline problems?" I ask. "The ones who *come*, yeah—and act out . . ." she replies, thinking. "And Samoans maybe . . ." she says, pausing again. "I think I'd say there were like three groups of people. The ones who are behavior problems, the ones who are totally disengaged and don't come, and the ones who come every once in a while," she says. "So you're saying the first group, behavior problems, is mostly African-American males?" I repeat, trying to understand. She nods. "And are the other groups African-American males too?" I ask. "No . . . they're very mixed, at least for me," she begins, going into her class to tell the kids to get packed up to go to the library. As they start coming outside to wait near her, I expect her to stop talking, but she doesn't. "I'd say the groups that aren't in there are Chinese and Filipino," she says, as we start walking down to the library. "So I'm confused—who's in these groups?" I ask. "In the 'totally not engaged' group, the no-shows, there are no Chinese, Japanese, or Koreans," she replies. [*Caught up in the analytic groove, I prompt further race-group comparisons:*] "And the Filipinos?" I ask. "They're in the 'out of it' group . . . oh, wait, that's the RSP's—wait—" she says. We're now walking with a black student from the library down to the attendance office. We arrive at the office, and she keeps talking. "Here," she says, grabbing a piece of paper and writing down the word "behavior." Under "*Totally Out Of It*," she writes

—Latino
—Af-Am.

Then she writes "*Coming 1–2 days/week*", and writes under that

—RSP

A black parent enters. We are surrounded by teachers now. [*Our racial descriptions become muted, yet they remain:*] "So in behavior problems, it's mostly these?" I say, pointing to the word "Af-Am." "Yes . . . and in the 'totally out of it's,' the no-shows, it's primarily—these," she says, pointing at the word "Latino." "This is totally unscientific—just my personal impression," she says, smiling. "It's all unscientific," I smile back.

Repeatedly, adults' private analyses of general achievement "patterns" eventually produced descriptions of racial orders. As this new teacher's comments about "Japanese and Koreans" indicated, adults' racialized achievement comparisons eventually flowed easily enough that speakers could even incorporate into their comparisons groups with no substantial presence at Columbus. While the behavior of comparing Columbus's racialized groups seemed initially awkward to some teachers, that is (analyzing achievement patterns in racial terms seemed "unscientific" to some and socially problematic to others), the basic logic of comparing racialized groups appeared automatic. Some teachers—particularly white teachers—would arrive eventually at race-group comparisons even after denying explicitly that racial patterns existed, as in this example involving Mr. Fitsner, a white teacher:

I am talking to Stephen (Fitsner) as we walk down the hallway together toward the department office. I ask him if he's been receiving attendance and suspension lists any more, as all faculty had received these lists a few times in their mailboxes earlier that semester. No, he says, probably because of the recent departure of one of the assistant principals. "It'd be nice to have them so we can know how many people are here every day, who's cutting," he says, describing an idea he has for the in-school suspension of "cutters." Once we are in the office, I ask, "Who do you get the sense is cutting your class?" "The mind-set here is that any slight obstacle in your way keeps you from coming to school," he replies, adding, "Like 'I'm bored,' etc. Some of the excuses are way too slight." "Do you see any pattern in who the cutters are?" I ask. He thinks, pauses, then says, "It's mostly the poor kids . . . the low-skilled. They vote with their feet, say maybe 'Mr. Fitsner's boring.' I take it to some degree on myself." "So you don't mean socioeconomically when you say 'poor'—you mean skills?" I ask. "Yes, skills," he says. "So do you see a pattern in who has the low skills?" I ask. He pauses. "No . . . it's pretty across the board . . . evenly spread . . . no particular ethnic groups . . ." he says.

"So it's pretty even keel . . . interesting . . ." I say. We chat about something else. In a few minutes, I return: "So it's interesting that you say there's no pattern, really . . ." [*My pressuring him to describe an achievement "pattern" before led him spontaneously to deny "ethnic" patterns, but now he proceeds with comparing and ranking the "skills" and achievement behaviors of Columbus's short list of racialized "groups":*] He says: "Black males have the most trouble with acting out, running around the halls, generally seeing what school is for. Black females seem to have less of a problem with motivation, though I see a lot of them running around in the halls . . . Latino students— I'm making huge generalizations now—[*he excuses himself for his racial comparisons, yet continues:*] tend to have lower skills, maybe because of changing schools so often, going back to Central America. Chinese students—I don't really have many Chinese students—but they're really not a problem, I think because of their culture. Filipino students—they have some similar problems with lack of motivation, skills, but they're much more—I dunno . . ." he pauses. (As he pauses, I think to myself, "He's going to say 'respectful.'") ". . . respectful," he finishes. He describes the behavior of a student (whom we both know to be black) and says, "Where a Filipino kid would never do that. Samoan students—" he shakes his head, smiling. "I need to learn more about their culture," he says, pausing. "They are *wild!* Running around the halls. They seem to be good-hearted folk, but . . ."

Even in actively resisting racial descriptions of achievement patterns (such as "no . . . it's pretty across the board . . . evenly spread . . . no particular ethnic groups"), speakers suggested how strongly achievement was linked to race in schooling logic. Indeed, Mr. Fitsner soon went on to compare the school's major "ethnic" groups to one another—and his comparisons were simultaneously descriptions of racial patterns and explanations for them. Predictably, these explanations focused primarily on the "cultural" achievement behaviors of the "ethnic groups" themselves: while Mr. Fitsner had "taken" achievement patterns "to some degree on himself" when speaking generally of student boredom, he veered quickly into comparisons of how Columbus's various "ethnic groups" approached school. As other notes indicate, even adults who identified themselves as members of the "groups" being explained promoted to me such "cultural" comparisons of students' achievement orientation and school behavior:

> I have just sat in the class of a new Filipino teacher. It is now lunchtime, and we are talking about the troubles he is having with three students from his class [*a black student, a Latino student, and a Samoan student*]. A few Filipino students are in his room for lunch. George, a Chinese boy from his class, comes in to learn some martial arts moves. "He's a good kid," the teacher explains to me. "I couldn't trust many others to control themselves." He says that George and Amalia (a Filipina girl who had also been in the class) "make the most of what's given them—they just do it, and ask for more." "But what makes them buy in, and not the other three?" I ask. "Background . . . race . . . color," he says, adding, "If they buy into English class—if they believe in authority, in the role of the teacher. It's cultural, really." "What do you mean?" I ask. "Like I relate better to kids who believe in authorities—Asian," he says after a pause, with a grin of embarrassment.

Such "cultural" explanations seemed ready support in private discussions about Columbus achievement patterns; with the school's handful of "white" students too numerically small to make it explicitly into such school-level comparisons, adults typically just compared Columbus's other five "groups" to one another. Over the phone one evening, for example, John, another Asian-American teacher, started speaking comparatively of how the advanced classes in his department were "almost all Chinese and Filipinos—very few Latinos, African-Americans, or Samoans." When I asked him what he "made of" this pattern, he replied bluntly, "I think they have more stable families—and a culture where education is truly valued, and not given lip service." Later in the conversation, he added that he thought such "valuing" of education was "not in black families—of course there are exceptions." "I have no proof," he added in a sheepish tone. "This is my own opinion."

As stated earlier, Columbus students typically did not offer "opinions" comparing the achievement of the school's "racial groups" at all. If prompted, however, on rare occasions students too could offer racial descriptions of achievement patterns within Columbus or within other district schools. Tina, a self-described "black" student, was telling me one day that she had been accepted at "academic" Whitman but didn't "want to be in that environment" because it wasn't "black" enough. When I asked her to describe who had gone to Whitman from her middle school, she responded, "Filipino kids, and of course Chinese kids." My notes provided only a handful of such comparisons, and a smaller handful of comments explaining these patterns as "cultural." For example, two former students, Filipina girls, talking to me about school differences during their free period one afternoon suddenly described several schools in the district as "upper class" and "Chinese style." After a few blurted questions from me about this claim, they were soon comparing the "cultural" achievement orientations of "Filipino" families to those of "Chinese" families:

> L says, "Columbus is really a low economic school. If you were at Roosevelt, Whitman, Newton, Jefferson . . . they're more upper class, more Chinese style." "What do you mean, 'upper class'?" I ask. "More Chinese style," she repeats. "What does that mean?" I ask. L says, "They push their kids. They *won't* go to Columbus, they wouldn't *let* them. The kids have to work hard." "Filipino parents aren't like that?" I ask. [*A blatantly comparative race question on my part, which produces more matter-of-fact racial comparisons:*] L: "Chinese parents don't care about being happy." C: "Filipino parents don't care where you go to school as long as you're going somewhere. It's your individual choice to learn, to do your work." L: "Filipino parents care about happiness, and reaching your goals." [*Here, I blurt out a long-held hypothesis about racial achievement patterns within Columbus:*] "Do you get the sense that the Filipino students *here are more successful?*" I ask. C says, as if realizing, "Yeah! The honors class is all* Filipino." L: "It *has* been always." [*And like a typical researcher, I return to urge explanations:*] "Why do you think? Weren't you saying that Filipino parents don't push their kids?" L: "But they stress the importance of reaching your goals, and education as the way to do that." C: "Like my mom, she never had the opportunity to go to school and stuff in the Philippines, so she encourages me to." L: "And *my* dad *had* the opportunity, and he took it, and he's successful now, and he's like 'don't you want to be like me?'" The bell has rung, and we are walking out of the quad. "It's all cultural, Ms. Pollock, I *told* you," L says.

The students had offered a quick racial comparison of student achievement orientation; I myself had turned the comparison into the organizing logic of our conversation. Learning to quietly compare the achievement of Columbus's major student "cultures" like this—comparing "blacks" to "Filipinos" to "Chinese" to "Latinos" to "Samoans"—was for adults, myself included, a key aspect of learning how to analyze Columbus's "diversity." Reconstitution itself was key in bringing this phenomenon to my attention, as it became possible to watch an entire staff of Columbus newcomers—many of whom had never worked before with Columbus's particular combination of populations—accommodate the familiar practice of racial achievement comparison to local demographics. On a tour of the school building on the first day of the new staff's orientation, for example, a newly hired Filipino teacher and I peered at a 1995 graduation picture that had been left on the wall in somebody's emptied classroom. "Hmm," he said quizzically as we left the room, as if to start a conversation. "Did that picture surprise you?" I asked. "Yes. I expected it would be more diverse," he said. "Mm-hmm," I said, hoping he'd say more. "I guess I thought there would be more African-Americans there. Maybe they didn't show up for the picture . . . or maybe they didn't graduate," he said. "I think it's some of the former and more of the latter," I said. We both laughed a little awkwardly.

Graduation pictures in the making prompted similar private racial comparisons from Columbus adults. On one morning that March, I came early to school to see about 150 graduating seniors get their picture taken in the school's interior quad. As my fieldnotes describe, the scene prompted both me and another teacher to start counting graduates in comparative racial terms:

> Before school, the senior picture is being taken . . . I count around 10–11 black kids. It's hard to count Latinos—I think that at the time I don't even think about doing that because most of what I notice is how few students are black. I see Katrina, Sarah, and two or three other black girls with senior sweaters on. Jim is the only black guy. Lavanne is the only black person in the student association front row. In the white shirt section in the back are Leslie, Takisha, Jay, LeRoy [*black students*] . . . Charles [*a black teacher*] comes over and says to me, "this is the senior class?" He is silent, then counts out loud. "What are you counting?" I ask. "African-American students," he says. "I counted eleven," I say. ". . . fourteen," he finishes. "They're mostly female, too," he adds. Someone comes up to ask me something and so we don't get to discuss his opinion of this.

Both before and after reconstitution, people at Columbus occasionally spoke publicly in such comparative race-group terms about the school's graduation demographics when referencing a handful of achievement programs based at outside institutions. Public faculty meetings and the school bulletin, for example, sometimes provided mention of the "African American" and "Latino retention programs," the two community college–based programs designed to increase "black" and "Latino" graduation rates through special college classes offered to a selected group of students who left Columbus midday. In 1997, similarly, a district-funded tutoring program was inaugurated to serve "Filipino" students at Columbus after school; the program was administered by a number of self-labeled "Filipino" teachers who suggested privately that most achievement programs ignored Filipino students altogether (as one teacher who came from another school to tutor explained, the tutoring program was attempting to heighten public awareness of the "psychology of the Filipino child"). A sign on some teachers' doors in 1996 publicly advertised a nearby university's "Filipino Academic Student Services" program, while a 1997 Columbus newsletter advertisement for a "Step to College" program at the local state university announced with similar racial bluntness, "Attention all Latinos—it's time we think about our future." The graduation program each year recognized students for "completion of the African American/Latino retention program." Some graduating students also received small scholarships from the district's "Organization of Filipino American Educators," "Alliance of Black School Educators," and "Latin American Teachers Association."

At the end of their careers at Columbus, students could be recognized publicly within district and higher education structures as race- or ethnic-group members who had achieved exceptionally. Their achievement, however, was not monitored so publicly in racial terms throughout their Columbus careers. As I realized over time, most students would become "Latino" or "black" or "Filipino" in public achievement talk only at the very end of the academic pipeline. After listening more closely to talk of the few racially targeted achievement programs operating at Columbus, further, I realized that only off-campus and after-school programs—run by people identified as members of the particular "race groups" in question—targeted students racially for academic assistance. Achievement programs taking place inside the Columbus building during the school day were never labeled racially. An "Extra Tutoring and Counseling" (ETC) program that existed before reconstitution, for example, targeted "bottom quartile" students with low test scores and grades for several daily class periods of academic attention. Nobody publicly discussed the program as being geared toward eliminating racial disparities, nor was the program's enrollment (which was majority black, with some Latinos and Samoans) discussed publicly as racially ordered. In the second year after reconstitution, similarly, Columbus instituted another program targeting students with low test scores and grades, identical in aim to the ETC classes that had existed before. Some teachers privately described the program as the school's effort at "helping black students without calling them 'black.' "

While people at Columbus regularly wondered in public about the school-wide graduation rate, further (people said that somewhere between 50 percent and 80 percent of Columbus freshmen ended up graduating), they never publicly counted the racial demographics of graduation. Corroborating suspected racial graduation patterns required quietly taking the list of graduates and comparing it to a school enrollment list that included the official racial self-identifications families had once given the district placement office. On this evidence, the majority of students who graduated from Columbus were labeled "Filipino" or "Chinese": "African American," "Hispanic," and "Samoan" students seemed disproportionately not to graduate. The website of the state Department of Education provided additional information on the students who graduated ready to attend the University of California (having passed a required sequence of science, math, and English classes); it demonstrated that Columbus's "black" and "Latino" students were—in comparison to the school's "Chinese" and "Filipino" students—drastically underprepared for college. Other student lists showed that "Filipino" and "Chinese" students dominated not only the honor roll, but state and national societies requiring high grade-point averages; and a quick look at Columbus classrooms demonstrated that the existing AP class, English, was disproportionately "Filipino," while the one calculus class available was almost exclusively "Chinese." Analyzing various lists from my own teaching year in 1996, similarly, I noticed that once I disaggregated the extreme cases in my lists—the students actually failing classes, getting expelled, or rarely coming to class at all—these students seemed startlingly "black" and "Latino."

Such racial tallies often felt crude, as they erased students' individual achievement trajectories.[7] Data on racial achievement patterns within Columbus also obscured the fact that all Columbus students were academically underprepared when compared to many other students in the district or state. Yet some disturbing racial achievement patterns *did* exist within Columbus—and while adults struggled privately to name and explain these patterns, in their public talk of academic achievement they almost never referenced students in racial terms at all. As the next section shows, adults at and around Columbus buried the link between race and achievement as often as they forged it.

Part 2: Burying the Link between Race and Achievement

In some public contexts, adults in the California City Unified School District indicated that counting achievers in racial terms was a basic procedure of the district's everyday objective: evaluating student performance. Printed lists of district goals made available to parents occasionally listed raising the achievement of "African-Americans" and "Hispanics" as one of the superintendent's top priorities. The district also publicly recognized some academic successes in racial terms, organizing public parades for "African-American" or "Latino" students with high grade-point averages; occasionally, marquees in town would publicly congratulate "African-American" students on making the district's honor roll. The subtitles of several voluntary district conferences, some of which were held at local hotels, also matter-of-factly labeled achievement a race issue, again particularly in reference to black and Latino students ("Utilizing the Prior Knowledge and Life Experiences of African American Students in the Achievement of Educational Excellence"; "Working Together to Improve Latino Educational Achievement"). Such titles, along with the occasional presence of administrators at these racially targeted achievement workshops, suggested that the district sometimes proceeded with an explicitly racial analysis of student achievement.

However, the district revealed its racial achievement analyses only sporadically. Even as it submitted disaggregated information to court monitors on the academic progress of each of its "racial/ethnic groups" in the mid-1990s, for example, the district typically distributed to the public only the most generalized versions of these data. With a little probing at the district office in the mid-1990s, California City residents could pick up books of statistics with charts and graphs displaying racially disaggregated scores on standardized tests. Yet the information available in these books, or even that available on the district web page reporting on the desegregation order, only demonstrated certain districtwide trends: none of this data allowed the public to compare race-group achievement within any particular school. When I walked into the district's testing and assessment office in 1996 asking for school-level scores that were racially disaggregated, an employee predictably handed me books that displayed only districtwide patterns. When I remarked that I had assumed school-level scores were public record, he informed me that such data was "not exactly public."

Only the state education department's website revealed how Columbus's different "race groups" were doing on standardized tests and college requirements, suggesting that it gets easier to publicly describe people in racial terms the further one gets from those being described. At top-level, closed district meetings, too, according to a high-ranking official of the city's teachers' union who spoke to me privately at the union office, "African-American and Latino students at the 25th percentile" or "low-achieving African-American and Latino students" was like a "cant, or mantra"; yet descriptions of existing racial achievement patterns typically vanished from district representatives' talk of "achievement" when they were speaking in the presence of teachers. While the superintendent occasionally pledged publicly in the newspaper that he was working to improve the achievement of "blacks" and "Hispanics," the district's handful of open-invitation professional development workshops targeting these populations were held primarily with volunteer attendance on non-school time. Further, while talk of "African-American" and "Latino" standardized test scores appeared sporadically in press releases on reconstitution (as one California City headline put it, "School Test Scores Good, Mostly: but C.C. High-Schoolers, Blacks, Latinos Still Lag"), district representatives did not inform Columbus faculty directly of racial patterns in the school's test scores, teachers later reported, until an orientation of a new group of staff two years after reconstitution. In presenting that year's incarnation of Columbus staff with the school's current test scores disaggregated by race, district representatives fleetingly suggested that teachers should notice the achievement patterns of "African-American" and "Hispanic" students. According to participants, however, the brief discussion did not address what to make of these racial achievement patterns or how to respond to them—and the staff did not publicly discuss test scores in racial terms again. Subsequent discussion of test results referred only generally to "the bottom quartile."

Throughout the district, race-group achievement comparisons appeared in some institutional locations and vanished in others, suggesting that the racial descriptions possible in policy or academic statements are often not so possible in the discussions between research/policy people and school people, or among school people themselves. Ironically, the kind of racial data that policymakers used to justify firing Columbus staff—racialized assessments of student academic performance—were exactly the kind of data that policymakers did not discuss openly at the school level, and exactly the kind of data that Columbus adults themselves did not publicly collect. Indeed, as a researcher I did not feel comfortable collecting racial achievement data publicly either. When I had become interested, during the 1996–97 school year, in seeing Columbus grades and absences sorted by race, I had predicted in my notes that "it will be almost impossible, politically, to get them from the principal"; when I mentioned to one white teacher that I wanted more quantitative data on absences and grades at the school, he replied, dramatically feigning paranoia, that it would be hard to get because "it could be *used*!" "I don't want to ask the principal," I sighed. "She'll kill you," he said decisively.

Over my three years of participant observation at Columbus, there was only one sequence of incidents in which adults on school grounds proposed publicly that Columbus faculty should analyze student achievement in racial terms. Together, the incidents suggested that although the question of how different race groups achieved permeated California City schooling discourse, this very question was not easily asked in public—or, for that matter, easily answered.

On a school holiday the winter after the new faculty had arrived post-reconstitution, a guest speaker, Mr. Trestor, addressed a small cadre of teachers in a voluntary workshop on school reform. Confessing that he was one of the original architects of the district's reconstitution experiment, Trestor said he was now a district consultant. He promptly gave the assembled teachers a quiz on the history of desegregation policy in the city, which teachers were amused to report they resoundingly "failed." Back in a full-group discussion, the principal answered many of the questions herself. When Trestor asked if anyone could tell him the basic goals of the city's desegregation agreement, for example, teachers balked, shaking their heads; to my surprise (given the school's de-raced reform discourse) the principal replied, "To equalize the achievement of African-American and Latino students, and to integrate the schools." Nodding, Trestor turned on the overhead projector and put up a sheet listing the "Goals of the Consent Decree" that predictably buried these race labels in the district's language of "all":

1. Integration of all CCUSD schools.
2. Academic excellence for all CCUSD students.

During the rest of the workshop, the words "African-American" and "Latino" did not reemerge from this usual talk of reforms designed to achieve generic "academic excellence"; the public discourse of "all" was as routine at the new Columbus as it had been at the old. Yet this was the first and only time that the specifically racial goals of reconstitution had been suggested publicly to the new staff, and in a conversation about achievement several weeks later, race labels briefly resurfaced. One of the teachers who had been present at the workshop, a white woman, was the editor of the Columbus teachers' newsletter, and she reported on the event on her front page. She reprinted Trestor's quiz and the district's "Philosophical Tenets," asking, "How many of you know that we are a Consent Decree school? More importantly, how many of you even know what the Consent Decree is?" Her article concluded with a race-and-achievement question that had never been asked at Columbus quite so publicly, before or after reconstitution. "And if the target population was African-American and Latino students," she wrote, "have we succeeded in our goal to improve their academic excellence?"

A few days after the newsletter came out, I went to talk to its author about the faculty's response to it. She said that most people had been debating one of the reprinted "Philosophical Tenets"—the one suggesting that teachers were responsible for student failure. "Hmm . . . and you had a line about—what was it? 'If serving African-American and Latino students was our goal, I'm not sure if we accomplished it,' or something like that. Have you had any response on that?" I asked. "No," she said, smiling wryly.

Her question linking achievement to race was to hang in the air without response during the days the newsletter was distributed. It then disappeared. The question of how achievement related to race, she suggested, was omnipresent but only sporadically articulated:

"But I think we've really failed miserably at that. I used to teach at the continuation high school, and all the kids there were African-American and Latin—there was like one Chinese kid and maybe two white kids. So to think those are the populations that get kicked out, that are the problem kids, the cast-offs . . . and at Columbus, those are really the groups that are failing overall," she said. "When you say that, what images come to your mind as evidence?" I asked. "My grades . . . the ones failing. When I call home with problems, it's mostly the African-American and Latin kids," she said. "What do you mean when you say 'problem'?" I asked. "Well, when I call home about a problem, a student not doing their work or being disruptive, it's almost always African-Americans or Latins. The ones that are being disruptive, distracting are almost always African-American; the ones that are not doing their work are about half African-American, half Latin," she said. "These are just my impressions. I think to check it, it should be done statistically," she continued, saying, "I should actually do that, look at my grades. Maybe I could do that for next time." "For the newsletter?" I asked. "Yeah . . . well, the only thing is that I'm sort of wary of doing that, because race is such a tough subject, and people could easily get offended. I wouldn't be *doing* it to offend people, just to inform them, to give them information, to point out a problem," she said. "Could you bring it up in a faculty meeting?" I asked. "I don't think Margaret [*the principal*] would want to hear it— she wants to discuss solutions, not problems," she replied. "And actually I'm not sure the other people would either. They want to *do* things . . . and the thing about bring-ing it up at faculty meetings is that nothing would get done."

Columbus teachers, of course, talked all the time in public about how to solve achievement "problems"; they just did not talk about how to solve achievement "problems" that seemed racially ordered. Describing racial achievement patterns, as she suggested, involved far more than simply provid-ing "information." In raising and marking especially "tough" academic "prob-lems" in racial terms, it veered into the territory of potential offense. While her article's title ("A Picture of Reality?") implicitly asked whether other people at Columbus saw racial achievement patterns, the newsletter editor was to find that her colleagues would not easily answer this question in public conversa-tion. One month later in a small-group meeting after school on the Columbus "vision," she spoke up again with her question about researching the link be-tween achievement and race. It was quickly, and actively, buried under general talk of "low" and "high" achievement:

> She says, "Can I just add one thing? This is just my trip right now . . ." She pauses. "I think if 30% of our students are failing . . . then we should really look at the *ethnicity* of who's failing and try to serve the needs of *those* kids. For example, I went to a workshop last week for a program to help African-American students. It was really wonderful. They have programs at the elementary level and for middle schools . . . but they don't have a pilot program in a high school yet, so . . ." she stops. Amy [*white teacher*] says, "I don't think we should just focus on the needs of the low-achieving students—I think we have to focus on the high-achieving students too." Someone murmurs assent. "We need AP classes here," Amy finishes. Lawrence [*black teacher*] turns to Kathy [*white teacher*] and says, "Are we gonna start tracking then?!" The principal says, "Can I respond to that? We *do* have AP classes here. The teachers need to know they have them and what they entail. There was a problem with de-termining who was supposed to be in them . . ." The conversation moves on to what to do next Monday at the staff development meeting.

In the privacy of her empty classroom some weeks later, the newsletter editor and I sat down and examined her class grades. As she had suspected, "black" and "Latino" students were indeed "statistically" failing disproportionately. Yet the subject of "the ethnicity of" who was "failing" or who was taking advanced classes at Columbus never emerged in public talk of student achievement, and I did not hear the newsletter editor raise her question about race and achieve-ment again for the rest of the school year.

At and around Columbus, it seemed, race-group achievement comparisons vanished at the very moments when adults came together to discuss improving academic achievement. Indeed, adults actively trained each other to bury any link between race and achievement, as my own experience proved. After I attended one contentious faculty meeting on school "problems" in the winter of 1997, an administrator approached me in a corner of the hallway:

> "I'm getting somewhat confused about the focus of your study," she said. "You seem very unfocused. I thought you were writing about diversity, so it seems odd to me that you haven't been to any of the places where diversity is explicitly addressed, like the clubs, the unity club . . . I keep being surprised at the places you show up. You seem to show up everywhere," she said. She was surprised, for example, that I had come to the recent workshop with Mr. Trestor. "Well, I think it's important to know how the district has dealt with diversity—that will be a piece of this," I said. "I think you're collecting too much data," she said. "Yeah, you're probably right," I said nervously.

Her comments suggested that "diversity" was supposed to remain in contained spaces, like Columbus's handful of racially targeted social "clubs." "Diversity" most certainly would not be explored publicly in a school reform workshop—a space for discussing how to improve student achievement. District representatives expressed to me even more explicit assumptions that a "diversity" study would steer clear of achievement issues. Months earlier, as I had struggled to get district clearance to continue my study of race talk (which I had anxiously titled "diversity talk" in my own colormute move) at the newly reconstituted Columbus, a district administrator explained the rejection of my first research proposal over the telephone (I eventually received clearance with the new principal's support). "Diversity" issues, she said bluntly, had nothing to do with "achievement":

> "We want research proposals that will increase the academic achievement of our students," she explained. "Research on diversity, curriculum, that's nice to know—but it's not of an immediate impact. It won't have an immediate impact on the achievement of students."

In contrast, some people suggested that a "diversity" study would de facto relate race to achievement, and that the subjects, when linked, would be too dangerous for the district to handle. On one of the anxious days after the rejection of this first research application, Maverick, the black security guard, explained my situation:

> "You know why they don't want you doing research here, it's because they're afraid you'll tell the *truth*. They're afraid you'll tell the truth!" he said. I admitted that I was shocked by the district's lack of interest in "diversity," given that the district's first "philosophical tenet" was that kids "need to learn to live in a world characterized by cultural diversity." "Di*ver*sity," he said, rolling his eyes. "Diversity is not the issue! The issue is *racism*," he said, looking straight at me. "How to function within a racist society. They're wondering why the kids are failing and why they can't read and why

they're ripping up the schools. They're afraid you'll tell the *truth*. I'm gonna tell it the first chance I get." He kicked some dust.

As Maverick put it, the district was afraid a "diversity" study might reveal the "truth" about the link between race and achievement—that in "a *racist* society*," the kids were *failing*. More importantly, he implied, the district was also afraid of the word "*why*"—afraid that my study might uncover a world of blame for racially patterned "failure." Schools, indeed, are institutions saturated with blame, in which a description of any achievement pattern immediately prompts an explanation of who is to blame for it. Describing a racial achievement pattern is particularly charged, as such descriptions typically either hint at the presence of "racism," or—depending on their location of blame—risk *being* "racist." It was not surprising, perhaps, that people at and around Columbus often repressed any mention of the racial patterns they found—or that when they did describe racial patterns, as the final section of this chapter demonstrates, they typically sought to explain them as the responsibility of others.

Part 3: The Role of Blame in Race and Achievement Talk

Around Columbus, a handful of arguments often circulated to explain various achievement patterns: "the district," "economics," "culture," and "parents." As seen in chapter 4, Columbus people, both adults and students, argued regularly that "the district" funneled students with academic and behavioral difficulties into "comprehensive" schools like Columbus rather than to the city's handful of "academic" schools; noting that students at these "comprehensive" schools were also majority low-income, they also argued that the district systematically distributed opportunities based on "economics." In contrast, private explanations by adults that implicated "culture," as well as those that implicated "parents," typically involved comparing race-group achievement within Columbus—and especially, as both Mr. Vane and Mr. Fitsner's comments (Part 1) indicated, comparing how Columbus's various racial or "ethnic groups" approached school. Particular "cultural" explanations, such as Mr. Fitsner's "Filipinos are more respectful," recycled often enough around Columbus that I could hear the ends of explanatory sentences before they were spoken. Indeed, descriptions of racial achievement patterns typically functioned simultaneously as explanations for them—often, explanations implicating the achievement behaviors of student "ethnic groups" themselves.

While some Columbus adults privately blamed student or district behavior for achievement patterns, the district's "reconstitution" strategy unsubtly placed responsibility for student failure on teachers and school administrators. As Payne (1984) argues, "When the problems of bad schools are not seen as resulting from the cultural characteristics of the children, they are likely to be seen as resulting from poor teachers rather than, say, poor superintendents. . . . In general, the higher one ranks in the hierarchy, the smaller one's chances of being studied as a possible cause of social problems" (13). Indeed, after reconstitution, descriptions of the old Columbus vaguely blamed the previous staff for everything from student achievement to the physical decline of the building. Districtwide, teachers anticipating the threat of reconstitution often argued that they were being blamed unfairly. When one 1997 districtwide professional development day for high school teachers began with a long motivational speech by an invited guest who warned that adults often labeled students as "unable to learn," a Hacienda High School teacher stood up and said loudly, "All of us being targeted for reconstitution have been told that *we* can't learn." Applause soon turned into a roar.

Controversy over the district's "Philosophical Tenets," written originally to articulate the basic philosophy of the Consent Decree, centered on "the eighth tenet," which read as follows in the late 1990s: "Teachers, administrators and staff are partners with students in the learning process. If students fail, all partners should accept full responsibility for this failure and take action to insure success." In the mid-1990s, the union president had forced the wording of this tenet to be broadened from "*teachers* will accept full responsibility for this failure" to the statement that included administrators and students themselves. A subsequent union president argued that parents should be implicated in the tenet as well.

Debating the players to blame for school failure was actually a process central to daily school life. Columbus teachers often blamed attendance problems on students' lack of motivation, even as they lambasted administrators for doing little to address truancy and tardiness. In turn, students routinely accused teachers of making classes "boring" and administrators of taking tyrannical measures to punish latecomers. Formal assessment events, like grading periods, were particular occasions for debating who was responsible for problematic outcomes; and in a district context where low student performance primarily seemed to make school-level adults look bad, school adults sometimes deleted evidence of poor performance altogether. As one Asian-American teacher complained to me in 1997:

> "Nobody will sit down and have honest discussion about the problems. Cite me one meeting where we were allowed to discuss problems *honestly.* Attendance is very bad, classes are really small. Let's get out the records and *discuss* them. Get out your roll books—who has *never come? Why* did you give people incompletes?"

While pleading for "honest discussion," of course, she herself indicated that discussion of achievement "problems" often led to disagreement about who was responsible for them. Earlier that year, Columbus had weathered substantial debate over whether to give "incomplete" rather than failing grades to students who had missed numerous classes and turned in insufficient work.

The district had allowed the "incompletes," an action that some teachers interpreted as an attempt to avoid claiming responsibility for the high volume of Fs at reconstituted Columbus. Thomas, a white teacher rehired from the previous staff, suggested to me one day that this battle over assessing students was deeply racialized. While teachers held both the district's practices (the "system") and students themselves responsible for student underachievement, he said, the district in turn blamed teachers, positioning them as "racist" people who created racial achievement patterns through their very expectations of students:

> He says the new teachers now were starting to make the same complaints about the system that were made before—about the disciplinary transfers into Columbus, and about how many "Special Ed" students Columbus had. "The principal said at a meeting that there were so many Special Ed kids here we should be considered a Special Ed school. And I was like, if Teresa [*the former principal*] had said that last year they would have used it as evidence to lynch her—if any teachers had said it it would've been interpreted as groaning. It would have been 'those old racist teachers, they have low expectations for their students,'" he said. "How big was the 'racist' part of the 'old racist teachers' thing?" I asked. "I think it was a *big* part of it all along—a *big* undercurrent," he said. "Why do you think that? Was it ever said explicitly?" I asked. "It was things said at board meetings about teachers having low expectations," he said, mentioning the board president [*a black man*], and the superintendent [*a Latino man*]. "But there are no high expectations here *or* there—I mean look at the 'incompletes,' how much lower can your expectations get? The kids knew they had to be here, they knew what they had to do," he finished.

To many teachers, the district's talk of "low expectations" was a veiled accusation that teachers themselves produced racial patterns by expecting reduced achievement—both from students of color as a block and from certain "race groups" in particular. For the district, notably, "low expectations" were evidenced when teachers gave students of color grades that were unacceptably low; for Thomas, "low expectations" were evidenced when teachers gave students of color unearned high grades with the district's blessing. Race labels rarely appeared in district talk of teachers' "low expectations," but some teachers also suggested that the district particularly blamed "*white*" teachers for having them: as one white teacher suggested to me in private during the reconstitution controversy, district evaluators thought that "kids here have disparity because teachers are racist," and that "people here are racist because they are white." At any school with "racial disparities," he added, the blame would always fall on "white teachers."

At one voluntary, after-school district workshop in 1999—subtitled "A Series of Workshops about African-American Students"—the superintendent gave an opening address that suggested with unusual directness that racial achievement patterns in the district were a result of educators' racialized expectations.

Arguing that in California City there was not yet "success for all students," the superintendent explained bluntly that the district was still "wrestling" with "instilling the expectation that all students regardless of race will achieve":

> The superintendent described a science fair he had attended recently, saying he was interested in "who was there, who wasn't there." "Not a single African American student participated in that project—and one Latino," he said. He suggested standing in front of libraries and museums and "counting the African American and Latino kids" who entered . . . There needed to be a host of professional development activities on these points, he concluded.

While the superintendent proposed "instilling" in the district's "professionals" the "expectation that all students regardless of race" could "achieve," he revealed his own racialized expectations regarding "success" patterns in the city's schools: indeed, he suggested waiting in front of libraries for such racial patterns to show up. Yet even as the superintendent implied that concerned adults *should* be on guard for such inequitable racial patterns, the district's sporadic "professional development" sessions rarely addressed the possibility of either dismantling *or* proactively utilizing such jointly held racial "expectations." Indeed, few district communications with teachers about improving schooling framed student achievers in racial terms at all. At these rare moments when district representatives even mentioned existing racial patterns in the presence of teachers, they usually simply implied that teachers were at fault for expecting these patterns—even as the district itself quietly continued to expect them too. Adults throughout California City, it seemed, both expected racial achievement patterns and critiqued other players for actually creating them— and in skirting any discussion of joint responsibility for such patterns, they precluded any joint discussions of how exactly the racial patterns they all expected might be avoided.

Those players who feel closest to the production of racial patterns, it seems, often become most afraid of mentioning their existence. After two years around Columbus, I myself would hear a student coming late to class and anticipate that she would be "black"; I regularly assumed that honor roll lists would largely display names that were either "Filipino" or "Chinese." By the time I attended the first rehearsal of a traditional Columbus ceremony in May 1996, in which my former sophomore students were to be recognized publicly as the school's new seniors, I wrote in my notes that I wanted to

> test my hypothesis that there won't be any African-American or Latino kids there, and sure enough, there aren't!

Even as I came so self-consciously to wait for students to achieve differently along racial lines, however, I said nothing publicly about the racial achievement patterns I actually saw. While arguing privately and in my writing that school and district adults were allowing racial achievement patterns to be reproduced unfettered, I never let on in public that I myself saw racial patterns within Columbus. Afraid of having to publicly explain such patterns—or, more precisely, afraid of the repercussions of publicly blaming groups of people right around me—I just waited quietly for racial patterns to manifest themselves every time I returned.

Conclusion

Americans share expectations of racial achievement patterns, yet we do not coordinate very often to prevent them. Having naturalized racial achievement patterns as normal school orders, we rarely talk seriously together of how our own practices might *undo* achievement patterns that are racial. Americans are experts at thinking communally about race and achievement problems, but novices at thinking communally about race and achievement solutions—and as the battle between competing explanations of racial achievement patterns rumbles on, the connection between race and achievement remains both an omnipresent presupposition of American educational discourse and schooling talk's most anxious void. Ironically, in many of our schools and districts, racial achievement patterns have become submerged problems waiting to be discovered as well as obvious problems waiting to be remedied. With race a hidden subject "at the outer limit of every actual discourse" about achievement, in schools and districts racial patterns in achievement appear to be secrets that at once must and must not be discovered, threatening patterns that are dangerous, difficult, and almost, as Foucault (1978) puts it, "too necessary to mention" (35). Paradoxically, we are most reluctant to compare and rank race groups precisely in the very social location where we are perhaps most programmed to compare and rank them—school.

Such silences are not, of course, specific to Columbus or California City. As many other researchers have noted, people often resist talking about racial achievement disparities even in blatantly stratified American schools and districts.[8] Silence about such patterns, of course, allows them to remain intact: racial patterns do not go away simply because they are ignored. Indeed, once people have *noticed* racial patterns, they seem to become engraved on the brain. They become, most dangerously, acceptable—a taken-for-granted part of what school is about.

Since schooling discourse so routinely frames racial achievement patterns as taken-for-granted orders, though, simply remarking upon existing patterns does not eradicate them either. Indeed, describing any racial achievement pattern matter-of-factly, in research or in the everyday life of schooling, always risks reinforcing an ingrained American assumption that race groups *will naturally* achieve differently. American racism has relied upon naturalizing a racialized hierarchy of academic and intellectual potential ever since racial categories were created and solidified with pseudo-science (see Gould 1981); American racism has always framed racial achievement patterns as natural facts. We thus risk making racial achievement patterns in our schools seem normal both by talking about them matter-of-factly, and by refusing to talk about them at all.[9]

Race and achievement talk is full of such Scylla and Charybdis traps—and we thus must harness our discourse on achievement a bit more knowingly. The answer, it seems, is neither to delete mention of racial achievement patterns, nor to speak of these patterns matter-of-factly as expected orders created by other people. Rather, the trick is to actively *denaturalize* racial achievement patterns: to name them and claim them as things that we, together, have both produced and allowed. For our own routine explanations for existing patterns typically displace onto others the responsibility for undoing the patterns we find: and in failing to frame achievement patterns as communal productions, we fail to understand the dismantling of such patterns as a mutual responsibility.

In a society that already thinks racially but hates to do so, as we have seen, people often resist mentioning the very racial patterns they seem most trained to reproduce. Yet undescribed racial patterns do not disappear. While *re-creating* racial patterns at Columbus was inextricably related to matter-of-factly *talking* about them, *not* talking about racial patterns was just as active in this reproduction. Columbus speakers were, unfortunately, caught in the messiest dilemma of racial description: although talking in racial terms can make race matter, *not* talking in racial terms can make race matter too. Actually, we are often painfully aware of this basic trap of race talk, a final American dilemma that the last chapter explores at length. Across Columbus, anxiously whispered concerns about the consequences of both talking and *not* talking in racial terms ran rampant.

Six

Although Talking in Racial Terms Can Make Race Matter, Not Talking in Racial Terms Can Make Race Matter Too

Between me and the other world there is ever an unasked question: unasked by some through feelings of delicacy; by others through the difficulty of rightly framing it. All, nevertheless, flutter round it. They approach me in a half-hesitant sort of way, eye me curiously or compassionately, and then, instead of saying directly, How does it feel to be a problem? they say, I know an excellent colored man in my town; or, I fought at Mechanicsville; or, do not these Southern outrages make your blood boil? At these I smile, or am interested, or reduce the boiling to a simmer, as the occasion may require. To the real question, How does it feel to be a problem? I answer seldom a word.
—W.E.B. Du Bois, *The Souls of Black Folk*, 1903

One day in 1997, I see Mr. Charles in the hallway during classtime. We banter about how things are going. He asks me again what my thesis is for my dissertation, and I say I'm interested in how people talk about diversity. He says I'm welcome to come to any of his classes. "They're pretty diverse—you can go to my student teacher's class. Actually, it's mostly African-American and so it has a real interesting dynamic," he says. "Why?" I ask. "Because it's student teacher team taught, and because the students are African-American. They actually have some African-American students coming really regularly, which is unusual I think." "For African-American students to come regularly?" I ask. "Yes," he says. "Do they not come regularly to your other classes?" I ask. "I think schoolwide . . . African-American students really aren't being well served," he replies. "I mean not just at Columbus—it's a districtwide problem. I have some friends who teach at other schools and they say the same thing. It's a problem that really needs to be addressed, it's not being addressed," he finishes.

The whole time we're talking, students—mostly black—are passing us in the halls. In fact, every kid, with the exception of two Latinos and a Filipina holding a pass, has been black since the beginning of second period. As I walked down the stairs I was amazed by how consistently black the cutters were. . . . While talking to Mr. C, I did see a Latino guy from Mr. P's class whom I had already passed in the hallway by the main office. "Again," the student sighed in resigned agreement, as I looked at him with raised eyebrows. He kept walking glumly, swatting at the walls. . .

Two black girls pass Mr. C and one, with a lollipop stuck in her bun of hair, says, "I left that test at home, can I bring it in tomorrow?" "Sure you can bring it in tomorrow," he says, adding, "You're going to class, right?" "Yeah," she says, walking off with her friend. Later in our conversation they pass us again (they must have circled the Quad). "I thought you were going to class," Mr. C says, smiling. She turns her head back to him with a big smile and turns back around and keeps walking forward. He turns back to me and keeps talking.

Periodically over the days and years at Columbus, the halls filled with waves of wandering students who had cut class. Some laughed and shouted to one another as they bounded through the corridors; others shuffled slowly, aimlessly, eyes down as they batted walls with folded papers. During the recurrent phases when class-cutters circled the halls in a regular stream, adults fretted constantly about "the hall wanderers" in both public and private discussions. Adults used the hallway as a barometer for assessing schoolwide order, and the hall wanderers indicated to adults not only academic disengagement but cracks in the schoolwide disciplinary system. "The hallways" served as a key symbol of the school's state of mind, and the topic always inspired in adults a kind of impotent fury.

The hallways were also a topic to which race was sporadically said to matter. In early 1997, a teacher suggested privately to me that I test a personal hypothesis of his that the hall wanderers were "90 percent black." The overrepresentation of "black" students was a pattern I had long suspected myself, and I decided to take his suggestion. After many hours struggling to tally the "race" of wandering students, I found that students who appeared black to me did indeed make up the majority of the hall wanderers, even though "blacks" comprised only a fifth of the official student population.

Curious to see if other adults had noticed this overrepresentation, I started paying more attention to people's talk of the hallways in our informal conversations. With startling regularity, I came to realize, people privately describing the hall wanderers with labored pauses, hedges, and disclaimers finally blurted out that the majority of hall wanderers seemed to be "black"—and most who did so then said decisively that they would not raise "the subject" with anyone besides one or two close friends. It was "an issue that needs to be addressed," most sighed, but many maintained that they would consider "racist" any actions to focus publicly on the "black students wandering in the halls." As they predicted, the word "black" never appeared once in public complaints about "the hallway"—and throughout my years at Columbus, the demographics of the hallways remained the same.

In private debates about the subject, these adults acknowledged that they were trapped in a most paradoxical situation. While publicly framing the hall wanderers as predominantly "black" could seem explicitly "racist," public silence on the hallway's racial demographics effectively allowed black students to miss class disproportionately, an institutional allowance that to many seemed no less "racist." Adults seemed somewhat less aware that the combined effect of nervously whispering the word "black" in private and knowingly deleting the word in public was actually to *highlight* the perceived relevance of blackness to the hallway "problem." In routinely focusing fleeting and anxious private analysis exclusively on the presumably unnameable role of "blacks" in the hallways, that is, adults repeatedly displaced analysis from their *own* roles in producing the hallway's racial demographics—and in packing the full anxiety of the hallway "problem" into the very *word* "black," they repeatedly framed black students themselves *as* a disproportionate Columbus "problem" that was alternately the focus of private attention and knowingly ignored. Indeed, in their everyday struggles over describing and *not* describing the hall wandering phenomenon in racial terms, as this chapter shows, Columbus adults actually exemplified the most confounding paradox of racial description: *although speaking in racial terms can make race matter, not speaking in racial terms can make race matter too.*

Knowing silences, I want to demonstrate, are themselves actions with racializing consequences: actively deleting race words from everyday talk can serve to increase the perceived relevance of race as much as to actively ignore race's relevance. As Blum (2002) writes, "we cannot deracialize a racialized group simply by refusing to use racial language" (169), and as Haney Lopez (1996) argues further of racial orders, "to banish race-words *redoubles* the hegemony of race," by "leaving race and its effects unchallenged and embedded in society, seemingly natural rather than the product of social choices" (177). Indeed, just as the person stuttering and hesitating before describing an individual partygoer across the room as "black" actually highlights the anxious relevance of race to his own observations, black students as a group at Columbus assumed a hypervisibility in the discourse of school problems even as people vigorously tried to avoid talking about "blacks." Further, adults repeatedly muttering *quiet* critiques and hypotheses about "blacks" routinely avoided a racialized analysis of their own practices of *serving* the school's black students—and in the absence of any wider debate about how race mattered to the actions of *various* players in the Columbus hallways, a framing of "black" students as a disproportionately problematic population just continued to echo throughout Columbus adults' private conversations.

As one black administrator put it to me, "black" students at Columbus somehow kept becoming this hyper-diverse school's "million-dollar question"—and as various players routinely muttered only quiet anxious analyses about the school's "black" population, "black" students themselves were not just made hypervisible but also simultaneously vigorously overlooked. Districtwide, in fact—as plans to "focus" on black students waxed and waned—the word "black" had long been the race label most systematically spoken and the one most systematically suppressed. Both actions, it seemed, could serve to fuse the very label "black" *to* the notion of "problems": for all discussion of "problems," as Du Bois wrote a century ago, came to "nevertheless, flutter round" the very word.[1]

Making the Word "Black" Especially "Problematic": The Variable Weight of Race Words

Imagine that every word is a stone. While some words drop into an existing pool of talk with no more consequence than a pebble, dropping certain heavy words creates noticeable social waves.[2] As we have seen, race labels can be particularly heavy stones in American talk—depending on who is talking about what to whom—but even these are not weighted equally. When using the words "black" or "African-American," most Columbus adults, particularly white adults, stuttered, mumbled, and paused measurably even in private—as they did before using no other race label. In one conversation, for example, Sarah, a white teacher, whispered hesitatingly and conspiratorially as she explained to me and Lou, another white teacher, her claim that the school seemed "Afrocentric":[3]

> "I dunno, it seems like the sports teams are almost all black," whispers Sarah. Lou says, "I dunno, the basketball team is. The badminton team is all Chinese." We all laugh.

While white Columbus adults often treated the word "black" with palpable whispered anxiety, few paused anxiously before labeling "Chinese" students. Speakers of all "races" also typically smiled or laughed when privately using the word "Samoan," often displaying little discomfort when describing the antics of "Samoan girls" or "Samoan boys." No one hedged or stuttered before saying the word "Filipino" either. But many adults privately using the word "black" paused and stuttered predictably; indeed, when they *resisted* using a racial label to describe someone, it was typically a "black" person they were struggling to describe. In the fall immediately after reconstitution, for example, a white teacher who substituted regularly at Columbus started talking to me in the dean's office:

> She says she has a lot of questions about reconstitution and if it's really serving the students. The noise in the dean's office is now getting really loud. There are about 10 black kids in the small space, talking loudly to each other. "Reconstitution ruined all these people's lives," she says, "and it doesn't seem to be serving the kids here well—particularly the students in this room here," she finishes, smiling with her

eyebrows raised. I smile back. "What about the students here?" I ask. ". . . As a group," she says hesitatingly. "What kind of group?" I ask. She pauses. "African-American students," she says, exhaling.

Of course there were occasional exceptions, adults who were quite direct in quietly using the word "black." One white teacher's private critique of "black" "cutters" was so unusually blunt that I remembered it for years afterwards as an example of talk that in its very accusatory bluntness indeed sounded racist:

> March 28th, 1995
> I am driving in the car with some colleagues. It is raining hard outside. Kay [*white*]: "Well, guess who will be cutting today? All the black kids."

Such talk pointedly critiquing "black kids" without hesitation was relatively rare around Columbus. Rather, white teachers often treated even basic references identifying students as "black" as if they were inherently critical, and as if the very word "black" risked offense. Usually, the only adults who seemed to describe individual students nonchalantly as "black" or "African-American" were adults who called *themselves* "black":

> Sam [*a black security guard*] and Mr. S [*a black teacher*] walked past in the hallway. "Who are you looking for?" Connie [*white teacher*] asks. Sam calls out, still walking, "A light-skinned Afro-American guy . . . acne."

For Columbus students of all "races," it is worth noting, using the word "black" to describe peers or adults typically seemed relatively unremarkable. Contrast, for example, the student practice of describing a "black" person whose name was not known (A: "Which security guard chased you?" B: "Black dude.") with the typical teacher practice (A: "Which student was in the hallway?" B: "Uh . . . football player . . . really tall . . . you know, has his hair in dreds . . . uh, wears a blue starter jacket . . . uh, he's African-American"). Describing individuals racially often seemed no more problematic to students than describing them as glasses-wearers or residents of particular neighborhoods, as two Filipino-looking boys talking about the author of a particular "tag" (graffiti signature) indicated: "I just know he's a white dude, goes to Lomond High," one said. "Who's 'butter'?" someone else asked him. "Mexican dude," he replied.

Occasionally, however, non-black students indicated that the adults in their lives did seem to treat "black" as a particularly problematic word. Talking in the park with several Filipina girls one day, for example, I noticed that the topic of romance had them suggesting the particular weight a reference to "blacks" could have in family discourse. Some parents, it seemed, used the word when critically comparing "blacks" to other racialized "groups":

> K said her family didn't like her boyfriend because he was Chinese. They think he will be the jealous type, who might beat her or something. "I told them they've been watching too many movies," she said, saying that she didn't like Filipino boys

because they were "all the same." "I'm doing all the groups," she added. She had had one Filipino boyfriend, now she had a Chinese boyfriend, and next she would try "a Latin guy." "A black guy!" Nina snickered, giggling nervously. K shook her head, laughing also. She said her family would never let her go out with a black guy. I asked why not. "They'd say, 'you know how dirty they are,' " she said. She laughed.

Students laughing nervously when describing their families' prejudiced evaluations of "blacks" typically denounced such parental usage, calling their parents "racist" for using the word "black" in exclusively critical statements. Yet these same students displayed no special discomfort with using the word "black" to describe their peers, and they also typically interacted easily with black students themselves; for non-black students, "black" was typically not a word loaded with danger. Around Columbus, the label "white" actually had students giggling nervously far more often: it was this label that seemed loaded with criticism and anxiety.[4] In discussions where the word "white" came up, students (ironically, particularly black students) occasionally commented that the very word sounded like a slur. When I said something about "white people" one day in my own class in October 1994, for example, Katrina, who sometimes described herself as "black and Panamanian," complained, "I'm part white and it sounds bad to keep saying that. Why don't you say, like, 'Caucasian.' " Similarly, after a Filipino teacher discussing poetry in his classroom in 1997 made a comment about "the white man," a black student responded, "You can't say 'white man'—it sounds racist. You can say Caucasian. If you say 'white man' it sounds like you have hate in your heart."

Using the label "white" thus sometimes raised Columbus student concerns about "sounding bad," since "white" adults at Columbus were often the focus of students' critical analyses. For Columbus adults, however, it was using the race label "black" that seemed sometimes to be inherently "racist"—for it was the word "black" that typically bore the full weight of private critique. Indeed, as the first section shows, in private metapragmatic talk—talk *about* talking— adults of all "races" talking critically about the students in the hallways acknowledged quite explicitly that they often anxiously deleted the very word.

Part 1: Pointing Out That "Black" Is Being Deleted

Mr. Fitsner, who in answer to my questions about achievement "patterns" had hesitatingly offered the litany of racialized comparisons discussed in chapter 5, had subsequently started talking specifically to me about "black" students in the hallway. He was soon commenting critically on this very act of speaking racially:

"So . . . you said earlier you think most of the kids in the halls and stuff are black?" I ask. "Black and Samoan, yes," he says. "Like in front of my door—the stairway on this floor—there's always 10–15 black males over there. It's like where they congregate. They're probably the ones who are cutting." "Is the faculty going to have a discussion about this?" I ask. "Well, I hope the committee work we're doing will accomplish that," he replies, mentioning a new committee he hopes to form on "cutters." He says he thinks they should find the worst ones first and make them serve in-school suspension all day. "So you'd work on a plan for cutters in general?" I ask. "Yes," he replies. "You wouldn't mention the 10–15 black males out there every day?" I ask. "No, because I think that's discriminatory," he replies, adding, 'There must be other places I don't know, where other groups congregate." He pauses. "So you'd focus on 'cutters,' " I repeat. "Yes—and *then*, *within* that group, identify people . . . and then make specific adjustments for them," he says, adding, "Like I wouldn't say, 'We need to work on our African-American graduation rates.' I would look at graduation in general."

Insisting that "general" rather than explicitly racial talk was the proper vehicle for discussing "cutters," Mr. Fitsner made it clear that publicly describing the hall wanderers as predominantly "black" seemed to him to be inherently "discriminatory." Part of this potential for "discrimination," he suggested, was the potential inaccuracy of overlooking the "cutting" of "other groups"; indeed, as Ann Ferguson (2000) writes, discipline of students in the United States routinely *does* exhibit "a systematic racial bias," as "African American males are apprehended and punished for misbehavior and delinquent acts that are overlooked in other children" (233). Other Columbus adults, however, worried that the act of mentioning "blacks" in the hallway seemed rather an inappropriate divergence from "colorblindness." Sarah, the white teacher who had whispered conspiratorially in the private conversation (recounted above) with myself and Lou that the school seemed "Afrocentric," continued that conversation by explaining that while the hall wanderers, too, seemed majority "black," mentioning the overrepresentation of "blacks" like this typically seemed inappropriate:

> "That's the first time I've said anything about it to anybody. There are only two or three people I think I even *would* say it to," she says. "Why?" I ask. "It's just not P.C., you know," she replies. "How's that?" I ask. "You know, P.C. is you're supposed to be color-*blind*—'They're all the same,' " she mimics in a simpery voice. "So you think that's the ethos of the school?" I ask. "Not at *all* for the *students*—for the *teachers*, though. No, the students are some of the most racist I've seen! I'm like, 'you can't *say* that!' " she says, with a shocked laugh.

While students at Columbus talked racially about school people with daily nonchalance, adults monitored far more closely what could and "could not" be said at the school, especially in reference to troubling school orders—and they repeatedly framed the word "black" as disproportionately risky. In describing what words sounded "racist" in the mouths of adults, other teachers also told me that Columbus adults particularly deleted talk of "blacks" in the hallway in favor of descriptions that were "colorblind," "in general," or "overall." One day over the phone during the winter break of 1996, John, an Asian-

American teacher, was complaining to me that the school's process of scheduling students for the next semester was still dangerously incomplete, and that he expected to have a lot of kids coming in and out of his classes during the first few days of school. Our conversation turned quickly to the general topic of kids missing class, and over the privacy of the phone lines John commented both that "African-Americans" made up the majority of the hall wanderers and that this very topic was not discussed publicly in racial terms. While the topic "needed to be talked about," John argued, he knew his colleagues would reference the issue of the hallway's racial demographics only under de-raced generalized "headlines":

Me: Do you think any kids are falling through the cracks this year?

John: *OH* yeah . . . kids wandering around in the halls—mostly African-Americans, males and females.

Me: Do people talk about the fact that it's mostly African-Americans wandering around in the halls?

John: No . . . it hasn't been brought up yet. (With a laugh in his voice) But it will very soon!

Me: Why, do you think?

John: It needs to be talked about.

Me: So you think it will be?

John: Overall under the headline of attendance and cutting. I'll bring it up, if no one else does.

As John himself soon demonstrated, Columbus adults both noted and followed local norms for talking about "African-Americans": in a lunchtime conversation with me and a few colleagues back at school once the semester began, John would indeed "bring up" the subject of "African-American students" in the hallways through a question about wandering "overall." In fact, it was he who would now suggest that I test his hypothesis that the hallways were "90 percent black." A white teacher, Thomas, was in the middle of telling me how he had a lot of "real behavior problems" with the class coming in after lunch, and John entered Thomas's classroom from the hallway commotion to join us:

John: (to me, walking towards us): In your research, have you ever thought about tallying up who's wandering in the hallways?

Me: I've done some.

John: What'd you find?

Me: I haven't fully tallied it up.

John: Because I'm wondering if my perception is true. (stops)

Me: What's your perception?

John: My perception is that it's 90 percent black.

Me: Really?

John: Well. . .

Me: I need to spend a day or two where that's all I do. (John nods)

Thomas: Yes, I think that's true . . . and in fact, my next class, they're—they're black too, the ones . . . (trailing off).

Another white teacher, Sam, came in the room to eat and asked what we were talking about. In his hesitant response, Thomas first reaggregated his comments about "blacks" into the more typical opening description of "the people wandering the halls":

Thomas: We're saying—about how the people wandering the halls . . . the majority are . . . [*keeps hedging*] the people, you know, (he points out to the currently bustling quad area in the middle of the school) behavior problems . . . the majority seem to be, African-American.

Sam: (sits down to eat) Oh, yes, statistically, that's definitely true.

John: I was saying she should do the research. The majority of them . . . (stops)

Sam: *We* should be doing the research. (*To John:*) You should do it in your unit on statistics, it's the perfect thing.

Me: Have the students research it?

John: I'd be afraid to touch that though, with the racial tensions in my class.

Me: You mean having the kids do it?

John: It's a problem that needs to be addressed. I'm not sure if it's something the students should do. I'd be afraid to.

(I ask Sam if he has done such research in his own class, and he says no.)

Me: (to Sam:) What did you mean "statistically"?

Sam: I mean . . . in my unit on statistics we talk about statistical significance. The proportion of them having problems, causing problems, in relation to their . . .

John: The rest of the population.

Sam: Yes, in relation to their proportion of the population at large. Whether it's statistically significant.

Me: Do you think everyone notices it?

Sam: I think you'd have to be an idiot not to. (I nod.) It's something that needs to be addressed.

John: It does.

While Sam had initially suggested that teachers and students could "research" the hallway's racial demographics together, John's stated fear of sparking preexisting "racial tensions" soon had all three steering away from the notion of raising the question at all. Indeed, having critically framed the hall wanderers, the quad's "behavioral problems," and the people "causing problems" in Columbus classrooms all as predominantly "African-American," all three teachers next started to offer explanations for why such "problems" involving "black" students were not thoroughly "addressed." The very act of speaking of "blacks" when discussing such "problems" and even when discussing hoped-for solutions, they suggested, threatened always to be "racist," because referencing "blacks" specifically always seemed potentially either inaccurate or inappropriate:

Sam: Well, it's being addressed in the sense of saying we're failing them, and that's really *true*. It's our biggest problem . . . *they're* the ones opting out (he points at the quad). But as far as what to *do* about it, that's not being addressed.

Me: Here?

Sam: Here, in California City, in the *nation* really.

Me: Why isn't it being addressed?

Sam: Well . . . I think it's a topic there really isn't open discussion on.

Me: Why?

Sam: (*punctuating his sentence with noticeably long pauses*): There are . . . well . . . really just so many things that aren't . . . politically . . . well, that aren't politically . . . acceptable . . . to be said . . . [*Basic problem of appropriateness*]

Me: So you mean it's an issue of political correctness that keeps the issue from being discussed?

Sam: Well . . . I didn't want to say *that*, but . . .

John: It's hard to even bring *up* the issue at all. You could be, you know, called a racist.

Sam: The conversation ex*pands* to include so many things that it becomes practically meaningless. [*Problem of accuracy: conversations quickly become analytically over loaded*]

Me: What would be something unacceptable to bring up?

Sam: The sources. It would just get too big, trying to *explain* it. People would talk about the historical reasons for it, but it's a contemporary problem. What to do now? Is it even necessary to go to high school? These things are too big, I'm having trouble putting it into words. [*Basic problem of accuracy*]

Thomas (smiling): You're not supposed to ask questions like that. [*Basic problem of appropriateness: the existence of proper and improper questions*]

Me (smiling): Like what's inappropriate to say?

Thomas: It's something that should be talked about though.

Me: Would you be comfortable bringing up the topic in conversation?

Thomas: It depends . . . I would to *you*, or to these guys.

Me: Because we're friends?

Thomas: No, not *friends*, but professional . . . I wouldn't to the principal for example. [*Problem of appropriateness: proper and improper audiences*]

Me: Why not?

Thomas: Well, first because of her position, as my boss. I'd have to be careful to see how she saw me. [*Problem of appropriateness: speakers can be perceived poorly*]

Me: How could she see you?

Thomas: Well . . . she might say "Yes, you're right," but she might also say, "I think you're being racist." She's a person of color, too, and that might affect things . . . (There is a long pause. Sam says he needs to "grade stuff," and John gets up too.)

Our own initial conversation on the overrepresentation of "black" students in the Columbus hallways had indeed "expanded" to consider broader school dilemmas (like teacher-administrator race relations) and larger societal inequities (such as how schools "in the nation" failed to adequately serve "African-Americans").

Yet while in our conversation we had just begun to expand from debating the failure of blacks to debating "society's" failure to serve them, the aborted critical analysis left "failing" black students themselves at its center. Further, while Sam had noted the primary need for Columbus adults to discuss what they could "*do* about" serving black students better, through a hurried metapragmatic conversation about how difficult it would be to "address" this "problem" without being "called a racist," all four of us may have been ensuring that none of the people present would be addressing it. A pervasive self-consciousness and critique about how adults deleted talk of serving "blacks" did not necessarily translate into proposals or plans to "address the issue" of serving them. Concluding that the school's "biggest problem" of "failing" "African-Americans" needed to be "addressed" (and notably referring to this "problem" for the second half of the conversation solely as "it"), everybody went back to class.

Out to pizza with a diverse group of teachers from their department after school that day, John, Sam, and I ended up in another conversation about school "problems" that momentarily centered on student "African-Americans." While it was Sam himself who now hesitatingly dropped the word "African-American" into the discussion about school "statistics," after another teacher quickly framed African-Americans themselves *as* "problems" Sam himself led the conversation away from analysis of the school's "statistics," creating a conversational vacuum that once again left "African-Americans" themselves positioned as disproportionately "problematic." This vacuum was the achievement of all players present: as I would write later in my notes (notably myself using the common language of "problems"), "Sam and John didn't pick up on this problem *now*, though they said earlier it 'had to be addressed.' Maybe because *I* didn't?"

> One [*white*] teacher says she heard the principal went to a teacher and said, "You failed too many kids." Sam says he thinks the principal probably wouldn't say it that way. "She thinks too much about her language. She's under so much pressure to get those three statistics—attendance, grades . . ." he trails off. "What else is it?" I ask. "I dunno . . . suspensions, African-Americans . . ." Sam replies. "There you go, *that* was a big problem at Columbus," says a new (*white*) teacher. "Yeah . . ." Sam responds. John looks at me. [*Sam takes it back to general issues:*] "But anyway, you gotta wonder what her motivation is on the grades and stuff," Sam says.

Routinely, those struggling to describe the school's "problems" with serving "African-Americans" ended up dropping the subject—but not before their own conversations, as here, had somehow managed to frame "African-Americans" themselves as "a big problem at Columbus." Talking quietly of various school "problems" at Columbus either directly or transitively, adults repeatedly, if sometimes unwittingly, latched the very word "black" to the word "problem." Adults complaining about Columbus's "Special Ed kids," for example, indirectly fused "black" to "problem" by using the terms "Special Ed" and "problem" interchangeably: as the majority of students designated for "Special Education" at Columbus were black (the result of years of questionable placements in the district's elementary and middle schools), people talking about "Special Ed kids" as "problems" were often talking about black students without talking about "black students."[5] (While a tiny number of the "Special Education" students at Columbus were in wheelchairs or in need of regular medical assistance, most students had been classified as "Special Ed" for presumed learning disabilities. This latter group of "Special Ed" students was typically discussed as a population with behavioral rather than learning "problems.")[6] In public, adults often framed "Special Ed" students as the school's central disciplinary "problems," regularly bemoaning the fact that Columbus had the highest proportion of "Special Ed" students in the district and often longing quite publicly to rid their classes and the school of "Special Ed kids." During a discussion following a staff development presentation on Special Education during my teaching year, I myself took some notes I entitled "Problems at Columbus." "There's no real policy to deal with disruptive students—they just get bumped school to school," I wrote, adding that it was apparently "very hard to kick out Special Ed kids. Why *do* we get an unfair distribution of problem kids? They should give more money and programs to kids with *problems!*"

As we walked back from lunch one day, a black Special Ed aide critiquing the process of Special Education placement sarcastically linked the terms "Special Ed," "black," and "problem" even as he suggested that most adults were reluctant to discuss this very taken-for-granted correlation:

> Describing the students he assisted in mainstream classes, he said, "Some of the quote 'normal' kids weren't as good as these Special Ed kids. I was like, '*Why* are you Special Ed?!'" "Why *are* they Special Ed?" I asked. "Discipline problems . . . a lot of them," he said, starting to frown slightly. "And for speaking ebonics," he added wryly. I nodded. "'I be going'—'no, it's *I went*,'" he said, mimicking a teacher. "It didn't used to be called ebonics, they called it 'ignorance' or 'black street slang,'" he added. "Do you talk about this in the department?" I asked. He smiled. "Some of it . . . but there are certain things we *don't talk about*," he said, dropping his voice to a dramatically prudish whisper.[7]

Another Special Ed paraprofessional, a white man, confirmed to me in a separate private conversation that many Special Ed placements in the district's schools seemed more discipline-related than disability-related. In doing so, he both pinpointed the overrepresentation of "black boys" and agreed that hardly anybody at Columbus seemed to address the school's overwhelmingly "black" "Special Ed" demographic explicitly:

> "Many or most don't even have diagnosed disabilities, they're in here because somewhere along the line someone got tired of them and put them in. Maybe they were being disruptive," he said. In a minute, he added, "There is a real overabundance

of black boys. It's really mostly them that got put in there." "Is there any attempt to address their overrepresentation?" I ask. "No, there's no attempt really," he says.

At times in private Columbus conversations, adult speakers notably extended this routine equation between "Special Ed," "black," and "problem" students to include analysis of the hallways' racial demographics. Yet while speakers sometimes noticed their own demographic correlations, few openly critiqued the racial patterns they were referencing as unacceptable disparities requiring remedy. Mr. Hernandez, a Latino teacher, was telling me one day about a small private meeting in which six faculty of color had been "talking about this handful of kids that's just *everywhere*—who never go to class." He recalled that one administrator had noted that the hall wanderers themselves were "mostly African-American"—and that she had made this correlation "through Special Ed." "We were talking about Special Ed," he explained, "and she said, 'You know, it's surprising that 95 percent of the kids in Special Ed are African-American males.'" They had then started discussing how "most of the kids in the hallways" were also "African American, to tell you the truth, boys." "Boys?" I repeated. "Yeah, mostly—well, a few female names came up," he replied. I asked him if this faculty group would be urging that the school "focus on these kids." "No," he replied. "It was just one of the small things we were talking about."

"Focusing" on black students only in such private musings on distressing school patterns, Columbus adults repeatedly stated quite knowingly that such demographic analyses would be absent from public discussion. Rob, a black teacher at the post-reconstruction Columbus, often pointed out to me that the very people quietly linking mention of "black" students to complaints about school "problems" were deleting the word "black" from their public analyses. He paraphrased Malcolm X for me to characterize such covert racial practice: "In the South we had to deal with the wolf. In California, we have to deal with the fox," he explained. Rob spoke often of hearing talk of black students "under" talk of certain "problem" topics, or, as he said to Maverick and me in the hallway one day, "between the lines":

> Rob comes over to join Maverick and me talking in the hallway during class. He says there's a big fight brewing, started by the union. "And you know who's gonna have problems, is *him*, and *him*, and *him*," he says, pointing at three black students who have just passed us walking down the hall. "It's all about 'the rules,' and you know when it's about 'the rules,' they mean *us*," Rob says. Maverick nods. "They're fittin' to have the niggers kicked out of here, 'cause some of these white teachers can't deal with them," Rob continues, adding, "You've got to read between the lines. We got a letter, all about following the rules. And you know all the rules in the handbook are about *us*," he repeats. Maverick nods, adding, "to keep us in line." "It's all racial," Rob finishes. "What do you mean?" I ask. "It's all about whether you take the extra time for the kids here. Do you treat the kids as if they're psycho, abnormal, from

another planet—like that woman who said she was getting pushed around," he says, referencing a [*white*] teacher who said students had pushed her while she was trying to keep them from entering the building during lunchtime. "You treat them like they're not normal in your world. These teachers, many of them, their secret fantasy is to teach in the suburbs, so they try to make this into the suburbs," he says, adding, "I went to an all-black school. Teachers went *home* with the kids." On a piece of paper, he draws one circle with "we" written inside of it. "In the black school, the whole circle was 'we.' Here, it's this" (he draws four non-intersecting circles, and explains): "*Administrators, teachers, students*. And in comes an instigator," he says, pointing to the fourth circle, "and it starts with 'U!'" I ask him how this union letter about "the rules" appeared to him to be "all racial." Smiling, Rob says, "it's not overt, it's covert." On its face, he says, the union letter was about teachers not wanting administrative duties like lunchtime monitoring.

Rob and Maverick's muttered analysis of their colleagues' troubled interactions with "blacks" intertwined black students and black adults as a community anxiously "dealt with" at Columbus; and as Rob admitted next, he himself strove purposefully to keep his interactions with non-black adults as congenial as possible. Even as Rob criticized others for putting talk of black students "between the lines," thus, he himself, he indicated, kept race words rather purposefully out of most of his statements to other faculty:

"This reading between the lines—is this something you talk about in public?" I ask. "No," he says. "Why?" I ask. "Because I don't want to make a lot of enemies. I've got a lot more power getting on those boards—I'm on all those committees. My grandmother told me you can do more with honey than with vinegar; I can work better with friends. If I went around saying all these things to people, went in and said 'you're doing this and you're doing that,' you think I'd be on all those boards?" he finishes. "You wouldn't get any support for what you'd say anyway," Maverick says. Rob nods. "So I tell a few jokes, be friendly. I know how to do politics, I'm in my 30s, not my 20s," Rob says, smiling. I ask him if he gets his ideas across eventually. "Yes, I know I do," he says. If he were to speak out a lot, he finishes with a smile, "They'd say 'OOH, he's *venomous*,' or 'a *black* man . . . he's *menacing*.'"

Some adults at Columbus remained colormute with colleagues due to fears of sounding "racist," "discriminatory," or "politically incorrect"; others, like Rob, remained colormute to keep "political" avenues open for further collaboration. Rob gleefully refused to mince race words with parents and students (he purposefully left a "white supremacy" flow chart on his chalkboard on Parents Night, for example), but in the public presence of other faculty, he typically chose not to decode the language he privately said was "racial." One faculty meeting that spring demonstrated this choice especially clearly. At the meeting, teachers were arguing with one another and administrators about the future of a recently distributed Columbus faculty survey; scanning the survey, I noticed that a question I had seen on a previous draft (asking whether teachers felt sufficient freedom to speak in faculty meetings) had been deleted from the final version. Rob himself soon demonstrated that faculty meetings were indeed not a place where people said all they were thinking. Rather, in such meetings people with deeply racialized analyses often resorted to murky racial insinuations:

> Rob comes over to join me at the doughnut table and points to the survey. "No. 9 is a racial question," he says to me quietly. I look at the question. It reads, "There have also been concerns about discipline procedures at Columbus High. In your experience, are current procedures effective/realistic?" "Why is it racial?" I ask Rob. He smiles. "I'm not going to dignify that with an answer," he replies, adding that he will "come out with his gloves on" when the results of this question come back. He turns to another black teacher and starts talking about school decision-making processes, this meeting's other main debate. "If it's majority rule, minorities will get shut down," he says. "Our kids will get shafted every time. They have different ideas of how to run things—we'll get fucked."
>
> Back in the large discussion on decision making, Rob raises his hand. "I don't want to stereotype anyone, but I feel if it's majority rule, I'm not going to agree and I won't get heard," he says. He comes over momentarily and asks me if he was clear. I say I'm not sure they got the implication about "stereotyping." He smiles and nods. Returning to the group, Rob states again that he's concerned about not being heard. [*Now he uses a more overtly race-related gesture:*] "Okay . . . 'cause I don't want to have to do *this*," he says, raising a black-gloved fist into the air with mock seriousness. "You *wanted* to do that," says Sarah [*a white teacher*], laughing. Rob is smiling. Others laugh.

Resorting to race loaded gestures and words in public exchanges, some Columbus adults attempted to insinuate race's relevance to the topics at hand; yet few Columbus adults went any further to decode such talk in public. Later in the meeting, musing about how various "minority" issues actually got "shut down" in Columbus conversations, I talked to Rob on the sidelines again, this time about another recurrent research question of mine—whether it would really make sense for the school to explicitly "focus on certain racial groups" for particular assistance if so many of the kids at Columbus were poor. He said it did make sense, and that this was the very kind of suggestion teachers of color deleted from public forums:

> "The overriding factor is socioeconomics, but it's about how a lot of factors work together. It still makes sense to see people as different. People talk about it in their groups—there are things people don't bring to the public forum. You should look at the Samoan group. They *really* segregate themselves," he says. "I wish I could be present at some of these moments when people met as separate groups," I say. "Well, you were at one, and it wasn't very comfortable, was it," he smiles. [*During an impromptu parent discussion in Rob's room on Parents Night, I had introduced myself to a group of black professional mothers discussing the "African-American retention program" as a researcher and former teacher interested in "issues of race at Columbus." Several of the*

women had responded brusquely that the concerns they had been raising were not "about race," but "about education." Rob had critiqued the mothers as "bourgeois" for an hour after they had left.] "Some people would be okay with you being there, I'm sure," Rob adds. "So why wouldn't they bring things up in the public forum?" I ask. "Well," he says, gesturing towards the rest of the staff, "history has shown that they won't act to fulfill your needs, so . . ." he shrugs, and adds, "They don't like to see people separately. They want to see Columbus as one big happy family, and all that bullshit."[8]

Rob himself, who muttered quietly to me like this about specific race "groups" and "race" issues in private almost every time I saw him, would resist "bringing" race issues to the public conversation one more time during this meeting. Ironically, it was after the principal asked the faculty to brainstorm a list of expectations they had for one another, and a white teacher immediately suggested "direct talk instead of euphemistic talk." Now, Rob would even refuse directly a black colleague's request for public "elaboration":

As the principal writes down "direct talk," I hear Lan [*an Asian-American teacher*] say quietly to Rob, "Like if things are bad, say they're bad, not that they're 'in process.' " Several other suggestions are made, and Rob then speaks out again: "Remember the bus ride we took through the neighborhood . . . why we took it," he says. [*As described further later in this chapter, a neighborhood bus tour from the staff's summer orientation had circled primarily through several mostly-black housing projects near Columbus.*] "Elaborate on that," says Ned [*a black teacher*] from across the room. "It's too deep for some of y'all . . . think about it," Rob says. Lan leans over to Rob and whispers, "They don't understand where you're coming from." Moments later, I hear her mutter something to him about "this *We are the World* shit." "We had 30 expulsions last month, and 60 suspensions!" Rob whispers agitatedly to her. To the large group, Rob finally says, "I want to know about the discipline policy—can Columbus create its own? My primary concern is, um—if we continue to expel so many students, what happens?"

Hearing Rob expose talk of "discipline" and "rules" as "racial questions" in private and then speak in labored, de-raced code of such topics in public demonstrated that even those most critical of racial deletions themselves deleted race words in potentially dangerous contexts.[9] As Rob put it on another occasion (ironically, when speaking to me), "Lots of black people lead sort of like a double life. They only talk about things like this to other black people." Rob called one black teacher who openly criticized school policies in faculty meetings "a sacrificial lamb": this was the teacher, in fact, who had asked him for "elaboration" in the conversation described above. This teacher actually himself never mentioned the school's "race groups" explicitly in public; indeed, he published his most critical commentaries on school life anonymously in the teachers newsletter. Only one of these anonymous commentaries ever included a pointedly racial sentence. "Has anyone noticed," he wrote, "the overabundance of African-American students cutting class in the hallways?"

Cloaked in anonymity and the relative safety of printed discourse, this news-letter piece provided in a single sentence the only explicitly racial public description of the hallways I would hear over three years at Columbus. Fearing being "shut down," closing off further collaboration, or even unintentionally demonizing Columbus's black students, even those adults most critical of col-ormuteness deleted the word "black" from most discourse on the subject—and in doing so, they often foreclosed the very conversations they privately demanded. My own actions at Columbus were no exception. When I started formally counting the students in the Columbus hallway, as the next section describes, I immediately became unsure even of the accuracy of my own per-ception that "blacks" predominated—and using the word "black" to describe the hallway to certain people who asked me about my observations somehow began to seem so potentially inappropriate as to jeopardize my own position. These twin concerns for accuracy and appropriateness, I was to find, permeated all Columbus adults' private talk about talking racially about the hallways; indeed, the possibility of being either inaccurate or inappropriate came to seem race talk's two central dilemmas. Even in my own fieldnotes, I too was wor-rying about describing the hallways' racial demographics; and my own self-conscious worries about describing the hallways' overrepresentation of "blacks" indicated an even deeper uncertainty about the appropriateness of isolating black students for analysis.

Part 2: Columbus Speakers Struggling to Describe the Hall Wanderers Accurately and Appropriately in Racial Terms

Many times over the years at Columbus, I myself had casually noted the large proportion of students in the hallway who were black; only as a researcher did I begin to count them. One day in 1995, 25 minutes after the class bell had rung, I wrote with surprise in my notes that of the 63 students still inex-plicably in the hallway, "44 of them were black!" A year and a half later, after John suggested directly that I count up the hall wanderers by race, I kept detailed tallies of the hallways for several weeks. While doing so, I filled my fieldnotes with numerous hedging disclaimers about the basic difficulty of accurately labeling individual strangers racially in a place as diverse as Colum-bus. In particular, I realized, describing Columbus's "mixed" students on sight as members of single racialized groups always seemed potentially inaccurate. Note my difficulties with describing the hall wanderers racially even to myself in my fieldnotes:

February 28, 1997
    A black guy walks slowly down one side of the quad. He seems slow, sad, alone to me in his baggy pants—they're inhibiting his knees. A black guy walks past and throws away some fast food garbage. A Latino guy walks by. Actually, I first think

he is white, but his plain, black leather Nikes and his wide beige pants make me think he's Latino. Many of the students walk by repeatedly. Out of 111 students who walk by in the part of the period when I am counting, 12 are (or seem to be) Latino boys, 8 are Latina females, 6 are Filipino boys, 7 are Filipina girls, one is a Chinese boy, five are Chinese girls, one is a Samoan boy, 4 are Samoan girls, one is a white boy and one is a white girl, 13 are kids whose race I can't figure out (a guy I would have assumed was Filipino, for example, is speaking Spanish), 32 are black males, and 20 are black females. Black students make up about 50 percent of the total, not counting the people who walk by repeatedly.

In retrospect, my notes' fairly self-conscious struggles with describing individuals in the hallway racially demonstrated one important blind spot about describing "blacks": while I admitted that I found it hard to tell whether students were "Latino" or "white" or "Filipino," I typically tallied students as "black" "males" or "females" rather than "can't tell" if they appeared physiologically "black" to me at first glance. Unwittingly implementing the traditional American "one drop rule," I challenged my own descriptions of "black" individuals in my notes only occasionally.[10] Taking a tally from an upstairs window one day, for example, I noticed that one student whom I thought was black got closer and was wearing a hair net. Nervously, I changed my tally to "Latino."

Just as I sometimes struggled with labeling individuals racially, I sometimes struggled with labeling demographic patterns racially. At many moments, the demographics of the students cutting class seemed far too complex to harbor any clear-cut pattern of "black" overrepresentation. Note a typical scene in the Columbus quad during homeroom period or "advisory":

Feb. 19th, 1997

In the quad, 15 minutes after the bell. A very diverse crowd of latecomers—even some Chinese-looking kids, some singly, some in groups. Blacks, Samoans, Latinos, mostly in pairs. At advisory, there are crowds of black, Samoan, and Latino kids in the quad. A few pass each other, greet pleasantly—not factionalized in any hostile sense. The dean [*a Filipino man*] comes out, stands looking, and says into his walkie-talkie: "Can we have some help out here in the quad?" He approaches two Filipino boys sitting on a stoop on the side (notably hardly any Filipinos here!) and says, "Why aren't you in homeroom? No, you have to go." He passes them. One stands up briefly, then sits down again! I see Steve [*a young white teacher*] talking to a black guy who's with a Samoan girl and a black girl. Steve looks red. "Why? Everybody and they *mama* . . ." says the guy (I assume he's saying, "isn't in advisory"). Steve retorts something I cannot hear. The kids walk away. "*Okay* then," Steve warns, walking quickly out of the quad toward the office.

"Everybody and they mama" did skip class at Columbus—the racial patterns I found continually leaked. Yet they also held water. As my notes suggested, there were few "Filipino" students in the hallways, and even fewer "Chinese-looking kids"; and a pattern of "black" overrepresentation *did* keep showing up in my tallies of the hall wanderers, especially of those students who wandered the halls in repetitive circles. During a class period the same day as this advisory scene, for example, 83 students walked past me and sixty of them looked "black"—despite the fact that "blacks," according to district records, accounted for only 20 percent of the school population.

Still, every time I confirmed the existence of this racial pattern in the Columbus hallways, I silently challenged the accuracy and implications of my own observation. I knew, for one, that not all the students cutting class stayed in the building: many students who cut classes left Columbus altogether to hang out in friends' houses, restaurants, stores, or their own homes while parents were at work, and some "cutters" did not show up to school at all. Remembering such analytic complexities while doing tallies, I often felt actually relieved to see an expected predominance of "blacks" in the hallways, as these statistics promised to support my running claim that this basic racial pattern in class absence—one that, in my mind, harmed black students themselves—truly existed. Knowing my own hopes for confirming a problematic demographic pattern in the hallways, however, I was always paranoid that I was artificially skewing the tallies to make patterns appear clear-cut. As I wrote in my notes at the end of one day of tallying, "I decide to go on for another 10 minutes—is it because I want the tally to look more black? I do want to 'prove' a particular disservice to them . . ." After many days of compiling these tallies, I found—and let me hedge here—that roughly 60 percent of the students visibly cutting class in Columbus's hallways were students who looked "black" to me, or looked like the kids usually labeled "black" by themselves and their peers.

As Mr. Hernandez explained to me in one informal taped interview in 1999, most public discussions did not allow time for such hedges, caveats, or qualifications about the potential inaccuracies of racial descriptions. Only small group conversations, he said, could allow speakers the opportunity to make these more complex claims:

> "Where you have maybe 6 or 7 people in a room, you can say 'OK, you know what I'm talking about when I say this.' You can listen to me and not judge that I'm making some categorical statement about all African-American freshmen. While in a group of 90 I don't think that that's possible—I don't know if there's a language to do that on a larger level. That's what I think is really hard, creating that language. To be able to do that without offending people, or without, um . . . you know, getting this reaction. OK . . . when really what you're—when really, what you're maybe trying to do is do something really positive, and talk about something constructively."

Even in groups of two, though, those wishing to "do something really positive" with racial descriptions seemed to feel they risked "offending people." I myself became exceedingly self-conscious about the appropriateness of mentioning the overrepresentation of "black" students in the hallways one day in 1997, when the new principal invited me into her office to report to her about "the corridors." My discomfort kept *me* silent even after several months of worrying particularly about black students who were being allowed to miss hours of class in the hallways, and after close to two full years spent quietly analyzing how people at Columbus and in California City were dealing with the court-noted needs of "blacks":

March 7th, 1997

The principal stops me in the hall and says, "You have 20 minutes we could talk?" She says she's interested in what I've seen here compared to last year—pluses and minuses, broad brushed impressions. "Like the kids in the corridor just now. Did you have the impression that last year the halls would've been clear?" she asks as we walk into her office. "From the students' perspective maybe. Because I know all you do here is watch," she adds. Once we are sitting in her office, she brings up the issue of hall wandering again, saying, "We're working on one thing at a time. We're getting better attendance because we're sending home about 30 letters a day. I think it's a small number of hall walkers, like 30, and we're getting to them by talking to them individually, not as a group or anything. And it's working." [*She talks for a time about the physical upkeep of the school. I then respond hesitatingly to her hall wandering question:*] "This might help you with the hall wanderers," I say. "I know a teacher who went to talk to one kid who was wandering and asked, 'what's going on?' And the kid said, 'I just don't know who to go to talk to.' For the sake of the kids, that might be something to know—I think the hall wanderers may feel sort of lost." The principal is nodding seriously.

As I wrote later in my notes, I abruptly realized during this discussion that every student I was envisioning was black. I then debated silently whether to reveal my observations about the hallway's racial demographics to the principal, worrying that mentioning a particular concern for the welfare of "black students" would seem so "negative and rabblerousing" that the principal might "boot me out" of the school:

I was thinking of Latrell Lewis, *again* a black student. I'm thinking now about mentioning black students in particular, their overrepresentation in all the situations I've mentioned so far—but I can't figure out how to say it. I feel nervous that she'd get the sense that I'm looking for this [*appropriateness anxiety*] and that she'd respond very negatively, that she'd question my data [*accuracy anxiety*]. But then I also think that she might not, and that she'd say, "I'm concerned about that too." But my fear for my position here wins out and I just say, "Yeah, if I think of anything else . . ." Interesting that self-protection took over though I *wanted* to say it for the sake of black students!

Something seemed inherently dangerous to me about using the word "black" even in *private* descriptions of the hall wanderers—even though I wanted to mention these demographics "for the sake of black students." For one, the very act of mentioning "blacks" threatened to focus analysis inaccurately or inappropriately *on* "blacks"—and given the risks to self and students of focusing on these students "in particular," even stating a perceived demographic fact seemed potentially quite problematic. Other teachers articulated similar concerns. After my lunchtime discussion about "African-Americans" with Sam, John, and Thomas, I had observed one of Thomas's afternoon classes and stayed afterwards to talk to him. I asked him whether our private lunchtime conversation about "black students" had been typical, and he offered a number of reasons why it was not typical at all:

"That conversation today was really the first one like it I've had," he says. "Really?" I ask. "Yeah. I don't think it's a matter of avoiding it—I just think there's so little time around here to talk about issues bigger than 'what am I going to do tomorrow.' Here the discussions are always in survival mode. Anyway, I don't want to focus on that or anything, to harp on it," he added, musing. "The ethnicity piece?" I asked. "Yeah . . . I mean the fact that they're *black*. I don't want to say it's *because* they're black—I'm not being prejudiced. I think maybe it's because of other things, and I don't know for sure because I haven't done the research or anything. [*Having stated his accuracy concern to me, he then starts comparing and explaining student behaviors in racial terms anyway:*] But something about the socialization of African-Americans— the street culture, and maybe because of the lack of values at home, that makes them different from the Filipino students here, or the Latinos. I have a class first period, and there's a group of Latinos in there, and they can get a little bit rowdy, but not nearly that much." As we are parting, he asks me to remind him of what I'm particularly interested in at Columbus. "Is it the relations between the students?" he asks. "Well, no—I'm interested in how people talk about the community, and diversity," I answer. "Oh," he says, nodding. "I'm particularly interested in what gets talked about, and what doesn't," I add. "Oh, so that's why you were so interested in that topic," he says. "Yeah," I nod. "It's kind of like a white elephant," he says. "What do you mean?" I ask. "Like the analogy—it's something you don't see because it's white and it blends in, but you keep bumping up against it. And they don't know what it is, so they don't talk about it," he says. "Do you agree with what Sam said, that you'd have to be an idiot not to notice it?" I ask. "I think it's hard not to see it—but I don't think it's a matter of being an idiot. I think it's a matter of being aware. Some people are more aware than others. So . . . race matters, huh?" He is smiling. "Exactly," I say.

As adults muttered quiet comments about the "fact" that the students congregated in the hallway were disproportionately "black," some proceeded to offer social or "cultural" hypotheses about the general behaviors of "blacks" in comparison to the school's other racialized groups. Given this explanatory habit, the worry that even mentioning a pattern involving "blacks" would itself seem like "harping" or "focusing" unfairly or "prejudicially" on black students "*because* they were black" was actually a well-founded concern. Further, muted statements about "blacks" alone isolated black students for critique and implied that "black students" *were* somehow inherently problematic "because they were black": for adults musing about black student behaviors avoided any analysis of the dynamics through which various players *other* than "blacks" helped produce an overrepresentation of "blacks" in the hall wandering "problem." Without analysis of how teachers disproportionately ejected or bored black students into the hallways, or how administrators disproportionately left them there to wander, or how other students chose to stay home rather than to roam, simply referencing "blacks" when complaining about the demographics of this difficult school "issue" *could* always be "prejudiced": for repetitive private statements about blacks in isolation left the analysis of the problem resting on the shoulders of black students alone. Yet as people knowingly resisted *any* shared analysis of phenomena like the hallway's racial demographics, the issue of how *adults served* black students at Columbus also remained in the corner unaddressed.[11] Confining the "white elephant" issue (a particularly ironic analogy in this case) of "blacks" involved in "problems" to fleeting suggestive and critical references, adults repeatedly, if unconsciously, returned quietly to frame black students themselves as disproportionately "problematic" people.

Other analysts have noted that many U.S. speakers frame any mention of problematic racial demographics as potentially "racist," and they have worried that this framing of race talk keeps speakers from pointing out "real" racism (see, e.g., Blum 2002). Yet simple racial descriptions *can* be racist, it seems, if they leave particular race groups dangling analytically as if they are somehow responsible in isolation for racial patterns. And at Columbus, self-conscious anxieties about describing and critiquing "blacks" often indicated a well-founded worry about this very kind of analytic reduction. Non-black students at Columbus, too, who typically expressed little concern that racial descriptions in general risked "prejudice," occasionally expressed concerns that using the label "black" when describing peers as troublemakers might be "racist." As one self-described "mixed" boy, talking about students who were "all loud and noisy down in the computer lab in the library," put it, "I'm not racist but the black kids, I hate how they behave, they really mess things up." Similarly, one Filipina girl apologized for a racial description she made in a letter about the hallways written to a white teacher as an assignment:

> "Dear Mr. J., My day has been bad. I'm just a little angry about these people that push you in the hallway . . . I'm not trying to be racise [*sic*] but the majority was black people. That's the reason why I hate going through the second floor because that's were [*sic*] they stay."[12]

Acknowledging similarly that the basic act of quickly and critically mentioning a disproportionate presence of "blacks" when describing the demographics of Columbus's hallways seemed potentially "prejudiced" or "racist," many Columbus adults admitted that they accordingly omitted even basic descriptions of the problem. Yet paradoxically, full deletion of such public descriptions had the white elephant of potential solutions, too, being bumped into repeatedly yet actively ignored. Mr. S, a teacher who described himself as "black," even suggested to me once that the overrepresentation of "black" students in the hallways was so "obvious" that it did not *need* to be articulated or addressed in so many words:

> "It's one of those things that goes without saying. You don't need to say it, it's obvious. Listen to the voices in the hallway," he said, gesturing towards the building. "The kids not going to class—they're mostly black."

Such knowing silences—which marked and accepted the overrepresentation of "blacks," while actively resisting debating a role for adults in preventing their disproportionate presence—were themselves a form of racializing action. For as adults at Columbus kept noticing black students in the hallways and choosing actively not to mention them, they helped black hall wanderers *become* a daily phenomenon that "went without saying"—a normalized part of school life. The focus of more anxious attention at Columbus than any other "racial group," "black students" were also actively *overlooked* more than any other racial group: and both acts, as the final section of this chapter shows, actually placed black students' blackness at their center. In essence, adults proceeding with a sigh as if they assumed that black students *would* be involved in Columbus "problems" both watched and ignored black students in particular *because they were black*. Quietly, Columbus adults both focused on and ignored black students in racial terms—and in private conversations, adults occasionally acknowledged that by anxiously surveilling and ignoring black students in particular *throughout* Columbus life, they themselves helped *create* as well as normalize the demographics of the hall-wandering "problem."

Part 3: Creating a "Problem" That "Goes without Saying," by Actively Watching *and* Ignoring People "Because of Race"

My own notes from my first day of teaching at Columbus in 1994 listed the names of seven students I wanted to monitor for disciplinary reasons. All seven, as I noted later, were black boys. On my second day, I made notes to call the homes of five girls and boys—all of whom again were black. I had starred two students (both black) literally as "A PROBLEM."

Describing Columbus life in my fieldnotes the following year, as I also noticed later, I tended similarly to quietly record the particular presence of "black" students at problematic moments:

> Dec. 5, 1996
>
> A lot of kids not going to class today—LOTS—*many* black. Most basically ignored Mr. Hernandez when he said "get to class." I passed the Dean's office today at 7th period and there were 5 kids there, all black.

Approaching Columbus as a researcher with increasing knowledge of legal and district expectations that the city's schools serve "African-Americans" in particular better, I found myself regularly wandering around Columbus silently looking for "black" students involved in troubling situations. As my ethnographic eye returned repeatedly to seek black students involved in "problems," however, it seemed that both I and the adults present were framing black students as the ones to watch. Inside and outside one white teacher's classroom in 1997, for example, I observed a host of exasperated adults immediately spotlight two black students as the center of disciplinary attention. Black students at Columbus, it often seemed, were ejected most visibly from classes before becoming most visible in the halls:

> After class has started, a black student, Roddy, enters the room and moves stuff around on the overhead projector. He goes to the very back of the room to sit. Another black student, Duke, comes back to sit with him. The teacher gives Roddy the option to move to his assigned desk or leave the room [*immediate disciplinary focus*]. Roddy decides to leave. Duke leaves with him. [*Now gone, they are still the center of adult attention:*] The teacher calls security on the phone and gives them the names of the two boys. In minutes, Roddy and Duke are brought back by the [Filipino] dean. [*They tell a story of being focused on:*] "They had us on the walkie-talkies! They were like, 'Roddy and Duke walking the halls!'" Roddy says, sitting down in the back of the class again. "I'm on work strike . . . I won't work! I won't work!" he adds, laughing. The teacher continues to explain the assignment. "My religion is that I don't do homework Monday through Thursday," Roddy says loudly. The teacher continues, *purposefully ignoring Roddy.*[13]

Right before class, this teacher had told me he was trying to figure out "how to deal" with Roddy, Duke, and several other students in his class (all of whom were black) with whom he was having consistent "problems." His planned classroom strategy seemed to involve both focusing disciplinarily on these black students and actively refusing to pay attention to them:

> He had seated them throughout the room to separate them, he said, but he was now thinking of "putting them all together in one group." [*focus*] If they worked, good, but if not, he said, he didn't care, and he would just show them their grades at the end of the period. [*ignore*] He said he was also thinking of putting Roddy and Duke up in front of the room to do their mother-capping games in front of everyone, [*focus*] to keep score, to "flirt with the danger."

Throughout Columbus classrooms and offices, I watched adults alternately focus angry disciplinary attention on black students and ignore them rigorously as a purposeful disciplinary strategy. Some adults, like Roddy and Duke's teacher, spoke surprisingly consciously of both tendencies in their own behavior—and at times, others even suggested that a tendency to simultaneously focus on and ignore black students dangerously undergirded schoolwide plans for educational reform. During the orientation for new Columbus faculty immediately after reconstitution, for example, I accompanied the new staff on a bus tour of students' neighborhoods that many Columbus adults referred to wryly after the fact as "the bus ride through the ghetto." The bulk of the tour, some noted, had been spent driving through several mostly-black housing projects and neighborhoods, rather than through the neighborhoods of small single and multi-family houses immediately around Columbus where the majority of the school's Filipino and Latino students lived. A number of faculty later whispered irritably that the tour had focused disproportionately on black students and their presumed "problems" in a way that promoted a reductive vision of the school's "blacks" as well. Even as the bus had driven through the Ridgetop housing project, where all the people visible on the streets looked African-American (and as a police officer on the bus, herself black, acted as tour guide), several teachers had spoken up to protest an implicit and uncomfortable focus on this population:

> The police officer says, "These people like respect—the first thing they say, when you come through here looking, is 'we're not animals.' So treat them with respect." "Then why're we doing this then?" asks Charles [*black teacher*] from the back. Kurt [*white teacher*], sitting next to him, says loudly, "The point was to see the neighborhoods where our kids live—the *full range* of living conditions." "And ethnic makeup," adds Charles.

The bus ride concluded with a debriefing session among the new faculty, in which subtle critiques of the ride itself intertwined with appreciative comments about the eye-opening glimpse of Columbus students' impoverished neighborhoods. Yet private critiques of the ride's racialized dynamics—its voyeuristic brief viewing of "the ghetto" and its disproportionate, seemingly patronizing focus on "blacks"—continued for some time. After a lunch break several days after the tour, I was walking back into the building with Charles, Kurt, and a white teacher, Liz, all of whom had taught previously at Columbus. With a frown, Kurt suddenly brought up the "bus ride through the ghetto":

> "It wasn't supposed to be that, but it was," he says, adding, "It was supposed to be a trip to see the various neighborhoods our students came from, and it was all Ridgetop." Charles nods, adding, "That's the problem I had with it—we were basically just going through *this* neighborhood, for example, on the way to the black ghettos." "But that's the principal's focus," Liz says, looking at Charles. She adds, "Not to mention the fact that our school is 40% Latino."

The bus ride had suggested to these teachers that the new Columbus would itself be disproportionately "focused" on black students from "the ghetto," despite the school's more complex demographics; they surmised that other populations, like "Latinos," would likely be overlooked in the rush to frame "blacks" as the school's key needy population. Yet Kurt predicted next that this very anticipated mental focus on needy students from "the black ghettos" would inevitably have school adults ignoring the actual needs of "black students." "Coddling" black students as a kind of "special" treatment, Kurt suggested, would in the end do "blacks" a particular disservice:

> "All the focus was on Ridgetop, 'these poor kids from these miserable lives,'" Kurt continues. "Then that leads to coddling them—low expectations. We figured out that the house program really worked for the whole school. But the Consent Decree was all about focusing on black students, on Port Place, Ridgetop and Chapman Place [*all housing projects*]—then they added Latinos, but it was really mostly about blacks," he says. "You should know where they come from, and then that's *it*—treat them the same as everybody else. Definitely. Treating them 'specially' means having lower expectations for them," he continues. "Like remember Mr. Septimo? He wouldn't ever give anyone lower than a 'C,' regardless of their homework or attendance, because he basically had been told so by the superintendent. The Consent Decree says you're supposed to raise those students' grades, so you do. The Consent Decree says you're supposed to suspend fewer black students, so you don't suspend them, for the same infractions. And this all leads to taking away those kids' opportunities for success."

Even in a multiracial school like Columbus, Kurt suggested, quiet, district-urged framings of need did seem to "focus" implicitly on imagining the particular "problems" of black students. Yet when "focusing" on black students' presumed particular "misery," Kurt suggested, adults at the school and district levels tended to just overlook actual performance or behavior rather than debate methods for *assisting* "blacks"—and in doing so, adults often just lowered their "expectations" and in the end sabotaged opportunities for black students themselves. If needs and outcomes were noted and regretted but not truly addressed, he implied, focusing on black students was not in itself a service. Ms. Tubbs, a teacher who identified herself as "black," described to me a related classroom-level paradox of focusing unproductively on the school's "blacks" one day after school in the spring of 1996. Columbus adults struggling with various disciplinary "troublemakers" in their own classes, she suggested, actively focused on "black kids" as students who would cause disproportionate problems, even while ignoring black students themselves as a way of avoiding problematic interactions. Her example implied that in an ironic form of focused ignoring, adults themselves particularly *allowed* black students to leave the classroom for the hallways:

> "When a black kid stands up and says, 'Fuck this shit,' and walks out, the teacher lets him, and says, 'Oh, I'm glad he's gone, I don't have to deal with him today!' It's an issue that nobody talks about," she said. What teachers typically decided to do with a "*black* student who's a troublemaker," she said, was "to say, 'don't bother him too much, don't ask too much of him, he's black.'" And they just let him sleep over there in the corner. That's the other side of the coin, you see!" she finished.

Again, a quiet focus that assumed that black students would *be* "trouble" seemed to have Columbus adults primed as much to ignore actual black students as to pay them focused attention. Explaining to me next why black students had been relatively absent from a recent public student protest against the district's decision to reconstitute Columbus (which had culminated in a student press conference held on the school lawn), Ms. Tubbs suggested that black students at Columbus routinely felt "ostracized" from such communal events precisely *because* teacher and administrator adults so often focused on them for meticulous disciplinary observation. Black students, she suggested, felt at once invisible and hypervisible:[14]

> "Black students here—everywhere, really—feel ostracized," she said. [*ignored*] "They have for a long time. They feel left out—after *years* of being ostracized. And they know that if they were to gather, in numbers, the teachers would start gathering, the cars would start circling, you know. [*focus*] Because the teachers wouldn't know what was going on. We are the most visible, just because of our skin color—and that's okay. But when other students are there, it takes them a while to tell—and when a black student is there, they know *immediately* a black student was involved," she said, raising her eyebrows. [*focus*] "So that is to say, out here that day the black students *weren't* gathering. They know they're seen as the troublemakers, that if they gather 10 more teachers come out to 'supervise.'" [*focus*] (She did finger quotes when she said this.) "They've learned by now—*we've* learned to stand on the fringe. [*ignored*] If they were to get involved in the protest, Mr. Manrell [*a black dean*] would be out here and the walkie-talkies would start flashing and beeping." [*focus*]

For Ms. Tubbs, black students existed socially on "the fringe" even while being made psychologically central to Columbus life: surveilled and "ostracized" simultaneously, Ms. Tubbs suggested, Columbus's black students found themselves both ignored and the center of negative adult attention. Meanwhile, other adults, describing this tendency to rigorously ignore black students in particular, claimed that a black student who was ignored by adults was receiving a racialized form of preferential treatment. In 1997, I was eating lunch outside with Sarah and Lou (both white teachers), when Sarah, having commented on the demographics of Columbus's sports teams, suddenly announced that she was "going to say something bold":

> "I think this school's really Afrocentric," she repeats. "Really? How so?" I ask. "I mean I look at my students and I'm like 'hel*l*o!' We got Lat*i*nos, we got Sam*o*ans, I got *To*ngans—*they* need programs too. I dunno, it just seems really Afrocentric to me, in everything we do. [*focus*] It just seems like those kids are being *allowed* so much. I mean I look out my window at 3 o'clock and there are 20 black kids sitting there ready to leave, and no one's saying *any*thing to them. [*ignore*] There's something weird going on."
>
> Lou says, "But those are the ones not going to class. I dunno, I see that as not serving them well enough. I mean I look out in the hallway outside my class and I'm

shocked. Eighty percent of the kids are black." "*Thank* you," Sarah says. "And they're only 20% of the school," Lou adds. "*Thank* you," Sarah says. "That's interesting—so *you* see it as a *focus* on black students," I say, looking at Sarah. "And *you* see it as *neglect* of them," I say, looking at Lou. They both nod.

Both teachers agreed on the hallway's racial demographics, and both agreed that the adults at the school helped condone and thus produce these demographics; what they could not agree on was whether black students themselves were being particularly disadvantaged or advantaged by adult silences. To Sarah, actively ignoring "blacks" was evidence of a school pro-black focus; to Lou, the active ignoring seemed like a failure by adults to serve blacks in particular. Truly, both watching *and* ignoring black students in particular could seem alternately unfair to black students themselves, and accordingly, Columbus adults often simply alternated the two strategies.

At less self-conscious moments, Columbus people simply displayed these simultaneous dynamics of "focus" and "neglect," without fully recognizing their ironic coexistence. In 1997, as described in the beginning of this chapter, I spent one painfully ironic half hour in the hallway talking to Mr. C, a white teacher who gradually arrived at the argument that Columbus—like other schools in the district—was not serving "black students" well enough. As we stood talking, black students wandering around the building passed us repeatedly. Mr. C greeted several students multiple times with a laugh and the friendly accusation, "I thought you were going to class!" He continued to say people needed to "address" the "problem" of serving "black" students—as we both stood there ignoring hall wanderers who were primarily "black."

Black students themselves also noted occasionally that adults knowingly allowed them to wander the halls unimpeded. During one class period in 1997, two students approached me as I was sitting outside listening to a black security guard tell a group of students in the far hallway to "*Go* to *class! Go! Go! Go! Go! Go!*":

> As I sit and write, two black guys I have met this year come by and sit down with me. They both have Valentine's balloon sticks stuck in their hair. "So you don't have class right now?" I say, smiling. "I don't answer questions like that for fear they may be held against me in a court of law," replies one guy. "So . . . whose class are you missing?" I repeat, smiling. "I don't answer . . ." he repeats. "I won't hold anything against you. I'm a researcher this year, I don't enforce," I say. [*Having chosen self-consciously to refrain from any teacher-like discipline, I, too, of course, was part of the hall wandering "problem."*] "Mr. Kong," he replies, saying he doesn't remember the name of the course. "English. I saw you before in Mr. Chuck's English class, you were super sharp," I say. "Thanks for the compliment," he replies, as his friend repeats, "Not just sharp, but *super* sharp." We joke about how one of them has to spend his Valentine's Day working at Kentucky Fried Chicken. Then I ask, "So how is it that it's so easy for you to cut class?" They smile. One says he has been cutting not just

for the whole day today, but for the last two weeks. The other says, "Usually when I walk around I'm in my big coat and my hood, and my glasses. I look so intelligent that nobody ever says anything to me." "So it's because you guys look so intelligent," I repeat, smiling. "I dunno. No one ever says anything. The rookie security guards just tell you to get to class, and you say 'I'm going,' and they leave you alone. And you're not lying, because you are going to class—just not this period!" he chuckles. "So your conscience is clear," I say. He says yes. I ask why no one else stops him. He describes an example where "some new teacher—I don't know his name—saw me and said 'go to class.' He maybe even followed me for a few minutes. Then I went down the quad hallway, and doubled back on the ground under the hallway. The teacher didn't do anything. He saw me and everything." He points out the teacher [*a white teacher*], who happens to be walking by.

Positing various explanations for why adults allowed them to wander the hallways, the black students I talked to offered even more explanations for why they themselves chose to wander. These explanations always indicated that the apparent student "choice" to wander the halls intertwined adults and students in a depressing feedback loop of mutual avoidance—and many of these explanations indicated further that school adults themselves played a role in making wandering seem preferable to attending class. Some students said they actively avoided classes in which they did not understand the work or didn't feel like doing it, or in which teachers talked too much. While some explained that they cut class to hang out with their friends (and some sighed that they were simply "trying to get out of this motherfucker"), others said classroom desks were just unbearably uncomfortable, while still others said classes were "just TOO LONG." As many students noted directly, further, students' very presence in the hallways served as an implied critique of adults' classroom practices, and some black students—notably choosing to wander in the building rather than skip school altogether like some of their peers—trudged through the hallways for countless repetitive hours. A classic afternoon of sitting in the dean's office in 1997 demonstrated to me that cutting class in the building involved alternately weathering the brunt of frustrated adult attention and waiting interminably in social purgatory, ignored by surrounding adults:

A black girl asks a second black girl why she's here. "To get a pass to class," the second girl replies. She sits for some time, encouraged by the first girl to do some skills worksheets out of a workbook in the office. Several periods later, she is still sitting, and a new black girl now also sitting in the office asks her the same question of why she is here. She now responds bluntly, "because I don't want to go to class!" All day, various kids are either sent between several holding rooms or left waiting here to call their parents or to talk to some administrator. Some suggest that they are simply pretending to be waiting for something. One black girl apprehended in the hallway by a teacher and the principal says that she had actually been going to class, but the teacher started "getting in her business and following her." She decided to come to the dean's office so she could call her mother, rather than "sit like a stupid" up in one of the holding rooms.

Mr. P [*a black administrator*] tells Tommy, another black student, that he can't be down here every day. "Teacher's prejudiced," Tommy says. "Everybody's prejudiced," Mr. P replies, looking at me. He adds to Tommy, "You can't stay in here." Over the next hour or so, various adults tell Tommy to go away, and he refuses. The dean actually walks him out of the office, but he comes back. After Tommy tells an ROTC adviser [*a white man*] who asks why he is in the dean's office that it is "none of his business," he is finally kicked out of the dean's office by Mr. P himself, who says, "you gotta get out of here, you can't stay here, I don't *care* where you go." Tommy tries numerous times to get back in to the now empty dean's office, in partnership with a Samoan boy who has also been in the office sporadically throughout the morning. At one point Tommy even throws his body against the door, which the ROTC adviser holds tightly shut. Afterwards, Tommy keeps knocking on the door intermittently. "That Tommy—he drives me crazy—he's been here since 8:30 this morning!" says the secretary [*a Latina woman*]. Half an hour later, Tommy comes back into the dean's office with Mr. P, who takes him into his private office for a discussion. "He needs attention and that's probably the only way he can get it," says another black student who has been waiting here trying to call her house.

Weathering intermittent bouts of disciplinary "attention," students across Columbus chose wandering over classroom life; a small subset of others escaped from school altogether. Trying to locate such paths of escape, I found that students ran rather unglamorously down back staircases covered with graffiti, through rear hallways missing chunks of wall, and out back doorways strewn with shards of broken window pane:

> I walk around the outer fence of the football field. About 5 holes have been clearly patched over. I find a hole and walk in, stepping on broken glass, and sit on the bleachers. Paint is chipped off, and a large "Columbus High" is covered with tags and tags with lines through them. A security guard wanders over to me and says he thought I was a student. Kids start to try to get out here around 10 minutes before the lunch bell, he explains. This is his post. "They get out through the gym locker room windows," he says, pointing across the field to windows in another area covered with graffiti. A black student suddenly appears next to us through the same hole in the fence I just entered through. The security guard tells him to stop. "I'll take him to the Dean's office, or I'll suspend him," he says to me. "C'mere," he says to the kid. "Why?" the kid asks. "Just c'mere," he says. The kid walks slowly across the field with him. I wait a few minutes until lunch. Five or six kids run out from the tennis courts and see the security guard, who gets up and walks them back into the building.

As students appeared and disappeared through holes in walls and fences, Columbus adults alternately detained black students and let them run. And as frustrated adults sometimes even hauled students just arriving at school straight to the dean's office, somehow black students at Columbus often seemed lost even when they were disciplinarily found. On a single day in the winter of 1996, a teacher, a student, and a security guard each mentioned to me in separate private conversations that certain subsets of Columbus students—the teacher mentioned "Latinos," and the student and security guard mentioned "blacks"—were particularly "getting lost" at Columbus, as their needs for focused adult attention went unmet. The next afternoon, I noticed that a black student waiting outside to leave campus actually had the words "lost soul" shaved into the back of his hair. I approached him to ask what the phrase suggested. As the last period of class ticked away, he explained that most of the students from his neighborhood—Ridgetop, the majority black housing project that had been the focus of the faculty "bus ride through the ghetto"— were "lost souls" floating through school without self-direction or targeted adult guidance. He himself was a "leader" and would make it, he posited, but the rest would falter. Later that spring, finally, I turned the corner outside of Columbus in time to see a black student attempting a lunchtime escape over the auditorium fence fall on his tailbone on the concrete. As adults ran toward him, he lay on the sidewalk writhing in pain; teachers circled around him and the principal cradled his head in anticipation of the approaching ambulance. Momentarily the center of adult attention, he was a paradoxical exception to black students' tendency to vanish in full view.

Ignoring and Overlooking Students in Racial Terms

Of the various "racial/ethnic" populations in Columbus and in California City, "black students" were most often the center of racialized adult attention— and they were also most often actively ignored. Language both mirrored and constituted both actions: while adult talk served primarily to frame black students as "problem kids" *with* "problems," adult silence actively ignoring black students also left them wandering "lost souls." While the word "black" was being self-consciously struck out of policy and school language, however, other race labels often went matter-of-factly unused, or used primarily in connection to certain predictable topics; and the populations *referenced* by the labels typically weathered an analogous experience.

The word "Samoan," for example, was almost completely absent from district talk, an absence indicating the district's basic lack of concern for this small population. And at Columbus, outside of some talk of school clubs or "multicultural" assemblies, the word "Samoan" emerged almost exclusively in unflattering talk of incidents of disciplinary conflict or student violence. Samoan students at Columbus, as some suggested, were thus framed largely as students prone to violence: reporting at one "Samoan club" meeting on some teacher complaints that "some guys were sticking around after volleyball practice and causing trouble," for example, a Samoan security guard sighed: "And they don't ever say last names you know, they just say 'a Samoan kid,' " he said, gesturing to indicate a big person. "That *hurts* me," he finished, patting his chest.

The word "Chinese," in contrast, rarely came up in *any* school or district talk of "problems," in public or private. While most Chinese students at Columbus struggled with the dire poverty and dislocation of being some of the school's most recent immigrants, the word "Chinese" typically just popped up quietly to describe students who were achieving admirably in classes. As in California City discourse at large, the latching of "Chinese" to academic or behavioral success stories imbued the very word with connotations of unassisted success, and Chinese students themselves often thus slipped under the attention radar. As I myself wrote in my notes in early 1996, "I keep forgetting the Chinese population (most are in ESL). Indicative of school at large (they're 'OK' so they don't get any attention)."[15]

Further, while Columbus housed only small populations of "Chinese" and "Samoan" students, "Filipinos" comprised a third of the student population; yet at Columbus and in district talk, "Filipino students" received almost no institutionalized attention as a distinct group. Filipino students, who dominated Columbus's student government, most of its upper-level courses, and its Junior ROTC corps (which took over the main quad with drum and step routines nearly every day after school), often functioned as the school's unmarked backdrop: one typically stood out in public Columbus activities when one was *not* Filipino (as I wrote in one set of notes, "Watching the ROTC squad march and then play kickball, I notice that I am counting all of the non-Filipinos first"). With "Chinese" students the focus of districtwide talk of exemplary achievement and "black" and "Latino" students the focus of districtwide anxiety about school failure, further, district talk rarely referenced "Filipino" students at all. In one district function for the "Filipino Educators Association" in 1997, as a Filipino teacher told me, Filipino community members had begun to demand that the district actively monitor "Filipino" student achievement—still low in districtwide and statewide terms—precisely because the topic was so absent from the district's public analysis. A union official, a white man, put it to me most bluntly in one private conversation: "Filipinos are neglected districtwide," he said, "because there is no Filipino voice."

As we have seen, further, talk of "Latino" students (linked almost always to talk of "African-Americans") did emerge sporadically in district talk of school reform and academic achievement, yet everyday talk of "Latinos" as a group was strikingly rare among Columbus adults even in private. Aside from occasional references to student-student relations (like the "Latino/Samoan blowout"), curriculum, or performances in "multicultural" assemblies, Columbus adults rarely even referenced "Latino kids" as a distinct school population in informal conversations. At over a third of the Columbus population by the district's count, "Latino" (or "Hispanic") students were actually the largest "racial/ethnic" population at Columbus; but "Latinos" (who, like the school's "Chinese," "Filipinos," and "Samoans," straddled the immigrant and non-immigrant population) tended to vanish completely from school discourse rather than be framed as an asset *or* "problem." Even in private talk, that is, Columbus adults never noticeably *avoided* using the word "Latino": they simply rarely mentioned that the school's "Latino" population existed. In the middle of my last year of research, I myself suddenly realized how comparatively little data I had been collecting on "Latinos":

> Focusing on Latino students too would be good, but I'm not sure that I can do this. First of all, so many of the students are in ESL that I really have little data on them from the last two years (this negligence on my part indicates to some degree, perhaps, the isolation of ESL students from the rest of the school). I preferred to go looking in places where there seemed to be more "problems"—a bias in itself . . .

Disproportionately present neither on the honor roll nor on the suspension list, Latino students themselves often literally vanished, unnoticed, from class rosters. At graduation in 1997, I was shocked to realize that many of the Latino students I had taught two years earlier were nowhere to be found. Overlooking "Latinos," it seemed, was the flip side of focusing on the Columbus population more relentlessly positioned as "problematic": in one private conversation on school achievement in 1999, an ESL teacher admitted to me that he really had no idea how "Latinos" were doing as a group at Columbus, but he was certain that "black" achievement at Columbus was under par. Oddly, while this teacher taught many Latino students, he taught no black students at all.[16]

Finally, while "black" students remained the anxious focus of most quiet adult analyses of Columbus "problems," perhaps most absent in adult talk was any sustained public analysis of the role of "white" people in those problems.[17] As one black security guard who had attended Columbus in the 1970s put it, "African-American" students at Columbus seemingly would always be "labeled 'most likely to cut' "; yet in analyzing issues like the hallway, few Columbus people pointed out that the adult population ostensibly permitting students to wander for hours was disproportionately white. In adult descriptions of the hallways, the word "white" showed up only when adults quoted students who spit out racial epithets in anger.

McIntyre (1997) has argued that white educators tend to resist analyzing the role "whites" themselves play in producing racial orders, instead displacing race analysis onto people of color exclusively.[18] At Columbus, a resistance to investigating the role "white" adults played in producing the "black" hall-wandering demographic definitely characterized white adults' daily talk about the hallways; indeed, adults of all "races" talked far more about the hall wanderers than about the role of adults themselves. At Columbus, however, "white" adults did not, as some scholars have argued generally about U.S. "whites," simply overlook or unwittingly "unmark" themselves as non-racial Columbus players.[19]

Rather, the role of "white people" in producing various racialized patterns at Columbus went anxiously and actively unanalyzed. While white adults privately admitted feeling *extremely* racialized in the Columbus context, particularly in their relations with their students (see chapters 2 and 4), and while some "white" teachers felt that subtly racialized district discourse positioned *them* as the district's central problem (see chapter 3), at the school and district levels the very word "white" deftly escaped *any* public attachment to schooling "problems." Districtwide, in fact, the word "white" appeared in little public adult talk of any schooling subject in California City, even though "whites" formed the vast majority of the district's staff as well as its population of most "advantaged" students. Further, private talk *about* race talk at the school level, centered typically on the social and practical difficulties of talking about "blacks," rarely addressed the possibility of talking about "whites" at all. While people at Columbus and in the district repeatedly made the label "black" the most problematic member of the racial vocabulary—and while they too talked more *about* talking about black students in law or policy than about any other local "racial" group—"white" people were, in some ways, race talk's real "white elephant." Adults of all "races" at Columbus and in California City called regularly for talk about "blacks," but they never called for public talk about "whites"; and no adult, in public, expressed particular concern over this omission.[20]

Conclusion

The everyday anxiety many Americans, particularly "whites," admit they face over labeling someone else as "black" or "African-American" (and the stumbling and pausing many Americans exhibit before using the very word) not only illuminates general fears of being "racist" by making others' "race" inaccurately or inappropriately relevant in one's words; it also suggests a tendency to associate the full danger of a racialized system with those described. Such anxiety about using the word "black" also suggests insidiously, as it has for several centuries, that simply labeling someone as "black" in the United States still feels to many "whites" and others like a dangerously negative evaluation. Indeed, that racial descriptions of patterns involving "blacks" *are* so often latched to racialized evaluations of "black" *people* reminds us that race and racism have always been at root *about* evaluating people—about creating hierarchies and displacing responsibility for social "problems" rather than simply describing "difference." At multiracial Columbus, analyzing various racially patterned "problems" indeed always seemed to involve pinning responsibility for those orders on racialized peoples, quietly placing blame somewhere along a tense wire stretched between the poles of "white" and "black." As Frankenberg (1995) writes, however, "To speak of whiteness is . . . to assign *everyone* a place in the relations of racism" (6)—and so talk and anxious silence most often focused on "blacks" alone.

As all race labels *are* linked inextricably to the nation's inequality system—and as all such words *are* so often used when placing responsibility for social problems reductively on particular "races"—it is no wonder that in various contexts they can seem too dangerous to use. Yet packing particular worry into particular race labels, it seems, often functions to ignore the racializing roles being played by members of other "groups," and by speakers themselves. In *refusing* to use the word "black"—or in stuttering before mentioning "blacks," or in prefacing a description of "black students" with "I'm gonna say something bold"—Columbus adults not only exhibited an understandable fear of reproducing anti-black "racism," but also helped *reproduce* such "racism," by placing the full weight and fear of racial inequality and tension on young "black" people rather than opening up the analysis of racial orders to include the school's adults. At Columbus, "black" students, as DuBois would have predicted long ago, remained alone at the center of race analysis even as adults dodging the possibility of "racism" particularly resisted using the very word.

Yet Columbus adults also resisted public race talk out of concerns that clumsy race talk could *harm* "black students," and indeed, sporadic and rushed public meetings, where teachers spoke to almost 100 peers under the evaluating gaze of powerful administrators, were perhaps *not* the best locations for thorough discussions of how various "races" played roles in various school "problems." Across Columbus, in fact, adults of all "races" quietly framed public forums as the settings least conducive to explicitly race-related interchange. Yet paradoxically, they noted, *without* noting race's relevance during schoolwide debates about "problems," there was no way to make schoolwide plans for erasing problematic patterns that were racial. And across Columbus, accordingly, well-meaning adults just kept waiting agitatedly for the word "black" to appear in other people's public discourse. In one faculty meeting several months into the 1996–97 school year, I went outside to get some fresh air with a white teacher who had returned to Columbus after reconstitution. Within minutes, he was arguing that the turnover would never be successful unless the new staff *stopped* "talking about themselves" and instead openly discussed the welfare of "black" students:

> He says that he thinks that "once people stop talking about themselves and start talking about what students need," things will come around at Columbus. Last year, he says, he felt many teachers "had their little group of hand-picked honor students and gave up on all the other kids." "And did you see who went to the Shakespeare Festival this year?" he asks. "No," I say. "There was only one black student, and that was Lavanne," he says, adding, "The rest were all Asian students, Filipinos. Nobody said, 'Let's make sure there are 25 African-American girls on that trip so they can go to experience and appreciate other cultures.' If they didn't get their homework

done, or get their parents' permission, they didn't go," he says. "Do you think the motive to get 25 black girls there is there this year?" I ask. "I think it's *coming*—I think it *will* get *said*," he replies. "When I see someone stand up at a meeting like the one this morning and say, 'I'm concerned about the situation of the African-American girls who roam the halls every day,' I'll know it's working," he finishes. "So you think someone will say this?" I ask. "I *think* so," he says. "Why don't you?" I ask. "Well, I kind of want to see if *they* say it," he says. "Because then I'll really know things are working here."

Postscript

On the telephone one night in 1998, I was talking to Tina, a recently graduated student who typically self-identified as "black." I told her I was trying to write a chapter about how teachers talked about the "black students" wandering in the hallways. I was arguing, I said, that teachers privately talked about the hallways in racial terms but never did so in public; my hypothesis was that both actions somehow seemed to frame "black" students as particularly problematic. She tsked, as I wrote in my notes:

> She said students really didn't talk about the hallway as racially patterned. They didn't "sit around and analyze that 20 percent of the people in the hallway were Filipino"—they talked about the specific individuals they saw wandering. She asked why teachers cared about the hallway so much anyway. I said that the hallway seemed to adults like the ultimate academic symbol—when you asked teachers how things were going, they would often say something about the hallways right away. She said she was surprised to hear that adults worried about the hallway so much. "Get a life!" she said. She said that at her workplace she didn't sit around and analyze who was going to the water cooler a lot. I said perhaps this was because nobody was evaluating her on how many people went to the water cooler. "The teachers were being evaluated by how many kids were in the hallway?" she asked. I said yes, teachers were being evaluated all the time—that's why they got reconstituted, because higher-ups decided the teachers weren't good enough. She said new teachers hadn't made a difference anyway. "You could get Jesus Christ in there and there would be kids in the hallway," she said. Kids were going to cut regardless, it was like nature. She said I could quote her on this.
>
> She said again that basically, students didn't think very much about racial patterns in the hallway—they thought more about the individual stories of their friends. Occasionally, she herself had walked around in the hallway with a number of other "black students," because "people tend to hang out with who they feel more familiar with and comfortable with, who is more like them." She would see another group of students in the hallway, she said, "and they would be black, but to us, they would just be Willie and his friends." Then they would see a group of "Filipino kids" and it would just be

"Ginny and so and so." Then they would pass a group of "Latin kids" but it would just be "Luis and so and so." She said they wouldn't say something like " 'there are too many Filipinos in the hallway'—we didn't talk about it because we didn't care," she said. She said that if you were in the hallway you got caught no matter what color you were, and that really none of her teachers treated people that way.

She had noticed a number of incidents in classes, though, she added, where a Filipino student and a black male student would each come in late, and the teacher always had something to say to the black male student. Other students had also pointed out to her how when two students of different races did the same thing, one got talked to and the other one didn't. And in regard to graduation, she said, students did sit around talking about the kids they knew who weren't graduating, and with her friends it was all black students they were mentioning. But you could ask a "Latin student" and they would probably mention the Latin students they knew who weren't graduating, or the Filipino students would list who they knew that wasn't graduating. She said again that it was more about knowing individual stories. Like Daniel Cruza [*a Filipino student*], she knew he didn't graduate because he dropped out of school in 10th grade to take care of his baby.

I mentioned how I had once seen a teacher who was black look at the senior picture crowd and count how few black students were there. She tsked and said this was like going to the prom and counting who was there and saying they were the ones who were going to graduate. She just stayed at the prom for 15 minutes. She herself wasn't about to get up early to go take the graduation picture, and she knew a lot of other students who didn't care either. She admitted, though, that at the end of senior year—when people were getting their caps and gowns, and at graduation itself—other students did notice that "there were hardly any black people there." But at first, she said again, people would stand around and talk about their individual friends, Sheri so and so who wasn't graduating. Then someone might say, "Huh, there's hardly any black people on the stage!" But then they would talk more about the specific people who didn't graduate. "We were more on a personal level," she said.

For Tina, as for all Columbus people, race did not *constantly* matter to how one perceived the other human beings at Columbus; indeed, on an individual level life often seemed to proceed "no matter what color you were." Yet even as Tina stated definitively at first that being "black" did not really matter substantially at Columbus (and as she argued throughout that students and adults viewed one another as "individuals" or "specific people" or "friends" rather than in race-group terms), she suggested that she had in fact noticed many ways in which being "black" was made to matter problematically at Columbus. Somehow, through a host of institutional processes and interpersonal actions in which Tina acknowledged that race *did* seem to matter, the graduation stage ended up with "hardly any black people" on it.

Unlike the adults with whom they shared Columbus life, students typically did not actively suppress race words in talking about school; whether Tina noted race's relevance rather depended on the moment you listened to her. Seeing such revealed color-consciousness get *actively* submerged beneath the surface of countless adult speakers' talk of "students" and "people," further, we realize that de-raced talk is actually *never* the discourse of people who do not, or cannot, "see" race. Rather, it is the talk of people wishing for race's irrelevance—and, at times, the talk of people reluctant to mention its actual importance. As Friedman (1997) argues, arguments for the possibility of absolute "colorblindness" make sense only for the "little green creature from Pluto" who knows nothing of the U.S. tendency to racialize. No matter how loathe many Americans are to view people in racial terms, it seems that at this point in history we cannot help but do so. Indeed, even when we resist seeing racial patterns with all our might, we sneak back directly or indirectly to notice the racial patterns we ignore. And when we notice racial patterns and say nothing publicly to dismantle them, we often help ensure these very patterns' matter-of-fact reproduction.

In such a racialized and racializing world, colormute talk takes work—and colormuteness itself has consequences. Columbus people made race matter every day by talking about school in racial terms—but adults in particular also made race matter every day by refusing actively to do so. Whispering in anxious frustration their perceptions of how race mattered problematically at Columbus, Columbus adults repeatedly suggested racialized "problems" that "needed to be addressed"—inequalities or tensions in curriculum, discipline, school reform, achievement, and the distribution of academic opportunity. Only muttering quietly about these racial patterns, however, Columbus and district adults helped ensure the replication of the very patterns causing them most grief. Had they talked more openly with one another about their wishes and proposed plans for certain racial patterns to disappear—and, in doing so, had they also talked openly together about the double-edged reality that both clumsy race talk and race silence could make things worse—they might have forged an explicit shared strategy for dismantling the particular racial orders that plagued them. It is to such conclusions about the possibilities of talking that we now turn.

Moving Forward

> The test of a first-rate intelligence is the ability to
> hold two opposed ideas in the mind at the same
> time, and still retain the ability to function.
> —F. Scott Fitzgerald, *The Crack-Up*, 1936

> Reality is not easy to condense.
> — George Spindler, Jan. 23, 1996

One day when I was teaching, Jake, a black student, interrupted a visiting South American video artist in the middle of a story about his dying friend to ask, "what race was he?" "I don't think that matters," the artist responded. "Does that matter?" I echoed. "Just answer the question," Jake replied. Nando, a Latino boy, said with a sly smile that he wanted to know too. " 'Cause you're racist!" said Ana, a "Chicana" girl, exasperatedly to Nando. "He was Caucasian—white," the artist replied after a pause. Jake glanced at Nando with a smirk, and then leaned back in his chair in silence.

When I taught at Columbus, daily life presented me with countless moments in which people's "race"—the racial identifications of students, or my own, or that of my colleagues, or the people we read and talked about—could be either highlighted or ignored. Making race explicitly relevant *or* denying the relevance of race could always be the wrong move. As I wrote in my notes to myself as a teacher, "Saying we should treat people all the same has to be said at different times from when we are celebrating how different they are."

Just as Jake had openly questioned how race was relevant to the guest speaker's narrative, then, I found myself wondering years later how exactly race had mattered to the eighteen-year narrative of Jake's own life. To sum up some of this book's central concerns about when to talk as if race matters, try to analyze for yourself the relevance of race to this final Columbus story—the story of the school world of Jake, a former tenth-grade student of mine who, as we put it so often in American speech, "just happened to be black."

In June of 1997, Jake found out on his graduation day that he hadn't earned enough credits to receive his Columbus diploma. I saw Jake in the hallway after a morning of senior celebrations; he looked angry and miserable, and he responded to my congratulations with the startling news that he wouldn't be graduating at all. I immediately went with Jake to his counselor, who counted up Jake's credits again and realized that the previous semester he himself had miscalculated the credits Jake needed for graduation. Noting that Jake had passed every class he had been told to take, the counselor chalked the snafu up to his own mistake, gave Jake some quick credits for some work experience, and told Jake he could graduate. Jake called his mother with a laugh. His father had driven up from the South to see the graduation, and now there was going to be something to see. Jake walked across the stage that evening, beaming in a borrowed cap and gown reserved by someone else who for some reason had not made it to graduation.

So how had race mattered to Jake's educational life, to the millions of individual and institutional acts Jake had experienced over more than a decade of American schooling? As a teacher, I had not been sure, but I had spent an awful lot of time analyzing the role being played by Jake himself. When I had Jake in my tenth-grade Ethnic Literature class, to me he was sometimes a "black kid" commenting on California City life, sometimes a "Columbus kid" who seemed unconscionably underskilled for his age; sometimes an "inner-city kid" regularly assigned by the district to inexperienced teachers like me since elementary school, sometimes a kid from "the projects" who waited up anxiously at night for his mother to come home from work, sometimes a "Special Ed" kid who had extra meetings with a counselor. He was sometimes the class's comedy valve, sometimes an earnest participant in classroom discussions, and sometimes, to a new teacher, seemingly a purposeful and gleeful pain in the ass. He was, to me, sometimes "black" by his own description, sometimes "black" in comparison to the "Latino" or "Filipino" students he sat next to in class, sometimes "black" in relation to the curriculum we were studying, sometimes "black" for me even when I wasn't thinking about it, and daily, as I aged as a teacher, "black" in comparison to my own increasingly obvious "whiteness." In various ways, thus, Jake's "race" seemed to matter to me regularly—far more at the time, I must admit, than did my own "race" or the "races" of all the other players busy creating racial patterns in Jake's life.

There were many such racial patterns. As a tenth grader—the year of his life when I knew him best—Jake spent numerous hours embroiled in disciplinary conflicts with me and many of his other teachers, most (but not all) of whom just happened to be "white." Among ourselves, we never discussed such conflicts in racial terms; we labeled ourselves racially to one another even more rarely than we racially labeled Jake and his peers. We did often note to one another, however, that an underlying factor in the classroom frustration we shared with our students seemed to be the fact that so many students at Columbus (along with many other students in the district who just happened to be "low-income minorities") had arrived at high school egregiously unversed in basic academic skills. The district only sporadically called this racialized pattern of student academic underpreparation unacceptable. Jake had also spent his educational life in buildings that had just happened to become full of holes and broken windows by the time the folks near his mostly "black" neighborhood who just happened to be "white" had moved away to attend the city's private and "academic" schools. No one in California City publicly denounced such district patterns of white advantage. By age 15, Jake had also been labeled a "Special Ed" student by school adults for many years, along with many other students at Columbus who similarly just happened to be "black"; no one at Columbus openly analyzed this stark and suspect pattern of race-group overrepresentation. But plenty of school people over the course of Jake's educational life had articulated "race's" relevance to other less inequality-loaded topics quite openly and easily. By the time Jake graduated at 18, for example, he had seen many fights between students get publicly framed as "racial riots" between members of antagonistic racial groups; he had completed numerous assignments in which his teachers asked him to frame himself as a race group member; he had sat through a series of classes in which students and adults talked about the history and literature of a series of presumably distinct "race groups"; and he had attended many assemblies in which his classmates lauded specific and sequential "cultures." The summer before his senior year, finally, most of the teachers monitoring Jake's academic progress had been replaced in a school reform stemming from a law written originally on behalf of "blacks" from "the ghetto"—like Jake himself. Because he ran into a former teacher who was willing to argue (with new counselors who also just happened to be white) for his right to graduate on the last day of his high school career, Jake had happened to walk across the stage a graduate who just happened to be "black"—a complex individual player in almost two decades of complex multi-player school interactions, many of which seemed quite racialized indeed.

Life at Columbus was simultaneously about Jake being just individual Jake—silly, witty, angry, insightful, and frustrated Jake—and part of a web of racialized patterns that could appear startlingly simple or intolerably complex. Further, any temporary understanding of how race mattered to Jake's schooling story, or any Columbus person's schooling story, would not solve the complex social problem of knowing how to *say, to others*, that race mattered to it. Plenty of people in Jake's life had chosen not to say anything at all, for describing aloud any seemingly racialized pattern in a person's life or in Columbus life at large always *did* risk being "racist," by inaccurately or inappropriately claiming that race was relevant to an individual or an institutional story or by incorrectly pinpointing the role of particular "racial" groups." In particular, any mention of Jake's *blackness*, if not contextualized by mentioning the roles others were playing in producing patterns weighing *on* "blacks," always *did* particularly risk making Jake and his "black" peers seem problematic *because they were* "black." Indeed, race talk about any "group" in isolation always risked blaming "problems" on that group alone, forgetting the various other players involved in creating orders that were racial. Further, a mention of any racialized graduation story would likely be immediately countered by someone mentioning the "Samoan" students who also vanished disproportionately from graduation, the "white" teacher who stayed late every night working with "black" students, the "black" student who sailed through Columbus in honors classes, the college-bound graduating "Filipino" students who were seemingly identically "disadvantaged" "low-income minorities."

With bystanders always ready to contest the accuracy or appropriateness of any proffered description of how race mattered, the overwhelming social complexity of race talk might stifle your willingness to analyze such stories in racial terms at all. Yet as you sat back in safer silence, you would also have to silently consider the dramatic effects that *not* describing such stories in racial terms had already had upon the school experiences of students like Jake—and the effect such silences were having upon your own experiences as well.

Occasionally celebrating the "diversity" of Jake or his peers, of course, would be relatively easy; it is the racial *inequalities* affecting individuals and institutions that people struggle most to describe.[1] As an academic, I have realized that professional analysts, too, have particular trouble talking about racial inequality: when analyzing inequality, we, too, both highlight and omit mention of race in countless problematic ways, and our race talk too often exacerbates our "race problems" even as we attempt to solve them. When researchers lump students into racial groups and matter-of-factly, relentlessly measure how these racial groups do on tests, we forget the fabricated and porous nature of race group boundaries; worse, we prime one another to view the racial achievement patterns we find as matter-of-factly expected orders. Yet when we *do not* mention how racial groups do on tests, we allow whatever problematic patterns actually exist to stand intact as if they are acceptable—and similarly expected. When we set out to study how much people "really" think race matters, we forget the scripts and pitfalls of direct questions; yet when we never talk to people in private about what they "really" think, we are left only with the partially honest and systematically silent scripts of public discourse. When we insist that Americans do not fit into simple race groups, finally, we allow ourselves to ignore the ways in which we still organize one another racially; yet when we fail to expose "race groups" as historical and cultural fabrications, we prompt Americans to take "race groups" for granted as natural facts. Race talk errors and analytic omissions, it seems, are as central to scholarship as they are to daily life; yet we typically critique the omissions of others rather than our own. As one African-American professor suggested to me at a meeting of the American Educational Research Association, a large number of scholars around us seemed to be making careers writing books trying to point out what everyone else was not saying about race. "Hmm," I said nervously. "Interesting."

People connected to U.S. schools often do *not* say things "about race" very loudly, out of fear—a fear that is partly exaggerated and partly very important. It *is* regularly unclear when talking about people racially makes things better and when doing so makes things worse—particularly because our race talk so often places blame for "problems" reductively *on* isolated "races," or reveals assumptions that racial inequality is either natural or someone else's problem. The solution is thus not that we simply start talking together *more* about race, but rather that we learn to talk more skillfully. We can begin to do so, I think, by talking together with critical consciousness about race talk itself.[2]

I have meant for this book to jump-start such discussions about race talk. This has not been a typical ethnography, in which the researcher helps her readers "to understand something of interest about a corner of the world they have not experienced directly themselves" (Lederman 1990, 82). Rather, I have intended for it to act as a mirror held up to familiar dilemmas, and I want to encourage readers to use Columbus people's particular stories as typical examples for analyzing self. Columbus was (and still is) not an unusual school, nor were (or are) Columbus's struggles unusual U.S. experiences; each of us navigates race talk dilemmas every day, whether we work in schools or not. In a country full of racial and racialized patterns, no one can escape the paradoxes and dilemmas of race talk; school people, who must navigate daily the nation's systems of diversity and inequality, simply experience these traps with particular intensity.

This has, simply, been a story about a group of Americans struggling over when race *should* matter—and with the knowledge that they were helping *make* race matter through their very talk and silence. Racial descriptions *do* always get something wrong, for they always prime us to invest in simple categories artificial at their origin; they *do* always risk "discrimination," by potentially making race relevant where it ideally should not be. Yet avoiding race talk can help to naturalize the racial inequality orders that have already been built and that we keep rebuilding every day. As philosopher Lawrence Blum notes, "racial thinking" itself can have "morally destructive consequences," yet "Jettisoning racial language and thinking would render us no longer able even to talk or think about racism, racial injustice, racial insensitivity, [or] institutional racism . . . and to make appropriate claims on the conscience of Americans" (2002, 164–66).

Since the six race talk dilemmas I have described here will not be solved (for such is the nature of a dilemma), it is up to us all to figure out how to manage them successfully.[3] Learning to navigate the traps of race in contemporary America requires *risk*, emotional, social, and intellectual; doing race talk *well* requires an immense amount of care, analytic energy, and time. But we can and must get good at talking "about race," and I have tried to provide a road map here for doing so. Each chapter in this book has offered both a dilemma and a suggestion for moving forward through it.

Dilemma 1. We Don't Belong to Simple Race Groups, but We Do.
Moving forward: The biggest paradox of race is that race groups are genetic fictions but social realities. When talking to one another and with young people about race, then, we must take more moments to talk *about racial categorization*

itself, in order to get adults and young people engaged in the revelation that the lines we draw around "races" are human-made.[4] To continue to challenge (as Columbus students did) the very idea of simple or biological "race groups," we might ask one another how our own complex families or identities already challenge the very notion of simple racial difference. Examining the history of "race group" formation, further (the book's introduction and notes provided one road map to find such work), we might discuss how race categories have always been birthed in inequality contexts—and how after several centuries of treating one another racially, Americans must strategically employ race labels purposefully in our attempts to make things equal. Countering racial inequality does not require a belief in the biology of race, but rather a knowledge of race's social reality.[5] We can thus reject approaches that either (a) reinforce the false concept of distinct or biological "race" groups, *or* (b) dismiss altogether the continuing relevance of racial categorization. Instead, we can foster a necessary practice of strategic *race-bending*—that is, of alternately defying and strategically using race categories to describe human beings.

Dilemma 2: Race Doesn't Matter, but It Does.
Moving forward: Chapter 2 outlined the difficulties of determining and articulating race's relevance to our everyday institutional relationships. Deleting race words from talk of an institution's power dynamics, the chapter demonstrated, can leave the question of race's relevance simmering within everyday interactions. Yet simply talking *more* about social relations in racial terms will not itself defuse social tensions over race: given our propensity to assume that "race groups" in our institutions will *not* "get along," matter-of-fact talk of polarized race relations can reinforce a public script normalizing racial conflict (and summative statements about the "Xs" vs. the "Ys" can mask the complex and important ways in which we *do* interact and befriend one another across "racial" lines). Rather than rest satisfied with silenced *or* too-easy talk about race's role in our relationships, then, we need to learn to inquire together about *how* race matters to our relationships, giving ourselves the necessary time for joint inquiry rather than proceeding with our habits of quick deletion or blunt summation. That is, we might learn to try to discuss, slowly and with compassion and a critical lens, personal experiences of how race does matter to our everyday relations, particularly those relations in connection to which we often anxiously deny race matters at all. In K–12 contexts, further, we can also examine suspension lists and classroom disciplinary records, asking whether any student "race group" seems disciplined disproportionately and whether adult "race" plays a role in this disproportion. As Patricia Williams (1995) writes, "One of the subtlest challenges we face . . . is how to relegitimate the national discussion of racial . . . tensions so that we can get past the Catch-22 in which merely talking about it is considered an act of war, in which not talking about it is complete capitulation to the status quo" (40). We must attempt to go

beyond simple statements *or* dismissals of race's relevance to our social relations—for when we do *not* make the time for discussing *how* race matters,
those who claim race *does* matter are reduced to strategic angry accusations of
race's relevance, while those who claim race does *not* matter are left worrying
in toxic silence that it does.

Dilemma 3: The De-Raced Words We Use When Discussing Plans for Racial Equality Can Actually Keep Us from Discussing Ways to Make Opportunities Racially Equal.

Moving forward: Acknowledging the understandable tendency to replace targeted language with language that is generally inclusive of "everyone," we
might discuss together whether any of the de-raced words of communal discourse are making it difficult to address inequalities that actually do still play
out along racial lines. We need to keep considering when speaking in aggregated terms about goals for "all" provides a necessary discourse of full inclusion—and when more precise mention of needy sub-populations in policy and
practice is necessary to accomplish inclusive reforms. We can acknowledge
that mentioning certain sub-populations does not entail neglect of those not
mentioned—even when we choose to focus temporarily on particular subgroups to remedy particular disparities.

Dilemma 4: The More Complex Inequality Seems to Get, the More Simplistic Inequality Analysis Seems to Become.

Moving forward: We need to talk more together about how we feel race *should*
matter in our attempts to distribute opportunities equitably. This requires
shared consideration of how opportunities are currently distributed racially.
Noting that vague analyses of disadvantage can make remedying disadvantage
impossible, we need to take the time to analyze the details of how race actually
still matters to the complex local systems of opportunity in our communities
and, particularly, within our districts and schools. This will most likely require
discussing how the simultaneously binary ("middle-class white"/"low-income
minority") and multiracial complexities of unequal opportunity in contemporary America play out in local inequality formations; simultaneously, we will
also have to debate how issues of immigration, language, and neighborhood
resources factor into local systems of race-class inequality. After clarifying the
arrangement of local opportunity, we must debate when actions targeting specific groups are necessary, and when such actions oversimplify or neglect wider
patterns of race, class, or language. We must also debate when discarding race
analysis prematurely neglects the continuing ways in which opportunities are
racially unequal. We can postpone acting on the wish to proceed as if race no
longer matters to our inequality systems until the moment when children truly
enjoy equal opportunities "regardless of race." Until then, we can maintain

policies that attempt directly to equalize the racial distribution of educational and life opportunities, so that one day we can finally stop thinking racially about who is unequal to whom. Rejecting race-based remedies out of hand is not yet the answer, despite the illusion of equity such deletions achieve.[6]

Dilemma 5: The Questions We Ask Most about Race Are the Very Questions We Most Suppress.

Moving forward: Noting that schools are key sites where the basic racial disparities in academic preparation that plague the nation are reproduced, we must begin to state that adequately and equitably educating Americans of every "race" is to the nation's benefit. Acknowledging further that racially disparate educational outcomes have become all too normalized in American logic, we might also begin, in and around our schools, to discuss how to use our ingrained expectations of racial achievement patterns to coordinate to prevent them. We can attempt, for one, to monitor our schools and districts preventatively for racially patterned opportunities or resource disparities; we can also work harder to remedy patterns in academic preparation or achievement the moment we notice them in school. Knowing that public blame wars goad players to shirk rather than accept responsibility for any existing racial orders, further, we must learn to proceed in our achievement talk with a language of communal responsibility. Fostering such a language truly shifts the typical blame culture of public schooling, which more often focuses blame reductively on students or on teachers. Truly dismantling racial achievement patterns requires stating explicitly that any existing such patterns are not just remediable problems, but problems shared by school people, communities, district people, and students—and we might thus learn to start all conversations about achievement with the stated plan that all players will work together to dismantle any racial patterns found.

Dilemma 6: Although Talking in Racial Terms Can Make Race Matter, Not Talking in Racial Terms Can Make Race Matter Too.

Moving forward: Finally, realizing that actively *deleting* race words from our everyday talk of social "problems" can actually help *increase* the role race plays in those problems, we might try talking more to friends and colleagues about any existing habits of colormuteness in our institutions. If there are racially disproportionate orders that we knowingly refuse to name, we can start by admitting to one another why it is so tricky to name them—and we can continue by debating whether and how to name them most productively. Acknowledging that just muttering quietly about particular "races" functions most dangerously to displace analysis of other players' roles in creating racialized patterns, we must also begin to frame all racial disparities as orders created by many players—players that even include ourselves.[7] We must attempt, in the end, to promote a brave policy of interrogating our *own* roles in producing inequitable racial orders—and planning with one another the acts we can undertake individually and together to dismantle the problematic racial patterns we have been taught to accept.

To talk more skillfully about race, then, I suggest that we frame all our conversations about racial orders with honest, critically conscious discussion of *race talk itself and its dilemmas*. If we start to talk more in our workplaces and educational settings *about how we talk* about race, we might learn together to treat race itself as a paradoxical human-made system of differentiation that we need alternately to oppose and actively wield. That is, we might realize that we must both resist and actively enlist race labels in order to be truly antiracist. We might also understand that we must choose well when to treat and not treat each other as racial beings, for navigating this core choice is actually the only way to move forward to racial equality.

There are many conditions necessary for such discussions about race and race talk. We need first to commit to building communities in which all participants trust that their comments will be both respectfully engaged and put to use; while participants "of color" may be emotionally scarred by experiences with racism, "white" participants may be scarred by experiences with unsuccessful race talk. Acknowledging both kinds of pain, we need to mix compassion for our conversation partners with compassion for those harmed explicitly by the orders being described, and mix a desire for interpersonal harmony with a drive for analytic sophistication. We each need a willingness to listen sometimes while others talk, and to talk sometimes while others listen. We need a willingness to experiment with small conversations and large ones, with single-"race" and mixed-"race" groupings for talking; in different ways at different times, participants "of color" and "white" people will feel silenced and fearful in interracial interactions. And, we each need a willingness to consider and admit how we play a role in creating and allowing racial orders. This will to struggle through conversations about our own racializing acts is the single most necessary condition for successful discussion. We can help create this will, I think, by proactively framing race talk dilemmas themselves as things that we share—for we might then eventually realize that we share not only worries about the consequences of talking racially, but also responsibility for the very racial orders we fear our race talk will reproduce.

In our conversations about race and race talk, then, we need to proceed always by asking good questions about *how* race matters, questions that disrupt our normal scripts, unthinking statements, or muffled complaints about race. We also need to learn to manage the discomfort of debating *when* race matters in our lives, when we think race *should* matter, and when and how even thinking of other human beings racially helps or harms a racialized society. We need to proceed in all such conversations about race and race talk with a willingness to inquire, an acknowledgment that we will make mistakes, and a commitment to inserting ourselves into analysis of "problems" and potential remedies. We need to stay aware, further, of the difficulties *others* face in talking about race, by acknowledging in these conversations that every speaker will make mistakes in talking about race precisely because racial inequality is a pernicious system; to disarm fears of error, we can state directly that the task at hand is to work together through inevitable errors. Admitting that race talk *can* be inappropriate or inaccurate, and that mentioning racialized populations when analyzing "problems" *can* risk making those populations themselves seem dangerously problematic, we can proceed with the explicit recognition that in our quests to make things better we will fail in countless small ways that we must continually repair. If we learned to undergird all race talk with the presumption that racial inequality itself could be and would be dismantled by communal effort, there would soon be no reason to fear race talk at all.

Given our racialized society and the mutually harmful consequences of colormuteness, it seems we actually have no choice but to rally the strength to keep talking. Race talk will continue to be full of pitfalls both social and analytic; but armed with a knowledge of these pitfalls and with compassion for those who traverse them with us, we can together muddle through the project of figuring out when and how to talk as if race matters. As we struggle through this joint analysis, finally, we must remember one thing above all: together, we are already making race matter every day.

Once I had written the bulk of this book, I shared my conclusions with educators, professional developers, district administrators, and students from high school to the doctoral level. While the students often primarily wanted to discuss the question of racial categorization itself, all of the educators I talked to—teachers, teachers in training, school coaches, principals-to-be, superintendents—requested that I provide a more specific guide to *how* to talk racially in school settings. They argued that they themselves "lacked the language" to talk successfully about race, as racial language was itself loaded, difficult, incredibly hard to make "positive." One superintendent said succinctly that she felt "handicapped by language" that was always "woefully inadequate."[1]

While these readers called particularly for applying this book's conclusions to professional development efforts, most ironically seemed to eye prior professional development about race with substantial skepticism. Many argued that such events (with a few notable exceptions, especially Glenn Singleton's "Beyond Diversity" seminars, which were recommended repeatedly) either skirted "real issues" (one teacher rolled her eyes recalling a training series focused on celebratory dance) or produced unsuccessful conversations about race that threatened community relations or raised "problems" without achieving clear "results." Others argued that when talk about things like achievement *had* become racial, it had slipped into well-worn explanatory tracks that blamed other players unproductively. Educators who had led such conversations with colleagues "about race" sighed that it took substantial time to turn conversations from "them" to "us." Most argued that conversations about race's relevance to discipline were equally rare or problematic, as were detailed discussions unpacking complicated local systems of inequality in educational opportunity.

Even if people in schools and districts agreed on the importance of discussing racialized patterns in schools, they said further, sufficient time was rarely allotted for such discussions. This lack of time to fully discuss how race mattered or should matter to various school issues prevented the necessary trust building that could allow people to respectfully disagree, debate, and problem-solve, since conversations about race typically had people butting heads about the causes of racialized problems and the best remedies for them. The programs expected to provide *solutions* to racial inequality, they said, thus often got implemented without adequate discussion of the programs' potential to actually remedy existing racialized problems.

All agreed that given these dynamics, school and district leaders needed to be particularly good not only at making *time* to talk about race and racial orders, but also at leading compassionate conversations about race in various kinds of settings. Many argued for the importance of small-group discussion time, where adults could debate and discuss racialized data and beliefs "at length" and "in depth"; others disagreed with an exclusive focus on small conversations, arguing that school or district leaders had to facilitate schoolwide and districtwide discussions in order to make systemwide improvements. But it was particularly important, most argued, for *white* teachers and administrators to join these various discussions about dismantling racial inequality, rather than leave it to colleagues of color to raise the "issue of race" as if only people of color were racialized or implicated in racialized orders.[2] Indeed, teachers and administrators of color agreed that the burden of bringing up race during colormute conversations eventually took a toll both personal and professional, and that trusting environments had to be slowly built so that all players felt ready to participate in discussions of race's relevance. School and district leaders thus also had to "instill hope" for those tired of "*just* talking about race," for those who felt talk was not action and in fact often used as a poor substitute for action.

Yet all argued that the very experience of struggling together in conversation to understand and attack racial inequality was itself an essential outcome of "talking about race." A shared "hashing out" of how race did matter or was going to matter to school reform plans or to school mission statements, they said, *was* progress toward racial equality; so were the arguments about racial inequality taking place at public meetings or in more intimate settings. As shared analysis *was* action, they implied, the line between "doing something" and "just talking" was thus actually blurred—even while working to stay engaged in solving problems *between* conversations was essential in order to make "real change."

Having heard these eloquent recommendations, I want to close with my own suggestions for educators in particular, who must lead and participate in the race conversations being called for here. The book has been designed to facilitate such conversations, for it is full of stories to debate—actual events that required Columbus people to choose to act. As a teacher, I have found that talking directly about real-life dilemmas is an excellent springboard for debating our opinions about inequality and how to remedy it. This book offers many examples to spark such school-, district-, or university-level conversations (What would *you* do if asked to focus on black and Latino achievement within a school with Columbus's demographics? Would *you* remark publicly on the hallway's racial demographics? Why or why not? When and how?). Eventually, educators can flag local examples of race dilemmas for discussion.

In all conversations about race, I think, educators should be prepared to do three things: *ask provocative questions, navigate predictable debates,* and *talk more about talking.* First, managing race dilemmas requires engaging colleagues in direct discussions *about* those dilemmas, which requires asking some *provocative questions* to get started. Some of the provocative questions suggested below (such as those about racial categorization) can be asked cold to groups of relative strangers. Others—particularly the questions about local inequitable orders—must wait until relations of trust have been built between participants, and until local power dynamics (between "racial/ethnic" groups, or between staff and administrators) have been sufficiently acknowledged. Depending on the local community, similarly, some of these questions can be immediately asked face-to-face, while others might best jump-start conversations if facilitators first request anonymous responses:

1. To manage Dilemma 1 (We Don't Belong to Simple Race Groups, but We Do), try admitting that it is never clear when it is useful to speak of others in simple racial terms, since a core American paradox is that we have made "race" groupings real even though they are genetically false. To build comfort with debating "race" itself, try creating opportunities with students and adults for talking *about racial categorization*. To get started, try asking these *provocative questions*: "When do you remember first being told you were a race-group member, or treated as if you were? When does being treated as a member of a "race" seem reductive or personally harmful to you? When does it bring you joy and a sense of community? When does speaking racially about ourselves and others seem necessary to make things more equal? How can we both represent simple race groups equitably in our curriculum and public events, *and* highlight our students' more complex, blurry diversity?"[3]

2. To manage Dilemma 2 (Race Doesn't Matter, but It Does), try admitting that since Americans sometimes want race to matter and sometimes want race not to matter, it is always unclear when we are making race matter appropriately. Suggest that our social relations are a key arena in which we worry about when and whether race appropriately matters—and suggest that it is thus important to inquire *how* race *does* matter to our social relations (among students, among educators and between educators and students). Before beginning such inquiry, try acknowledging directly that people often understandably don't want to talk about the ways race matters most problematically to them—and that we must thus *take the time* to go beyond simple statements or dismissals of race's relevance. To get started, try asking these *provocative questions*: "When do you think your 'race' matters to your students? When does your students' 'race' matter to you? When would we each prefer to be approached instead as individuals, 'regardless of race'? How do we *talk* here about race's relevance to student relations, and to our own relations with students? What are the consequences of each habit of talk?"

3. To manage Dilemma 3 (The De-Raced Words We Use When Discussing Plans for Racial Equality Can Actually Keep Us from Discussing Ways to Make Opportunities Racially Equal), try discussing directly whether any de-raced equality words being used with good intentions (such as talk of "all students") might be making it difficult to analyze school or district inequalities that still are structured racially. Examining the language of the school or district mission statement and/or current published reform plans, try asking these *pro-*

vocative questions: "Is racial equality being adequately addressed and achieved by our reforms as stated? When would targeting 'race groups' in our reforms help children more? When would racial equality actually be best achieved by reforms designed for 'all'?"

4. To manage Dilemma 4 (The More Complex Inequality Seems to Get, the More Simplistic Inequality Analysis Seems to Become), try suggesting directly that given the confusing structures of today's inequality systems, we tend to oversimplify our analyses of inequality whenever we can. Adding that vague analyses of inequality make it impossible to *equalize* opportunity, acknowledge that it is a necessary (though time-consuming) task to analyze the details of *how* race actually still matters to the very complicated local systems of opportunity in our communities and within our schools. To get started in this analysis, try asking these *provocative questions*: "In the complex systems of opportunity in our school, district, and community, how is inequality structured along racial lines? How do issues of language, immigration status, or family income factor in? Are we adequately addressing all groups' needs? Since inequality systems include various factors intertwined with race, would it make sense to analyze our inequalities through several simultaneous lenses? Or should we target specific forms of inequality separately?"

5. To manage Dilemma 5 (The Questions We Ask Most about Race Are the Very Questions We Most Suppress), try starting all conversations about achievement with the stated recognition that racially unequal educational outcomes have become all too much an accepted part of American culture. Point out directly that Americans thus tend either to ignore racial achievement patterns as if they are acceptable, or mention them matter-of-factly as if they are natural. Suggest that it is necessary to talk about racial achievement patterns instead with the understanding that they can and must be communally dismantled. Try acknowledging, too, that U.S. talk about achievement is saturated with blame, and that public blame wars tend to prime players to displace rather than accept responsibility for racial orders. Suggest instead that we do best when we proceed with an urgent language of communal responsibility—that is, with the understanding that all players will and can work together to dismantle any racial patterns found.

To get started analyzing achievement, try asking these *provocative questions*: "Do racial achievement patterns exist in our schools and district? Are we treating them as if they are normal or acceptable? How are we each involved in producing them? How could we each be involved in remedying them? And who else needs to get involved in the analysis and remedy?"

6. Finally, to manage Dilemma 6 (Although Talking in Racial Terms Can Make Race Matter, Not Talking in Racial Terms Can Make Race Matter Too), try mentioning directly that while talking racially about problems often seems like it will make those problems worse, *not* talking racially about those problems can keep them permanently racial. To manage this dilemma, try acknowledging directly that talking about race is difficult—and then try talking more

explicitly with colleagues *about* any existing habits of colormuteness in the school or district. To get started talking about the local consequences of both talk and silence, try asking these *provocative questions*: "Are there are racially disproportionate orders in our own institution that we knowingly refuse to name? Why do we refuse to name them—and how could we name them most productively? What are the consequences of muttering quietly about racial orders? Who gets focused on and overlooked in our quiet analyses? When we would do best to analyze racial patterns in large group meetings, and when in small-group settings? What's the gain and loss of each strategy?"

When having the conversations about race that will ensue from these provocative questions, we can anticipate likely arguments with our colleagues or outside players. Preparing ourselves to engage those arguments with compassion and understanding, and anticipating the likely guilty or angry reactions from our colleagues (and ourselves!), we should thus always *be ready to navigate predictable debates about*:

1. Counterexamples casting doubt on the racial patterns we name
2. The relative importance of race and class
3. The role of players not in the room
4. The role of players in the room
5. Whether race is "really important" to individuals or institutional orders
6. The contours of local inequality formations (e.g., "What about the Filipinos? They have needs too")
7. The needs of specific language or immigrant groups
8. The accuracy of racial claims (e.g., "Well, there are also Samoans living in that neighborhood, even though it's predominantly black")
9. Whether it makes more sense to expand the analysis to a more general unit (e.g., "Well, all teenagers have problems"; "Well, all the kids here are needy")
10. The appropriateness of racialized claims (e.g., "That's racist. This isn't a racial issue, it's a kid issue.")
11. The question of whether perceiving colleagues or students racially is itself discriminatory (e.g., "When can we get over this racial thing and just see people as people?")
12. And finally, arguments about the unclear boundaries of "race groups" themselves (e.g., "Race is a fiction," or "My daughter is mixed—where does she fit in?")

All these rejoinders *are* valid arguments in different contexts, and both discussion leaders and participants must be ready to debate them in a respectful manner. Indeed, in any race discussion, one must be ready to debate three basic issues:

1. The players involved in the phenomenon. Are all necessary players included in our analysis?
2. The precision of our analysis. Have we precisely described the problem in all its complexity?

3. The placement of responsibility and blame. Is our talk placing blame or responsibility accurately and fairly? Have we displaced responsibility from any key players?

Finally, when talking with colleagues about race and racial orders, I suggest again that we remember always to keep talking self-consciously about race talk and its dilemmas. Doing so positions us properly as problem solvers—and it also frames race talk dilemmas as shared dilemmas to be navigated together. Let me repeat some final hints for how to *talk more about talking about race*:

1. Acknowledge the difficulties we all face in talking about race. Acknowledge explicitly that every speaker will make mistakes in talking about race precisely because racial inequality is a pernicious system. Acknowledge that both speaking and not speaking racially *can* always be wrong.

2. To disarm fears of error, try stating directly that the task at hand is to work together through inevitable errors: in our quests to make things better we will fail in countless small ways that we must continually repair.

3. Admit that race talk *can* always be inappropriate or inaccurate, and that it is thus always a struggle to determine how to discuss race most productively.

4. Admit that mentioning racialized groups when analyzing "problems" *can* risk making those groups themselves seem dangerously problematic.

5. Acknowledge that you will be proceeding in all conversations "about race" with an explicit willingness to inquire, and an expectation that we will not find simple answers.

6. State that you want to allow for debate about when we think race *should* matter, and when and how even thinking of other human beings racially helps or harms a racialized society.

7. State a commitment to inserting yourself into all analyses of "problems" and potential remedies—and urge that others do the same.

If we begin to consider and discuss race talk itself with more critical consciousness, I think, the communal risks of talking in racial terms will come to seem strategically navigable. Becoming *confidently* self-conscious about race talk, that is, we will finally realize the power and importance of struggling together through the basic dilemmas of talking racially.

Notes

Introduction

1. For discussion of the process through which pseudo-scientists reinforced the socially constructed "race" categories of "black," "white," and "Indian" (central to the institution of slavery) through massaging "biological" findings about genetically insignificant variations in human physical appearance, see Stanton 1972, Gould 1981, Stocking 1982, Banton 1998. Smedley (1999) provides a particularly useful discussion of how "race" was created as a North American system of "black"/"white"/"red"difference based fundamentally on categorizations and rankings of exterior appearances. For discussion of the extension of "race" categories over several centuries of immigration and colonial expansion to include the both-imposed-and-chosen racialized categories "Asian" and "Hispanic"/"Latino," see Espiritu 1992, Almaguer 1994, and Delgado and Stefancic 1998. The classic evidence against the existence of biological "races," of course, is the fact that the handful of groups Americans call "race" groups are actually more genetically diverse *within* themselves than between themselves (see Montagu 1997 [1942]).

2. Minow (1990) provides an eloquent discussion of this tension in U.S. legal analysis; see also P. Williams (1997) and Appiah and Gutmann (1996).

3. Van Den Berghe contrasts a general U.S. anxiety about race to Brazilians' happier national discourse on race's supposed irrelevance. Of course, the Brazilian mantra that race does *not* matter much in Brazil has been challenged by many scholars, who have argued that Brazil is an extremely race-conscious (and racially stratified) nation in which speakers simply resist conversations about racism. See, e.g., Twine (1998) and Sheriff (2000). Sheriff argues that this resistance to discussing racism is consistent across the Brazilian population's racialized spectrum: " '*Ninguem gosta de falar* [no one likes to talk about it],' I was told over and over," she writes (117).

4. Proposition 209 also called for a halt to race-conscious outreach programs in public employment and contracting. The opening text of the proposition, which eventually amended the California Constitution, read as follows: "*The state shall not discriminate against, or grant preferential treatment to, any individual or group on the basis of race, sex, color, ethnicity, or national origin in the operation of public employment, public education, or public contracting.*" For sociological examination of the proposition and its development, see Chavez 1998.

5. Similarly, after the *Hopwood* decision in Texas ruled the consideration of race in law school admissions impermissible at the state university, admissions officers at private Rice University also decided to delete race words from admissions talk. According to the *New York Times*, "Almost overnight, the admissions officers at Rice stopped saying aloud the words 'black,' 'African-American,' 'Latino,' 'Hispanic' or even 'minority' in their deliberations. The next year, the proportion of black students admitted in the freshman class fell by half; the proportion of Hispanics fell by nearly a third." ("Using Synonyms for Race, College Strives for Diversity," December 8, 2002.)

6. Acknowledgments, of course, to Cornel West (1993).

7. Scholarly or political talk of an American "we" is made suspect by many authors, who argue that any claim of "an overarching 'we-ness' across ethnic and racial difference" is itself a "colorblind" fantasy (Thompson 1999, 141).

8. Frankenberg (1993) has argued that "race evasive discourse" is a "*white*" American habit, exhibited particularly by "whites" who, by insisting on essential human "sameness," avoid all direct references to race as if such references are inherently "racist." "From this point of view," Frankenberg notes, "there are apparently only two options open to [whites]: either one does not have anything to say about race, or one is apt to be deemed 'racist' simply by virtue of having something to say" (33).

9. Gunnar Myrdal (1944), of course, famously described the "American dilemma" as the simultaneous existence of an ideology of equality and the practice of racial inequality (for further discussion, see "An American Dilemma Revisited," *Daedalus* 1995). Despite the obvious problem that "American" marks all the Americas and not just the United States, I utilize the term in this book because of its preeminence in U.S. ideological and political discourse, particularly about race and racism. See also Hochschild 1984, Hochschild and Scovronick 2003.

10. For foundational scholarship on race and schooling, see Woodson 1972 [1933]. On slave literacy, see also Genovese 1974; on the history of desegregation (including the lesser-known history of battles for integrating "Mexican-Americans" and "Chinese"), see, e.g., Kluger 1975, Wollenberg 1976, Weinberg 1977, Kirp 1982, Anderson 1988, Orfield and Eaton 1996, Wells and Crain 1997, Donato 1997. For a basic outline of the history of (and debates over) affirmative action in college admissions, see, e.g., Takagi 1992, Curry 1996, Edley 1996, Lydia Chavez 1998. On debates over "multiculturalism," see Taylor 1994, Banks 1995, Hu-Dehart 1996, Nieto 2000.

11. To begin an examination of the central role of schooling in the reproduction of U.S. racialized categories, identities, and power structures, see, e.g., McCarthy and Crichlow 1993, Ladson-Billings and Tate 1995, Tatum 1997, Fine, Weis, and Powell 1997, Kincheloe et al. 1998, Nieto 2000 (for discussion in a South African context, see Dolby 2001; for a Canadian example, see Yon 2000). Indeed, schools are institutions where people reproduce many such systems of difference and inequality: as others have argued, schools in the U.S. and elsewhere also help produce people who are "ethnic" or "indigenous" (Lukyx 1996), classed (Willis 1977, Eckert and McConnell-Ginet 1995, Varenne, Goldman, and McDermott 1997), gendered (Thorne 1993, Luttrell 1996), citizens of nations (Levinson 1996), "abled"/"disabled" (Varenne and McDermott 1998, Mehan 1996) and members of various local status groups (Eckert 1989). For more on the racialized distribution of educational opportunity *through* schooling, see, e.g., Payne 1984, Oakes et al. 1990, Kozol 1991, Valencia 1991, Carnoy 1994, Delpit 1995, Orfield and Eaton 1996, Secada et al. 1998, Noguera 2000, 2001.

12. For such scholarship on "race"-group linguistic patterns, see, e.g., Labov 1972, Kochman 1981, Bucholtz 1995, Smitherman 2000, Morgan 2002. Many of these scholars and others have long argued that this kind of "group"-specific talk matters particularly in *school*: see also, e.g., Cazden, John, and Hymes 1972, Philips 1972, Erickson and Mohatt 1982, Heath 1983, Foster 1997, Baugh 1999. Linguistic anthropologists and sociolinguists have also been particularly interested in how people using specific words or languages create a sense of themselves as distinct populations (see, e.g., Gumperz 1982, Silverstein 1985, Gal 1989, Urciuoli 1996, Bailey 2000). For an important

synthesis of anthropological theory on everyday ideologies *about* language and language use, see Schiefflin, Woolard, and Kroskrity 1998.

13. For further theoretical discussion of these contemporary and historical methods of everyday racialization in the U.S.—practices, that is, through which we place one another into groupings we call "racial"—see Goldberg 1990, Roediger 1991, 1994, Frankenberg 1993, Omi and Winant 1994, Delgado 1995, Bucholtz 1995, Jackson 2001. On the production of racial difference via the employment of popular culture, see Roediger 1998, Perry 2002, Carter forthcoming; through housing and neighborhood "choice," see Patillo-McCoy 1999, powell, Kearney, and Kay 2001; through social association, see Tatum 1997. Much influential theory on race-making also has emerged from scholars working in a European/diasporic context; see Fanon 1990 [1952], Hebdige 1979, Hewitt 1986, S. Hall 1991, 1992, 1996, 1998; Mercer 1990, Gilroy 1991, 1993a, 1993b; Rampton 1995. "Race" grouping has been framed in scholarship as the production both of *categories* central to inequality systems and of community-specific *practices*. West (1992), for example, describes "blackness" in one formulation as (1) the experience of inhabiting a category of people who must weather the constant probability of subjugation by "whites," and (2) the experience of enjoying the cultural practices shared by a community strengthened by resistance to such subjugation. Many authors have similarly named "whiteness" as both a category of privilege and a set of practices embodying that privilege (see Roediger 1994, Delgado and Stefancic 1997, Lipsitz 1998, Kincheloe et al. 1998, Thompson 1999). Frankenberg (1993), for example, frames "whiteness" as "a location of structural advantage, of race privilege"; a "standpoint; a place from which white people look at ourselves, at others, and at society"; and "a set of cultural practices that are usually unmarked and unnamed" (1).

14. Appiah (1996) calls *identification* this process of shaping lives and "life projects" around ascribed racialized labels (78).

15. Words not only invite or deter actions from others, but act on people to in a sense *create their identities and worlds*. For classic analyses arguing generally that language shapes the world we live in, see Whorf 2000 [1940], Althusser 1971, Foucault 1972, Wieder 1974. Scholars of "speech act" theory (Austin 1962, Searle 1969 [for discussion, see also Hanks 1996]), and those working within the tradition of conversation analysis, have long been particularly interested in words as actions that produce real-world consequences. On conversation analysis, see, e.g., Cicourel 1970, Moerman 1988, Duranti and Goodwin 1992, Goodwin and Goodwin 1992, Tedlock and Mannheim 1995 (for useful syntheses of such research on discourse as social action, see also Briggs 1986, Mishler 1986). Mehan (1996) argues further that a "social constructionist" tradition of research has been particularly concerned with how institutional orders, including school orders, are "both generated in and revealed by the language of the institution's participants" (243). "Because language *is* action," Mehan writes, "different uses of language constitute the world differently" (262, emphasis mine). Critical Discourse Analysis scholarship (Fairclough 2001) has also argued particularly that language helps produce existing power relations even while displaying those relations; language, as Fairclough writes in summation, particularly "contributes to the domination of some people by others" (3). Critical theorists of race, finally (see, e.g., Delgado 1995, Delgado and Stefancic 1998), have looked particularly at how race labeling practices have organized U.S. history, while theorists who explore gender and sexuality (Thorne 1993,

Spivak 1993, Hall and Bucholtz 1995, Ortner 1996, Butler 1997) have also explored the systemic and everyday social consequences of labeling.

16. In a longitudinal study of the self-identifications of immigrant youth (and teenage children of immigrants) in California, Rumbaut (forthcoming) noted the youths' conflation of "national-origin," "ethnic," and "race" categories. Rumbaut noted that racialized state political battles over resources (battles often fought in schools) had California youth (1) choosing to label themselves with what Rumbaut calls "pan-ethnic categories" (like "Latino," "Asian," and "black") and/or "national-identity" categories (like "Filipino" or "Mexican"), and (2) calling all of these labels their "race." For further discussion of youth worldwide negotiating over (and eliding) meanings of "race," "ethnicity," and "nationality," see, e.g., Gilroy 1993a, Sansone 1995, Amit-Talai and Wulff 1995, Sharma, Hutnyk, and Sharma 1996, K. Hall 2002, Maira 2002.

17. For more analyses of "race" as a system of distributing power to simplified groups (as opposed to the heritage-connoting, voluntary-group-association term "ethnicity"), see Omi and Winant 1994, Harrison 1995, Sanjek 1996.

18. In contrast, Schofield (1995) describes a strikingly self-consciously "colorblind" school of the 1970s–80s (with demographics listed as 50% "black," 50% "white") in which labels were almost completely absent from daily discourse. "In almost 200 hours of observations in classrooms, hallways, and teachers' meetings . . . fewer than 25 direct references to race [for the author, direct uses of the words "black" and "white"] were made by school staff or students," she writes (254).

19. Moerman (1988) notes that "study of actual occasions has demonstrated that all terms for persons are said and understood by people with real interests. Those people actively orient to their immediate situation and type of occasion, to the setting, to when during the occasion the reference occurs, to the kinds of actors present, to social actions both ongoing and hinted at. All those factors—and more—influence the terms they use" (98). Gumperz and Hymes (1972) called the knowledge necessary to communicate appropriately in such various cultural contexts "communicative competence" (vii).

20. For important work on "race" and identity development in the U.S., see, e.g., Cross 1991, Tatum 1992, 1997; Ward 2000.

21. For Appiah (1996), "identification" in a more comprehensive sense is always intertwined with "identity," since the very application of race labels helps shape how "an individual intentionally shapes her projects—including her plans for her own life and her conception of the good—by reference to available labels, available identities" (78). In so defining "identification," Appiah builds on the work of Ian Hacking on "making up people": Hacking writes that "numerous kinds of human beings and human acts come into being hand in hand with our invention of the categories labeling them" (Hacking 1992, cited in Appiah 1996, 78). I am concerned in this book primarily with the basic identificatory act of labeling itself, and with its effects in "shaping" shared social orders. For some nice examples of anthropological work that looks similarly closely at the processes and consequences of categorizing kinds of people (and negotiations over such categorization), see, e.g., Moerman 1968, Frake 1980, 1998, Bucholtz 1995, Mehan 1996, Bailey 2000, Jackson 2001. For some foundational work on categorization and labeling as a universal human process, see Levi-Strauss 1963; for an excellent discussion of contemporary anthropology's concerns with the very process of delineating "kinds of people" in an increasingly globalizing world, see Appadurai 1996.

22. Through historical inquiry, we have watched not just public figures (see Jordan 1974 on Thomas Jefferson's pivotal racializing role in U.S. history) but also 18th- and 19th-century American and European scientists actually devise racial categories and struggle to rank them according to existing social perceptions (see, e.g., Gould 1981, Stocking 1982, Banton 1998, Baker 1998, Smedley 1999). Historical scholarship has also illuminated moments when people confronting the seamless continuum of human diversity struggled to keep social race categories intact, arguing passionately, for example, that some people were simply "black" and others simply "white" (see, e.g., Roediger 1991, Haney Lopez 1996, Davis 1997, Sollors 2000). Examining centuries of racial formation in America has also demonstrated how populations once categorized as members of tribal, religious, or national groups ended up "racial" (see Genovese 1974, Espiritu 1992, Omi and Winant 1994, Almaguer 1994, Ignatiev 1995, Sacks 1997).

As suggested here, anthropology itself played a key role in creating such "racial" categories in the first place; it has since taken on the responsibility of calling them into question. At the turn of the 20th century, skull-measuring anthropologists were still arguing vehemently that racial groups were biologically distinct populations that could be "scientifically" ranked on a scale of human worth; yet other anthropologists began to step in to debunk as pseudo-science the idea that race groups could be placed on any legitimate hierarchy (see, e.g., Boas 1895; for discussion, see Stocking 1982, Baker 1998). By midcentury, anthropologists were arguing loudly that "races" did not exist at all, pointing out that the world's so-called "racial groups" were more genetically diverse *internally* than different from each other (for a seminal contribution, see Montagu 1997 [1942]). Anthropologists now routinely frame racial categories as historical, cultural, and political creations rather than natural or "biological" realities. Current public education work by the American Anthropological Association emphasizes the genetic fiction of "race" (Overbey and Moses 2002). Our most nuanced spokespersons emphasize that after centuries of acting as if race categories exist, we have basically created a world in which they do (Harrison 1995, American Anthropological Association 1998). This argument will be explored further in chapter 1.

23. Thorne (1993) found similarly that the study of gender in childhood typically framed gender as a set of traits owned by boys and girls themselves (the typical question of childhood gender studies, she writes, is "are girls and boys different?"). Thorne shifted in her own fieldwork to ask, "How do children actively come together to help create, and sometimes challenge, gender structures and meanings?" (4). Gender, Thorne concluded, "is not something one passively 'is' or 'has' "; rather, people " 'do gender' " (5). Appadurai (1996) articulates similar concerns about how the concept of "culture" is used in much theory and research. Even using "culture" as a noun, he argues, implies that "cultures" are easily delineated "things" owned by specific people. Rather, he notes, the social or "cultural" practices of "cultural groups" (and the maintenance of boundaries between such groups) are being negotiated constantly (12–13).

24. In treating race talk as directly representative of inner thoughts and feelings, much research on race thus gets trapped in attempts to infer speakers' "real" intentions (for comment, see Connolly and Troyna, 1998; see particularly Hammersley 1998). For an analysis of the many such pitfalls involved in research on everyday language, see Mertz 1992, Briggs 1986, Frake 1980. On the "ethnography of communication," long known for explorations of patterns in the way "natives" talk, see the foundational work of Hymes (1962, 1964) and Gumperz and Hymes (1972).

25. In this book, I call "private" any talk occurring in informal groups of two, three, or four people, while I call "public" the talk of more formal interactions involving additional participants (including written documents circulated to numerous readers).

26. For concise discussion of anthropology's contemporary problems with describing "kinds of people," see Marcus and Fisher 1986, Clifford and Marcus 1986, Appadurai 1996, Gupta and Ferguson 1997.

Chapter 1

1. For more discussion of the historical process of slotting people into "race" groups, often called racialization (and what Omi and Winant (1994) call "racial formation"), see Roediger 1991, Espiritu 1992, Almaguer 1994, Haney Lopez 1996, Davis 1997, Sacks 1997, Saragoza et al. 1998.

2. For other useful articulations of this paradox, see also Winant 1998, John Jackson 2001, and the American Anthropological Association's "Statement on 'Race'" (1998). Haney Lopez (1995) similarly argues succinctly that "race is neither an essence nor an illusion" (193).

3. Baker (2000) makes this useful distinction between "identity" and "identification" in his discussion of a late-1990s controversy over a "mixed-race" category of the U.S. census. While proponents of the "mixed-race" category demanded that the Census allow individuals to accurately record their complex *identities*, Baker suggests, opponents (like the NAACP) argued that distributing resources necessitated simpler, lump-sum racial *identification*. For further analysis of this controversy, see Cose 1997.

4. Again, that students called all six categories "racial" corroborates the findings of Rumbaut (forthcoming), who notes that in California's demographically and politically complex setting, young people called both "pan-ethnic" labels like "Latino" and "black" and "foreign national" labels like "Filipino" "races." Rumbaut noted "a substantial proportion of youths who conceived of their nationality of origin as a fixed racial category."

5. For further framing of such youth practices (particularly hip-hop artifacts and behaviors) as a global youth culture, see Gilroy 1993a, Sansone 1995, Dolby 2001.

6. Other scholars have noted such strategic employment of simple self-categorizations within inequality contexts. Gayatri Spivak (1987) coined the phrase "strategic essentialism" to refer to the use of simple, primordial categories to reference groups for those groups' own political benefit (despite the reductive consequences of such primordialism). British sociologist Stuart Hall has been central in framing race categories as "strategic places from which to speak" when navigating inequality systems (see Sharma, 1996, 34, for further discussion). Paul Gilroy (1993b) has described the strategic use of race categories to label communities bounded by historic struggles against racism and racial inequality as a tactic of "anti-anti-essentialism." Omi and Winant (1994) document many examples of purposeful racialization, or the seizing of race categories to describe selves in order to wield community and political power in the context of inequality structures. Finally, much anthropological work, such as work on indigenous rights movements, has also explored dynamics of "strategic essentialism." As Hodgson (2002a) argues, many anthropologists, building also on philosopher Charles Taylor's work on "the politics of recognition" (see Taylor 1994), have argued that indigenous peoples who "demand that their rights be acknowledged must fill the places of recognition that others provide . . . [e]ven as they seek to stretch, reshape, or even invert the meanings implied" (Li 2001, cited in Hodgson 2002a, p. 1041).

7. Similarly, in a recent ethnography of adults in Harlem, John Jackson (2001) argues that everyday "jostling for certainty over which particular *behaviors* are labeled black or white" (187, emphasis mine) opens up a space for contesting the very idea of racial difference. Jostling over how particular people are labeled, I would argue, similarly always demonstrates that racial difference is produced rather than "natural."

8. Throughout my research, I particularly asked students "Who's 'we'?" in the midst of our conversations in order to get them to articulate their running classifications of self and others. For another application of this fieldwork strategy of attending closely to shifting youth "we's," "they's," and "I's," see also Varenne 1982.

9. For a similar example of U.S. youth play over classification, see Bailey 2000, who demonstrates Rhode Island youth contesting racialized ("black") and national-origin ("Dominican"/"Spanish") classifications through the use of various languages in informal conversations. By switching rapidly between Standard English, African-American Vernacular English, and Spanish, Bailey writes, the youth studied used language as "the key to racial/ethnic identity, preceding phenotype." Yet even while these youth used language to *contest* racialized classifications (such that someone who "looked" "black" could prove he "was" instead "Spanish" by speaking Spanish), Bailey notes that they also used race labels to *impose* racialized "social classification[s] based on phenotype" on one another (557).

10. For analysis of the often painful "What are you?" self-identification questions forced upon U.S. individuals who appear to strangers to be "mixed," see Root 1996, Williams 1996. Gal (1995) has made similar claims about gender-bending, suggesting that any discussion of crossing gender lines actually requires the use of mutually exclusive categories of "male" and "female."

11. For more examples of people struggling to define the category "Latino," see Delgado and Stefancic 1998, Suarez-Orozco and Paez 2002.

12. Ironically, in the autobiographical *Down These Mean Streets*, Piri Thomas describes his own youthful dilemmas of racial self-classification, particularly his own negotiations (as a darker-skinned member of his family) with U.S. definitions of "blackness." See Thomas 1973.

13. As Taylor (1994) writes, "People do not acquire the languages needed for self-definition on their own. Rather, we are introduced to them through interaction with others who matter to us" (32).

14. For historical parallels in American fiction on the sudden revelation of racialized classificatory information, see Chesnutt 1968 [1899], Johnson 1965 [1912]. For commentary, see Sollors 2000.

15. For further examples of young people simultaneously crossing and policing race-group borders, see Gilroy 1993a, Roediger 1998, Perry 2002, Maira 2002, Carter forthcoming.

16. For more discussion of the simplifying effects the discourse of "cultural" exchange often has on classifications of "peoples," see Appadurai 1996; see also Hodgson 2002b. Suarez-Orozco and Suarez-Orozco (2001) have argued that for immigrant youth in particular, the very "entry into American identities today is via the culture of multiculturalism," which quickly socializes "children of color" into the nation's simplified "racial regime" (Suarez-Orozco 2001, 357).

17. For evidence of children and adults re-creating such simple race taxonomies in U.S. preschools, see Van Ausdale and Feagin 2001.

18. Suarez-Orozco and Suarez-Orozco (2001) have pointed out that the lump-sum category "Latino" often artificially masks the diversity of various Spanish-speaking national origin populations across the Americas and Europe. Others (e.g., Saragoza et al. 1998) have argued similarly, but added that "Latino" has become a racialized category precisely because "Latinos" in the U.S. share experiences with systems of racialized inequality. Rumbaut (forthcoming) has noted the particular impact of California politics on fostering youths' racialized self-identifications as "Latino" (or, in some locations, "Mexican"). California's Proposition 187, which attempted to deny social and educational services to immigrants deemed "illegal," prompted many youth respondents in Rumbaut's longitudinal sample to change primarily "mixed" self-identifications to single racialized ones (one girl who had described herself as a "mixed chocolate swirl" before Proposition 187, for example, labeled herself racially "Mexican" after weathering the political battles of the mid-1990s). Rumbaut notes that many of these political battles engaged youth in and around schools. Felix Padilla (1985, cited in Saragoza et al. 1998, p. 48) has termed " 'situational' Latino politics" the tactic of strategically using the racialized/pan-ethnic/national allegiance "Latino" to increase the group's empowerment and to improve members' chances of garnering resources within inequality systems. For a similar analysis of "Asian-American" group formation, see Espiritu 1992.

19. As Winant (1998) writes, the very idea of racialized difference serves both to allocate resources *and* to "provid[e] means for challenging that allocation" (90).

20. As British anthropologist E. R. Leach wrote when describing the function of rituals in a complex Burmese society (the Kachin) in the 1950s, "If anarchy is to be avoided, the individuals who make up a society must from time to time be reminded, at least in symbol, of the underlying order that is supposed to guide their social activities. Ritual performances have this function for the participating group as a whole; they momentarily make explicit what is otherwise a fiction" (Leach 1954, 16). More recently, Rosaldo (1993) has argued that, "Although certain rituals both reflect and create ultimate values, others simply bring people together and deliver a set of platitudes that enable them to go on with their lives" (20). "Multicultural" assemblies at Columbus accomplished both aims.

21. Many observers have charged "multicultural" curricula with oversimplifying human diversity (McCarthy 1998) and for setting up precisely these sorts of racialized conflicts (Schlesinger 1998). Yet multicultural education, of course, sets out unapologetically at times to represent basic "groups" equally in order to remedy a simple history of ignoring these very "cultures" (see Nieto 2000 on multicultural education's project of actively "affirming diversity"). Wallace (1993) thus notes that she has become a "reluctant supporter" of "multiculturalism" precisely because its "opportunity for ongoing critical debate" about difference and inclusion counters the dominant discourse of " 'color-blind' cultural homogeneity" (252). Banks (1995) argues further that true multiculturalism, far from simplistically "including" "content about ethnic groups" (316), typically embeds curricular reform in a larger context of schoolwide change. "Multicultural education" is best defined, Banks writes, "as a restructuring and transformation of the total school environment so that it reflects the racial and cultural diversity that exists within U.S. society and helps children from diverse groups to experience educational equality" (329). For further elaboration of the full sociopolitical context of the "multicultural education" project, see Nieto 2000. For a useful sample of research on multiculturalism, see Banks and Banks 1995; see also Sleeter and Grant 1987. On "multicultural education" as practiced in various locales worldwide, see Grant and Lei 2001.

22. Lipsitz (1998) argues that simple-race "identity politics" often leave "white" people unmarked, never acknowledging the particular role "whiteness" plays "as an organizing principle in social and cultural relations" (1). This argument has been central to whiteness studies, from W.E.B. Du Bois to James Baldwin to the present (see Thompson 1999 for an excellent review). Accordingly, scholars calling themselves "critical multiculturalists" (Kincheloe and Steinberg 1998) argue that multiculturalists in education must be "fervently concerned with white positionality," with the construction of whiteness, and with white privilege, "in their attempt to understand the power relations that give rise to" racial inequality (3). Mohanty (1993) argues more generally that "difference" in multicultural education should never be framed just as "benign variation" (a framing that to Mohanty suggests an "empty pluralism"), but rather as always "asymmetrical" and "situated within hierarchies of domination and resistance" (42).

23. One predecessor's words offer some final guidance for understanding how people both defy social categorizations in daily life and employ these categorizations in order to create and navigate a predictable social structure. When anthropologist E. R. Leach began work with the Kachin in Burma in the 1950s, he found, as he wrote, that Kachin social organization seemed startlingly in flux. Like many British anthropologists of his time, Leach had been interested initially in the Kachin's social ranking system; yet among the Kachin, he quickly realized, such rankings were clear-cut "in theory" but not in practice. "Although a man's rank is in theory precisely defined by his birth," Leach (1954) explained, "there is an almost infinite flexibility in the system as actually applied" (167). Leach argued that acting *as if* things were simply ordered, however, was itself a key part of cultural practice. That is, while there might be debate over who would serve as the Kachin chief, the *category* of "chief" was a given. Delineating such simple social categories, he argued, was thus not just "an analytical device of the social anthropologist": "it also corresponds to the way that Kachins themselves apprehend their own system through the medium of the verbal categories of their own language" (ix). The "verbal categories" of Kachin talk described how Kachin people "apprehended" their social categories, not necessarily how they always lived them—but as there would always be a "chief," conceptual social schemes in the end organized lives in practice as well as in theory.

24. On the concept of working-class youth only "partially penetrating" the class system in Britain (that is, challenging the middle-class authority of schooling even while slotting themselves into working-class jobs), see Willis 1977.

25. See, e.g., Heath 1995. For a similar argument about the dwindling demographic future of U.S. "races," see Sanjek 1996.

26. As one think tank reported on a public speech by Connerly on his proposed "Racial Privacy Initiative,"

> Mr. Connerly (like so many Californians) is a prime example of the absurdity of racial classification. His heritage includes Irish, African and Choctaw native American ancestors. His wife is Irish. His son married a Vietnamese girl.
>
> "But when people find out my grandchildren are Ward Connerly's grandchildren, they often say, 'Oh, you're black,' " he told the audience. "This initiative is for the growing population of kids who don't know what box to check—and shouldn't have to decide. Please give them freedom from race and let them just be Americans." See "Editorial: Undermining Identity Politics. American Civil Rights Coalition, April 5, 2002. (http://www.acrc1.org/editotial. htm) [*sic*]

27. As Loury (2000) argues in a foreword to a study supporting affirmative-action policies, "The implicit assumption of color-blind advocates is that, if we would just stop putting people into these [administrative] boxes, they would oblige us by not thinking of themselves in these terms. But, this assumption is patently false" (Bowen and Bok 1998, xxviii).

28. Appiah (1994) suggests that a "multicultural" "politics of recognition" in itself forces on individuals an oversimplifying account of group "authenticity," forcing people to make public and central single, over-scripted identities that they might rather keep personal, negotiated, and partial. Nieto (2000) accordingly outlines the "major pitfall" in even writing a book *about* "multicultural education": "the information presented can be overgeneralized to the point that it becomes just another harmful stereotype" of any student "group" (8). Gonzales and Cauce (1995) argue most generally that "the crux of the difficulty that we face in trying to deal effectively with race and ethnicity within the educational system" is, "How does one recognize ethnic differences and support ethnicity as an important dimension of self-definition without paradoxically encouraging group divisions and intergroup tensions that often result when ethnic categories are emphasized?" (140–41).

29. At the higher education level, a lively exchange between anthropologists (Dominguez 1994) shows "minority intellectuals" arguing over the same central double-bind—not wanting to hyper-racialize faculty or authors of color, yet needing to retain "racial talk" itself in order to equalize academic opportunity and diversify syllabi (Dominguez 1994, 335).

30. Taken in isolation, the claim that race groups do not genetically exist indeed has some public figures arguing that racial inequality must also be a cultural construction. Popular lore holds that during one discrimination suit being argued to the Supreme Court, for example, Justice Scalia leaned over to a prosecuting lawyer and asked if race was a cultural construction; as the startled lawyer struggled to respond, Scalia asked whether a discrimination suit was necessary or even possible if race categories were constructed falsehoods. After a statement was issued by the American Anthropological Association in 1998 suggesting the now prominent anthropological viewpoint that race categories are cultural constructs, for another example, a letter appeared in the Association's *Anthropology Newsletter* from an anthropologist asserting that as race categories were cultural constructions, there was no need for affirmative action in recruiting graduate students of color to his university. Notably, a key backer (with Ward Connerly) of California's Proposition 209, which attempted to outlaw "race-based" equality remedies in the state's public institutions (see this introduction), was a little-known anthropologist, Glynn Custred. Custred reportedly explained his actions with the quip, "As an anthropologist, I know that when you've got diversity, you've got a problem" (Chavez 1998, 1).

Chapter 2

1. Legal scholars have been particularly active in laying out the contours of the American debate over "colorblindness" and race-consciousness, as it is rooted in commentary about the U.S. Constitution. Justice Harlan wrote in his famous *Plessy v Ferguson* dissent (1896) that while his colleagues on the Supreme Court were enshrining the

doctrine of "separate but equal" race-segregated facilities, the Constitution's equality provisions were instead designed to be "colorblind." Almost a century later, Justice Blackmun argued in *Bakke* (1978) that "in order to get beyond racism, we must first take account of race. In order to treat persons equally, we must treat them differently." Navigation between the two theoretical poles of "colorblindness" and race-consciousness has characterized much of U.S. discourse on race and equality. As Crenshaw (1997) writes of this polarization, "The goal of a color-blind world is one in which race is precluded as a source of identification or analysis; its antithesis is color consciousness of any sort" (103). For further discussion, see, e.g., Edley 1996, Skrentny 1996, Friedman 1997, Guinier and Torres 2002.

2. As Danielsen and Engle (1995) point out more generally, "On one hand, lawyers and activists have sought to design legal remedies for broad classes of disadvantaged groups, focusing on generally drawn status categories to define these groups. On the other hand, the same group remedies have often sought to transcend these categories by making it unlawful to take them into account" (xiv).

3. Other scholars of racialized discourse have noted the coexistence of raee conscious/anti-race or even racist/antiracist ideologies within the discourse of individual speakers. See Hatcher and Troyna 1993 on such coexistence in children's talk; see also Blum (2002) and Wetherell and Potter (1992) on adult talk. See Frankenberg (1993) on tensions between "color-evasive" and "race-cognizant" discourses in the talk of white women in particular. Philosopher Amy Gutmann (1994) notes that the question of when to treat one another racially is a core question of U.S. political discourse as well. She asks, "Apart from ceding each of us the same rights as all other citizens, what does respecting people as equals entail? In what sense should our identities as men or women, African-Americans, Asian-Americans, or Native Americans, Christians, Jews, or Muslims, English or French-Canadians *publicly* matter?" (4, emphasis in original).

4. Columbus did, therefore, achieve for students what Metz (1994) and others have described as one characteristic of a "truly 'integrated' " school: adults and students did attempt to "self-consciously [create] intellectual and social engagement across racial and ethnic groups" of students (Fine, Weis, and Powell 1997, 248).

5. In her own study of patterned silence about the existence of racism in Brazil, Sheriff (2000) argued that studying silence was methodologically so problematic that she chose to focus only on "metadiscursive" talk *about* not talking—that is, "informants' elicited statements *about their silence*, rather than silence and/or unmediated linguistic behavior itself" (115, emphasis mine). In contrast, I chose to study unsolicited gaps in natural everyday talk as well as unsolicited talk about such silences. Both deleting race labels and talking about such deletions, I argue here, are common U.S. speech events and both appropriate and possible for study.

6. The assumption that such prompted talk "about race" is always a direct representation of informants' "attitudes," rather than a strategic response to prompting, runs throughout various methods of race research (Studs Terkel thus confidently titles his collection of interview data *Race: How Blacks and Whites* Think and Feel *about the American Obsession* [1992, emphasis mine]). For more commentary on survey and interview research on racial/political attitudes, see Sears, Sidanius, and Bobo 2000 (in which various contributors argue over whether, for example, "prejudice" "really" underlies whites' stated opinions on race). See Hammersley (1998) for more commentary on interview research on race in schools: Hammersley argues that adult talk about race is

often taken as suspect, while student talk about race is taken as unnuanced description of fact. Mishler (1986) demonstrates more generally that much interview research ignores the effect of the interview situation, often separating answers from the context of the questions asked and erasing the interviewer entirely from the text presented. As Mertz (1992) argues even further, the assumption that talk is a purely descriptive "window" on the "real world," rather than a strategic act in itself, actually plagues all research using talk as data.

7. Peshkin, who was himself white, received similar answers to his direct questions from students of all "ethnicities." "White" students responded that "being white" made little difference at school; similarly, "When I asked black students about the importance of being black if someone wanted to know them well, they did not rank it highly," he reported (191). Interviews with "Filipino" students also suggested that "during their high school years, their ethnicity is not salient" (208). Peshkin also concluded that

> At school, non-newcomer Mexicans basically see being Mexican as a fact of little consequence, as I learned when I asked students if being Mexican affected their life in and out of class. Specifically, did being Mexican make a difference regarding the grades they got, how teachers treated them, being popular, getting elected to office, who'd they vote for, what clubs they'd join, success in sports, getting in trouble, getting their share of what the school had to offer? Overwhelmingly, students saw little or no relationship between their ethnicity and any of these points: it was neither helpful nor unhelpful to be Mexican [184].

Peshkin admitted that his direct questions about "identity" were methodologically problematic, acknowledging retrospectively that his explicit interviews on student "ethnicity and identity" had not captured the "inconsistencies" of racial identity at his field site (177–78).

8. Schofield (1999) found that "white" and "black" educators asked directly about race by a team of interviewers repeatedly denied altogether that race was relevant even to *student* relations at their "50 percent African American and 50 percent White" middle school (249). Powell (in Fine, Weis, and Powell 1997) found similarly that in "family group" support sessions for small teams of teachers, adults responded to direct brief questions about race's relevance by dismissing race's relevance altogether. Longer conversations, she argues, allowed participants to take apart their own "coded" language and instead debate race's relevance.

9. For general discussion of interviewers' routine failure to consider interviews as communicative events (thus regularly ignoring or overriding respondents' communicative norms), see Frake 1980, Briggs 1986, Mishler 1986. See also Eckert and McConnell-Ginet 1995.

10. In another California school ethnography, Olsen (1997) found that students were ready to draw such racialized maps upon request. Eckert and McConnell-Ginet (1995) and Varenne (1982) found students similarly ready in interviews with language describing school "cliques."

11. Throughout American literature and historical record, actually, eating together has been framed as a quintessentially anxious type of racial contact (see Pollock 1992; see also Sollors 2000). Beverly Tatum (1997) provides a particularly thoughtful discussion of this very trope of lunchtime seating in schooling discourse ("why are all the black kids sitting together in the cafeteria?"); Tatum argues that organizing social relations and social space racially is actually a developmentally natural act for students of

color coming of age in multiracial places. In an investigation of a South African high school, notably, Nadine Dolby (2001) recorded analogous racial descriptions of lunchtime and teatime spatial arrangements (80).

12. Similarly, in an analysis of the discourse on "Navajo"-"Anglo" relations in a Utah school district, Deyhle (1995) demonstrates that occasional talk of group conflict among youths obfuscated discussion of larger racialized dynamics between Navajo students and Anglo adults.

13. In the O.J. Simpson trial of 1995, Fuhrman became known as a white police officer who openly used the word "nigger" in his testimony.

14. For further analysis of "whiteness" as a state of being that is inherently *about* struggling to retain power, see Lipsitz, *The Possessive Investment in Whiteness* (1998). On white teachers and white privilege in particular, see, e.g., Sleeter 1993b, Kincheloe et al. 1998.

15. For further critical analysis of racialized school dynamics over disciplinary "control," see Devine (1996), Ferguson (2000), and Noguera (2001).

16. Student accusations of adult "racism" at Columbus waffled between critiques of "racist" individuals and critiques of a "racist" institution at large. For discussion of how definitions of "racism" have historically expanded from the former to encompass the latter, see Blauner (1994) and Blum (2002). Blauner notes that while many white Americans still too often define "racism" narrowly as referring exclusively to interpersonal acts rather than institutional orders, many African-Americans have also been "critical of the use of racism as a blanket explanation for all manifestations of racial inequality" (22). Yet "the 'inflated' meanings of racism are already too rooted in common speech to be overturned by the advice of experts," Blauner writes, and besides, no term seems as accurate *as* "racism" for "convey[ing] the pervasive and systematic character of racial oppression" (23).

17. Crenshaw notes that in the O.J. Simpson saga, the (white) public's skeptical reaction to claims of race's relevance to the case evidenced a false assumption that the U.S. social and legal systems were colorblind in the first place. "The frequent deployment of the metaphor of 'the race card' . . . presumes a social terrain devoid of race until it is (illegitimately) introduced," she writes (104). For Crenshaw, such presumptions of race's irrelevance exemplify the practice that Gotanda (1991) calls "non-recognition," in which a "technique of 'noticing but not considering race' implicitly involves recognition of the racial category and a transformation or sublimation of that recognition so that the racial label is not 'considered.' " In the early days of the O.J. case, Crenshaw explains as an example, "the wishful belief that race would *not* play a role was accompanied by a studied practice of denying the rather obvious racial dimensions of the case" (100, emphasis mine).

18. Schofield (1999) found that an adult "colorblind perspective" in a 1970s East Coast school even mitigated against discussing a black suspension rate four times that of whites. "The disparity in suspension rates," she writes, "was never treated as a serious issue that needed attention" (257).

19. In a study of a West Coast elementary school, Ann Ferguson (2000) found similar controversies between students and adults over interpreting disciplinary incidents as racially biased. While one student "positions himself as black and, as such, racially marked for special (mis)treatment," Ferguson recounts, "The teacher is adamant about discrediting this interpretation of the event because to allow it to be credible is to call

into question the neutral, universalistic impartiality of the rule/authority structure. It is also to call into question her own sincere presentation of self as unbiased" (222).

20. Cochran-Smith (1995a) urges similarly that teacher educators should help teachers-to-be explore and discuss directly the complexities and dilemmas of race's relevance in their schools.

Chapter 3

1. In this process, I follow the work of Mikhail Bakhtin (1981), who wrote that any utterance can be "exposed ... as a contradiction-ridden, tension-filled unity" of "embattled tendencies in the life of a language" (272); he even posited that we can hear the "internal dialogism of the word" (280). David Roediger (1991) has similarly described the historical evolution of race-loaded yet de-raced words in the United States. Roediger has, for example, examined how race got buried in the early American term "working man," which came to represent "whiteness" and freedom in contrast to the "black"-loaded "slave."

2. Almost all desegregation cases in the U.S. have focused on moving "black" students into proximity with "white" ones (some rare cases have focused on "Hispanics"; see, importantly, *Keyes v School District No. 1*, 1973). More rarely, as critics have pointed out, have policymakers focused on moving white students into proximity with black students. For general analysis of desegregation, see Kirp 1982, Yudof, Kirp, and Levin 1992, Orfield and Eaton 1996, Wells and Crain 1997. On the particular segregation of Mexican-Americans, see Donato 1997. For some discussion of the history of segregating Asian-American students in California, see Wollenberg 1976.

3. In this chapter's brief discussion of the facts of California City's desegregation history, I have relied at times upon a secondary source that here goes uncited (by permission of the author) to protect California City's anonymity.

4. Here and throughout this chapter, the italics in court opinions represent my added emphasis.

5. This de-racing of policy talk was perhaps one local example of a national trend: throughout the 1980s, many scholars have argued, national discussion of racial equity became submerged within a discourse of improving education for "everyone" in the nation (for discussion, see Secada 1989, Weinberg 1991, Takagi 1992). Weinberg notes that explicit talk of racial equality was "omitted" from K–12 educational discourse during the 1980s even as talk of "excellence for all" mushroomed (1991, 4). While some of this erasure of specific race words might have reflected increasing diversity nationwide, it was also quite possibly a deliberate resistance to racially targeted policy. Omi and Winant (1994) have recounted the purposeful erasure of racial data from policy recordkeeping during the Reagan Administration in the 1980s, leaving one government official to comment that "if abuse exists, we will not be able to find it" (134). Kymlicka (1995) describes how decades earlier, an international logic of "protecting vulnerable groups directly" shifted to a logic of "universal human rights" within liberal human rights discourse after World War II; "Guided by this philosophy, the United Nations deleted all references to the rights of ethnic and national minorities in its Universal Declaration of Human Rights" (3). Yet such generalized language, Kymlicka suggests, has since proved inadequate to address group-specific needs. "It has become increasingly clear

that minority rights cannot be subsumed under the category of human rights," Kymlicka argues, since generalized human rights discourse and strategy often do not articulate how specific minority rights issues will be resolved (4–5).

6. In a historical examination of U.S. efforts to target poverty assistance to needy populations, Skocpol (1995) praises a strategy of "targeting within universalism": that is, she argues that programs offering benefits to "all Americans" were successful at " 'helping the poor by not talking about them' " (Hugh Heclo, cited in Skocpol, 265). Policies specifically designed to give programs and benefits directly to "minorities," Skocpol argues, have tended to both anger mainstream voters and stigmatize the groups targeted for assistance. Rarely, she argues, "do advocates of targeted benefits or specially tailored public social services face up to the problem of finding sustained political support for them" (252). Yet California City's desegregation experiences suggest that once universalistic discourse is set in motion, this very discourse can preclude targeting efforts: for once "all" talk is hegemonic, any targeting efforts seem to some to be inherently "unfair."

7. In many contexts other than schooling, such processes of disaggregating and reaggregating descriptions of the world have struck anthropologists as key cultural acts. Doing fieldwork in the Philippines, for example, anthropologist Charles Frake (1980), famous for his investigations of everyday categorization processes, became fascinated by an everyday process of amateur disease diagnosis that involved speaking either specifically or generally about categories of illness. Frake argued that such shifting diagnoses were social rather than purely medical acts: many diagnoses, for example, demonstrated the necessity of speaking "at just a level of generality that specifies the pertinent information but leaves other, possibly embarrassing, information ambiguous" (116).

8. In the intervening years, former Columbus teachers have wondered aloud to me whether any Columbus actions during the school's probation year could have staved off the district's reconstitution fervor. Some have argued that while they privately focused on discussing the particular welfare of students who happened to be black, the house and academy programs simply *were* about attempting to serve the entire student body better—and that "parading out black students" at the qualitative presentation accordingly would have seemed perfunctory or even offensive.

9. Most reconstituted Columbus teachers found new jobs in other schools across the district. Ironically, most of the young teachers who were hired to staff Columbus after reconstitution have since left not just Columbus, but the teaching profession.

Chapter 4

1. Anthropologists have long contended that people spend a great deal of time analyzing the world structurally, defining various groups of people in contrast to one another (for a primary example, see Levi-Strauss 1963). As anthropologists have realized more recently, people also regularly debate the accuracy of their own analyses. The contemporary world, many have suggested, is full of heightened analytic complications, both for professional analysts and for people analyzing the social world in their daily lives (see, e.g., Wolf 1992, Rosaldo 1993, Appadurai 1996).

2. Many scholars have examined American debates over racial analyses of inequality—and racially targeted equalization policies (see, e.g., Sears, Sidanius, and Bobo

2000, Hochschild and Scovronick 2003). Gutmann (1994) argues most broadly that "questions concerning whether and how cultural groups should be recognized in politics are among the most salient and vexing on the political agenda of many democratic and democratizing societies today" (5). Wells and Crain (1997) argue that "the vast majority of Americans . . . are not now ready to move beyond a universal or equal opportunity agenda to a more proactive particularistic or race-specific one designed to produce equal results" (6), adding more specifically that "most *whites* believe that the race-conscious agenda is distinctive in its moral challenge to fundamental American values" (11, emphasis mine). Bobo (1988), similarly, argues that "whites" in particular tend to disapprove of "specific policies aimed at improving the social and economic position of *blacks*" (emphasis mine; cited in Wells and Crain 1997, 9), yet he also points out (Bobo 2000) that much research on public opinion has promoted a "distorted view" that whites monolithically oppose racialized equalization policies (138). Indeed, just as many whites support various race-based equalization strategies, many controversially popular authors of color have argued against race analyses of "disadvantage" (see, e.g., D'Souza 1995, McWhorter 2000). Curry (1996) provides an excellent core sample of a national debate over racialized analysis of opportunity (affirmative action). For a series of arguments about racialized policy and "American values," see Edley 1996. See also Guinier and Torres 2002, who argue strongly for race analysis in monitoring inequality problems.

3. As stated in this book's introduction, the opening text of the proposition, which eventually amended the California Constitution, read as follows: "*The state shall not discriminate against, or grant preferential treatment to, any individual or group on the basis of race, sex, color, ethnicity, or national origin in the operation of public employment, public education, or public contracting.*" See Lydia Chavez 1998. In various such so-called "race-neutral" or "colorblind" policy shifts in education in particular, Blum (2002) notes, "complex questions about the purposes of educational institutions, the character of 'merit' and 'qualification' and the like, are swept aside in the face of the view that it is simply wrong to take account of applicants' racial identity in admissions" (91).

4. In an edited volume exploring the question of affirmative action in a staunchly "multiethnic America," Skrentny (2001) has argued that "late-twentieth-century American demographic" changes, particularly those related to immigration, "will ensure that if the twentieth century had the problem of the color line, the twenty-first will have the problem of color lines" (2). With the question of *which* "groups" should benefit from affirmative action still unanswered, he argues—and with the question of who "really" has been harmed by discrimination also up for debate—"the way affirmative action draws color lines has been, is now, and will be increasingly an object of contention in twenty-first-century America" (8).

5. Similarly, Sheriff (2000) noted that Brazilian informants talking to her about the relevance of race in Brazil "qualified" everyday descriptions of racial inequality by insisting that such inequality was "driven not by distinctions of color but by class" (119).

6. For further analysis of absent discussions about the needs of "ESL" or "LEP" students in U.S. schools, see Olsen 1995.

7. The legal basis of this requirement stems from the 1974 Supreme Court case *Lau v. Nichols*. For discussion, see Crawford 1995. See also ARC Associates (*Revisiting the Lau Decision: Twenty Years After*), 1996.

8. Linda Chavez, a conservative commentator and long-time public opponent of race-based affirmative action policies, similarly preempts race analysis with class analy-

sis: "the time has passed when every member of a racial minority is truly 'disadvantaged,'" she explains (1996, 321). Affirmative-action supporter Manning Marable, however, argues that the race/class debate, which usually ends with the trumping of race *by* class, is a "false debate." To reach the "long-term goal of a color-blind society," he argues, American analysts simply cannot "become neutral about the continuing significance of race in American life" (1996, 15). For an excellent discussion of the complexities and dilemmas of *class* analysis in the U.S., see Schram 1995.

9. By the mid-1980s, Douglass (2001) notes, UC Berkeley's Asian-American population similarly had far exceeded their proportion of the state's overall student population, and the word "disadvantaged" accordingly ceased for some to accurately describe the state's Asian-American population. "They had become overrepresented, and hence no longer a 'disadvantaged' group" in the language of admissions policy (128).

10. On the concept of "foreignness," see Mia Tuan, *Forever Foreigners or Honorary Whites? The Asian Ethnic Experience Today* (1998).

11. As Wang and Wu (1996) argue of affirmative action, similarly, "One of the increasingly prominent fallacies in the attacks on affirmative action is that Asian-Americans are somehow the example that defeats the rationale for race-conscious remedial programs" (191). Instead, policymakers considering race-based equalization plans "should also be sensitive to the tremendous diversity within the Asian-American category. Including some but not all Asian-American groups may be justified under certain circumstances. Policy makers may legitimately consider the differences in economic, immigration, and historical background between the Asian groups in determining whether they should be included in an affirmative action policy" (199–200).

Chapter 5

1. The practice of ranking presumed scholastic ability racially even precedes the availability *of* schooling to all the nation's "races." In his basic writings on race in America, for example, Thomas Jefferson outlined his presumptions of "Negro" slaves' mental inferiority (Jordan 1974), jumpstarting centuries of pseudo-scientific research on race and "natural" ability even as slaves were officially forbidden to become literate. In well-known contemporary findings, Claude Steele (1992) has shown that racialized test scores are not pure reflections of cognitive skills, but rather patterns produced by the continued racialized social context *of* testing (in which the test-taker of color is still seized by the fear of proving that she is, as expected, less "able"). For a good discussion of the racialized nature of many tests themselves, see Hilliard 1990.

2. For foundational anthropological work disproving false assumptions of "racial" intellectual difference, see, e.g., Boas 1895, Montagu 1997 [1942]. For many years, subsequent anthropological research on "cultures" and schooling produced very important work in the "cultural" explanations vein, particularly analyzing disconnections between student and teacher discourse styles in classrooms shared by white teachers and students of color. For reviews, see Trueba and Wright 1992, Jacob and Jordan 1993. More recently, anthropologists of education have questioned their own assumptions about (and accounts of) "cultural" difference. For a useful confessional account of misgivings over such a research approach to simplified "cultural" difference, see McDermott 1997.

3. For histories of how opportunities to learn have been distributed along racial lines in the United States, see Weinberg 1977, Tyack 1980, Olson and Wilson 1984, Anderson 1988, Donato 1997. For analysis of the continuing racialized distribution of opportunities between and within schools, see Oakes et al. 1990, Kozol 1991, Darling-Hammond 1999; for an excellent systemic analysis of race and opportunity, see Valencia 1991.

4. See, e.g., Fordham and Ogbu 1986; Gibson, 1988. For further discussion, see Gibson 1997. For critiques of Ogbu's theory, see O'Connor 1997, and Carter, forthcoming. O'Connor, for example, demonstrates that students of color who perceive a racialized opportunity system and struggle systematically to overcome it achieve highly.

5. Ogbu's "why" questions could also produce racial explanations that were, ironically, staples of the very cultural deprivation studies Ogbu said he abhorred:

Anthropologist: Why is it that the Mexican-American students are absent from school so much?

Student: you know the best thing I think for it is that it has to do with the family. [106]

6. The question of learning how to ask questions of respondents has long been a serious concern in interpretive social science (for discussion, see Mishler 1986, Briggs 1986). Strangely, it seems less common to make this concern central to research on race (see also chapter 2).

7. On one of the first days of my Ethnic Literature classes in 1994, I asked students to interview one another and inform the class of what languages their partner spoke, where he/she had been born, and how he/she self-identified "ethnically." In my second-period class, six out of the fifteen students who ended up attending regularly had been born in other countries, including the Philippines, El Salvador, Taiwan, Italy, and Jamaica; the remainder had been born in California City. The students born in California City included a student who described himself as "Latin"; a male student (who spoke Tagalog); a female student who was "part African-American and part Filipino" (and understood Tagalog); a Latina student (who spoke Spanish); a female student who was "Asian-American," a male student who was "Filipino-American," a female student who was "African-American," and a student who said he was "born in Africa" and spoke multiple languages (I jotted this down dutifully and found out later that he was joking).

By graduation three years later, one student born in the Philippines, the one born in El Salvador, and the one born in Jamaica had been dropped because of low attendance. Of the nine students born in California City, four had not graduated from Columbus. They were the "Latin" student and the Latina student, whose whereabouts I did not know, and two "African-American" students, one male and one female, who had not received enough credits by their senior year. There were, then, a total of seven students who did not graduate: one Filipino student, three Latino students, and three black students. Walking triumphantly down the aisle were: the Filipino student, born in the U.S.; the "part African-American and Filipino" female student, born in California City; the Filipino student born in the Philippines; the "Asian-American" female student born in California City; a "Filipino-American" student born in California City; the female student born in Taiwan; and a Filipino student born in California City. Seven students, thus, had graduated: all were Filipino, part Filipino, or "Asian."

My other classes showed similar patterns. In my fifth-period class, nine out of twenty students had been born in other countries, five in the Philippines and the others from

Jordan, El Salvador, Jamaica, and Vietnam. Most of the Filipino students in the class, including two students born in California City, described themselves as "Filipino" and spoke both Tagalog and English. Other students born in California City included a student who described herself as "Spanish and white" and spoke some Spanish; a student born in a neighboring city who described herself as "black" and said that she spoke "a little Mexican/Spanish"; a male student who "spoke a little Chinese" and was "Chinese-American"; a male "Latino" student who spoke Spanish; and a female student born in Georgia and a female student born in California City who both described themselves as "black." Three years later, missing from graduation were the female "Spanish and white" student, who had transferred to another school in the district; the female black student born nearby who had done the same; an ethnic "Mexican" born in California who had missed too much school because she had to take care of her child; a Filipino student born in California City who had been dropped for lack of credits in his sophomore year; the male "Latino" student born in California City, and the male student born in Jamaica, who had also been dropped for lack of credits; two male black students (one born in Texas and one born in California City) whose whereabouts I did not know; and one black student born in California City, who had not received enough credits for graduation in her senior year. Nine students, thus, were missing: three Latinos, five blacks, and one Filipino. Graduates included three Filipina students born in the Philippines; a female student born in Jordan; a male Filipino student born in the Philippines; a male Filipino student born in California City; the male Chinese-American student born in California City; the male student born in Vietnam; the male Salvadoran student; and the female black student born in Georgia. There were, in total, ten students who graduated: five Filipinos, two Asians, one Latino, one black, and one (in the district's terms) "other non-white."

In my sixth-period class, five out of 16 students had been born in other countries, three in the Philippines, one in China, and one in Europe (though she was Filipino) to military parents. The rest of the students had been born in California City, with one student born in another city in California. The students born abroad described themselves as "Filipino," with the exception of one "Chinese" male student and one student who described herself as "Filipino and Spanish"; most spoke Tagalog and English (the "Chinese" student spoke Chinese). The students born in California City described themselves in various ways. A male student was "half Filipino, half white"; a female student was "Filipino, speaking no other languages"; a male student was "black and white"; a male student spoke "Spanish and English"; a "white" female student spoke English; a male "African-American" student spoke "no other languages"; a male student was "Filipino, knows Tagalog and English"; a female student was "Filipino, no other languages"; a male student was "Guatemalan" and spoke Spanish; a male student was "black" and spoke English; and a female student was "Hawaiian, no other languages." Three years later, five of the students were missing from graduation: the Filipina student born in Europe, whose whereabouts were unknown since her junior year; a Latino student born in California City who had been expelled in his sophomore year; an "African-American" student born in California City who had transferred to another school in the district in his senior year; a Filipino student who had been born in the Philippines; and the Filipino student born in another California city, whose whereabouts were unknown. There were thus five students who did not graduate: three Filipinos, one Latino, and one black. Graduates included: the male "half Filipino, half white" student;

two Filipina students born in California City; the male "black and white" student; the male student born in China; the "white" female student born in California City; the "Filipino and Spanish" female student born in the Philippines; the "Guatemalan" male student born in California City; a "black" male student born in California City, who had found hours before graduation that he was indeed eligible; the Filipina student born in the Philippines; and the "Hawaiian" female student. Eleven students had graduated: five Filipinos, one Latino, one white, two black, two "others."

I did not have "ethnic" classification notes for my third-period class, which had been far too rowdy in the first few days for me to do the introductory activity. A class list, however, demonstrates that three years later 19 out of the 29 students were not present at Columbus' graduation. I will use the racial self-descriptions they used throughout the year. Missing were: four Filipino students (three boys, one girl), whereabouts unknown, most dropped because of poor attendance; a Filipino student who had left school to take care of his child by working in the fast food industry; three black male students, two of whom had been transferred involuntarily to other schools because of disciplinary conflicts; three black female students, whereabouts unknown; a Latina student who had transferred to a school where students did most of their work at home; a Latino student who had moved, whereabouts unknown; a half-Asian student who was graduating one year late because of his poor attendance; a black student who was graduating one year late because of time off for his career in the entertainment industry; a black student who had been expelled in her sophomore year; a Latino student who had dropped out of school because of his lack of credits; and a Latino student and a Filipino student who were still in school but did not have enough credits for graduation. Nineteen students, thus, were missing: six Filipinos, four Latinos, eight blacks, and an "other." Graduates included two black female students, two female and one male Filipino students, a female student from Pakistan, a male Vietnamese student, a male white student, and a Latino student.

8. See, for example, Metz 1978, Olsen 1995, Noguera 1995, Schofield 1995, Lipman 1998, Markus, Steele, and Steele 2000.

9. In an analysis of a controversy over grading Native Alaskans at the University of Alaska–Fairbanks, Gilmore, Smith, and Kairaiuak (1997) demonstrate that both clumsy talk and silence about race and achievement can leave intact damaging assumptions of differential ability.

Chapter 6

1. For discussion of how analyses of school "problems" routinely come to center on "black" students in particular in American schooling discourse (rather than on institutional arrangements also involving non-black students and adults), see Payne 1984, Linda Powell 1997, Lipman 1998, Ferguson 2000, Noguera 2001. Ferguson argues that "in the school setting," for example, it is often "assumed that it is the cultural difference [black] kids bring to school that produces the existing pattern of punishment rather than institutional operations themselves" (20). For a review of studies demonstrating that blackness is an anxious focal point of analysis in multiracial systems internationally (a kind of focus that, we shall see, often leaves whiteness particularly unmarked and unanalyzed, even as whiteness is framed as blackness's polar opposite), see Harrison

1995. Toni Morrison (1992) has observed that blackness has always been a focal point even in white Americans' constitutions of American whiteness.

2. Analysts of "hate speech," particularly critical race theorists, have explored the particular social weight of racial epithets in American discourse (see, e.g., Matsuda et al. 1993, Gates 1994), and other analysts have explored the social weight of the word *"racist"* (see, e.g., Blum 2002). Fewer have explored the variable weight of race labels themselves.

3. "Afrocentrism" is, of course, more accurately framed as a curricular, pedagogical, and political philosophy. See Asante 1998.

4. bell hooks (1998) has written of associations between whiteness and terror in "the black imagination." In her own childhood in the segregated South, she writes, "black folks" openly "associated whiteness with the terrible, the terrifying, the terrorizing" (44). Still today, she writes, "all black people in the United States, irrespective of their class status or politics, live with the possibility that they will be terrorized by whiteness" (50).

5. Lipman (1998) reports a related speech pattern she found in a school in the U.S. South: "All of the students identified by teachers as 'problems' were African-American," she writes. "However, the teachers assiduously avoided discussions of race and racial identification" (112).

6. For discussion of the rampant overrepresentation of black students nationally in "Special Education" classes for the supposedly disabled—an overrepresentation that has demonstrated, to many analysts, the placement of students on racialized disciplinary grounds rather than true "disability"—see Markowitz, Garcia, and Eichelberger 1997, Losen and Orfield 2002.

7. For critical analysis of how many school adults frame the use of "ebonics," or black vernacular English, as problematic in school settings, see Delpit 1995, Perry and Delpit, 1997. Both authors argue that black vernacular must be built upon, rather than outlawed or simply sanctioned, in schooling attempts to teach standard English.

8. Delpit (1995) and Lipman (1998) argue that teachers of color get particularly "shut down" in multiracial faculties' discourse, even when such discourse involves serving students of color. At Columbus, players of various "races" often seemed equally colormute. Sheriff (2000) writes that "customary silences" about racial orders in Brazil, too, are "practiced by different and opposed groups"; yet she points out, importantly, that such silences tend "to be constituted through, and circumscribed by, the political interests of dominant groups," particularly whites (114).

9. Similarly, Ferguson (2000) has noted that in the West Coast school she studied, "African American staff members and a few white adults speak bitterly and with frustration—but cautiously and privately—about the way that race makes a difference in the treatment of children. In public discussions, however, they rarely mention race because they know that raising the issue is volatile, divisive, and will result in their own marginalization" (220–21).

10. The "one drop rule" refers to a socio-legal (and scientifically erroneous) definition pervasive throughout American race history, in which a person with any known "drop" of so-called "black blood" was defined as "black." For discussion, see Davis 1997; see also Sollors 2000. See Clifford (1990) for some discussion of the tendency for ethnographic fieldnotes themselves to both reflect and reproduce ethnographers' preexisting categorical schema.

11. Irvine (1990) argues that "Two primary factors contribute to the unequal treatment of black students in school: prejudicial attitudes and lack of appropriate training ... they are both alterable and modifiable through in-service staff development and preservice teacher education programs" (115). See her chapter 6 for suggestions for such professional development.

12. In her study of an extremely colormute middle school several decades ago, Schofield (1999) found students (including black students) suggesting in interviews that *any* identification of their peers by race would make other students or teachers "think I'm prejudiced" (255).

13. See Devine (1996) on the explosion of police-like paraphernalia (like walkie-talkies and, in increasing proportions, metal detectors) in U.S. schools.

14. Ralph Ellison, of course, described the simultaneous hyper-invisibility and centrality of black Americans in the national psyche (1994 [1952]), as has Toni Morrison (1992).

15. For more discussion of how assumptions of unassisted success (often called the "model minority myth") make various Asian-American struggles invisible, see Chun 1980, Takagi 1992, Sue and Okazaki 1995, Lee 1996.

16. Pachon (1996) argues that Latinos also get particularly overlooked in "minority outreach programs," as such programs typically have been "considered to have reached all minority groups once they officially targeted African-Americans (however poorly)" (186).

17. Courtney Cazden notes that in her classic work *White Teacher* (1979, 130), veteran teacher Vivian Paley "agonizes over why she so often speaks of 'the black girls,' " while wondering herself why she "never needed a collective 'white' to help me identify characteristics that individual white children shared" (cited in Cazden, forthcoming, 11). In *White Teacher*, Paley recounts how her student teacher pointed out that Paley commented "three times as often about black children in this class, even though there are only ten blacks to twenty whites" (xvii). McIntyre (1997) has written of white preservice teachers' particular reluctance to discuss their *own* whiteness.

18. McIntyre labels "white talk" the kind of teacher talk about race that serves to "insulate white people from examining their/our individual and collective role(s) in the perpetuation of racism" (45). McIntyre's own work calls for white educators to investigate "white identity," interrogate their own "uncritical acceptance of racist actions" (7), and pinpoint their own roles in producing racial inequalities.

19. As Frankenberg (1993) writes, "whites" often escape public race analysis as if they are not implicated in racial orders or even "racial" at all. Instead, she argues, racial discourse in the U.S. "frequently accords a hypervisibility to African Americans" (even while, she adds, giving "a relative *invisibility* to Asian Americans and Native Americans; Latinos are also relatively less visible than African Americans in discursive terms" [12]). Giroux (1997), however, has argued that contrary to much of whiteness theorizing, contemporary white people—especially, increasingly, white youth—are *very* conscious of being "white." The crux of the problem for today's "whites," Giroux argues, is rather what to *do* about whiteness, and how to avoid white defensiveness or retrenchment (294).

20. Noting the absence of "whites" and "whiteness" from race analysis has been a hallmark of "whiteness" scholarship, which attempts to make whiteness more central to analysis of racial orders (see Thompson 1999 for an excellent review; see also Kincheloe et al. 1998). From W.E.B. Du Bois to James Baldwin to the present, Thompson notes, theorists of "whiteness" in the U.S. have argued that while whiteness is normal-

ized to appear almost non-racial (such that analysis focuses always on the "pathologies" of "others" while "whites" and whiteness emerge unscathed), whiteness and thus "white" people have always been at the core of racial orders, indeed the privileged class against which "disadvantage" is measured and the norm against which other "races" are constructed as "deviant" (150). Accordingly, *naming* whiteness and the role *of* whites is framed in whiteness scholarship as particularly central to antiracist efforts. "Only by undercutting the systematic privileging and normalizing of whiteness whereby racism is defined as *other* people's problem can we-ness [that is, a shared American equality project] be reconstructed as interracial," Thompson writes (155).

Moving Forward

1. Richard Wilk (1995) has said as much of "cultural" celebratory events in Belize: "Ethnicity is officially sanctioned and is even supported by a government 'Director of Culture,' as long as it remains focused on self-consciously artistic performance. Safe ethnic culture is ornamental, attractive to tourists, part of an international genre of 'our nation's wonderful diversity'; it is mostly disengaged from the concerns with land, labor and rights which predominate in ethnic discourse at the community level" (128).

2. Fairclough (2001) suggests similarly that it is politically empowering for communities to carefully consider their own language use.

3. I thank the expert professional development coaches I have talked to in California for this insight, and for the Fitzgerald epigraph to this chapter.

4. Haney Lopez (1995) argues similarly that "human interaction rather than natural differentiation must be seen as the source and continued basis for racial categorization" (196).

5. Blum (2002) argues similarly, as have many scholars (e.g., Omi and Winant 1994, Winant 1998) that "recognizing racial wrongs does not require acceding to the reality of race" (that is, as biological fact), but rather to the reality and history of *racialization* (166). To "move ahead, then, in abandoning the false and destructive idea of race while retaining our ability to name and deplore racism and other racial wrongs," Blum notes, we must denounce the concept of "races" yet retain the concept of racialized groups (166). In the end, Blum argues finally, "race *equality* is empirically more likely to diminish a destructive racial consciousness than is a ban on the public use of racial categories" (203, emphasis mine).

6. As Amy Gutmann (1996) argues, U.S. society is still too racially unequal for exclusively "colorblind" policy: "Without color conscious policies, we would not be acting in ways that benefit the least advantaged and that bring our society closer to the time when color blindness can be fair to everyone, regardless of color" (177–78).

7. Thompson (1999) names "colortalk" this kind of talk that "explicitly names the mechanisms" by which racialized orders are "maintained" (144).

Practically Speaking

1. Marilyn Cochran-Smith (1995b) confesses similar concerns in her analysis of teacher education work. "How can we open up the unsettling discourse of race," she asks, "without making people afraid to speak for fear of being naïve, offensive, or using the wrong language? Without making people of color do all the work, feeling called

upon to expose themselves for the edification of others? Without eliminating conflict to the point of flatness, thus reducing the conversation to platitudes or superficial rhetoric?" (546). Cochran-Smith found that having student teachers consider their own autobiographies in reference to key readings about racial privilege and identity was a helpful starting point.

2. Many others have written of the importance of establishing (and training) white educators as key discussion partners in anti-racism work. See Titone (1998), who argues for "educating the white teacher as ally": white antiracist educators, Titone writes, should ideally be "willing to initiate, and able to hold a group in, discussions of racial issues and education, even emotional and confrontational ones" (167). Sleeter (1993b) argues more generally in a debate on white university-level educators in *Educational Researcher* that "White people tend to retreat from identifying racism with ourselves; we have strategies that enable us to talk about racial issues, but at the same time remove our own responsibility from scrutiny" (14). See also Lawrence and Tatum (1997), who argue for the need to build trusting contexts for white educators to discuss race in teacher education programs.

3. This strategy of talking more *about* racial categorization is, to me, analogous to Lisa Delpit's strategy of talking more explicitly *about* language use in the classroom. Through talking *about* how distinctions between "standard" and "non-standard" English are central to the "culture of power" in schools and society, Delpit writes, students trapped between "standards" began "to understand how arbitrary language standards are, but also how politically charged they are" (1995, 44).

Bibliography

Almaguer, Tomas. 1994. *Racial Fault Lines: The Historical Origins of White Supremacy in California*. Berkeley: University of California Press.

Althusser, Louis. 1971. Ideology and Ideological State Apparatuses. In *Lenin and Philosophy, and Other Essays*. London: New Left Books.

American Academy of Arts and Sciences. 1995. An American Dilemma Revisited. *Daedalus*, Winter.

American Anthropological Association. 1998. AAA Statement on "Race." *Anthropology Newsletter*. May 17, p. 1.

Amit-Talai, Vered, and Helena Wulff, eds. 1995. *Youth Cultures: A Cross-Cultural Perspective*. London: Routledge.

Anderson, J. 1988. *The Education of Blacks in the South, 1860–1935*. Chapel Hill and London: University of North Carolina Press, 1988.

Anzaldua, Gloria. 1987. *Borderlands/La Frontera: The New Mestiza*. San Francisco: Spinsters.

Appadurai, Arjun. 1991. Global Ethnoscapes: Notes and Queries for a Transnational Anthropology. In *Recapturing Anthropology: Working in the Present*, edited by Richard G. Fox. Santa Fe, NM: School of American Research Press.

———. 1996. *Modernity at Large: Cultural Dimensions of Globalization*. Minneapolis: University of Minnesota Press.

Appiah, K. Anthony. 1994. Identity, Authenticity, Survival: Multicultural Societies and Social Reproduction. In Charles Taylor, K. Anthony Appiah, Jürgen Habermas, Steven C. Rockefeller, Michael Walzer, Susan Wolf, *Multiculturalism: Examining the Politics of Recognition*, edited by Amy Gutmann. Princeton, NJ: Princeton University Press.

———. 1996. Race, Culture, Identity: Misunderstood Connections. In *Color Conscious: The Political Morality of Race*, edited by K. Anthony Appiah and Amy Gutmann. Princeton, NJ: Princeton University Press.

Appiah, K. Anthony, and Amy Gutmann. 1996. *Color Conscious: The Political Morality of Race*. Princeton, NJ: Princeton University Press.

ARC Associates. 1996. *Revisiting the Lau Decision: Twenty Years After*. Oakland: ARC Associates.

Asante, Molefi K. 1998. *The Afrocentric Idea*. Philadelphia: Temple University Press.

Austin, J. L. 1962. *How to Do Things with Words*. Cambridge, MA: Harvard University Press.

Bailey, Benjamin. 2000. Language and Negotiation of Ethnic/Racial Identity among Dominican Americans. *Language and Society* 29: 555–82.

Baker, Lee. 1998. *From Savage to Negro: Anthropology and the Construction of Race, 1896–1954*. Berkeley: University of California Press, 1998.

———. 2000. Profit, Power, and Privilege: The Racial Politics of Ancestry. Paper presented at the Annual Meeting of the American Educational Research Association, New Orleans, LA, April 25.

Bakhtin, Mikhail. 1981. *The Dialogic Imagination*. Austin: University of Texas Press.

Banks, James A. 1995. Multicultural Education and the Modification of Students' Racial Attitudes. In *Toward a Common Destiny: Improving Race and Ethnic Relations in America*, edited by Willis D. Hawley and Anthony W. Jackson. San Francisco: Jossey-Bass Publishers.

Banks, James A., and Cherry A. McGee Banks, eds. 1995. *Handbook of Research on Multicultural Education*. New York: Macmillan.

Banton, Michael. 1998. *Racial Theories*. 2d ed. Cambridge: Cambridge University Press.

Barth, Frederick. 1969. *Ethnic Groups and Boundaries*. Boston: Little, Brown and Company.

Baugh, John. 1999. *Out of the Mouths of Slaves: African-American Language and Educational Malpractice*. Austin: University of Texas Press.

Behar, Ruth, and Deborah A. Gordon, eds. 1995. *Women Writing Culture*. Berkeley: University of California Press.

Bell, Derrick A. 1992. *Faces at the Bottom of the Well: The Permanence of Racism*. New York: Basic Books.

———. 2000. *Race, Racism, and American Law*, 4th ed. Gaithersburg, MD: Aspen Law & Business.

———, ed. 1980. *Shades of Brown: New Perspectives on School Desegregation*. New York: Teachers College Press.

Blauner, Bob. 1994. Talking Past Each Other: Black and White Languages of Race. In *Race and Ethnic Conflict: Contending Views on Prejudice, Discrimination, and Ethnoviolence*, edited by Fred L. Pincus and Howard J. Ehrlich. Boulder, CO: Westview Press.

Blum, Lawrence A. 2002. *"I'm Not a Racist, But . . .": The Moral Quandary of Race*. Ithaca, NY: Cornell University Press.

Boas, Franz. 1895. Human Faculty as Determined by Race. *Proceedings of the American Association for the Advancement of Science* 45: 301–27.

Bobo, Lawrence. 1988. Group Conflict, Prejudice, and the Paradox of Contemporary Racial Attitudes. In *Eliminating Racism: Profiles in Controversy*, edited by Phyllis A. Katz and Dalmas A. Taylor. New York: Plenum.

———. 2000. Race and Beliefs about Affirmative Action: Assessing the Effects of Interests, Group Threat, Ideology, and Racism. In *Racialized Politics: The Debate about Racism in America*, edited by David O. Sears, Jim Sidanius, and Lawrence Bobo. Chicago: University of Chicago Press.

Bowen, William G., and Derek Bok. 1998. *The Shape of the River: Long-Term Consequences of Considering Race in College and University Admissions*. Princeton, NJ: Princeton University Press.

Briggs, Charles L. 1986. *Learning How to Ask: A Sociolinguistic Appraisal of the Role of the Interview in Social Science Research*. Cambridge: Cambridge University Press.

Bucholtz, Mary. 1995. From Mulatta to Mestiza: Passing and the Linguistic Reshaping of Ethnic Identity. In *Articulating Gender: Language and the Socially Constructed Self*, edited by Kira Hall and Mary Bucholtz. New York: Routledge.

Butler, Judith. 1997. *Excitable Speech: A Politics of the Performative*. New York: Routledge.

Carnoy, Martin. 1994. *Faded Dreams: The Politics and Economics of Race in America*. Cambridge: Cambridge University Press.

Carter, Prudence. Forthcoming. *Not in the "White" Way: Aspirations, Achievement and Culture among Low-Income African American and Latino Youth.* Oxford University Press.

Cazden, Courtney. Forthcoming. Teacher and Student Attitudes on Racial Issues: The Complementarity of Practitioner-Research and Outsider-Research. In *Talking, Reading, Writing and Race: Contributions of Literacy Research to Racial Understanding,* edited by S. Greene and D. Abt-Perkins. New York: Teachers College Press.

Cazden, Courtney, Vera P. John, and Dell Hymes, eds. 1972. *Functions of Language in the Classroom.* New York: Teachers College Press.

Chavez, Linda. 1996. Promoting Racial Harmony. In *The Affirmative Action Debate,* edited by George E. Curry. Reading, MA: Addison-Wesley.

Chavez, Lydia. 1998. *The Color Bind: California's Battle to End Affirmative Action.* Berkeley: University of California Press.

Chesnutt, Charles W. 1968 [1899]. *The Wife of His Youth and Other Stories.* Ann Arbor: University of Michigan Press.

Chun, K. 1980. The Myth of Asian American Success and Its Educational Ramifications. *IRCD Bulletin* 15 (1 and 2). New York: Teachers College, Columbia University.

Cicourel, Aaron. 1970. The Acquisition of Social Structure: Towards a Developmental Theory of Language and Meaning. In *Understanding Everyday Life,* edited by J. Douglas. Hawthorne, NY: Aldine.

Clifford, James. 1990. Notes on (Field)Notes. In *Fieldnotes: The Makings of Anthropology,* edited by Roger Sanjek. Ithaca, NY: Cornell University Press.

Clifford, James, and George E. Marcus. 1986. *Writing Culture: The Poetics and Politics of Ethnography.* Berkeley: University of California Press.

Clifton, R. A. 1994. Race and Ethnicity in Education. In *International Encyclopedia of Education.* 2d ed. Edited by T. Husen and T. N. Postlethwaite. Oxford: Elsevier Science.

Cochran-Smith, Marilyn. 1995a. Color Blindness and Basket Making Are Not the Answers: Confronting the Dilemmas of Race, Culture, and Language Diversity in Teacher Education. *American Educational Research Journal* 32 (3), Fall: 493–522.

———. 1995b. Uncertain Allies: Understanding the Boundaries of Race and Teaching. *Harvard Educational Review* 65 (4), Winter: 541–71.

Cohen, Carl. 1995. *Naked Racial Preference: The Case against Affirmative Action.* Lanham, MD: Madison Books.

Conchas, Gilberto Q. 2001. Structuring Failure and Success: Understanding the Variability in Latino School Engagement. *Harvard Educational Review* 71 (3): 475–504.

Connolly, Paul, and Barry Troyna, eds. 1998. *Researching Racism in Education: Politics, Theory and Practice.* Buckingham: Open University Press.

Cose, Ellis. 1997. *Colorblind: Seeing beyond Race in a Race-Obsessed World.* New York: HarperCollins Publishers.

Crawford, James. 1995. *Bilingual Education: History, Politics, Theory, and Practice.* 3d ed. Los Angeles: Bilingual Educational Services, Inc.

Crenshaw, Kimberle Williams. 1997. Color-Blind Dreams and Racial Nightmares: Reconfiguring Racism in the Post-Civil Rights Era. In *Birth of a Nation'hood: Gaze, Script, and Spectacle in the O.J. Simpson Case,* edited by Toni Morrison and Claudia Brodsky Lacour. New York: Pantheon Books.

Cross, William E. 1991. *Shades of Black: Diversity in African-American Identity.* Philadelphia: Temple University Press.

Curry, George E., ed. 1996. *The Affirmative Action Debate.* Reading, MA: Addison-Wesley Publishing Company, Inc.

Danielsen, Dan, and Karen Engle. 1995. Introduction. In *After Identity: A Reader in Law and Culture,* edited by Dan Danielsen and Karen Engle. New York: Routledge.

Darling-Hammond, Linda. 1999. Race, Education, and Equal Opportunity. In *The African American Predicament,* edited by C. H. Foreman. Washington, DC: Brookings Institution Press.

Davis, F. James. 1997. *Who Is Black? One Nation's Definition.* University Park, PA: Pennsylvania State University Press.

Delgado, Richard, ed. 1995. *Critical Race Theory: The Cutting Edge.* Philadelphia: Temple University Press.

Delgado, Richard, and Jean Stefancic, eds. 1997. *Critical White Studies: Looking behind the Mirror.* Philadelphia: Temple University Press.

———. 1998. *The Latino/a Condition: A Critical Reader.* New York: New York University Press.

Delpit, Lisa. 1995. *Other People's Children: Cultural Conflict in the Classroom.* New York: New Press.

Devine, John. 1996. *Maximum Security: The Culture of Violence in Inner-City Schools.* Chicago: University of Chicago Press.

Deyhle, Donna. 1995. Navajo Youth and Anglo Racism: Cultural Integrity and Resistance. *Harvard Educational Review* 65: 403–44.

Dolby, Nadine. *Constructing Race: Youth, Identity, and Popular Culture in South Africa.* Albany: State University of New York Press, 2001.

Dominguez, Virginia R. 1994. A Taste for "the Other": Intellectual Complicity in Racializing Practices. *Current Anthropology* 35 (4), August–October: 333–48.

Donato, Ruben. 1997. *The Other Struggle for Equal Schools: Mexican Americans during the Civil Rights Era.* Albany: State University of New York Press.

Douglass, John Aubrey. 2001. Anatomy of Conflict: The Making and Unmaking of Affirmative Action at the University of California. In *Color Lines: Affirmative Action, Immigration, and Civil Rights Options for America,* edited by John David Skrentny. Chicago: University of Chicago Press.

D'Souza, Dinesh. 1995. *The End of Racism: Principles for a Multiracial Society.* New York: The Free Press.

Du Bois, W. E. B. 1965 [1903]. *The Souls of Black Folk.* In *Three Negro Classics.* New York: Avon Books.

Duranti, Alessandro, and Charles Goodwin, eds. 1992. *Rethinking Context: Language as an Interactive Phenomenon.* Cambridge and New York: Cambridge University Press.

Eckert, Penelope. 1989. *Jocks and Burnouts: Social Categories and Identity in the High School.* New York: Teachers College Press.

Eckert, Penelope, and Sally McConnell-Ginet. 1995. Constructing Meaning, Constructing Selves: Snapshots of Language, Gender, and Class from Belten High. In *Articulating Gender: Language and the Socially Constructed Self,* edited by Kira Hall and Mary Bucholtz. New York: Routledge.

Edley, Christopher. 1996. *Not All Black and White: Affirmative Action and American Values.* New York: Hill and Wang.

Ellison, Ralph. 1994 [1952]. *Invisible Man*. New York: Modern Library.

Emerson, Robert M., Rachel I. Fretz, and Linda L. Shaw. 1995. *Writing Ethnographic Fieldnotes*. Chicago: University of Chicago Press.

Erickson, Frederick, and Gerald Mohatt. 1982. Cultural Organization of Participation Structures in Two Classrooms of Indian Students. In *Doing the Ethnography of Schooling: Educational Anthropology in Action*, edited by George D. Spindler. New York: Holt, Rinehart and Winston.

Espiritu, Yen Le. 1992. *Asian American Panethnicity: Bridging Institutions and Identities*. Philadelphia: Temple University Press.

Fairclough, Norman. 2001. *Language and Power*. 2d ed. London: Longman.

Fanon, Franz. 1990 [1952]. The Fact of Blackness. In *Anatomy of Racism*, edited by David Theo Goldberg. Minneapolis: University of Minnesota Press.

Ferguson, Ann Arnett. 2000. *Bad Boys: Public Schools in the Making of Black Masculinity*. Ann Arbor: University of Michigan Press.

Ferguson, Ron F. 1988. Teachers' Perceptions and Expectations and the Black-White Test Score Gap. In *The Black-White Test Score Gap*, edited by C. Jencks and M. Phillips. Washington, DC: Brookings Institution Press.

Fine, Michelle. 1991. *Framing Dropouts: Notes on the Politics of an Urban Public High School*. Albany: State University of New York Press.

———. 1997. Witnessing Whiteness. In *Off-White: Readings on Race, Power, and Society*, edited by Michelle Fine et al. New York: Routledge.

Fine, Michelle, Lois Weis, and Linda C. Powell. 1997. Communities of Difference: A Critical Look at Desegregated Spaces Created for and by Youth. *Harvard Educational Review* 57 (2), Summer: 247–85.

Fine, Michelle, Lois Weis, Linda C. Powell, and L. Mun Wong, eds. 1997. *Off-White: Readings on Race, Power, and Society*. New York: Routledge.

Flores, Penelope V. 1998. Filipino American Students: Actively Carving a Sense of Identity. In *Struggling to Be Heard: The Unmet Needs of Asian Pacific American Children*, edited by Valerie Ooka Pang and Li-Rong Lilly Cheng. Albany: State University of New York Press.

Fordham, Signithia. 1996. *Blacked Out: Dilemmas of Race, Identity, and Success at Capital High*. Chicago: University of Chicago Press.

Fordham, Signithia, and John U. Ogbu. 1986. Black Students' School Success: Coping with the Burden of "Acting White." *The Urban Review* 18 (3).

Foster, Michele. 1997. Ebonics and All That Jazz: Cutting through the Politics of Linguistics, Education, and Race. *The Quarterly of the National Writing Project* 19 (1): 7–12.

Foucault, Michel. 1972. *The Archeology of Knowledge and the Discourse on Language*. Translated by A. M. Sheridan Smith. New York: Pantheon Books.

———. 1978. *History of Sexuality*. New York: Random House, Inc.

Frake, Charles. 1980. *Language and Cultural Description*. Stanford, CA: Stanford University Press.

———. 1980 [1961]. The Diagnosis of Disease among the Subanun of Mindanao. In *Language and Cultural Description*. Stanford, CA: Stanford University Press.

———. 1980 [1964]. Notes on Queries in Ethnography. In *Language and Cultural Description*. Stanford, CA: Stanford University Press.

Frake, Charles. 1980 [1975]. How to Enter a Yakan House. In *Language and Cultural Description*. Stanford, CA: Stanford University Press.

———. 1998. Abu Sayyaf: Displays of Violence and the Proliferation of Contested Identities among Philippine Muslims. *American Anthropologist* 100 (1): 41–54.

Frankenberg, Ruth. 1993. *White Women, Race Matters: The Social Construction of Whiteness*. Minneapolis: University of Minnesota Press.

Fraser, Steven, ed. 1995. *The Bell Curve Wars: Race, Intelligence, and the Future of America*. New York: Basic Books.

Friedman, Lawrence M. 1997. *Brown* in Context. In *Race, Law, and Culture: Reflections on "Brown v. Board of Education,"* edited by Austin Sarat. New York: Oxford University Press.

Gal, Susan. 1989. Language and Political Economy. *Annual Review of Anthropology* 18: 345–67.

———. 1995. Language, Gender, and Power: An Anthropological Review. In *Articulating Gender: Language and the Socially Constructed Self*, edited by Kira Hall and Mary Bucholtz. New York: Routledge.

Gates, Henry Louis. 1992. *Loose Canons: Notes on the Culture Wars*. New York: Oxford University Press.

———, ed. 1994. *Speaking of Race, Speaking of Sex: Hate Speech, Civil Rights, and Civil Liberties*. New York: New York University Press.

Geertz, Clifford. 1973. *The Interpretation of Cultures*. New York: Basic Books.

Genovese, Eugene D. 1974. *Roll, Jordan, Roll: the World the Slaves Made*. New York: Vintage Books.

Gibson, Margaret A. 1988. *Accomodation without Assimilation: Sikh Immigrants in an American High School*. Ithaca, NY: Cornell University Press.

———, ed. 1997. Ethnicity and School Performance: Complicating the Immigrant/Involuntary Minority Typology. *Anthropology and Education Quarterly* 28 (3).

Gilmore, Perry, David M. Smith, and Apacuar Larry Kairaiuak. 1997. Resisting Diversity: An Alaskan Case of Institutional Struggle. In *Off-White: Readings on Race, Power, and Society*, edited by Michelle Fine et al. New York: Routledge.

Gilroy, Paul. 1991. *"There Ain't No Black in the Union Jack": The Cultural Politics of Race and Nation*. Chicago: University of Chicago Press.

Gilroy, Paul. 1993a. Between Afro-Centrism and Eurocentrism: Youth Culture and the Problem of Hybridity. *Young* 1, 2.

———. 1993b. *The Black Atlantic*. Cambridge, MA: Harvard University Press.

———. 2000. *Against Race: Imagining Political Culture beyond the Color Line*. Cambridge, MA: Belknap Press of Harvard University Press.

Giroux, Henry A. 1997. Rewriting the Discourse of Racial Identity: Towards a Pedagogy and Politics of Whiteness. *Harvard Educational Review* 67 (2), Summer: 285–320.

Goldberg, David Theo, ed. 1990. *Anatomy of Racism*. Minneapolis: University of Minnesota Press.

Gonzales, Nancy A., and Ana Mari Cauce. 1995. Ethnic Identity and Multicultural Competence: Dilemmas and Challenges for Minority Youth. In *Toward a Common Destiny: Improving Race and Ethnic Relations in America*, edited by Willis D. Hawley and Anthony W. Jackson. San Francisco: Jossey-Bass Publishers.

Goodwin, Charles, and Marjorie Harness Goodwin. 1992. Assessments and the Construction of Context. In *Rethinking Context: Language as an Interactive Phenomenon*, edited by Alessandro Duranti and Charles Goodwin. Cambridge and New York: Cambridge University Press.

Gotanda, Neil. 1991. A Critique of Our Constitution is Colorblind. *Stanford Law Review* 44 (1): 1–68.

Gould, Stephen Jay. 1981. *The Mismeasure of Man*. New York: W. W. Norton and Company.

Grant, Carl A., and Joy L. Lei. 2001. *Global Constructions of Multicultural Education: Theories and Realities*. Mahwah, NJ: Lawrence Erlbaum Associates, Inc.

Grant, Carl A., and Christine E. Sleeter. 1986. *After the School Bell Rings*. Philadelphia: The Falmer Press.

Gregory, Steven. 1996. "We've Been Down This Road Already." In *Race*, edited by Steven Gregory and Roger Sanjek. New Brunswick, NJ: Rutgers University Press.

Gregory, Steven, and Roger Sanjek, eds. 1996. *Race*. New Brunswick, NJ: Rutgers University Press.

Guinier, Lani, and Gerald Torres. 2002. *The Miner's Canary: Enlisting Race, Resisting Power, Transforming Democracy*. Cambridge, MA: Harvard University Press.

Gumperz, John J., ed. 1982. *Language and Social Identity*. Cambridge: Cambridge University Press.

Gumperz, John J., and Dell Hymes, eds. 1972. *Directions in Sociolinguistics: The Ethnography of Communication*. New York: Holt, Rinehart and Winston.

Gupta, Akhil, and James Ferguson, eds. 1997. *Anthropological Locations: Boundaries and Grounds of a Field Science*. Berkeley: University of California Press.

Gutmann, Amy. 1994. Introduction. In Charles Taylor et al., *Multiculturalism: Examining the Politics of Recognition*, edited by Amy Gutmann. Princeton, NJ: Princeton University Press.

———. 1996. Responding to Racial Injustice. In *Color Conscious: The Political Morality of Race*, edited by K. Anthony Appiah and Amy Gutmann. Princeton, NJ: Princeton University Press.

Hacking, Ian. 1992. Making Up People. In *Forms of Desire: Sexual Orientation and the Social Constructionist Controversy*, edited by Edward Stein. New York: Routledge.

Hall, Kathy. 2002. *Lives in Translation: Sikh Youth as British Citizens*. Philadelphia: University of Pennsylvania Press.

Hall, Kira, and Mary Bucholtz, eds. 1995. *Articulating Gender: Language and the Socially Constructed Self*. New York: Routledge.

Hall, Stuart. 1991. Old and New Identities, Old and New Ethnicities. In *Culture, Globalization and the World-System: Contemporary Conditions for the Representation of Identity*, edited by Anthony D. King. Binghamton: State University of New York Press.

———. 1992. New Ethnicities. In *"Race," Culture and Difference*, edited by James Donald and Ali Rattansi. Newbury Park, CA: Sage Publications in association with the Open University.

———. 1996. Minimal Selves. In *Black British Cultural Studies: A Reader*, edited by Houston A. Baker, Jr., Manthia Diawara, and Ruth H. Lindeborg. Chicago: University of Chicago Press.

Hall, Stuart. 1998. Subjects in History: Making Diasporic Identities. In *The House That Race Built*, edited by W. Lubianao. New York: Vintage Books.

Hammersley, Martyn. 1998. Partisanship and Credibility: The Case of Antiracist Educational Research. In *Researching Racism in Education: Politics, Theory and Practice*, edited by Paul Connolly and Barry Troyna. Buckingham: Open University Press.

Haney Lopez, Ian F. 1995. The Social Construction of Race. In *Critical Race Theory: The Cutting Edge*, edited by Richard Delgado. Philadelphia: Temple University Press.

———. 1996. *White by Law: The Legal Construction of Race*. New York: New York University Press.

Hanks, William F. 1996. *Language and Communicative Practices*. Boulder, CO: Westview Press.

Harrison, Faye V. 1995. The Persistent Power of "Race" in the Cultural and Political Economy of Racism. *Annual Review of Anthropology* 24: 47–74.

Hatcher, Richard, and Barry Troyna. 1993. Racialization and Children. In *Race, Identity and Representation in Education*, edited by Cameron McCarthy and Warren Crichlow. New York: Routledge.

Heath, Shirley Brice. 1983. *Ways with Words: Language, Life and Work in Communities and Classrooms*. Cambridge: Cambridge University Press.

———. 1995. Race, Ethnicity, and the Defiance of Categories. In *Toward a Common Destiny: Improving Race and Ethnic Relations in America*, edited by Willis D. Hawley and Anthony W. Jackson. San Francisco: Jossey-Bass Publishers.

Hebdige, Dick. 1979. *Subculture: The Meaning of Style*. London: Routledge.

Henry, Jules. 1963. *Culture against Man*. New York: Vintage Books.

Herrnstein, Richard, and Charles Murray. 1996. *The Bell Curve: Intelligence and Class Structure in American Life*. New York: Simon & Schuster.

Hewitt, Roger. 1986. *White Talk Black Talk: Inter-Racial Friendship and Communication amongst Adolescents*. Cambridge: Cambridge University Press.

Hilliard, Asa. 1990. The Limitations of Current Academic Achievement Measures. In *Going to School: The African American Experience*, edited by K. Lomotey. Albany: State University of New York Press.

Hochschild, Jennifer. 1984. *The New American Dilemma: Liberal Democracy and School Desegregation*. New Haven: Yale University Press.

Hochschild, Jennifer, and Nathan Scovronick. 2003. *The American Dream and the Public Schools*. New York: Oxford University Press.

Hodgson, Dorothy L. 2002a. Introduction: Comparative Perspectives on the Indigenous Rights Movement in Africa and the Americas. *American Anthropologist*, 104 (4), December: 1037–49.

Hodgson, Dorothy L., ed. 2002b. *In Focus: Indigenous Rights Movements*. Special issue of *American Anthropologist* 104 (4), December.

hooks, bell. 1998. Representations of Whiteness in the Black Imagination. In *Black on White: Black Writers on What It Means to Be White*, edited by David Roediger. New York: Schocken Books.

Hu-Dehart, Evelyn. 1996. P.C. and the Politics of Multiculturalism in Higher Education. In *Race*, edited by Steven Gregory and Roger Sanjek. New Brunswick, NJ: Rutgers University Press.

Hymes, Dell. 1962. The Ethnography of Speaking. In *Anthropology and Human Behavior*, edited by T. Gladwin and W. Sturtevant. Washington, DC: Anthropological Society of Washington.

———. 1964. Introduction: Toward Ethnographies of Communication. In *The Ethnography of Communication*, edited by John J. Gumperz and Dell Hymes. Washington, DC: American Anthropologist.

Ignatiev, Noel. 1995. *How the Irish Became White*. New York: Routledge.

Irvine, Jacqueline Jordan. 1990. *Black Students and School Failure: Policies, Practices, and Prescriptions*. New York: Greenwood Press.

Jackson, Jean E. 1990. "I Am a Fieldnote": Fieldnotes as a Symbol of Professional Identity. In *Fieldnotes: The Makings of Anthropology*, edited by Rodger Sanjek. Ithaca, NY: Cornell University Press.

Jackson, John L., Jr. 2001. *Harlemworld: Doing Race and Class in Contemporary Black America*. Chicago: University of Chicago Press.

Jacob, Evelyn, and Cathie Jordan, eds. 1987. *Explaining the School Performance of Minority Students*. Special issue of *Anthropology and Education Quarterly* 18 (4).

———. 1993. *Minority Education: Anthropological Perspectives*. Westport, CT: Ablex Publishing.

Johnson, James Weldon. 1965 [1912]. *The Autobiography of an Ex-Colored Man*. In *Three Negro Classics*. New York: Avon Books.

Johnston, R. C., and Viadero, D. 2000. Unmet Promise: Raising Minority Achievement. *Education Week*, March 15 (vol. 19, no. 27), pp. 1, 18–21.

Jordan, Winthrop D. 1974. *The White Man's Burden: Historical Origins of Racism in the United States*. London: Oxford University Press.

Kay, Paul. 1975. *Tahitian Words for Race and Class*. Berkeley: University of California, Language Behavior Research Laboratory.

Kincheloe, Joe L., and Shirley R. Steinberg. 1998. Addressing the Crisis of Whiteness: Reconfiguring White Identity in a Pedagogy of Whiteness. In *White Reign: Deploying Whiteness in America*, edited by Joe L. Kincheloe et al. New York: St. Martin's Press.

Kincheloe, Joe L., Shirley R. Steinberg, Nelson M. Rodriguez, and Ronald E. Chennault, eds. 1998. *White Reign: Deploying Whiteness in America*. New York: St. Martin's Press.

Kirp, David. 1982. *Just Schools*. Berkeley, CA: University of California Press.

Kitano, Harry H. L., and Roger Daniels. 1988. *Asian Americans: Emerging Minorities*. Englewood Cliffs, NJ: Prentice-Hall.

Kluger, Richard. 1975. *Simple Justice*. New York: Vintage Books.

Kochman, Thomas. 1981. *Black and White Styles in Conflict*. Chicago: University of Chicago Press.

Kozol, Jonathan. 1991. *Savage Inequalities*. New York: Harper.

Kymlicka, Will. 1995. *Multicultural Citizenship*. New York: Oxford University Press.

Labov, William. 1972. *Language in the Inner City*. Philadelphia: University of Pennsylvania Press.

Ladson-Billings, Gloria, and William Tate. 1995. Toward a Critical Race Theory of Education. *Teachers College Record* 97: 47–68.

Lawrence, Sandra M., and Beverly Daniel Tatum. 1997. White Educators As Allies: Moving from Awareness to Action. In *Off-White: Readings on Race, Power, and Society*, edited by Michelle Fine et al. New York: Routledge.

Leach, Edmund. 1954. *Political Systems of Highland Burma*. London: Athlone Press.

Lederman, Rena. 1990. Pretexts for Ethnography: On Reading Fieldnotes. In *Fieldnotes: The Makings of Anthropology*, edited by Roger Sanjek. Ithaca, NY: Cornell University Press.

Lee, Stacey J. 1996. *Unraveling the "Model Minority" Stereotype: Listening to Asian American Youth*. New York: Teachers College Press.

Lemann, Nicholas. 1999. *The Big Test*. New York: Farrar, Strauss and Giroux.

Levinson, Bradley. 1996. Social Difference and Schooled Identity at a Mexican *Secundaria*. In *The Cultural Production of the Educated Person: Critical Ethnographies of Schooling and Local Practice*, edited by Bradley A. Levinson, Douglas B. Foley, and Dorothy C. Holland. Albany: State University of New York Press.

Levinson, Bradley, Douglas Foley, and Dorothy Holland, eds. 1996. *The Cultural Production of the Educated Person: Critical Ethnographies of Schooling and Local Practice*. Albany: State University of New York Press.

Levi-Strauss, Claude. 1963. *Totemism*. New York: Penguin.

Li, Tanya Murray. 2001. Masyarakat Adat, Difference and the Limits of Recognition in Indonesia's Forest Zone. *Modern Asia Studies* 35 (3): 645–76.

Lipman, Pauline. 1998. *Race, Class, and Power in School Restructuring*. Albany: State University of New York Press.

Lipsitz, George. 1998. *The Possessive Investment in Whiteness: How White People Profit from Identity Politics*. Philadelphia: Temple University Press.

Losen, Dan, and Gary Orfield, eds. 2002. *Racial Inequity in Special Education*. Cambridge, MA: Harvard Education Publishing Group.

Lukyx, Aurolyn. 1996. From Indios to Profesionales: Stereotypes and Student Resistance in Bolivian Teacher Training. In *The Cultural Production of the Educated Person: Critical Ethnographies of Schooling and Local Practice*, edited by Bradley A. Levinson, Douglas B. Foley, and Dorothy C. Holland. Albany: State University of New York Press.

Luttrell, Wendy. 1996. Becoming Somebody in and against School: Toward a Psychocultural Theory of Gender and Self Making. In *The Cultural Production of the Educated Person: Critical Ethnographies of Schooling and Local Practice*, edited by Bradley A. Levinson, Douglas B. Foley, and Dorothy C. Holland. Albany: State University of New York Press.

———. 2002. *Pregnant Bodies, Fertile Minds: Race, Gender and the Schooling of Pregnant Teens*. New York: Routledge.

Maira, Sunaina Marr. 2002. *Desis in the House: Indian American Youth Culture in New York City*. Philadelphia: Temple University Press.

Marable, Manning. 1996. Staying on the Path to Racial Equality. In *The Affirmative Action Debate*, edited by George E. Curry. Reading, MA: Addison-Wesley.

Marcus, George E., and Michael M. J. Fisher. 1986. *Anthropology as Cultural Critique: An Experimental Moment in the Human Sciences*. Chicago: University of Chicago Press.

Markowitz, Joy, Shernaz B. Garcia, and Joy Eichelberger. 1997. *Addressing the Disproportionate Representation of Students from Racial and Ethnic Minority Groups in Special*

Education: A Resource Document. Office of Special Education Programs, U.S. Department of Education, March 14.

Markus, Hazel R., Claude M. Steele, and Dorothy M. Steele. 2000. Colorblindness as a Barrier to Inclusion: Assimilation and Nonimmigrant Minorities. In *The End of Tolerance: Engaging Cultural Differences,* edited by Richard A. Shweder, Martha Minow, and Hazel Rose Markus, special issue of *Daedalus* (Fall), pp. 233–59.

Matsuda, Mari J., et al. 1993. *Words That Wound: Critical Race Theory, Assaultive Speech, and the First Amendment.* Boulder, CO: Westview Press.

McCarthy, Cameron. 1998. *The Uses of Culture: Education and the Limits of Ethnic Affiliation.* New York: Routledge.

McCarthy, Cameron, and Warren Crichlow, eds. 1993. *Race, Identity, and Representation in Education.* New York: Routledge.

McDermott, Ray. 1997. Achieving School Failure 1972–1997. In *Education and Cultural Process: Anthropological Approaches,* 3d ed., edited by George Spindler. Prospect Heights, IL: Waveland Press, Inc.

McIntosh, Peggy. 1989. White Privilege: Unpacking the Invisible Knapsack. *Peace and Freedom* July/August: 10–12.

McIntyre, Alice. 1997. *Making Meaning of Whiteness: Exploring Racial Identity with White Teachers.* Albany: State University of New York Press.

McWhorter, John H. 2000. *Losing the Race: Self-Sabotage in Black America.* New York: The Free Press.

Mehan, Hugh. 1996. Beneath the Skin and between the Ears: A Case Study in the Politics of Representation. In *Understanding Practice: Perspectives on Activity and Context,* edited by Jean Lave and Seth Chaiklin. Cambridge: Cambridge University Press.

Mercer, Kobena. 1990. Black Hair/Style Politics. In *Out There: Marginalization and Contemporary Cultures,* edited by Russell Ferguson, Martha Gever, Trinh T. Minhha, and Cornel West. Cambridge, MA: MIT Press.

Mertz, Elizabeth. 1992. Language, Law, and Social Meanings. *Law and Society Review* 26 (2): 413–45.

Metz, Mary Hayward. 1978. *Classrooms and Corridors: The Crisis of Authority in Desegregated Secondary Schools.* Berkeley: University of California Press.

———. 1994. Desegregation as Necessity and Challenge. *Journal of Negro Education* 63: 64–77.

Minow, Martha. 1990. *Making All the Difference: Inclusion, Exclusion, and American Law.* Ithaca, NY: Cornell University Press.

Mishler, Elliot G. 1986. *Research Interviewing: Context and Narrative.* Cambridge, MA: Harvard University Press.

Moerman, Michael. 1968. Being Lue: Uses and Abuses of Ethnic Identification. In *Essays on the Problem of Tribe,* edited by Jane Helm. Seattle: University of Washington Press.

———. 1988. *Talking Culture: Ethnography and Conversation Analysis.* Philadelphia: University of Pennsylvania Press.

Mohanty, Chandra Talpade. 1993. *Beyond a Dream: Deferred Multicultural Education and the Politics of Excellence.* Minneapolis: University of Minnesota Press.

Moll, Luis C., and Stephen Diaz. 1993. Change as the Goal of Educational Research. In *Minority Education: Anthropological Perspectives,* edited by Evelyn Jacob and Cathie Jordan. Westport, CT: Ablex Publishing.

Montagu, Ashley. 1997 [1942]. *Man's Most Dangerous Myth: The Fallacy of Race.* Walnut Creek, CA: Altamira Press.

Morgan, Marcyliena. 2002. *Language, Discourse and Power in African American Culture.* Cambridge: Cambridge University Press.

Morrison, Toni. 1992. *Playing in the Dark: Whiteness and the Literary Imagination.* Cambridge, MA: Harvard University Press.

Myrdal, Gunnar. 1944. *An American Dilemma: The Negro Problem in Modern Democracy.* New York and London: Harper and Brothers Publishers.

Nieto, Sonia. 2000. *Affirming Diversity: The Sociopolitical Context of Multicultural Education.* New York: Addison Wesley Longman, Inc.

Noguera, Pedro. 1995. Ties That Bind, Forces That Divide: Berkeley High School and the Challenge of Integration. *University of San Francisco Law Review* 29, Spring: 719–39.

———. 2000. Where Race and Class Are Not an Excuse. In *A Simple Justice,* edited by W. Ayers, M. Klonsky, and G. Lyon. New York: Teachers College Press.

———. 2001. The Trouble with Black Boys: The Impact of Social and Cultural Forces on the Academic Achievement of African American Males. *Harvard Journal of African American Public Policy.*

Oakes, Jeannie, with T. Ormseth, R. Bell, and P. Camp. 1990. *Multiplying Inequalities: The Effects of Race, Social Class, and Tracking on Opportunities to Learn Mathematics and Science.* Santa Monica, CA: Rand Corporation.

O'Connor, Carla. 1997. Dispositions toward (Collective) Struggle and Educational Resilience in the Inner City: A Case Analysis of Six African-American High School Students. *American Educational Research Journal* 34, Winter: 593–629.

Ogbu, John. 1974. *The Next Generation: An Ethnography of Education in an Urban Neighborhood.* New York: Academic Press.

Olsen, Laurie. 1995. School Restructuring and the Needs of Immigrant Students. In *California's Immigrant Children: Theory, Research, and Implications for Educational Policy,* edited by R. G. Rumbaut and W. A. Cornelius. San Diego: Center for U.S.-Mexican Studies, University of California San Diego.

———. 1997. *Made in America: Immigrant Students in Our Public Schools.* New York: The New Press.

Olson, James Stuart, and Raymond Wilson. 1984. *Native Americans in the Twentieth Century.* Urbana: University of Illinois Press.

Omi, Michael, and Howard Winant. 1994. *Racial Formation in the United States: From the 1960s to the 1990s.* 2d ed. New York: Routledge.

Orfield, Gary, and Susan Eaton. 1996. *Dismantling Desegregation: The Quiet Reversal of Brown v. Board of Education.* New York: The New Press.

Ortner, Sherry. 1984. Theory in Anthropology since the Sixties. *Comparative Study in Society and History* 26 (1): 126–66.

———. 1996. *Making Gender: The Politics and Erotics of Culture.* Boston: Beacon Press.

Outlaw, Lucius. 1990. Toward a Critical Theory of "Race." In *Anatomy of Racism,* edited by David Theo Goldberg. Minneapolis: University of Minnesota Press.

Overbey, Peggy, and Yolanda Moses. 2002. AAA Public Education Initiative Moves Forward. *Anthropology News,* November, p. 1.

Pachon, Harry P. 1996. Invisible Latinos: Excluded from Discussions of Inclusion. In *The Affirmative Action Debate,* edited by George E. Curry. Reading, MA: Addison-Wesley.

Padilla, Felix M. 1985. *Latino Ethnic Consciousness: The Case of Mexican Americans and Puerto Ricans in Chicago*. Notre Dame, IN: University of Notre Dame Press.

Page, Reba Neukom. 1991. *Lower Track Classrooms: A Curricular and Cultural Perspective*. New York: Teachers College Press.

Paley, Vivian Gussin. 1979. *White Teacher*. Cambridge, MA: Harvard University Press.

Patterson, Orlando. 1997. *The Ordeal of Integration: Progress and Resentment in America's "Racial" Crisis*. New York: Basic Books.

Pattillo-McCoy, Mary. 1999. *Black Picket Fences: Privilege and Peril among the Black Middle Class*. Chicago: University of Chicago Press.

Payne, Charles M. 1984. *Getting What We Ask For: The Ambiguity of Success and Failure in Urban Education*. Westport, CT: Greenwood Press.

Perry, Pamela. 2002. *Shades of White: White Kids and Racial Identities in High School*. Durham, NC: Duke University Press.

Perry, Theresa, and Lisa Delpit, eds. 1997. *The Real Ebonics Debate: Language, Power, and the Education of African-American Children*. Special issue of *Rethinking Schools* 12 (1), Fall.

Peshkin, Alan. 1991. *The Color of Strangers, the Color of Friends: The Play of Ethnicity in School and Community*. Chicago: University of Chicago Press.

Phillips, Susan. 1972. Participant Structures and Communicative Competence: Warm Springs Children in Community and Classroom. In *Functions of Language in the Classroom*, edited by Courtney Cazden, Dell Hymes, and Vera P. John. New York: Teachers College Press.

Pollock, Mica. 1992. Guess Who's Not Coming to Dinner. Unpublished paper, Harvard College.

———. 1993. The Survival of the Fairest: The Racialization of American Beauty Culture, 1870–1930. Senior Honors thesis, Harvard College.

powell, john a., Gavin Kearney, and Vina Kay, eds. 2001. *In Pursuit of a Dream Deferred: Linking Housing and Education Policy*. New York: Peter Lang.

Powell, Linda C. 1997. The Achievement (K)Not: Whiteness and "Black Under-achievement." In *Off-White: Readings on Race, Power, and Society*, edited by Michelle Fine et al. New York: Routledge.

Rampton, Ben. 1995. *Crossing: Language and Ethnicity among Adolescents*. London: Longman Group Ltd.

Roediger, David R. 1991. *The Wages of Whiteness: Race and the Making of the American Working Class*. London: Verso.

———. 1994. *Towards the Abolition of Whiteness*. London: Verso.

———. 1998. What to Make of Wiggers: A Work in Progress. In *Generations of Youth: Youth Cultures and History in Twentieth-Century America*, edited by Joe Austin and Michael N. Willard. New York: New York University Press.

Roman, Leslie G. 1993. White Is a Color! White Defensiveness, Post-Modernism, and Anti-Racist Pedagogy. In *Race, Identity, and Representation in Education*, edited by Cameron McCarthy and Warren Crichlow. New York: Routledge.

Romo, Harriet D., and Toni Falbo. 1996. *Latino High School Graduation: Defying the Odds*. Austin: University of Texas Press.

Root, Maria P. P., ed. 1996. *The Multiracial Experience: Racial Borders as the New Frontier*. Thousand Oaks, CA: Sage Publications.

Rosaldo, Renato. 1993. *Culture and Truth: The Remaking of Social Analysis*. Boston, MA: Beacon Press.

Rose, Tricia. 1994. *Black Noise: Rap Music and Black Culture in Contemporary America*. Hanover, NH: Wesleyan University Press, published by University Press of New England.

Rumbaut, Rubén. 1996. *The New Californians: Assessing the Educational Progress of Children of Immigrants*. California Policy Seminar Brief Series, April.

———. Forthcoming. Sites of Belonging: Acculturation, Discrimination, and Ethnic Identity Among Children of Immigrants. In *Discovering Successful Pathways in Children's Development: New Methods in the Study of Childhood and Family Life*, edited by Thomas S. Weisner. Chicago: University of Chicago Press.

Sacks, Karen Brodkin. 1997. How Did Jews Become White Folks? In *Critical White Studies*, edited by Richard Delgado and Jean Stefancic. Philadelphia: Temple University Press.

Sanjek, Roger. 1996. The Enduring Inequalities of Race. In *Race*, edited by Steven Gregory and Roger Sanjek. New Brunswick, NJ: Rutgers University Press.

Sansone, Livio. 1995. The Making of a Black Youth Culture: Lower Class Young Men of Surinamese Origin in Amsterdam. In *Youth Cultures: A Cross-Cultural Perspective*, edited by Vered Amit-Talai and Helena Wulff. London: Routledge.

Saragoza, Alex M., Concepción Juarez, Abel Valenzuela, Jr., and Oscar Gonzalez. 1998. Who Counts? Title VII and the Hispanic Classification. In *The Latino/a Condition: A Critical Reader*, edited by Richard Delgado and Jean Stefancic. New York: New York University Press.

Schiefflin, Bambi R., Kathryn A. Woolard, and Paul V. Kroskrity. 1998. *Language Ideologies: Practice and Theory*. New York: Oxford University Press.

Schlesinger, Arthur M., Jr. 1998. *The Disuniting of America: Reflections on a Multicultural Society*. New York: W. W. Norton.

Schneider, Anne, and Helen Ingram. 1993. Social Construction of Target Populations: Implications for Politics and Policy. *American Political Science Review* 87 (2), June: 334–47.

Schofield, Janet Ward. 1999. The Colorblind Perspective in School: Causes and Consequences. In *Multicultural Education*, 4th ed., edited by James Banks and Cherry A. McGee Banks. Boston: Allyn and Bacon.

School Colors. 1994. *Frontline* Production. WGBH Educational Foundation, Center for Investigative Reporting, and Telesis Productions International; Scott Andrews, director. Alexandria, VA: PBS Video.

Schram, Sanford F. 1995. *Words of Welfare: the Poverty of Social Science and the Social Science of Poverty*. Minneapolis: University of Minnesota Press.

Searle, John. 1969. *Speech Acts: An Essay in the Philosophy of Language*. London: Cambridge University Press.

Sears, David O., Jim Sidanius, and Lawrence Bobo. 2000. *Racialized Politics: The Debate about Racism in America*. Chicago: University of Chicago Press.

Secada, Walter G. 1989. Introduction. In *Equity in Education*, edited by Walter G. Secada. New York: The Falmer Press.

Secada, Walter G., R. Chavez-Chavez, E. Garcia, C. Munoz, J. Oakes, I. Santiago-Santiago, and R. Slavin, 1998. *No More Excuses: The Final Report of the Hispanic Dropout Project*. Washington, DC: U.S. Department of Education.

Sharma, Sanjay. 1996. Noisy Asians or "Asian Noise"? In *Dis-Orienting Rhythms: The Politics of the New Asian Dance Music*, edited by Sanjay Sharma, John Hutnyk, and Ashwani Sharma. London: Zed Books.

Sharma, Sanjay, John Hutnyk, and Ashwani Sharma, eds. 1996. *Dis-Orienting Rhythms: The Politics of the New Asian Dance Music*. London: Zed Books.

Sheriff, Robin E. 2000. Exposing Silence as Cultural Censorship: A Brazilian Case. *American Anthropologist* 102 (1): 114–32.

Silverstein, Michael. 1981. The Limits of Awareness. Sociolinguistic Working Paper No. 84. Austin, TX: Southwest Educational Development Laboratory.

———. 1985. Language and the Culture of Gender: The Intersection of Structure, Usage, and Ideology. In *Semiotic Mediation: Sociocultural and Psychological Perspectives*, edited by E. Mertz and R. Parmentier. New York: Academic Press.

Skelton, Tracey, and Gill Valentine, eds. 1998. *Cool Places: Geographies of Youth Cultures*. London: Routledge.

Skocpol, Theda. 1995. Targeting within Universalism. In *Social Policy in the United States: Future Possibilities in Historical Perspective*. Princeton, NJ: Princeton University Press.

Skrentny, John David. 1996. *The Ironies of Affirmative Action: Politics, Culture, and Justice in America*. Chicago: University of Chicago Press.

———, ed. 2001. *Color Lines: Affirmative Action, Immigration, and Civil Rights Options for America*. Chicago: University of Chicago Press.

Sleeter, Christine. 1993a. Advancing a White Discourse: A Response to Scheurich. *Educational Researcher* 22 (8), November: 13–15.

Sleeter, Christine. 1993b. How White Teachers Construct Race. In *Race, Identity, and Representation in Education*, edited by Cameron McCarthy and Warren Crichlow. New York: Routledge.

Sleeter, Christine E., and Carl A. Grant. 1987. An Analysis of Multicultural Education in the United States. *Harvard Educational Review* 57 (4), November: 421–44.

Smedley, Audrey. 1999. *Race in North America: Origin and Evolution of a Worldview*. 2d ed. Boulder, CO: Westview Press.

Smitherman, Geneva. 2000. *Talkin That Talk: Language, Culture, and Education in African America*. London and New York: Routledge.

Sollors, Werner. 1986. *Beyond Ethnicity: Consent and Descent in American Culture*. New York: Oxford University Press.

———. 2000. *Interracialism: Black-White Intermarriage in American History, Literature, and Law*. New York: Oxford University Press.

Spindler, George. 1963. The Transmission of American Culture. In *Education and Culture: Anthropological Approaches*. New York: Holt, Rinehart and Winston.

Spivak, Gayatri Chakravorty. 1987. Subaltern Studies: Deconstructing Historiography. In Spivak, *In Other Worlds: Essays in Cultural Politics*. New York: Routledge.

———. 1993. *Outside in the Teaching Machine*. New York: Routledge.

Stanton, William Ragan. 1972 [1960]. *The Leopard's Spots: Scientific Attitudes toward Race in America, 1815–59*. Chicago: University of Chicago Press.

Steele, Claude. 1992. Race and the Schooling of Black Americans. *Atlantic Monthly*, April.

Steinberg, Laurence, with B. Bradford Brown and Sanford M. Dornbusch. 1996. Ethnicity and Adolescent Achievement. *American Educator* 20 (2), Summer: 28–44.

Stocking, George W., Jr. 1982. *Race, Culture, and Evolution: Essays in the History of Anthropology*. Chicago: University of Chicago Press.

Suarez-Orozco, Carola, and Marcelo Suarez-Orozco. 2001. *Children of Immigration*. Cambridge, MA: Harvard University Press.

Suarez-Orozco, Marcelo. 2001. Globalization, Immigration, and Education: The Research Agenda. *Harvard Educational Review* 71 (3), Fall: 345–65.

Suarez-Orozco, Marcelo, and Mariela M. Paez, eds. 2002. *Latinos: Remaking America*. Berkeley: University of California Press.

Sue, Stanley, and Sumie Okazaki. 1995. Asian-American Educational Achievement: A Phenomenon in Search of an Explanation. In *The Asian American Educational Experience: A Source Book for Teachers and Students*, edited by Don Nakanishi and Tina Yamano Nishida. London: Routledge.

Takagi, Dana Y. 1992. *The Retreat from Race: Asian-American Admissions and Racial Politics*. New Brunswick, NJ: Rutgers University Press.

Tatum, Beverly Daniel. 1992. Talking about Race, Learning about Racism: An Application of Racial Identity Development Theory in the Classroom. *Harvard Educational Review* 62 (1): 1–24.

———. 1997. "*Why Are All the Black Kids Sitting Together in the Cafeteria?*" and Other Conversations about Race. New York: BasicBooks.

Taylor, Charles. 1994. The Politics of Recognition. In Charles Taylor et al., *Multiculturalism: Examining the Politics of Recognition*, edited and introduced by Amy Gutmann. Princeton, NJ: Princeton University Press.

Tedlock, Dennis, and Bruce Mannheim, eds. 1995. *The Dialogic Emergence of Culture*. Urbana: University of Illinois Press.

Terkel, Studs. 1992. *Race: How Blacks and Whites Think and Feel about the American Obsession*. New York: New Press.

Thomas, Piri. 1973. *Down These Mean Streets*. New York: Knopf.

Thompson, Audrey. 1999. Colortalk: Whiteness and *Off-White*. *Educational Studies* 30 (2), Summer: 141–60.

Thorne, Barrie. 1993. *Gender Play: Girls and Boys in School*. New Brunswick, NJ: Rutgers University Press.

Titone, Connie. 1998. Educating the White Teacher as Ally. In *White Reign: Deploying Whiteness in America*, edited by Joe L. Kincheloe et al. New York: St. Martin's Press.

Trueba, Henry T., and Pamela G. Wright. 1992. On Ethnographic Studies and Multicultural Education. In *Cross-Cultural Literacy: Ethnographies of Communication in Multiethnic Classrooms*, edited by Marietta Saravia-Shore and Steven F. Arvizu. New York: Garland Publishing.

Tuan, Mia. 1998. *Forever Foreigners or Honorary Whites? The Asian Ethnic Experience Today*. New Brunswick, NJ: Rutgers University Press.

Twine, France Widdance. 1998. *Racism in a Racial Democracy: The Maintenance of White Supremacy in Brazil*. New Brunswick, NJ: Rutgers University Press.

Tyack, David. 1980. *The One Best System*. Cambridge, MA: Harvard University Press.

———. 1993. Constructing Difference: Historical Reflections on Schooling and Social Diversity. *Teachers College Record* 95 (1), Fall: 8–34.

Urciuoli, Bonnie. 1991. The Political Topography of Spanish and English. *American Ethnologist* 18 (2): 295–310.

———. 1996. *Exposing Prejudice: Puerto Rican Experiences of Language, Race, and Class*. Boulder, CO: Westview Press.

Valencia, Richard. 1991. The Plight of Chicano Students: An Overview of Schooling Conditions and Outcomes. In *Chicano School Failure and Success: Research and Policy*

Agendas for the 1990s, edited by Richard Valencia. London and New York: The Falmer Press.

Van Ausdale, Debra, and Joe R. Feagin. 2001. *The First R: How Children Learn Race and Racism*. Lanham, MD: Rowman and Littlefield Publishers.

Van Den Berghe, Pierre. 1996. Race Relations/Racism. *Encyclopedia of Cultural Anthropology*. Volume 3, edited by David Levinson and Melvin Ember. New York: Henry Holt and Co.

Varenne, Herve. 1982. Jocks and Freaks: The Symbolic Structure of the Expression of Social Interaction among American Senior High School Students. In *Doing the Ethnography of Schooling*, edited by George Spindler. New York: Holt, Rinehart and Winston.

Varenne, Herve, Shelley Goldman, and Ray McDermott. 1997. Racing in Place: Middle-Class Work in Success/Failure. In *Education and Cultural Process: Anthropological Approaches*, 3d ed., edited by George Spindler. Prospect Heights, IL: Waveland Press, Inc.

Varenne, Herve, and Ray McDermott. 1998. *Successful Failure: The School America Builds*. Boulder, CO: Westview Press.

Wallace, Michele. 1993. Multiculturalism and Oppositionality. In *Race, Identity, and Representation in Education*, edited by Cameron McCarthy and Warren Crichlow. New York: Routledge.

Wang, Theodore Hsien, and Frank H. Wu. 1996. Beyond the Model Minority Myth. In *The Affirmative Action Debate*, edited by George E. Curry. Reading, MA: Addison-Wesley.

Ward, Janie Victoria. 2000. *The Skin We're In: Teaching Our Teens to Be Emotionally Strong, Socially Smart, and Spiritually Connected*. New York: Fireside.

Waters, Mary. 1999. *Black Identities: West Indian Immigrant Dreams and American Realities*. New York: Russell Sage Foundation; Cambridge, MA: Harvard University Press.

Weinberg, Meyer. 1977. *A Chance to Learn: A History of Race and Education in the United States*. Cambridge: Cambridge University Press.

———. 1991. The Civil Rights Movement and Educational Change. In *The Education of African-Americans*, edited by Charles C. Willie, Antoine M.Garibaldi, and Wornie L. Reed. New York: Auburn House.

Wells, Amy Stuart, and Robert L. Crain. 1997. *Stepping over the Color Line: African-American Students in White Suburban Schools*. New Haven: Yale University Press.

West, Cornel. 1992. Black Leadership and the Pitfalls of Racial Reasoning. In *Race-Ing Justice, En-Gendering Power: Essays on Anita Hill, Clarence Thomas, and the Construction of Social Reality*, edited by Toni Morrison. New York: Pantheon Books.

———. 1993. *Race Matters*. Boston: Beacon Press.

Wetherell, Margaret, and Jonathan Potter. 1992. *Mapping the Language of Racism: Discourse and the Legitimation of Exploitation*. New York: Harvester/Wheatsheaf.

Wexler, Philip. 1992. *Becoming Somebody: Toward a Social Psychology of School*. London: The Falmer Press.

Whorf, Benjamin Lee. 2000 [1940]. Science and Linguistics. In *The Routledge Language and Cultural Theory Reader*, edited by Lucy Burke, Tony Crowley, and Alan Girvin. London: Routledge.

Wieder, D. L. 1974. *Language and Social Reality: The Case of Telling the Convict Code.* Paris: Mouton.

Wilk, Richard. 1995. Learning to Be Local in Belize: Global Systems of Common Difference. In *Worlds Apart: Modernity through the Prism of the Local,* edited by Daniel Miller. London: Routledge.

Williams, Patricia J. 1991. *The Alchemy of Race and Rights: Diary of a Law Professor.* Cambridge, MA: Harvard University Press.

———. 1995. *The Rooster's Egg: On the Persistence of Prejudice.* Cambridge, MA: Harvard University Press.

———. 1997. *Seeing a Color-Blind Future: The Paradox of Race.* New York: Noonday Press.

Williams, Teresa Kay. 1996. Race as Process: Reassessing the "What Are You?" Encounters of Biracial Individuals. In *The Multiracial Experience: Racial Borders as the New Frontier,* edited by Maria P. P. Root. Thousand Oaks, CA: Sage Publications.

Willie, Charles V., Antoine M. Garibaldi, and Wornie L. Reed. 1991. *The Education of African-Americans.* New York: Auburn House (William Monroe Trotter Institute, University of Massachusetts Boston).

Willis, Paul. 1977. *Learning to Labor: How Working-Class Kids Get Working-Class Jobs.* New York: Columbia University Press.

Winant, Howard. 1998. Racial Dualism at Century's End. In *The House That Race Built,* edited by W. Lubiano. New York: Vintage Books.

Wolf, Margery. 1992. *A Thrice-Told Tale: Feminism, Postmodernism, and Ethnographic Responsibility.* Stanford, CA: Stanford University Press.

Wollenberg, Charles M. 1976. *All Deliberate Speed: Segregation and Exclusion in California Schools, 1855–1975.* Berkeley: University of California Press.

Woodson, Carter Godwin. 1972 [1933]. *The Mis-Education of the Negro.* New York: AMS Press.

Yon, Daniel. 2000. *Elusive Culture: Schooling, Race, and Identity in Global Times.* Albany: State University of New York Press.

Yudof, Mark G., David L. Kirp, and Betsy Levin, eds. 1992. *Educational Policy and the Law.* 3d ed. St. Paul, MN: West Publishing Company.